The Pilgrims and Pocahontas

The Pilgrims

and

Pocahontas

RIVAL MYTHS OF
AMERICAN ORIGIN

Ann Uhry Abrams

Westview Press
A Member of the Perseus Books Group

Copyright © 1999 by Ann Uhry Abrams

Published in 1999 in the United States of America by Westview Press, 5500 Central Avenue, Boulder, Colorado 80301-2877, and in the United Kingdom by Westview Press, 12 Hid's Copse Road, Cumnor Hill, Oxford OX2 9JJ

Library of Congress Cataloging-in-Publication Data
Abrams, Ann Uhry.
  The Pilgrims and Pocahontas : rival myths of American origin / Ann
Uhry Abrams.
      p.   cm.
  Includes bibliographical references (p.   ) and index.
  ISBN 0-8133-3497-7 (hc)
  1. Pilgrims (New Plymouth Colony)   2. Massachusetts–History–New
Plymouth, 1620–1691.   3. Pocahontas, d. 1617.   4. Jamestown (Va.)–
History.   5. Massachusetts–History–New Plymouth, 1620–1691–
Folklore.   6. Jamestown (Va.)–Folklore.   I. Title.
F68.A16   1999
974.4'02–dc21   99-10926
                                                                                              CIP

Design by Heather Hutchison

10   9   8   7   6   5   4   3   2   1

*This book is dedicated to
the late Lillian B. Miller*

Contents

List of Illustrations ix
Preface: Finding the Myths xiii

Part 1
Exploring the Myths

1   Invented Traditions   3
2   Myths and History   15
3   Ancestors and Commemoration   35

Part 2
Articulating the Myths

4   Lady Rebecca or the Forest Siren?   51
5   The Landing of the Forefathers   73
6   Vanishing Indians and Noble Women   109
7   Compact with Destiny   139

Part 3
Combating the Myths

8   Saints and Sinners   165
9   Prelude to Battle   193
10   The Pilgrims Versus Pocahontas   221

Part 4
Transforming the Myths

11   The Pilgrims Triumphant   245
12   The Myths Triumphant   261

Notes   283
Selected Bibliography   347
Index   363

Illustrations

1.1   *Plymouth Rock in town square,* engraving,
      early nineteenth century   7
1.2   Base of Plymouth Rock embedded in wharf,
      photograph, before 1859   8
1.3   Jamestown church tower, photograph, c. 1906   9

3.1   John Gadsby Chapman, *Baptism of Pocahontas,*
      oil on canvas, 1837–1840   36
3.2   Robert Walter Weir, *Embarkation of the Pilgrims,*
      oil on canvas, 1837–1844   36
3.3   John Vanderlyn, *Landing of Christopher Columbus,*
      oil on canvas, 1837–1847   38
3.4   William Henry Powell, *De Soto discovering the Mississippi,*
      oil on canvas, 1855   38
3.5   Antonio Capellano, *Preservation of Captain Smith by
      Pocahontas,* sandstone, 1825   41
3.6   Enrico Causici, *Landing of the Pilgrims,* sandstone, 1825   41
3.7   Enrico Causici, *Conflict of Daniel Boone and the Indians,*
      sandstone, 1826–1827   41
3.8   Nicholas Gevelot, *William Penn's treaty with the Indians,*
      sandstone, 1827   41
3.9   Pilgrim Hall with circular iron fence enclosing upper part
      of Plymouth Rock, mid-nineteenth century, engraving   46

4.1   Simon Van de Passe, *Matoaks als Rebecka,* engraving, 1616   52
4.2   Robert Vaughan, *King Powhatan comands C. Smith to be
      slayne, . . . ,* engraving, 1624   52
4.3   Simon Van de Passe, *Captain John Smith,* engraving, 1616   53

4.4   Robert Vaughan, *Map of Virginia*, engraving, 1624   54
4.5   Alonzo Chappel, *Pocahontas saving the life of Capt.*
      John Smith, engraving, 1861   61
4.6   Thomas Sinclair, *Captain Smith rescued by Pocahontas*,
      lithograph, 1841   61
4.7   A. C. Warren, *Captain Smith rescued by Pocahontas*,
      engraving, mid-nineteenth century   63
4.8   Edward Henry Corbould, *Smith rescued by Pocahontas*,
      engraving by George Virtue, c. 1850   63
4.9   *Pocahontas*, after the Turkey Island portrait, lithograph,
      1830s   70
4.10 Thomas Sully, *Pocahontas*, oil on canvas, 1840s   70
4.11 Robert Matthew Sully, *Pocahontas*, oil on canvas,
      early 1850s   70
4.12 Robert Matthew Sully, *Pocahontas*, oil on canvas,
      early 1850s   70

5.1   Detail of cartouche by Thomas Jefferys, *A Map of the*
      most inhabited part of New England . . ., engraving, 1774   78
5.2   Samuel Hill, *Invitation to Forefathers' Day dinner*,
      engraving, c. 1798   79
5.3   Michele Felice Corné, *Landing of the Pilgrims*,
      oil on canvas, 1800–1810   81
5.4   Michele Felice Corné, *Landing of the Pilgrims*,
      oil on canvas, 1800–1810   81
5.5   Anonymous, *Landing of the Pilgrims at Plymouth,*
      Dec. 22nd, 1620, engraving, c. 1840   83
5.6   H. Carmienecke, *Landing of the Pilgrims at Plymouth,*
      December, 1620, heliotype, 1856   83
5.7   S. E. Brown, *Landing of the Pilgrim fathers*,
      engraving, c. 1841   85
5.8   Anonymous, frontispiece in *Historical, Poetical, and*
      Pictorial American Scenes, engraving, 1851   85
5.9   Nathaniel Currier, *Landing of the Pilgrims at Plymouth*
      11th Dec. 1620, lithograph, c. 1850   86
5.10 Samuel F. B. Morse, *Landing of the forefathers*,
      oil on canvas, 1811   92
5.11 Henry Sargent, *Landing of the fathers*, oil on canvas,
      1815–1824   99

5.12 Unknown artist, *Edward Winslow,* oil on canvas, c. 1650   100
5.13 Sargent's *Landing of the fathers* in Pilgrim Hall, Plymouth,
     photograph, c. 1870   107

6.1 John Gadsby Chapman, *Baptism of Pocahontas,*
     oil on canvas, 1837–1840   115
6.2 John Gadsby Chapman, *The coronation of Powhatan,*
     oil on canvas, 1836   117
6.3 John Gadsby Chapman, *The warning of Pocahontas,*
     oil on canvas, 1836   117
6.4 John Gadsby Chapman, *Pocahontas saving the life of
     Captain John Smith,* oil on canvas, 1836   118
6.5 John Gadsby Chapman, *Good times in the New World*
     (or *The hope of Jamestown*), oil on panel, 1841   118
6.6 John Gadsby Chapman, *Baptism of Pocahontas,* oil sketch   123
6.7 John Gadsby Chapman, key to the *Baptism of Pocahontas,*
     engraving, c. 1840   123

7.1 Robert Walter Weir, *Embarkation of the Pilgrims,*
     oil on canvas, 1837–1844   147
7.2 Robert Walter Weir, key to *Embarkation of the Pilgrims,*
     engraving, c. 1844   150
7.3 Tompkins H. Matteson, *Signing of the Mayflower Compact,*
     oil on canvas, c. 1850   161

8.1 John McRae, after Henry Brueckner's *The marriage of
     Pocahontas,* lithograph, 1855   171
8.2 Anton Hohenstein, *The wedding of Pocahontas,*
     lithograph, 1867   173
8.3 Emanuel Leutze, *English Puritans escaping to America,*
     engraving, 1847   181
8.4 Charles Lucy, *Departure of the Pilgrim fathers,*
     oil on canvas, 1847   183
8.5 Charles Lucy, *The first landing of the Pilgrims, 1620,*
     engraving, c. 1850   184
8.6 Charles Cope, *Departure of the Pilgrim fathers from
     Delft Haven, 1620,* engraving, c. 1854   186
8.7 William Bartlett, "Leyden Street," engraving, 1853   188
8.8 William Bartlett, "Pilgrim costumes," engraving, 1853   189

8.9 Peter Frederick Rothermel, *Landing of the Pilgrims at Plymouth Rock*, oil on canvas, 1854   189

9.1 John W. Ehninger, "Priscilla and John Alden," illustration for *Courtship of Miles Standish*, 1859   208
9.2 John W. Ehninger, "The council," illustration for *Courtship of Miles Standish*, 1859   208
9.3 John Gilbert, "Priscilla at the wheel," illustration for *Courtship of Miles Standish*, 1859   209
9.4 John Gilbert, "The wedding procession," illustration for *Courtship of Miles Standish*, 1859   209

11.1 George Henry Boughton, *Pilgrims going to church*, oil on canvas, 1867   254
11.2 Victor Nehlig, *Pocahontas saving the life of John Smith*, oil on canvas, 1870   254
11.3 George Henry Boughton, *Priscilla and John Alden*, engraving, 1889   256
11.4 Howard Chandler Christy, "Priscilla Mullen and John Alden," illustration for *Courtship of Miles Standish*, 1903   256

12.1 Hammatt Billings, Plymouth Rock canopy, photograph, c. 1866   262
12.2 Hammatt Billings, national monument to the forefathers, Plymouth, Mass., photograph, n.d.   263
12.3 McKim, Mead, and White, Plymouth Rock canopy, photograph, c. 1925   266
12.4 Jamestown Church, Jamestown, Va., photograph, 1994   268
12.5 William Ordway Partridge, *Pocahontas*, Jamestown, Va., bronze, 1907–1922   270
12.6 U.S. government obelisk, Jamestown, Va., photograph, 1994   274
12.7 Excavations at Jamestown, Va., photograph, 1997   280
12.8 James Fort, Jamestown settlement, Va., c. 1997   281
12.9 Interior scene, Plimoth Plantation, photograph, c. 1997   281

Preface: Finding the Myths

*T*hree sisters surrounded me in an antique-laden living room in a Richmond assisted-living facility; the purpose of our visit was to talk about their ancestor Pocahontas, for whom the eldest of the three was named. In their laps were scrapbooks, clippings, and photographs—memories of days long past when they had viewed the grave of their Indian antecedent in England or had gathered with other descendants of John Rolfe and Pocahontas to celebrate the founding of Jamestown. They told of ancestral links to Tidewater plantations, where many of the tables and chairs in the room had originated, and reminisced about how the name "Pocahontas" had been passed from generation to generation in their family. Each of these women related different stories about the proud lineage that they shared with other leading Virginians whose common progenitor was John Bolling (1675–1729), great-grandson of Pocahontas and John Rolfe. They seemed most pleased that their roots went back to the daughter of a tribal chief, and they chuckled when describing the times either they or their children had dressed in native costume to portray their illustrious ancestor.

A few months later, I was in the library of the Mayflower Society in Plymouth, hearing similar reminiscences from a spry descendant of eleven different Pilgrim families. With charts and histories to document her lineage, the octogenarian explained how generations of her family had occupied homes in the same neighborhood, only a few miles from where her ancestors had landed in 1620. Although Plymouth had changed dramatically during her lifetime, she found that living with memories of the Old Colony provided a sense of comfort and continuity. Therefore, she drove to the Mayflower Society at least once a week to chat with other descendants, read about recent genealogical findings, hear lectures, enjoy teas or receptions, and learn more about the colony populated by her forebears.

The memories of these women in two very different locales taught me a great deal about the topic I had long been researching, for perpetuation of the Jamestown and Plymouth legends had spun a web of myths, many anchored in verifiable fact but most based on fabrication. That perfect past—whether plantation luxury or village austerity—was an elusive dream that none of these intelligent women entirely believed or fully doubted. Telling stories of hardships endured or ideals pursued, these elderly keepers of the ancestral legacies had become living personifications of the myths themselves. The hospitable ladies of Virginia pointed with pride to the desk owned by a famous ancestor who had lived on a plantation now opened to the public; the bright-eyed citizen of Plymouth talked eagerly about watching an expedition in her neighborhood where archeologists uncovered the foundations of a seventeenth-century house built by one of her Pilgrim ancestors. In revisiting those vestiges of past lives that helped define their own existences, they all seemed suddenly transformed into the mythic characters they had so long commemorated.

Whether told with soft accents or broad vowels, the stories these women related were similar; only the characters varied. From the vantage point of the waning twentieth century, it seems almost impossible to think that these legends—the retellings of which are now so trivialized—once shaped the perceptions of generations and even underlay the mutual hostility that nineteenth-century residents of Virginia and Massachusetts felt for each other. As I returned home to incorporate the interviews into this book, I remembered most vividly those two settings—the library and the living room—and in more ways than one, they have shaped my understandings of the two opposing origin myths.

One critical reality in studying these various restructurings of colonial history is the fine line that divides fact from fiction. In his classic anthropological study, Mircea Eliade explains that an "origin myth narrates and justifies a 'new situation'—new in the sense that it did not exist *from the beginning of the World.*" These origin myths, writes Eliade, "continue and complete the cosmogonic myth; they tell how the world was changed, made richer or poorer." According to Eliade, "*it is the first manifestation of a thing that is significant and valid,* not its successive epiphanies" (italics in original). Therefore, "the child is taught not what its father and grandfather did but what was done for the first time by the Ancestors, in mythical Times."[1] Virginians and Bay Staters of the early nineteenth century took the shards of information about their first English settlers and molded them into elaborate tales. Based on a few documented facts, each origin myth expanded by drawing from the ongoing tide of history and each was reconfigured according to predominant ideologies.

The Virginia and Massachusetts origin myths embody the character of two diverse societies and often serve as rationales for their opposing ideologies. The Virginia story is looser, less focused, and therefore riddled with incongruities. A shipload of single men founded Jamestown, and yet Virginia's origin myth revolves around a female.[2] In the antebellum period, Pocahontas represented a wide spectrum of ideals. As a Native American, she symbolized uncorrupted nature and inherent common sense; as a woman, she stood for both the strength and weakness of the perceived feminine character; and as an Anglican convert, she personified the path Indians should follow if they wished to survive in Christianized America. For the diverse population of antebellum Virginia, these multifaceted perceptions of Pocahontas were fluid enough to satisfy the aristocratic and leisure-loving plantation class as well as the tough and persevering pioneer.

Whereas the Virginia legend focused on a female, the Massachusetts myth centered on a patriarchal hierarchy, even though women composed a relatively large percentage of the Plymouth population. The nucleus of the Pilgrim migration was paternalistic and family oriented; the heroes were men leading a biblical-style mission. Compared with Virginia's poetic blend of manor and forest, the forebears of Massachusetts were stoic, their activities cerebral. Steeped in the structured canons of Western European classicism, theology, and law, they maintained a strict, unbending set of rules to reinforce their religious convictions. Mythical Plymouth shines as a harmonious utopia populated by like-minded, high-principled individuals working together to produce a perfect society. In short, the Pilgrim myth exalted the educational and cultural refinements of Western civilization; the Pocahontas myth glorified a symbiotic relationship between man and nature.[3]

In an attempt to unravel various manifestations of the Virginia and Massachusetts origin myths and see how they determined each region's historical identity, I have followed numerous paths of inquiry. From bulging folders containing photocopies of articles, poetry, and artwork, I devised a methodology that places writings and illustrations of the first Jamestown and Plymouth settlements against a backdrop of contemporaneous political and social concerns. That course led me down two different analytical paths. Following one trajectory, I investigated whether individuals refashioned the origin myths as a means for dealing with contemporary problems; following the other, I questioned whether constant repetition of the myths determined the way residents of nineteenth-century Virginia or Massachusetts actually interpreted current events. In short, my goal has been to study the two origin myths to discern how they influenced regional behavior and, conversely, to find out how contemporaneous events induced mutations of the two legends.[4]

Research for this project has had its difficulties, one of the most challenging being the unequal distribution of published material. Not only were such great nineteenth-century historians as George Bancroft, Jared Sparks, and Francis Parkman all New Englanders, but the great preponderance of twentieth-century intellectual historians have also written abundantly about the first settlers of Massachusetts and have virtually ignored early Virginia.[5] There are valid reasons for this disparity. New England has a vast concentration of universities that turn out students interested in exploring regional beginnings. This is not merely a modern phenomenon. In the seventeenth century, when the Puritans sought to establish their own educational system free from any taint of Anglican interference, seventeenth-century Puritan clergymen began writing the histories of their migrations; thus, its orientation was theological analysis. The Virginia legend more readily found its way into poetry and fiction and a romanticized legend developed from a story related by John Smith in his *Generall Historie* of 1624. Told mostly by borrowing from (and corrupting) that source, the Virginia origin myth remained fluid and imaginative, with little of the didacticism found in the Pilgrim legend.

Because my interest lay in the myths themselves rather than in a thorough investigation of the original settlements, I narrowed my primary research to the nineteenth and early twentieth centuries, with the greatest concentration on the antebellum period, a time when residents of the United States were creating a viable history to define the beginnings of their new nation. I soon discovered that the prevalence of the origin myths in early nineteenth-century culture produced a subtle combativeness between regions, centered on which group of ancestors most influenced American society. That intriguing observation led me into a variety of explorations that brought me face-to-face with my next obstacle. In honing in on the individual myths, I often tended to overemphasize their importance, especially as a component in the complex ideological baggage that pitted Massachusetts and Virginia against each other before and during the Civil War. Therefore, I have tried to integrate the rivalry based on seventeenth-century history into considerations of the more substantial issues that drove the two sections to war. Yet within my attempt to balance these ingredients, I deliberately point out how arguments over larger questions often contained bombastic or derogatory references to the Jamestown and Pilgrim legends.

During the antebellum years, the two myths frequently found their way into political oratory and were popular subjects for artists and writers. Obviously, I could not investigate all sources, and thus I had to limit my analysis to selected examples. Even after paring down the number of works to investigate, the challenge of simultaneously exploring both myths seemed daunting. For one thing, I found it difficult to separate specific data on early Jamestown or Plymouth from the history of the larger Massachusetts and Virginia colonies. Nevertheless, I had to understand the broader historical and social structure of nineteenth-century America in order to learn why the Jamestown and Pilgrim myths varied as times changed. Thus, I have occasionally found it necessary to provide an overview of the broader cultural milieu in order to place the myths in their proper historical context. Terminology also often posed problems. Most troublesome were the designations of "Puritan" and "Pilgrim," which frequently overlap, partly because many of the early writers and orators—either intentionally or inadvertently—conflated the two societies and partly because in certain contexts the two groups hardly seemed to differ. A different grammatical problem stemmed from the absence of a noun formed from the word "Massachusetts" to match the term "Virginian." When appropriate, I have used "Bay Stater" to describe a resident of Massachusetts as a corollary to the term "Virginian." In the antebellum years, the Old Dominion had a unique sense of its origins that was distinct from its Southern neighbors. However, in the more homogeneous New England, where the leadership of all six states was dominated by descendants of the early Puritan settlers, the sense of ancestral beginnings crossed state boundaries. Thus, for comparative purposes, I also use the pair "New England" and "Old Dominion," in the belief that it is appropriate to contrast the residents of an entire region with those of a single state.

In reading general histories, I was often stymied by the term "national ideology." Despite the many writers who propose that such a consensus existed during the antebellum period, I found that few people in Boston, Richmond, or even Washington, D.C., were theorizing about the nation as a whole.[6] Instead, the antebellum United States was a crazy quilt of localized interests. From county to county—and even neighbor to neighbor—conflicting viewpoints flourished. Many Virginians, for example, opposed secession but defended slavery or, conversely, detested slavery but championed states' rights. The same dichotomy was true in Massachusetts, where abolitionists were idolized, despised, tolerated, or ridiculed depending on the mood of individual communities or households. Consequently, to presume that all nineteenth-century Virginians waxed poetic about Pocahontas would be as inaccurate as assuming that everyone in Massachusetts felt nostalgic about the Plymouth settlers. Nineteenth-century residents of Massachusetts and Virginia cared far more about developments of their own time and place than incidents that had occurred two centuries earlier. But they were not indifferent about their regional histories. Antebellum Americans had been so saturated with the origin myths that they accepted them as gospel. And because perceptions of those colonial beginnings differed on opposite sides of the Mason-Dixon line, attacks on regional legends usually sparked impassioned written and oral rebuttals.

Scholars in the 1980s and 1990s have been exploring various aspects of colonial Virginia and Massachusetts, with new findings appearing almost weekly. Anthropologists, archeologists, geographers, and demographers have supplemented the work of historians; and studies of colonial America now take into account the lives of both Native Americans and African Americans. Now, at the end of the twentieth century, some scholars are considering the influences of and interchanges between British American and Caribbean or Latin American cultures, while still others are unearthing data on the English worlds from which the first Massachusetts and Virginia settlers originated.[7] These numerous historical inquiries—combined with the plethora of nineteenth-century cultural, social, and political histories—provided me with a thorough, if sometimes overwhelming, ground for studying the original Jamestown and Plymouth colonies.[8] Since the late 1960s, scholars of nineteenth-century America have tried to erase past omissions in questions of slavery, African-American society, women's roles, the encounter between Europeans and Native Americans, and the lives of the indigenous peoples. This necessary correction has dominated scholarly analysis of nineteenth-century American history and culture.[9] But despite the vast array of such studies, I found only sporadic interest in the origin myths, a gap that I hope this volume will fill.[10]

Although histories have proven invaluable sources for the social and political background against which these origin myths developed and mutated, my most fruitful research came from slogging through volume after volume of antebellum magazines, journals, and newspapers. More often than not, these periodicals contained a variety of descriptive prose, verse, and illustrations designed to convey regional ideals and retell the history of the early settlements. I also found rewards in reading political speeches and sermons, for in most cases, the creators alluded to the origin myths in order to reinforce familiar prejudices or press personal points of view. For example, an orator addressing one of the many New England Societies that had been established throughout the nation almost always entitled his address "The Landing of the Pilgrims." In considering that subject, clergymen and visiting dignitaries would restructure the origin myth to conform with their own opinions about such controversial matters as the schism within the Congregational Church or the abolition of slavery.

Prints, paintings, and sculpture have proven to be equally loaded with information. By examining thematic similarities in works of art and studying the nuances inherent in specific compositions, I have been able to better understand manifestations of the origin myths. Novels, poems, and plays about Pocahontas and the Pilgrims—that have no doubt shaped more perceptions of colonial beginnings than the most serious and scholarly historical studies—are invaluable. Because certain images recur repeatedly in literature and art, I have deliberately selected examples that seem either typical or unique; and conversely, I have either avoided or ignored several well-known authors, whose works have been overinterpreted. Instead, I ferreted out more obscure writers, who were sometimes more successful at capturing popular perceptions.

I have divided this book into four sections. The first one, entitled "Exploring the Myths" (Chapters 1–3), examines the two legends as invented regional traditions and looks at the sources that originated the stories as well as the views of contemporary scholars about the actual Jamestown and Plymouth colonies. The second section, "Articulating the Myths" (Chapters 4–7), looks at specific examples of the visual and literary representations of the Pocahontas and Pilgrim legends during the antebellum years. These include an exploration of the opposing interpretations of Pocahontas as a forest nymph and Anglicized princess; the landing on Plymouth Rock as a metaphor for the Pilgrim myth; literary and visual representations of Pocahontas as a symbol of Indian removal and women's rights; and the Mayflower Compact as a rationale for justifying biased nativism and Calvinist proselytizing. The third section, "Combating the Myths" (Chapters 8–10), considers the Jamestown and Plymouth origin myths as one component in the heated cauldron of sectional differences that eventually boiled over into civil war. After the Northern victory, the Pilgrims emerged as the nation's primary ancestors, while only Virginians continued to revere the Pocahontas legend as an explanation of the state's beginnings, which is the subject of the fourth section, "Transforming the Myths" (Chapters 11–12). This section examines the way the war changed American perceptions about the two legends that culminated in the tercentenaries of Jamestown in 1907 and Plymouth in 1920–1921.

Exploration of these origin myths involves a drama that leaps between centuries and cultures. Such notable men as Samuel F. B. Morse, Lyman Beecher, Alexis de Tocqueville, Henry Wadsworth Longfellow, William Gilmore Simms, Charles Sumner, Wendell Phillips, John Brown, Henry Adams, and Mark Twain make cameo appearances; and such respected but little-studied artists as Henry Sargent, Robert Walter Weir, and John Gadsby Chapman play starring roles, as do the writers John Brougham, Felicia Hemans, Lydia Sigourney, and Seba Smith. Other lesser-known writers–John Davis, James Nelson Barker, Robert Treat Paine Jr., Joseph Croswell, John Esten Cooke, Charlotte Barnes, Emily Clemens Pearson, George Washington Parke Custis, and Robert Dale Owen–play supporting parts. All share a common interest in reinterpreting the origin myths of Virginia and Massachusetts. And by looking closely at this wide spectrum of personalities and styles, we enter a realm of make-believe that transformed two stories about the early settlement of the American continent into intricate mythological constructions.

Research for this book has occupied the better part of the 1990s, and within those years, I have been helped by numerous individuals. I therefore wish to thank the following people who have made this endeavor possible. In Virginia, I received special favors from Ann Southwell, Barbara Batson, Robert Mayo, Roger Stein, Mark Cattanach, Nancy Egloff, Debby Padgett, Rodney Taylor, William Rasmussen, and numerous others at the Virginia Historical Society, the Valentine Museum, the Virginia State Library, and the Jamestown-Yorktown Foundation. In Massachusetts, I was helped by Georgia Barnhill, Peggy Baker, James Baker, Jeremy Bangs, and the staffs of the American Antiquarian Society, the Pilgrim Society, the Massachusetts Historical Society, the Houghton Library of Harvard University, and the Boston Public Library. I am also grateful to Ellen Miles, Wendy Wick Reaves, William Truettner, Pat Lynagh, and all of my colleagues at the National Portrait Gallery and National Museum of American Art. A special thanks to Marie Nitschke, Marie Hampton, Linda Matthews, and the rest of the staff at Emory University's Woodruff Library. I also wish to thank Kathryn Grover, whose advice and help was invaluable, and I appreciate the contributions of Paul Staiti, Wendy Greenhouse, Vivien Fryd, Barbara Mitnick, and John Seelye (who gave me advice many years ago). And there is no way I can express the proper gratitude to Anne Palumbo for her wisdom, editorial expertise, and constant encouragement. And last, but never least, I want to thank all my patient and understanding family–my mother, Alene Uhry; my children, Alan, Margaret, Laurie, John, Andy, and Mary; and my grandchildren, Patrick,

Daniel, Sarah, and Edward. Of course, this book would never have gone to press without the assistance of Edward Abrams, who has not only endured my obsession with the Pilgrims and Pocahontas but has enthusiastically become an active participant in my long years of research and writing.

Ann Uhry Abrams
Atlanta, Georgia
February 1999

Part One

EXPLORING
THE
MYTHS

1

Invented Traditions

$\mathcal{T}$wo familiar tales constitute the genesis chapter of American history. One explains the origins of Virginia; the other describes the founding of Massachusetts. Most nineteenth-century Americans accepted the stories as verifiable explanations of how the first two English colonies in North America began and revered them as if they were divine revelations. Each of the two legends not only lent credence to regional identities but also fostered a panoply of rituals that helped shape two distinct and often rival cultures.

The oldest is the story of Pocahontas, daughter of the Indian chief Powhatan. As a child of twelve, she purportedly prevented her father's men from executing John Smith, legendary founder of the Jamestown Colony in Virginia. That heroic deed is credited with saving Jamestown from destruction and preserving the North American continent for future English colonization. She allegedly brought food to the Jamestown settlers and warned them of raids by her tribesmen; during these frequent visits, Pocahontas became so enamored with the British way of life that she spurned her pagan past, joined the Anglican Church, and wed the Englishman John Rolfe. Offspring of that union ostensibly married into families of English Cavaliers and sired the upper echelon of the Old Dominion's plantation society.

The Massachusetts legend centers upon a pious band of Pilgrims who broke with the Church of England and separated from other Puritans in order to worship as they pleased. Their quest for religious freedom took them from Britain to Holland and ultimately to America, where they could raise their families in an atmosphere of religious tranquillity. According to their legend, the Pilgrims—led by church elders William Bradford, William Brewster, John Carver, and a soldier named Miles Standish—wrote a compact on board the *Mayflower* that presumably established the fundamentals of the future U.S. Constitution. After the Pilgrims landed on Plymouth Rock, they were said to have cooperated with the Indians and endured a hard life in the wilderness in order to establish a homogeneous republican society.

Whether the events at the core of these tales actually happened remains a subject for scholarly debate. But as Drew Gilpin Faust observed when considering Confederate nationalism, the important issue was not *whether* the guiding myths were based on "genuine" or "spurious" history but rather that the legends themselves "must be treated . . . as facts, analogous to any other historical data."[1] In other words, if the stories were perceived as having happened, they must be regarded as historical evidence that affected attitudes and produced verifiable consequences.

Creative minds in Massachusetts and Virginia often embellished the simple tales with other well-known characteristics of colonial America. The concept of Old Dominion chivalry, for example, came not from the wilderness outpost established by the Virginia Company in 1607 but from the plantation society that developed during the late seventeenth and eighteenth centuries. Similarly, New England's origin myth sprang from an amalgam of the Plymouth story with the more extensive history of the Massachusetts Bay Colony. Current events also shaped restructuring of the origin legends. On the eve of the American Revolution, residents of Plymouth turned the Pilgrims' exile from England into the perfect metaphor for American independence; as Virginians drew together under attacks against slavery during the 1850s, the Jamestown myth emerged as a rationale for defending the plantation society. For almost four centuries, legend piled upon legend and myth upon myth so that only shards of truth lie buried beneath a mountain of make-believe.

A number of rites and rituals brought the genesis parables to the people. Eric Hobsbawm characterizes these commemorations as "invented traditions" and defines them as "a set of practices, normally governed by overtly or tacitly accepted rules." These "ritual or symbolic" acts "seek to inculcate certain values and norms of behaviour by repetition," and continuing ritual "automatically implies continuity with the past."[2] Pilgrimages to Jamestown to commemorate the founders constitute one such practice, as do the annual celebrations of the Pilgrims' landing. The original settlers knew nothing of these ceremonies; rather, succeeding generations *invented* them to inspire regional loyalties. Constantly represented in works of art and literature, such rituals provoke a general impression of patriotism or honor, and they transform these abstract feelings into tangible verbal or visual realities.

The "invented traditions" of Virginia and Massachusetts filled the cultural and historical void created by separation from the English motherland. Independence meant abandoning the British royal heritage and state-controlled religion. This loss necessitated not only writing a unique U.S. history but also manufacturing social, moral, and ritual customs to go along with it. When the Revolution suddenly removed colonists from ties to the Old World, a new one had to be restructured with regional lore at its foundation. Americans of the postcolonial period were really a disparate people, living apart in their separate regions with their own traditions to remember and local stories to tell. Even though most American citizens of the early nineteenth century had European roots, they had little to unite them as a nation. Hence, the parables of regional beginning provided sustenance and security to a new nation searching for familiar, yet particularized, historical anchors.

Despite the religious character of its colonial beginnings, Massachusetts did not elevate the Plymouth settlers to sainthood until after the United States became a nation. The term "Pilgrim" was in fact first used by Congregationalist minister Chandler Robbins in a sermon of 1793.[3] Residents of Massachusetts readily adopted the name. How better could they characterize the *Mayflower* passengers than to depict them as devout refugees traveling a long distance to perform a holy mission? At the time, the Congregational Church was losing its hegemony in Massachusetts, and ministers were frantically attempting to unite their straying parishioners. Thus, reminders of mythic heroes who settled on the shores of Plymouth Bay provided a convenient focus for redirecting attention to the cohesiveness of an earlier—if mythical—world.[4]

During the antebellum period, the Pilgrims were regarded as biblical patriarchs who came to America to spread their doctrine across a pagan land. In a speech in 1839, future congressman and senator Robert Winthrop—a direct descendant of John Winthrop, founder of the Massachusetts Bay Colony—said that the settlers of Plymouth "made the wilderness to them like Eden" and laid "the foundations of Civil Freedom" that formed the nucleus of future U.S. law and education.[5] For Winthrop, the Pilgrims were seen as saintly figures who migrated from their comfortable European homes only to pursue a sacred mission. Accordingly, Plymouth was considered to be "holy" territory. A speaker there in 1853 compared "the patriotic descendant of the Pilgrim and the Puritan" wandering around the "consecrated grounds" of Plymouth to the "Christian traveller" visiting "the scenes where once occurred those miracles and events so memorable in the sacred history."[6] Clearly, the town had become a Puritan Jerusalem, drawing thousands to renew their ties to the past by viewing Plymouth Rock, the region's most important icon.

Actually, the famous boulder had lain partially buried in its antediluvian resting place, largely unnoticed during most of the colonial period. Then in 1741, a ninety-five-year-old descendant of the early colonists designated it as the spot where the forefathers had landed.[7] With the large rock now distinguished from all others in the harbor, the town of Plymouth grew increasingly conscious of its unique treasure, even though a wharf concealed it from public view. Following an anniversary celebration of the *Mayflower*'s landing in 1774, a party of merrymakers decided to remove Plymouth Rock from its dockside moorings and transport it to safer ground. Equipped with a yoke of oxen and several large screws, they slowly tugged and heaved the weighty hunk of granite until, much to their dismay, the relic split apart; the upper half was on their pulley, but the lower portion remained buried in the ground.

Instead of admitting that they had destroyed the "sacred" rock, the men devised a brilliant alibi—the fracture was an act of fate that symbolized America's need to sever its attachment to Britain. As proof of their patriotism, the men hauled the upper portion to the center of town and dropped it next to a liberty pole (Fig. 1.1). Forgotten in this maneuver was the bottom half, which remained partially submerged beneath the wharf (Fig. 1.2). Although the two granite pieces would continue to exist separately for more than a century, the incident suggested that Plymouth Rock had become the perfect icon to embody the Pilgrims' mission.

By the mid-nineteenth century, the rock had acquired an aura of sanctity that commanded expressions of religious reverence. The English writer William H. Bartlett, who visited the town in 1852,

FIGURE 1.1   Plymouth Rock in Town Square, *engraving, early nineteenth century.*
Courtesy of the Pilgrim Society, Plymouth, Mass.

equated it with such international shrines as "the Mosque of Omar at
Jerusalem and the Temple at Mecca" and commented on its sacred
aura felt across "the bounds of the great republic."[8] God and patriotism were united in the broken piece of granite that substituted for
the Catholic or Anglican relics forbidden by the Puritan founders. In
speaking and writing about the Pilgrims, New Englanders were
therefore allowed to express an ecclesiastical fervor otherwise forbidden in their Calvinist-dominated region.

Virginia's origin legend prompted a different kind of veneration,
although one also fraught with religious overtones. Their icon was
an old brick church tower, the only remnant of the original
Jamestown settlement (Fig. 1.3). Because its survival seemed to suggest the presence of supernatural beings, clergymen often visited
the site. "We come as pilgrims to-day to a sacred shrine," intoned
the Reverend Randolph Harrison McKim, who led a conference of
Episcopal bishops there in 1898. "For on this spot, two hundred
and ninety-one years ago, was planted, by the right hand of the
Lord our God, a vine of civilization and liberty and religion, which

FIGURE 1.2   *Base of Plymouth Rock embedded in wharf, photograph, before 1859. Courtesy of the Pilgrim Society, Plymouth, Mass.*

has spread over the land."[9] As late as 1941, a visitor to Jamestown referred to the site as "holy ground" permeated by "a certain brooding presence of great spirits."[10]

Pocahontas was similarly revered. Biblical references proliferated in literature and oratory. A poet of 1857, for example, called her a "vision fair as heaven" and described her as the "dove of mercy" who delivered "God's ark" from "the billows dark."[11] In a period when Bay Staters were commemorating their ancestors as godly patriarchs, Virginians were imagining their legendary heroine as an ethereal angel. Although nuances often varied, both regions were employing religious language to describe their colonial beginnings.

According to Raymond Firth, such symbolic triggers as Plymouth Rock and the Jamestown tower "have become important, not for what they represent, but for what they themselves are thought to express and communicate." They, in fact, embody a "higher form of reality."[12] For a nation that wrote separation of church and state into its Bill of Rights, the origin legends formed a bridge between the secular and spiritual realms. The heroes and heroines of Jamestown and Plymouth emerged as ideal actors for two quasi-religious passion plays that combined regional chauvinism, ancestor veneration, and a need for illustrating historical beginnings with an assortment of rites and rituals.

FIGURE 1.3   *Jamestown Church tower, photograph, c. 1906. Courtesy of the Association for the Preservation of Virginia Antiquities, Richmond, Va.*

Virginia and Massachusetts developed certain practices to honor their ancestors, most of which centered upon the day the forebears purportedly landed.[13] The *Mayflower* ostensibly entered Plymouth Bay on December 22, which just happened to be the winter solstice, an ancient European date for celebration.[14] Although European Christians shifted the focus of the pagan holiday to incorporate the birth of Christ, the Puritan establishment frowned upon any formal observation of Christmas, considered to be a "popish" or Anglican rite.[15] Instead, New Englanders observed Forefathers' Day each December. From the first celebration of 1769, Plymouth commemorated the Pilgrims' landing with a parade, followed by a banquet at which well-known orators or clergymen were invited to speak.[16] The holiday soon spread to other Massachusetts towns and traveled with their residents as they moved out into new territories around the nation. But these emissaries soon discovered that in areas with ancestors of their own, the Pilgrims' landing seemed hardly relevant, especially when its celebration conflicted with Christmas.

Consequently, missionaries of the Massachusetts legend began to promote Thanksgiving. Although today that holiday is synonymous with commemorating the Pilgrims, there was no such connection before the latter part of the nineteenth century. Until well after the Civil War, Thanksgiving was a religious observance for New England families and had no direct link to the Plymouth settlers. The story of how the holiday evolved from a regional day of family-oriented prayer and feasting into a major national event is a tale of Yankee ingenuity, female determination, and the Massachusetts mission to disseminate its values to the entire nation. Most people believe that the November holiday started after the 1621 harvest, but that was not the case. Several of the *Mayflower* passengers recorded that the colonists shared their plentiful harvest with the Wampanoags, the Indians who had helped them learn to farm and hunt, but no evidence indicates that any autumnal festival occurred on a regular basis.[17]

The modern holiday is actually the product of a gradual evolution. The title itself had a different meaning in the early years. Spelled with a lower case "t" throughout the eighteenth century, the word applied to a day of prayer proclaimed by colonial (and later state) governors several times during the year. Although in the young republic various presidents would frequently set aside days for expressing gratitude, only New Englanders observed Thanksgiving annually.[18]

In the early nineteenth century, the holiday usually took place on a Thursday during the autumn, although the date varied depending on the whims of individual governors. The observation began with morning church services, after which family members would gather for a leisurely meal. In 1851, New England novelist Sylvester Judd described an early nineteenth-century Thanksgiving as "a day devoted to mirth, gratefulness, hospitality, family love, eating, drinking."[19] During the same period, a contributor to Plymouth's *Old Colony Memorial* pointed out the more somber aspects of the holiday. "Multitudes" of New England families, he explained, gathered each year "around the old hearthstone" to renew "their pledge, in a language more sacred and more reliable than that of words, to love one another and seek each other's peace and prosperity, till thanksgiving days are transplanted from earth to heaven."[20]

As Calvinist missionaries traversed the continent in the 1830s and 1840s, they encouraged New England–style Thanksgivings as annual events, although the holiday had no national sanction. Then along came Sarah Josepha Hale, the indomitable editor of *Godey's Lady's Book.* Each issue of her magazine carried articles describing the New England celebration, but beyond that, Hale also petitioned governors of various states to declare a holiday each November. Within a few years, she began issuing similar requests to the White House.[21] In response to Hale's pleading, Abraham Lincoln proclaimed the first nationwide Thanksgiving to commemorate Union victories of 1863.

The custom took root rapidly after the war ended. Caught up in the exaltation of victory, Northerners embraced the holiday and encouraged subsequent presidents to authorize yearly Thanksgivings. For understandable reasons, postwar Southerners remained reluctant to observe a New England festivity sanctioned by the government to thank God for their own defeat. Nevertheless, by century's end, the tradition had gained so much momentum that Thanksgiving was celebrated annually around the United States. With the heightened interest in colonial America during the late nineteenth century, the Pilgrims were incorporated into the holiday lexicon, a conflation of history and regional lore that united Forefathers' Day with Thanksgiving. Finally, in 1939, Franklin Roosevelt fixed the celebration on the third Thursday of each November, where it has remained ever since.[22]

Virginia's favorite ritual was the pilgrimage to Jamestown. The first took place on May 13, 1807, when Virginia celebrated the two-hundredth anniversary of John Smith's landing. Organized by citizens of Petersburg and Norfolk—with help from students at William and Mary College in Williamsburg—this Jamestown commemoration deliberately emulated the Forefathers' Day celebrations of Plymouth.[23] The so-called jubilee consisted of prayers and speeches at Jamestown, followed by a celebration at Williamsburg's Raleigh Tavern. After singing a selection of hymns and patriotic ballads, the diners raised their glasses to "the memory of our gallant Ancestors—may the ethereal Spirit, which animated their dauntless souls, be the never failing inheritance of their posterity." The jubilee ended with resolutions to "commemorate the event of the first settlement" of the nation annually and hold "Virginiads" at Jamestown every five years.[24]

Although those events never materialized, nineteenth-century Virginians did periodically visit the deserted island where the first Englishmen had settled. In a mood of somber reverence, they wandered through the graveyard, offered prayers by the old church tower, and experienced a sense of communion with the souls of the regional ancestors. This ritual, along with those taking place annually in Plymouth, acquired the coloration of a pious quest, thus creating a spiritual aura that transformed the ancestral myths into regional religions. Whether the objects "worshipped" were material or human, the attempts to preserve them and keep them under the protection of faithful followers comforted believers with the assurance that the hallowed colonists would survive in perpetual memory.

Stripped of the rich royal heritage of the British Empire, the United States had to create its own aristocracy. The determining factor was the date of an ancestor's arrival. Bloodlines traceable to Plymouth or Jamestown formed an American upper crust that imitated and gradually replaced the lost British nobility. Edith Bolling Wilson, the second wife of President Woodrow Wilson, recorded a revealing example of America's peculiar ancestral pedigree. When she accompanied her husband to the Paris Peace Conference of 1919, Mrs. Wilson was taken aback by the haughtiness of a French nobleman. How dare he snub her, she complained. Didn't he realize that *she* was "directly descended from a princess" and thus belonged to "the only aristocracy in America?" The first lady was, in fact, so proud of her descent from John Rolfe and Pocahontas that she ascribed her dark hair, close-set eyes, and "love of the woods" to an inheritance from her Indian ancestor.[25]

Edith Wilson's pride in her lineage is no isolated incident, for scores of prominent Virginians still begin their family trees with Pocahontas and John Rolfe, whose granddaughter Jane married Robert Bolling, and the children of this union have been credited with siring Virginia's most elite dynasties.[26] For centuries, heirs of that legacy drew a clear distinction between their deified Indian ancestor and all other "savages." She was regal, she converted to Christianity, her father was an "emperor," and her marriage to Rolfe produced a perfect blend of forest and field. Because the first Jamestown settlers were all male and no doubt quite a few interracial couplings took place, exaggerated claims about Pocahontas's ladylike behavior, regal demeanor, and Christian faith served as an elaborate rationale to justify the mixed blood flowing through many Old Dominion veins.

Virginians' delight in genealogical links to John Rolfe and Pocahontas differs only in degree from Bay Staters' pride in claiming ancestors aboard the *Mayflower*. This heredity received its official sanction in 1769, when descendants of the Plymouth settlers founded the Old Colony Club. Initially opened only to "respectable" young *Mayflower* offspring, the organization added a clause to its bylaws forbidding members from "intermixing with the company" of the town's taverns. Thus protected against an incursion of Plymouth's riffraff, the founders had little trouble persuading those of like backgrounds to join; within a year, the roster displayed an impressive number of Watsons, Wadsworths, Winslows, and Lothrops, all boasting about their ancestors aboard the *Mayflower*.[27]

Almost a century later, the writer-physician Oliver Wendell Holmes commented on that exclusive pedigree. A New Englander, he said, "claims his descent from the Pilgrims of Plymouth" either "literally" or "virtually," thus "no man need ask more than once why we have entered that third circle of intimate communion, which is narrower than the common communion, . . . narrower than the common citizenship."[28] As Holmes's statement infers, the *Mayflower* progeny constitutes an exclusive American elite. In designating the Pilgrims as ancestors, New Englanders were not only linking their families with the region's first comers but also tying their present lives with the supposed virtues of Plymouth's past. The Pilgrim legend seemed immune from the rigidity and biases connected with the Massachusetts Bay Puritans, thus the *Mayflower* passengers emerged as the ancestors of choice—chaste, pious, and courageous.[29]

As the Tidewater progeny moved southward, they sired an exclusive gentry of "first" plantation families; and as children and grandchildren of the original Plymouth settlers moved westward, they spawned America's entrepreneurial and professional upper crust. In hopes of maintaining their ancestral heritage, these migrating descendants sought to unite with others of similar backgrounds. Offspring of old Puritan families formed New England Societies, the oldest chapters being in the port cities of New York (founded in 1805) and Charleston, South Carolina (founded in 1819). Due to their ef-

forts, obelisks and statues dedicated to the Plymouth settlers filled
city parks, words spoken by the Pilgrims resounded from pulpits and
lecterns, and books about the early Plymouth and Massachusetts
colonies stocked library shelves around the nation.[30] Similar regional
clubs for displaced Virginians eventually came into being, although
New England organizations predated them by more than a half century.[31]

A distinctive secular "religion" evolved as a corollary to the quest
for ancestors among the first English settlers in North America. In
the nonwestern and Native American worlds, where ritual ancestor
worship links spirits of the dead with deeds and aspirations of the living, past and present merge into a bond of continuing traditions.[32]
Akin to but distinctive from such types of veneration, European
Americans developed their own rationale for worshiping their forebears, although they rarely attempted to conjure up the actual spirits
of the long-dead progenitors. Such ghostly emanations and notions
of reincarnation seemed antithetical to Protestant beliefs, so in the
United States, a pair of semisecular parables created the saints and
martyrs for America's two regional bibles.

Almost four centuries of carefully crafted mythmaking have provided the United States with a kaleidoscopic history of its early settlements. Nineteenth-century Virginians pictured their "Cavalier ancestors" as champions of liberty and openness, loyalty and honor,
bravery and courtliness; Bay Staters boasted about their Pilgrim forefathers' high moral standards, individual piety, congregational autonomy, educational superiority, and governmental stability. As each
variant of these ancestral rituals carried successive generations further from the original models, American ancestor worship progressed to an unprecedented level of idolatry. Somewhere beneath
the bravado and swagger lies a knot of verifiable fact. It is essential
now to seek those fragments of historical documentation to demonstrate how scant evidence about Jamestown and Plymouth served as
the launching pad for so many diverse myths.

2

Myths and History

*A*lthough Captain John Smith remained in Jamestown for only two years, his gargantuan legacy outweighs the length of his stay and the durability of his actual contributions to development of the colony. His reputation as a courtly knight and courageous administrator is firmly anchored to the core of the Old Dominion's origin myth. Charles Campbell, the state's most respected antebellum historian, described Smith as "the father of the Colony"; an anonymous contributor to the *Southern Literary Messenger* labeled him "the Columbus of the Virginia colonization," who "exhibited the adventurous daring of a fearless soldier, and the resources of an officer." This writer further embroidered his description by asserting that as a "real knight errant," Smith "kept at bay hundreds of savages by his cool valour and dexterity" and "by his head and heart alone" saved the colony "from anarchy, from starvation, from destruction."[1]

Pocahontas occupied the opposite end of the symbolic spectrum. Admired for her ladylike demeanor and brave yet feminine aplomb, her mythic character countered Smith's rugged gallantry and strong-willed authority. William Henry Foote, for example, wrote in *Sketches of Virginia* (1850) that the "influence of that admirable girl, Pocahontas, is an exhibition of the power of loveliness and gentleness over [the] barbarians." Not only was she "the beauty of her tribe," he wrote, but she was "as gentle and kind as she was beautiful."[2] For Foote and other antebellum Virginians, Pocahontas exemplified the quintessential blend of female grace, aristocratic dignity, and the refreshing innocence of her woodlands upbringing.[3]

❧

These character portrayals—and indeed almost all information pertaining to the settlement of Jamestown—are derived from three publications that John Smith issued during his lifetime: *A True Relation*, written originally as a letter and published by Smith in 1608; *Proceedings of the English Colonie in Virginia*, included in *A Map of Virginia* (1612); and the best-known, the *Generall Historie of Virginia, New England, and the Summer Isles* (1624).[4] The first two offer only brief descriptions of conditions in Virginia, but the *Generall Historie* gave the British public its first detailed glimpse into life in an American settlement written by one of the original settlers. Although other explorers and geographers had described the topography, vegetation, and indigenous peoples of Virginia, none could compete with Smith for presenting firsthand observations about the new world.[5] Not only had he lived at Jamestown for two years and governed the settlement for part of that time but he was able to narrate an intriguing adventure filled with romance, brutality, and human interaction.

The *Generall Historie* is actually a long, rambling pastiche through which Smith strove to explain his role in the colonizing venture. Two years prior to its publication, a brutal Indian raid had almost destroyed the entire English population in and around Jamestown, and London's near-bankrupt Virginia Company—which was still in charge of the venture—bore the brunt of royal accusations. Hoping to disassociate himself from the failing corporation, Smith produced documents and anecdotes that exonerated his decisions, emphasized his skills in running the colony, and underscored his expert dealings with the Indians.[6] The captain's twentieth-century biographer, Philip L. Barbour, describes the book as "a thorough, somewhat egocentric compendium of facts as John Smith saw them, elaborated by extensive quotations from other, and usually unacknowledged, sources."[7]

Even though the *Generall Historie* was a hodgepodge of borrowed material and exaggerations, it became the primary source for stories about the early Jamestown settlement. Most important, it was the fountainhead for *all* data about Pocahontas, or Matoaka, described by Smith as a "poore innocent," a "tender Virgin" who "much exceedeth any of the rest of . . . [her people] for wit and spirit." Indeed, he wrote, she was the "only Nonpareil" of the land. Most significantly, it was in the *Generall Historie* that the famous rescue story was first introduced to the public.

Smith presented himself as a fearless fighter who had exhibited his martial expertise in Hungary and Turkey before crossing the Atlantic and then applied those skills to dealing firmly but fairly with the "Salvages." But he was stymied, he claimed, by the unqualified leaders dispatched by the Virginia Company because they repeatedly interfered with his attempted peace negotiations and conspired to strip him of all authority. According to his description, these incompetent appointees caused scores of men to die of starvation, succumb to Indian attacks, or fall victim to internal bickering. Smith, however, claimed that after he assumed leadership of Jamestown, the Indian threat abated and conditions in the fort improved. Although other sources confirm that Smith's more structured administration corrected previous errors, he clearly exaggerated his accomplishments to deflect criticism.

In 1609, Smith was wounded in an accident and returned to England for medical attention. His narrative about the Virginia settlement after that date was by necessity a miscellany gleaned from others. In relating those happenings, Smith told how conniving men in the settlement persuaded Pocahontas that he was dead, how Captain Samuel Argall captured her and held her prisoner, after which she became a Christian and wed the planter John Rolfe. Smith also implied that *he* had been responsible for convincing Queen Anne (the wife of James I) to receive Pocahontas at the Court of St. James; he also related the details of his emotional reunion with Pocahontas in Brentford, England.[8] When Pocahontas and her family were ready to depart for America, Smith wrote, she suddenly became ill and succumbed to a "religious and godly" death.[9]

The story of Pocahontas in the *Generall Historie* constitutes the nucleus from which all future embellishments have mutated. And it was Smith who first assigned Pocahontas a cardinal role in the British colonization of America, thus suggesting that by saving his life, she had assured survival of Britain's first stronghold on the continent. Even Bostonians of the late eighteenth century touted Pocahontas's heroism as a creditable moral lesson for young Americans to emulate.[10] It was only in the nineteenth century, as Virginia and Massachusetts began sparring with each other, that Smith's writings came under scrutiny. After the Civil War, a group of enterprising New Englan-

ders discounted as fantasy Smith's description of the rescue by Pocahontas.[11] For the next seventy-five years, Smith and Pocahontas were
minimized in most general U.S. histories and, except in Virginia,
were considered to be semifictitious characters.[12]

During the 1950s, the tide began to turn as scholars sought to redeem the captain's reputation, and within the next half century, re-
examinations of the *Generall Historie* have further vindicated the author. Among other things, their explorations have demonstrated that
Smith's meticulous and accurate descriptions of Indian rituals not
only provided important guidelines for future immigrants but also
recorded ceremonies and practices that were soon to disappear.[13] Others have found evidence to indicate that Pocahontas did indeed exist.
Several seventeenth-century writers confirmed her visit to England,
and recent anthropologists have tied incidents that Smith described to
practices followed by Eastern Algonquian tribes. Some even suggest
that Powhatan staged his daughter's intervention in the attempted execution as a face-saving maneuver designed to preserve Smith's life
and achieve peace with the colonists without jeopardizing his own
stature as a tribal chieftain. They claim that viewed in this context, the
rescue scenario was a traditional Powhatan rite aimed at initiating
Smith into the tribe and forcing him to respect the chief's authority.[14]
But regardless of Smith's reasons for writing it, the *Generall Historie*
has endured over the centuries and remains the most authoritative–if
controversial–chronicle of the first Virginia settlement.[15]

In recent years, scholars have attempted to piece together a factual
account of early seventeenth-century Virginia based upon demographic, ethnographic, and archeological research. These findings,
combined with the writings of Smith and his contemporaries, provide a fairly balanced, albeit fragmentary, picture of the Jamestown
Colony. Although Smith and his nineteenth-century defenders imply
that he alone led the expedition of 1607, he was actually one member of a seven-man council hired by the Virginia Company to ex-
plore the area and bring back minerals and other possible money-
making raw materials.[16] The other commissioners[17] were an
assortment of explorers, military men, and "gentlemen" (a class distinction that could mean anything from educated non-laborers to

younger sons of noble families). Their companions aboard the *God-speed, Susan Constant,* and *Discovery* included several blacksmiths, a few masons, two surgeons, a tailor, and a barber. None had experience in either farming or surviving under adverse circumstances. Earlier attempts at colonization, most notably the ill-fated community on Roanoke Island, had vanished without a trace. Consequently, the party dispatched by the Virginia Company realized it was up against overwhelming odds. Because the sponsors had advertised the voyage as a quest for importable raw materials, most of the men joined the expedition in hopes of financial gain. But few of these adventurers anticipated the challenges that lay ahead.[18]

Around their triangular fort lived one of North America's mightiest Algonquian-speaking nations, the Powhatans. Their chief, or *weroance*–a man named Wahunsonacock, called Powhatan by the English–had either conquered or had allied with tribes stretching east to west from the Chesapeake Bay to modern Richmond and north to south from the Potomac to the Carolina coast. Encounters between the Englishmen and Native Americans represented classic examples of misunderstanding and misinterpretation, inevitable in the struggle for power between two antithetical cultures. At first there were some attempts at mutual cooperation, as the Indians warily sized up the new arrivals and sought ways to integrate them into their lives. But as this was happening, the Englishmen were consumed by the challenge of sheer survival.

Unprepared for summer on the Virginia coast, scores of settlers died from dysentery, malaria, and other diseases breeding in the tepid swamp and from fevers and infections. George Percy lamented, "There were never Englishmen left in a forreigne countrey in such miserie as wee were in this new discovered Virginia."[19] Men who survived the heat and illness starved to death because they knew nothing about subsistence farming. Exacerbating the battle to survive were acrimonious power struggles within the fortified town. Although the Virginia Company initially selected Edward Maria Wingfield to head the governing council, he was unable to control the deteriorating morale in the settlement, and the sponsors replaced him with Smith. Most accounts confirm that his firm leadership improved conditions within the fort, and he also eased tensions with the Powhatans by partaking in certain tribal rituals that facilitated the exchange of imported goods for food.[20]

Researchers have also substantiated Smith's claim that after his departure in 1609, Indian attacks increased, the food supply dwindled,
starvation was rampant, and the men once more dissolved into internal bickering during a period often called "the starving time."[21] Recent findings by archeologists suggest that the food shortage (and
subsequent strained relations between the Jamestown settlers and Indians) may have been caused by a severe drought in the region,
which made the English even more dependent on imported goods.[22]
But whatever the cause, the lack of food was intensified by a deficiency of eligible workers and was rendered even worse when the
supply-bearing ships unloaded a mixed lot of young and inexperi-
enced indentured servants seeking a better life.[23]

The picture brightened, however, in 1611, when the new governor,
Sir Thomas Dale, imposed a set of rules for organizing the colony;
and the prospects for success improved even more the following
year, when John Rolfe planted an experimental crop of West Indian
tobacco. Although the marriage of Pocahontas and John Rolfe
around 1613 or 1614 is often given a romantic gloss, there is ample
reason to believe that it was arranged for economic and political reasons. At the time he married Powhatan's daughter, Rolfe himself acknowledged that he needed to placate the Indians in order to save
his nascent tobacco enterprise. In an oft-quoted letter to Governor
Dale, the planter requested the marriage "for the good of this plantation, for the honour of our countrie, for the glory of God, for my
owne salvation, and for her converting to the true knowledge of God
and Jesus Christ." Apparently the union worked to improve relations
with the Powhatans, for intermittent tribal attacks did cease, at least
temporarily.[24] As the men began farming tobacco in Jamestown's
outlying areas, the harsh conditions of the frontier outpost grew
gradually better. The cooperative efforts needed for exporting shipments of tobacco to England afforded residents their first opportunity to rise out of the doldrums and work together in anticipation of
building a viable society.[25]

The journey of Rolfe and Pocahontas to England was also apparently a maneuver designed to improve conditions. Governor Dale
accompanied them, taking along a party of Algonquians, all supposedly Christian converts; his purpose was to demonstrate the "civilizing" efforts of the Virginia Company and thereby encourage more
accomplished people to immigrate. Of all the Indian "specimens,"

Pocahontas was the greatest trophy because she was advertised as the "emperor's" daughter. In light of that distinction, the Stuart court provided her with a generous living allowance during her stay in England.[26] After she died in 1617, followed by Powhatan the next year, the peaceful interregnum secured by Rolfe's marriage began to unravel. The English had pushed so far into Indian territory that in retaliation, Powhatan's brother Opechancanough conducted a brutal raid on the settlers in 1622 and almost wiped out the entire population.[27] By then, however, the tobacco trade was well entrenched, Englishmen were no longer confined to the makeshift fort, and a wider migration was altering the balance of Virginia's population. Shiploads of English entrepreneurs accompanied by women and children were creating a network of autonomous and self-sufficient tobacco plantations along the banks of the James River and eventually up and down the Rappahannock, York, and Potomac Rivers. Fueled by the tremendous profits to be gained from exporting the "noxious weed," planters embarked upon a way of life and commerce that would dominate the region for the next two centuries.[28]

The success of independent tobacco plantations brought eventual wealth to the owners but did little to enrich the coffers of the Virginia Company. Organized as a capital venture to benefit its shareholders, the corporation had originally envisioned the colony as a way station for trading and exporting unprocessed commodities, but it never contemplated having to reap benefits from agricultural pursuits. In a frantic attempt to retain control of the venture, the Virginia Company passed several reforms, among them formation of a General Assembly (or House of Burgesses) that began meeting in 1619. Despite these measures, planters' profits from tobacco exports still accrued to the Virginia Company, thus leaving them little incentive for efficient production, and the colony began once again to sink into despondency, inactivity, and waste. Finally, in 1624, the testimony of John Smith—supported by more recent visitors to Jamestown—convinced the Crown to revoke the corporation's charter and assume operation of the colony. A succession of royal governors tightened the reins of administration and regulated the society that had faltered so drastically under the Virginia Company's purview. Although royal officials controlled most colonial affairs, they did permit the House of Burgesses to make certain decisions that allowed propertied individuals a measure of self-governance.

The planter class inspired an additional component to Virginia's origin myth: the image of the Cavalier aristocrat who fled after Oliver Cromwell and his Puritan army ousted the Stuart monarchy in 1640. Those members of the rural gentry—most from the western counties of southern England—have long been credited with fathering almost all of the tobacco planters who modeled their homes and their lives after the British country estates they left behind. However, studies of immigration patterns have dispelled much of that myth by suggesting that only a small minority of Virginia's plantation owners were actually transplanted Cavalier noblemen. But this small population of immigrants did intermarry with children of the royal governors or local planters and therefore exerted a disproportionate amount of influence on the ensuing Tidewater lifestyle.[29]

It is difficult to pinpoint the first appearance of the enslaved black laborers upon whom those planters would come to depend. Although it is recorded that a Dutch trader brought twenty West Africans to Virginia in 1619, so little is known about this first black "cargo" that no one has been able to prove or disprove whether they were immediately forced into bondage.[30] Subsequently, many Africans were shifted from the Caribbean to Virginia plantations, but slavery did not become the backbone of the colony's economy until the last decades of the seventeenth century. For at least sixty years after John Rolfe introduced tobacco to Jamestown, most Virginia planters employed indentured Europeans, whose temporary labor was cheaper than purchasing Africans. Nevertheless, the exigencies of tobacco farming required backbreaking work that neither indentured servants nor Native Americans were willing to endure. Not only were slaves the property of the owner and thus lifetime employees but planters could aggrandize their "investments" with the birth of each new generation. Consequently, the number of enslaved Africans, who composed only 3.5 percent of Virginia's total population in 1640, had risen to 42 percent by 1710. Five years earlier, the House of Burgesses had passed a slave code, and from that point until the Civil War, Virginians combined the concepts of medieval vassalage with British ideas of "Negro inferiority" and developed a labor force that would first build and later destroy the Old Dominion.[31]

Because most plantations that lined the rivers had their own docks for shipping crops to England, Jamestown itself played only a minimal role in the tobacco trade. Nevertheless, even though its population continued its downward spiral, Jamestown remained Virginia's provincial capital throughout the seventeenth century. Dissatisfied with the power wielded by the English overlords, Nathaniel Bacon and his followers hastened the demise of Jamestown when they raced through the capital burning everything in sight in 1676, followed by a year of intermittent warfare against Governor Sir William Berkeley and other officials. In the wake of Bacon's Rebellion, Jamestown lay in ashes, and although inhabitants did attempt to rebuild to some extent, a second fire in 1698 finished the job. One year later, the Virginia capital moved to Middle Plantation (renamed Williamsburg), and Jamestown was left to decay and finally disappear.[32]

Just as the core of Virginia's origin myth came almost entirely from John Smith's *Generall Historie*, its Massachusetts counterpart also sprang from one source—the memoir written by Plymouth's second governor, William Bradford.[33] But the two books had very different histories. Smith's publication had been available ever since it first appeared in 1624, whereas Bradford's history (which passed to his descendants after his death in 1657) was never even printed until the latter half of the nineteenth century. Over the years, a few clergymen and scholars were permitted access to the governor's manuscript, several of whom incorporated portions into their own writings. It was from these deliberately selective and didactic interpretations that the Pilgrim myth evolved.[34] Reverend Thomas Prince, who used the manuscript for his 1736 history, stored the document in the library of Boston's Old South Church, where it remained until reported missing in the late 1770s. Since the last person to have studied Bradford's manuscript was Massachusetts governor Thomas Hutchinson, many believed that the loyalist official took it with him to London when he fled Boston on the eve of the Revolution.

Bradford's work surfaced in the 1850s in a footnote of Bishop Samuel Wilberforce's *History of the Protestant Episcopal Church in America*. Upon notification that the lost manuscript was lodged in the Church of England's Fulham Library, Charles Deane, a retired businessman and amateur historian working at the Massachusetts Historical Society, immediately arranged to have the text copied for publication. That first edition of 1856 was of immense value, not only to historians and antiquarians but to all those who claimed descent from the Pilgrims. Bradford had recorded the names of every passenger aboard the *Mayflower*, a list that no doubt delighted the legitimate offspring and disappointed those whose ancestors' names were absent. After Deane's 1856 publication, the original manuscript remained in London for another forty years while Bostonians attempted to convince Anglican prelates to relinquish it, a deed finally accomplished in 1897.[35]

The positive reception accorded Bradford's history contrasts sharply with the skepticism and controversy surrounding John Smith's *Generall Historie*. In fact, few have doubted the authenticity of Bradford's account, nor has the sincerity of its author been disputed. However, there is little question that Bradford, like Smith, was writing from a biased perspective. Beneath every paragraph of his convincing and often lyrical prose lie the beliefs of the small, renegade cult to which he belonged. Although ostensibly the history was not written for publication, it *was* recorded with posterity in mind. For this reason, Bradford included incidents and observations that would enhance his own reputation as governor and omitted those that might cast doubts on his abilities.

Most of the seventeenth- and early eighteenth-century clergymen who perused Bradford's manuscript and incorporated portions into their own writings described the Pilgrims' voyage from Europe to America as if it had been a religious hegira. And because the Congregational Church had roots in English Puritanism, most of these clerical historians portrayed the arrival of the Separatists who landed at Plymouth in 1620 as the first step in the larger Puritan migration to New England. For two centuries, this reading of colonial history predominated and contributed greatly to the myth that the first settlers of Massachusetts were pious Puritans who immigrated to obtain religious freedom. This is not exactly the way Bradford wrote it. His narration is a well-crafted justification of the circumstances surrounding the Separatist migration from England to America. Historians over the years have added data, some apocryphal and some documented, to expand Bradford's text, but most did little to contradict his version of events.[36]

The governor's history begins at the turn of the seventeenth century, when an offshoot Puritan sect (often called Brownists after the earlier breakaway Puritan, Robert Browne) began worshiping at the estate of William Brewster in Scrooby, Nottinghamshire. Led by the pastor John Robinson, these rebels followed an orthodox brand of Calvinism based on congregational autonomy, exclusivity, and rule from within each church by a mutually approved covenant. Rejecting any uniform code of behavior and the political and missionary aspirations of the mainstream Puritans, Robinson formally broke with the movement in 1604. His rebellion not only defied both the Anglican Church and the Puritan establishment but also rendered his flock the scourge of all religious authorities.[37] In those "ignorante and superstitious times," Bradford wrote, the Church of England "begane to persecute all the zealous proffessors in the land . . . if they would not submitte to their ceremonies, and become slaves to them and their popish trash."[38]

In 1608, Robinson and his flock moved to Leyden, Holland, where they hoped to maintain their religious independence, living there without undue interference from the Dutch and little attrition of the faithful for about a decade. But when local officials began to threaten their autonomy and younger members of the congregation started leaving the fold, some of the contingent contemplated moving away from all alien influences.[39]

Only about forty of the original secessionists emigrated in 1620, leaving Robinson and the majority of the congregation behind in Leyden. Leaders of the emigrating band procured financial backing from a group of London merchants and gained permission from the Virginia Company to inhabit the upper portion of its vast North American holdings. To ensure a substantive return on their investment, the London sponsors demanded that the small religious band travel with a company of "strangers" who would share in building the colony. These "strangers," one of whom was Miles Standish, composed more than half of the 104 emigrants. Leaders of the group hired two ships–the *Mayflower* and the *Speedwell*–but after arriving on the Cornwall coast and discovering that the *Speedwell* was not seaworthy, all were crowded aboard the *Mayflower* and on September 16, 1620, set sail from Plymouth, England.[40]

After four months at sea, the *Mayflower* terminated its voyage on Cape Cod, well north of the land that the Virginia Company had designated. For several weeks, the ship remained moored near present-day Provincetown while a few of the men scouted the terrain, eventually finding a protected bay with a good harbor and steep hill that assured ample fortification for the settlement.[41] Although the Pilgrim myth depicts the emigrants from Leyden as the first Englishmen to land in Massachusetts, they had been preceded by others. Several expeditions (especially one headed by John Smith) had already surveyed the coastline, named many of the rivers and bays, and spread the European diseases that wreaked havoc on the native population. In addition, a scattering of English and French trading posts dotted the coastline.

Before moving ashore to their selected site, which they named Plymouth after their point of departure, the "saints" and "strangers" forged the legendary Mayflower Compact. The document—now well entrenched in Pilgrim folklore as the nation's first republican constitution—was actually a covenant to guarantee congregational autonomy, provide a secure system for governing the new colony, and certify the Separatists' hegemony over the diverse population of "strangers." Establishment of an administrative authority was especially important because no ordained clergyman had migrated with the breakaway group, thus the colony depended on church elders for both spiritual and secular guidance.[42]

A December landing meant the settlers had to endure a New England winter, during which nearly half of them perished. Nevertheless, within a year, the surviving *Mayflower* passengers had established a functioning society that blended the customs they left behind with their ideals of independence from outside interference. Agreements outlined in the Mayflower Compact endowed individual householders (who had to be accepted church members) with control over most civic and religious matters, and these "freemen" comprised the General Court, which made laws and levied taxes.[43]

Bradford's account mentions two English-speaking natives, Samoset and Squanto, or Tisquantum.[44] Other sources confirm that these two men taught the residents of Plymouth the secrets of farming in the new land and helped ensure a forty-year period of relative peace by negotiating a treaty with Massasoit, chief of the Wampanoags. For the Plymouth settlers, Samoset and Squanto—whose lives seem to have been suspended between their own culture and that of the English—provided an essential bridge to ease the emigrants' transition from their accustomed "civilized" world to life in a strange land.[45]

As ships arrived intermittently from England and delivered more "strangers" to Plymouth, inevitable internal dissension arose, so that the first decade of colonization was an uphill battle to maintain congregational autonomy and church domination of the secular society. In 1621, three years after becoming governor, Bradford described a trying confrontation with John Lyford, an attractive clergyman from England. Bradford explained that upon his arrival, Lyford had agreed to accept Plymouth's brand of separatism, but his compliance ended when he combined forces with another newcomer, John Oldham, to challenge the elders' authority. The two men "grew very perverse," Bradford wrote, "and shewed a spirite of great malignancie, drawing as many into faction as they could." Other colonists "did nourish and back them in all their doings," and before long, many began to "speak against the church" and hold "nothing but private meetings" with much "whisperings among them."[46] In other words, an insurrection was brewing. When Lyford and his colleague tried to notify London authorities that they were being stifled by the Plymouth leaders, Bradford intercepted the letters, accused the two men of provoking a schism within the Plymouth church, and brought the "strangers" to trial. Not surprisingly, the tribunal of church elders convicted Lyford and Oldham of attempted subversion and banished them from the colony.[47] It was a story that future interpreters of the legend would reinforce and parody.

Another perceived threat came from Merry Mount. Founded originally as a trading post by an English captain named Wolastone (or Wollaston), the Merry Mount settlement soon fell into the hands of Thomas Morton, whom Bradford called a "petie-fogger" with "more craft than honestie." The governor not only condemned Morton's "Athisme" but also deplored his "quaffing and drinking both wine and strong waters in great exsess" with the Indians and inviting their women "for their consorts, dancing and frisking togither" and even "worse practises."[48]

Morton's greatest sin, in Bradford's eyes, was erecting a maypole, which the governor interpreted as a blatant demonstration of paganism. Indeed, the entire Merry Mount Colony, even the symbolism of its name, represented the impious hedonism of the Elizabethan world from which the Plymouth settlers had escaped. John Endecott, a visiting Separatist minister on his way to establish a settlement at Salem, hastened into action; he tore down Morton's maypole and threatened to oust all of the participants from the colony. But "thinking him selfe lawless," Bradford wrote, Morton began arming the Indians for defense. This potentially dangerous act of defiance provoked the Plymouth governor to consult with other settlement leaders and "suppress Morton and his consortes before they grewe to further head and strength." Ultimately, Bradford dispatched Miles Standish "to take Morton by force," whereupon he was brought to Plymouth and kept under arrest until he could be deported. Morton retaliated by publishing the *New English Canaan*, a scornful anti-Puritan tract that ridiculed and condemned the rigidity of all Massachusetts colonists.[49]

Bradford perceived Morton and his Merry Mount settlement as an exemplification of the worldly sin and temptation that was anathema to the Plymouth Separatists. If the governor overreacted to Morton's debauchery and to the apostasy of Lyford and Oldham, it was his way of maintaining control of the colony against constant threats of religious and social defection. However, despite all his efforts, Bradford could maintain neither the coherence nor the single-mindedness experienced during the first few years of settlement. By the time he left office in 1644, more than 634 male heads of household lived in the Plymouth Colony, although only 232 of them were freemen with voting privileges. "Strangers," therefore, greatly outnumbered "saints," and new generations would be forced to coexist in a far more diverse world where true congregational exclusivity and independence would be difficult to maintain. Such changes had forced many families to move to more remote areas. In reporting this dispersal of the nuclear congregation, Bradford remarked sadly:

> And thus was this poore church left, like an anciente mother, growne olde, and forsaken of her children, (though not in their affections,) yett in regarde of their bodily presence and personall helpfullness. Her anciente members being most of them worne away by death; and these of later time being like children translated into other families, and she like a widow left only to trust in God. Thus she that had made many rich became her selfe poore.[50]

This poetic passage is a fitting epitaph for the first Plymouth Colony as the steady influx of migrants from England challenged the Separatists' hold on the once-cohesive village.

By far the greatest threat to the Plymouth Colony's hegemony was John Winthrop's arrival at Boston in 1630 with a boatload of mainstream Puritans. During the next twelve years, between 20,000 and 25,000 Puritans flooded into Massachusetts Bay in what became known as the Great Migration. Within twenty years, they had spread their culture into Connecticut, Rhode Island, and other segments of what by then could be rightly termed New England. The British emigrants who arrived between 1620 and 1642—most from East Anglia and Yorkshire—were a diverse lot of farmers, artisans, merchants, and lower gentry. They were, in fact, similar to inhabitants of Plymouth Colony in both background and places of origin. Recent case studies indicate that although the majority of these migrants relocated because they were dissatisfied with conditions in Stuart England, there was far less religious or social conformity than the myths would have one believe.[51]

During the latter half of the twentieth century, numerous scholars have written about the beliefs and influence of New England's Puritan founders. Perry Miller opened the debate in 1952 with his seminal essay, "Errand in the Wilderness." His thesis was that the Puritans of Massachusetts Bay believed they were embarking upon a divine mission to establish a perfect "city on a hill" where their religion could flourish unfettered by governmental interference and they could implant their beliefs on the tabula rasa of the American wilderness.[52] In the years since Miller published his thesis, scholars have hotly debated the sources and meaning of that Puritan "errand," some expanding the idea of a divine mission and tying it to later American culture, others arguing that few immigrants believed they were missionaries, and still others pointing to inherent differences between English and American Puritanism that provided New England society with its unique culture.[53]

Almost all towns had a Congregational Church, with its hierarchy of elders monitoring the activities of parishioners and judging all phases of colonial life. Consequently, a unique—and often paradoxical—form of secular republicanism coexisted under the shadow of a highly regulated ecclesiastical governing board. To balance this, New England villages had British-style courts of law and town councils that gave citizens a hand in secular governing. The curious opposition of strict regulation and popular participation had its pedagogical component in a system of public education designed to control and shape the schooling of all the colony's children in both secular and spiritual matters.[54]

In hopes of maintaining the church's dominant role, seventeenth- and eighteenth-century clerical historians minimized the colony's di-

versity and blurred the differences between the Plymouth and Massachusetts Bay colonies. But there were clear distinctions between the
two, at least before 1660.[55] Each migrating party to Massachusetts
Bay traveled with a clergyman and a clearly defined religious program; the *Mayflower* contingent, by contrast, had no ordained minister and policies that were far more flexible. This was especially true
in terms of church admission. Plymouth elders were less stringent
when judging those eligible to accept the covenant and become full
members of the Congregational Church. And although the Plymouth elders did monitor the lives of their parishioners, they admin-
istered their guidance more leniently than their counterparts in
Massachusetts Bay.[56]

These differences became less noticeable after the 1660s, when
large numbers of mainstream Puritans began infiltrating into the Plymouth enclave, intermarrying with its residents, and eventually diminishing the Separatists' individuality. Isolation from the motherland also helped drive the English neighbors to depend on each
other for mutual defense. Yet despite increasing interchanges, Plymouth thrived as an independent colony until the 1670s, when in a
series of Indian raids (known as King Philip's War), whole villages
were slaughtered, thus reducing Plymouth's manpower and straining
its financial coffers.[57] In the aftermath of that confrontation, the two
colonies drew closer together, and finally, in 1691, when an edict
from the Crown demanded that Plymouth be annexed to Massachusetts Bay, the Old Colony ceased to exist.

Because Virginians and New Englanders reconfigured their origin
legends to meet concurrent objectives and ideals, the *real* histories of
Jamestown and Plymouth have been buried under a palimpsest of
apocryphal tales. To penetrate those layers, it helps to compare the
first two English settlements, which had more in common than nineteenth-century mythmakers dared admit. Both were products of Ja-
cobean England, and both began as outposts on the edge of a continent populated by natives whose sheer numbers and strange customs
provoked continuing anxieties. Colonists in both places harbored
similar stereotypical notions about the "savages" upon whom they
depended for trade and assistance; and all British migrants believed

that they would be disseminating their particular lifestyles across an empty pagan and uncivilized land.[58] The first colonists lived in the same kind of simple homes, and a disproportionate number of them succumbed to illness. English was the language of both settlements, although the inhabitants spoke with different accents. They also dressed alike, but in Virginia—where class distinctions were more prevalent—clothes often connoted social rank.[59]

John Pory, who spent three years as secretary to the governor and council of Virginia, stopped in Plymouth on his way back to England in 1622 and recorded his observations in a series of letters. Most of his remarks concerned geographical formations, climate, topography, vegetation, agricultural products, fishing, Indians, and other topics that interested the early settlers. When comparing the situation in Plymouth with that of Virginia, Pory commented favorably about "the wholesomeness and plenty of the country" and found the residents of "New Plymouth" to be "free from wickedness and vice" and their "industry" as "appeareth by their building" seemed "stronger" than any he had seen in Virginia.[60] Such observations drove John Smith to openly criticize the Brownists of Massachusetts. He had apparently tried to persuade some of the first migrating parties to hire him as a guide and was furious when they refused his services. If they had followed his instructions, Smith charged, they would have avoided "a wonderfull deale of misery" because the "Brownists" were guilty of "pretending onely Religion their governour, and frugality their counsell, when indeed it was only their pride, and singularity, and contempt of authority" that guided them.[61]

Those were the opening salvos in a war of words that would escalate as time went on. In making such comparisons, both Pory and Smith were confirming what later generations would repeat, for although the two colonies shared a motherland and lived similarly precarious existences, there were visible contrasts that made each distinctive. The first and most obvious, as Pory observed, was geographical. The Jamestown site was a mosquito-infested peninsula (eventually becoming an island); its soil was soggy, its climate sultry. The *Mayflower* passengers were more fortunate. They selected a protected bay, the earth proved to be fertile, the air usually clear, the hilly terrain excellent for defense. Because John Smith and other explorers had published their experiences and proffered advice to future immigrants, the settlers of Plymouth had a decided advantage over the men who had landed at Jamestown thirteen years earlier, totally unprepared to survive in a hostile environment.

Another point of comparison is the two colonies' attitudes toward Native Americans, for both appropriated tribal lands with little concern for the cultures they were uprooting. Nineteenth-century New Englanders claimed that the Puritans had formed benevolent missionary societies and had attempted to Christianize the natives, whereas the Jamestown settlers had blatantly preempted huge tracts of Powhatan territory. To that assertion, nineteenth-century Virginians replied that their Northern counterparts' bible-toting forays into Indian territory were mere subterfuges for taking Indian lands.[62] From the perspective of the late twentieth century, both parties seem equally guilty. The Puritans used the guise of preordained duty to mask their territorial conquests; the Virginians elevated an Indian "princess" above the tribes that her putative descendants were displacing. That rationale not only legitimized the interracial heritage of many Old Dominion planters but also provided a fictitious "deed" for occupying the territory "inherited" from their Powhatan ancestors.[63]

Unlike the powerful and often hostile Powhatans of Virginia, the Wampanoags of Massachusetts proved no real threat to the earliest Plymouth residents. It was only after the Puritans began more aggressive attempts to convert the Indians that open warfare ensued. In the Tidewater, the first Anglican (and Puritan) clerics actively sought native converts; however, their congregations, which were composed of tobacco planters and small farmers, were more concerned with acquiring tillable acreage than in saving souls. Encroachment onto their lands provoked the Powhatans to retaliate, most notoriously in the two incursions of 1622 and 1644–1646. However, in the long run, the steady flow of immigrants ultimately gave English settlers the upper hand.[64]

Settlers in both regions duplicated the environment they had left across the ocean, but the models in Massachusetts were East Anglican and Yorkshire villages rather than the estates of the West Country. Most of Plymouth's original residents came as family units bonded by a common religion and dedicated to founding an enduring society. Because the nucleus of the colony had lived and worked together as exiles in Holland, its members were able to reproduce the composition of that close-knit community in America, and each new village within the Plymouth Colony structured itself similarly.

When the Massachusetts Bay settlers began building their own villages, they copied the Plymouth model. Although New England towns rarely developed into those idyllic havens—with mutually supported moral codes and fully representative governments—about which nineteenth-century mythmakers boasted, the majority of the communities that stretched from Cape Cod northward along the Maine coast and westward into New Hampshire and the Connecticut Valley had a homogeneous population, shared similar lifestyles, and existed in relative harmony. Because the bulk of the families settled New England between 1620 and 1642 and only a sprinkling of new immigrants came afterward, the society of colonial Massachusetts avoided sweeping changes and thus remained relatively static. Virginians, from the start, never pretended to be alike. The original Jamestown fortress was populated exclusively by men who had come on a commercial venture with little thought of settling permanently. In fact, like John Smith, many returned to England shortly after arriving. In contrast with their New England counterparts, who prided themselves on their cooperative village lifestyle, Virginians in all walks of life valued autonomy and independence. Not only did a gulf separate the minority of wealthy planters from the large majority of small farmers but both segments chose to live great distances from their neighbors.

Residents of Massachusetts were determined to educate their young within the colony to avoid sending them abroad for schooling; this prompted the founding of Harvard College in 1636 and establishment of a system of public schools in every township. Virginians had no such educational goals. Although many of the original Jamestown settlers had attended a university before coming to America, the early Virginia colonists did not have any kind of public schools until the end of the seventeenth century. The rural nature of the colony meant that most parents taught their children at home and the few who had financial means sent male offspring to England for their education. Despite plans for founding a Virginia college during the early years of settlement, none came into being until William and Mary opened its doors in 1693, fifty-seven years after the founding of Harvard.

The religious uniformity of the Massachusetts Bay Colony was also absent in the Old Dominion. Colonial Virginia was officially Anglican, but large enclaves of Quakers, Catholics, and Puritans coexisted in the Tidewater; by the second half of the eighteenth century, Lutherans, Presbyterians, Baptists, and eventually Methodists dominated the western part of the colony. Virginians were far more receptive to religious diversity than their counterparts in New England.[65]

The Virginia and Massachusetts colonies also had their economic differences. Even though most of colonial New England was agricultural, the coastal areas engaged in fishing, shipbuilding, and other nautical enterprises. From these grew the very successful mercantile trade that transported raw materials from New England and the West Indies to Europe in exchange for finished goods. And to the shame of later generations, New Englanders also profited from the slave trade. Virginia planters were certainly thriving from the growing African population, upon which they depended for farming the "noxious weed." Although Yankee ingenuity and enterprise is legendary, many have underestimated the Old Dominion's commercialism. Instead of coordinating with others to create a cooperative export-import business comparable to that in New England, the independent Virginia planters were highly competitive with their neighbors.[66] Rivalry for the export market generated the pattern of independent living that gave seventeenth-century Virginia the appearance of feudal England, with its powerful landowners, hierarchical government structure, and diversified population of small farmers, who had little representation in the House of Burgesses.

The fates of the two earliest English settlements were also opposite. When Plymouth and Massachusetts Bay merged in 1691, only minor territorial and administrative differences disturbed the relatively peaceful transition, and Plymouth remained a viable community. Jamestown, however, vanished completely when the capital moved to Williamsburg. Clearly, the differences between the original Plymouth and Jamestown settlements outweigh the similarities. Nineteenth-century Bay Staters and Virginians magnified those points of divergence when they constructed elaborate legends to emphasize the assets of their own past and vilify the shortcomings of their opponents. Despite earnest attempts to reconstitute a historical environment, the tastes and trends of each generation have totally subsumed the past—and in between lies a huge historical abyss that has been continually replenished with fantasy.

3

Ancestors and Commemoration

$\mathcal{T}$wo paintings in the rotunda of the United States Capitol–John Gadsby Chapman's *Baptism of Pocahontas* (Fig. 3.1) and Robert Walter Weir's *Embarkation of the Pilgrims* (Fig. 3.2)–provide interesting insights into the development of the origin myths during the early nineteenth century. The very location of the two works at the heart of the nation's government reveals that during the first half of the nineteenth century, paintings depicting the Pilgrims and Pocahontas were considered important enough to deserve that place of honor. However, the congressional decision to commission the murals in 1836 was not easily obtained. Four paintings by the artist John Trumbull portraying episodes from the Revolutionary War already hung in the rotunda, and during the late 1820s, Congress decided to finance four additional historical compositions.[1] More than a decade would elapse before the legislature authorized the project.

When the House of Representatives first discussed additional rotunda paintings in January 1828, congressmen from various parts of the country began arguing over favorite regional topics and debate became mired in partisan opinions. In the meantime, prominent painters complicated matters by petitioning their representatives for the highly coveted commission. With no chance of reaching a consensus over either artists or subject matter, the House tabled the bill and sent it back to the Library Committee where it had originated. Over the next few years, different representatives reintroduced the

FIGURE 3.1 *John Gadsby Chapman*, Baptism of Pocahontas, *oil on canvas, 1837–1840. Architect of the Capitol, U.S. Capitol, Washington, D.C.*

FIGURE 3.2 *Robert Walter Weir*, Embarkation of the Pilgrims, *oil on canvas, 1837–1844. Architect of the Capitol, U.S. Capitol, Washington, D.C.*

proposal, but arguments on the House floor prevented it from passing. Finally, in 1836, the measure slipped through without debate. It named four artists—Chapman, Weir, John Vanderlyn, and Henry Inman—and asked them to restrict their choices of subject matter to "the discovery of America; the settlement of the United States; the history of the Revolution; or the adoption of the Constitution."[2]

With Trumbull's paintings already depicting the two latter subjects, the artists commissioned in 1836 decided to illustrate the "discovery of America" and "settlement of the United States." Vanderlyn announced that he would paint the *Landing of Christopher Columbus* (Fig. 3.3); Chapman chose the settlement of Virginia; Weir said he would select a scene from the colonizing of Massachusetts; and Inman agreed to paint Daniel Boone crossing the Alleghenies as a representation of the Western migration. But Inman died before he could complete the assignment, and Congress chose William H. Powell to take his place. Powell, however, rejected Inman's topic in favor of *De Soto Discovering the Mississippi* (Fig. 3.4).

Although not initially planned that way, the four paintings commissioned in 1836 complement each other. Two tell of Spanish exploration and two of English settlement. Vanderlyn imagined Columbus and his party marching triumphantly onto the Caribbean island while awestricken Indians hide behind a tree (Fig. 3.3); Powell showed De Soto on his horse accompanied by a formidable bevy of armed explorers invading a village of natives (Fig. 3.4). These were the notorious Spanish Conquistadors making their bold and often ruthless incursions into Indian lands. By the time Vanderlyn had installed his painting in 1847 and Powell had hung his in 1855, the United States was in the process of acquiring vast territories originally occupied by Spain. Therefore, the paintings by Vanderlyn and Powell suggest that Spanish and Catholic influences would disappear when Anglo-Americans "liberated" the lands.

And that is just the process portrayed in the other two paintings installed at midcentury in the Capitol rotunda. Chapman's *Baptism of Pocahontas* (Fig. 3.1) and Weir's *Embarkation of the Pilgrims* (Fig. 3.2) make it quite clear that Protestants conducted the civilizing process. Chapman pictured Pocahontas being baptized into the Church of England and thereby abandoning her pagan past for indoctrination into English religion and culture. The Indians she has spurned surround her, still wearing "savage" clothing, while she is completely

FIGURE 3.3   *John Vanderlyn,* Landing of Christopher Columbus, *oil on canvas, 1837–1847. Architect of the Capitol, U.S. Capitol, Washington, D.C.*

FIGURE 3.4   *William Henry Powell,* De Soto Discovering the Mississippi, *oil on canvas, 1855. Architect of the Capitol, U.S. Capitol, Washington, D.C.*

covered in virginal white. Behind her stands John Rolfe, her future husband, who is helping her through the civilizing process; his presence at the ceremony assured their illustrious offspring that their families were sired by practicing Protestants.

Weir showed a different application of Protestant civilizing. His Pilgrims kneel in prayer aboard their ship bound for America, their gentle and dignified presences invoke the piety and devotion of those preparing to face the unknown and spread their beliefs across the nation. Their clothes are typical of antebellum portrayals of the *Mayflower* passengers. In fact, artists varied the dress according to their own whim, some following current styles, others inventing costumes to fit the implied message of the work. Not until the mid-nineteenth century did the familiar stiff, drab Pilgrim "uniform" come into being.[3]

The message underlying the paintings by Chapman and Weir (as well as those by Vanderlyn and Powell) was that of salvation. Pocahontas *saved* Virginia for the Anglican Church; the faith of the Pilgrims *saved* the United States from paganism. In this way, Chapman and Weir embellished the Massachusetts and Virginia origin myths with suggestions that God willed the transportation of Protestantism to America.

A writer for the *New-York Mirror* commended the artists for selecting "four points in our history which happily harmonize one with the other, and all evince views at once patriotick, poetical and philosophick." He was especially taken with Pocahontas and the Pilgrims as subjects. Chapman, he wrote, would paint

> scenes in Virginia, illustrating the colonization of that portion of America; where both Europeans and aborigines displayed in vivid colours, the chivalry of the one, and the native heroism of the other, Smith and Rolfe, Powhattan and Pocahontas, live in every memory. . . . [Weir] represents the departure of the pilgrims to seek a refuge in the wilderness from church and state tyranny. Those pilgrims who founded an empire *on a rock*; an empire which no storm can overthrow, and whose *prosperity* must *revolutionize* the world.[4]

The columnist not only praised these historical events as being "truly grand and fitted for the capitol" but said the artists "have done honour to themselves and to their country by their selection of subjects . . . [that] commemorate four distinct seeds, from which have arisen plants uniting and forming a great tree."[5]

Those "distinct seeds" may be found elsewhere in the U.S. Capitol rotunda. Antonio Capellano's *Preservation of Captain Smith by Pocahontas* (Fig. 3.5), Enrico Causici's *Landing of the Pilgrims* (Fig. 3.6) and *Conflict of Daniel Boone and the Indians* (Fig. 3.7), and Nicholas Gevelot's *William Penn's Treaty with the Indians* (Fig. 3.8) are relief panels above the principal doors that lead to the legislative chambers. These reliefs—carved by Italians and installed during the 1820s—depict the origin myths of Virginia, Massachusetts, the West, and Pennsylvania. All portray an encounter between fully clothed Europeans and half-dressed natives and thus emphasize the contrast between civilization and savagery, a theme repeated in other artistic embellishments of the Capitol building.[6]

In Capellano's *Preservation of Captain Smith*, a kneeling Pocahontas, wearing only a feathered skirt, lifts her arms in a gesture of supplication, while a fully dressed John Smith rests his head upon her breast. Behind them stand three menacing Indians, two aiming tomahawks toward the supine figure of Smith, as Powhatan (in the center) raises an arm to deter the fatal blow. It is a spectacle of brutality repelled by the intervention of a nubile young woman. This relief panel combines sensuality with heroism to convey a dual characterization often found in Pocahontas illustrations. Another Italian sculptor, Enrico Causici, presented a different cultural encounter in his interpretation of the Massachusetts origin legend. The panel pictures a rowboat with three Pilgrims (woman, man, and child) landing on Plymouth Rock; there to greet them is an Indian wrapped in animal skins, offering the strangers an ear of corn. This rather bizarre juxtaposition of characters reveals that the Pilgrims arrived as a family and, unlike their counterparts in Virginia, inspired the friendship of local tribes, not their enmity.

Similar depictions of the Pilgrims and Pocahontas appeared frequently in prints of the antebellum period. During the mid-nineteenth century, one of the most lucrative and popular ways to market artworks was the subscription print, usually issued by either an art union or printmakers such as Nathaniel Currier and, later, Currier and Ives.[7] These lithographed, engraved, or etched reproductions of paintings and drawings allowed average people to purchase inexpensive pictures and provided artists with a venue for distributing their works. Historical topics were always in demand, and "The Rescue of John Smith" and "The Landing of the Pilgrims" frequently surfaced as favorites. Thus, not only did these subjects appear as murals and sculp-

FIGURE 3.5   *Antonio Capellano,*
Preservation of Captain Smith by
Pocahontas, *sandstone, 1825. Architect of the
Capitol, U.S. Capitol, Washington, D.C.*

FIGURE 3.6   *Enrico Causici,*
Landing of the Pilgrims, *sandstone,
1825. Architect of the Capitol, U.S.
Capitol, Washington, D.C.*

FIGURE 3.7 (LEFT)
Enrico Causici,
Conflict of Daniel
Boone and the
Indians, *sandstone,
1826–1827. Architect
of the Capitol, U.S.
Capitol, Washington,
D.C.*

FIGURE 3.8
(RIGHT)
Nicholas Gevelot,
William Penn's
Treaty with the
Indians, *sandstone,
1827. Architect of the
Capitol, U.S. Capitol,
Washington, D.C.*

ture in the U.S. Capitol but similar representations in homes around the nation indicated that all varieties of Americans enjoyed viewing re-creations of the origin legends.

The Virginia and Massachusetts myths were also repeated often in antebellum American literature, although Bay Staters were far more prolific than Virginians. This imbalance began because the first settlers of Massachusetts had migrated from England to establish an independent Puritan society. To maintain the faith of their followers, spiritual leaders constantly reiterated the founders' religious quest while also examining their own personal orientation to that mission. In the process, clergymen recorded the legends of origin as a means of better understanding their secular and religious responsibilities. Many published those findings in volumes that not only remained in circulation for two centuries but underwent frequent revisions by each new generation of clerical scholars.

No such storehouse recorded the history of colonial Virginia. One cause of this disparity was the preponderance of publishing houses in the Northeast that produced a seemingly endless supply of sermons and narratives relating the history of Massachusetts. Another difference obviously lies in the diverse composition of the two communities. Virginians were less concerned with soul-searching and sermonizing about their ancestors' motivations for settling the Chesapeake. Because they were hoping to structure their society on the British model, they were not as intent as their Massachusetts counterparts about developing a separate culture and justifying it through analytical writings.

Annual Forefathers' Day celebrations also contributed to the preponderance of publications about the Massachusetts origin legend. Each year in Plymouth, Boston, and around the country, noted orators were delivering speeches, while well-respected poets were composing "hymns" to be sung at the banquet table. One of the most prominent was William Cullen Bryant, a native son of Massachusetts, who wrote the following tribute early in his career:

> *Wild was the day; the wintry sea*
> *Moaned sadly on New England's strand,*

When first, the thoughtful and the free,
Our fathers, trod the desert land.

Green are their bays; and greener still
Shall round their spreading fame be wreathed
And regions now untrod, shall thrill
With reverence, when their names are breathed.

They little thought how pure a light
With years, should gather round that day;
How love should keep their memories bright
How wide a realm their sons should sway.

Till where the sun, with softer fires,
Looks on the vast Pacific's sleep,
The children of the pilgrim sires,
This hallowed day like us shall keep.[8]

Like numerous others in the Forefathers' Day repertoire, Bryant's verses repeated a popular concept—the landing at Plymouth was directly related to the fate of the nation. The fathers not only anticipated the Constitution but laid the groundwork for the conquest of the continent. The metaphorical "desert land" in which Bryant located the regional ancestors lay not in coastal New England but far away in the ever-expanding West. The Pilgrims thus braved the "wintry sea" to spread their doctrines from coast to coast.

Compared to their counterparts in Massachusetts, antebellum Virginians produced far fewer literary works about the Jamestown's heroes during the first decades of the nineteenth century. As most professional publishing took place above the Mason-Dixon line, Virginia authors had less access to the wider literary markets. Before Richmond's *Southern Literary Messenger* started featuring historical accounts of colonial Virginia during the 1840s, literary treatment of the Pocahontas story came either from outsiders (who often derided the legend) or from loyal progeny whose tributes to their Indian ancestor remained buried in notebooks and diaries.

Blair Bolling, a direct descendant of Pocahontas and John Rolfe, compiled one such memorial in the early nineteenth century and illustrated it with his own sketches. Amid diary entries, Bolling provided a detailed account of his ancestors' history in England and Virginia, including descriptions of the plantations owned by his relatives. Bolling also reproduced a long epic poem about Pocahontas written in 1813 by a Richmond woman named Elizabeth Hening. Although totally lacking in literary grace, the verses Bolling transcribed in his formal script provide a rare indication of how Virginians were shaping the origin myth during the opening years of the early nineteenth century.

The poem, entitled "Savage Magnanimity," tells how Pocahontas "through the forest stole with noiseless feet" to warn John Smith and his English colleagues about a murderous attack planned by her father's band of "furious savages." Through the "gathering storm" she fled, and when she reached her destination, the heroine found the "gallant Smith . . . in sleep profound" and her breast "heaved . . . with many an anxious sigh" as she warned him that her father's "warrior band" was coming to "spill" the "sleeping white man's blood."

The poem ends with a very revealing tribute to Pocahontas:

> *Heroic maid, thine is that hallowed love,*
> *That flows unmingled from a source above,*
> *From earthly dross refined by angels' art,*
> *The pure emotion of a spotless heart . . .*
> *Let those who bend at Mammon's golden shrine,*
> *And take with falsehood's lips the vows divine,*
> *Who wed the gold that fills the miser's chest,*
> *And swear to love while hatred fills the breast,*
> *Blush if they can that in a savage mind,*
> *A love should dwell so noble, so refined.*[9]

In these few lines, Hening included a number of paradoxes that pervade the Virginia origin myth. Not only was Pocahontas both a "heroic maid" and sensuous child of the forest, but all other Indians—including her own father—were considered to be "savages." She acquired her "spotless heart" and rose above her "savage mind" through acceptance of Christianity (the "hallowed love" that came from "above") and that revelation replaced the "earthly dross" with "angels' art." This purification through baptism rendered her a worthy ancestor for Blair Bolling and other elite Virginians.

Bryant and his fellow New Englanders were describing their regional origins in terms of "thoughtful and free" missionaries disseminating their beliefs to "regions now untrod," at the same time Virginians were recounting a romantic adventure. Although both the Pilgrims and Pocahontas braved the perils of nature to carry out a "sacred mission," the former were believed to have been motivated by theological and civil obligations, the latter driven by emotional instincts. These basic differences were to pervade transmission of the origin myths and determine their meanings for the remainder of the nineteenth century.

In 1820, residents of Plymouth formed a new organization known as the Pilgrim Society to commemorate the bicentenary of the *Mayflower*'s landing.[10] Its first project was construction of Pilgrim Hall, the oldest ancestral memorial in the United States (Fig. 3.9). Original specifications called for a two-story structure with the lower section reserved for "public entertainment" and the upper one equipped with a "handsomely appointed" assembly room along with ample areas to display "antiquaries" and house a library.[11] Within two years, the trustees had purchased a lot on Court Street and hired Alexander Parris, one of the best-known architects in Massachusetts, to design the structure. Steeped in the neoclassicism of Charles Bulfinch and Benjamin Latrobe, Parris—who was then designing Quincy Market in Boston—proposed a seventy-by-forty-foot building with a granite exterior and the requisite two floors of exhibition space. In September 1824, the cornerstone of Pilgrim Hall was in place, and by December of that year, the building was ready for the Forefathers' Day banquet.[12]

By 1824, Plymouth had become a popular tourist attraction, with visitors traveling from around the region to touch its famous boulder and chip off bits of its upper portion to take home as souvenirs. To avoid total destruction of the "sacred" rock, the Pilgrim Society moved quickly to transport the icon from the center of town and enclose it within an iron fence in front of their Court Street property. In succeeding years, the organization began buying and demolishing old wharves and warehouses along the bay with the idea of transforming the harbor into a showplace with the boulder as its centerpiece.

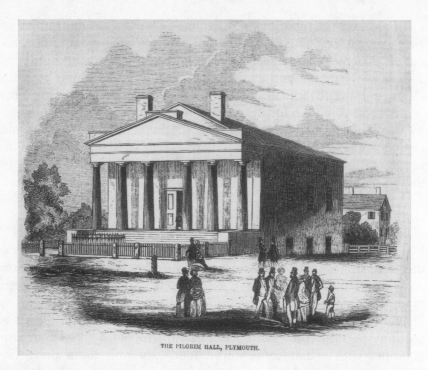

THE PILGRIM HALL, PLYMOUTH.

FIGURE 3.9   *Pilgrim Hall with Circular Iron Fence Enclosing Upper Part of Plymouth Rock, mid-nineteenth century, engraving. Courtesy of the Pilgrim Society, Plymouth, Mass.*

On August 1, 1853, the 233rd anniversary of the Pilgrims' departure from Holland, the Pilgrim Society inaugurated its campaign to build a canopy over the rock with an all-day celebration in Plymouth. Festooned in garlands and flags, the town went to great lengths to welcome 2,500 visitors who converged there from all corners of the nation. Massachusetts senators Charles Sumner and Edward Everett, governor John Clifford, and numerous local dignitaries addressed the crowd. A columnist for the *New York Courier and Enquirer* urged readers to contribute to the fund-raising drive but at the same time criticized residents of Plymouth for keeping the bottom half of their treasure submerged under a wharf. The citizens of New York, he taunted, would never "allow a memorial so precious to be buried up, obscured amidst wooden warehouses—with an old wooden wharf pushing its impudence into the waters, as if with a most radical progress." New Yorkers, he said "would sell the Battery and mortgage the Park" to avoid such a disgrace.[13] Fourteen years would elapse before a canopy covered the bottom part of the rock and an additional thirteen more would go by before the two halves of the boulder were united.

Jamestown had no buildings to commemorate Virginia's earliest settlers. The site of the first colony was a mosquito-ridden swamp, cut off from the mainland by the meandering James River, which kept propelling its way inland. The only reminder of the early colony was the old church tower that loomed over the tombstones and submerged foundations. In the mid-eighteenth century, the tobacco planter Richard Ambler had built a large house on the far side of the island, and over the next hundred years, various occupants tended their crops among the ruins. Otherwise, the property remained tranquil and vacant except for the occasional boat that stopped en route from Richmond to the Chesapeake. The desolation and remoteness of the spot added a ghostly overlay that seemed to characterize the Virginia origin myth.

Two men who visited Jamestown in 1817 responded to that mystique very differently. John Henry Strobia, a passenger on the New York–bound schooner *Logan*, spent several days at Jamestown while the ship's captain awaited a favorable wind. As he toured the island, Strobia experienced "a thousand Ideas and emotions, too rapid to be remembered or described," musing on the gallant and romantic Smith and the "tutelary angel," Pocahontas. He looked "upon the scenes" of Jamestown's history "with the eyes of a patriotic lover," even though only ruins of the early colony remained. A few months later, Henry Beaumont of Yorkshire, England, saw the overgrown marshlands quite differently, remarking only on "Reeds which were nearly eight feet in height" and old houses "Built of Brick which had fallen down and which appeared to have been long abandoned."[14] These two contrary views reveal a great deal about the power of preconditioning. Steeped in Virginia's origin myth, Strobia thrilled to emanations of Jamestown's historic past; lacking those associations, the Englishman saw only desolation and decay.

To the properly indoctrinated, Jamestown, like Plymouth, had become a perfect embodiment of the origin myth as it evolved in the nineteenth century. Ruins on a deserted island at the mouth of the James seemed haunted by the past. The broken gravestones and decaying brick tower recalled a courageous Indian girl and a fortress on the edge of a hostile continent; the eerie silence inspired romantic imaginations to run free and folklore to fill the air. At the same time, the bustling town on the edge of Plymouth Bay employed Yankee energy to concoct a more stolid fantasy. Buildings rose and rituals recurred to remind New Englanders that the Pilgrims had established the tangible foundation for an orderly and productive society. One urban, one pastoral, the two sites of early settlement formed perfect backdrops against which imagined dramas would unfold.

Part Two

ARTICULATING THE MYTHS

4

Lady Rebecca or the Forest Siren?

When the Disney Studio's 1995 animated feature *Pocahontas* presented Virginia's origin legend as a romance between a dashing, young John Smith and a sexy, fully developed Indian woman, it allied with one side of an age-old controversy. Disney officials seemed unconcerned about their departure from the *real* legend, because the Pocahontas story has always been interpreted in two opposing fashions. One version is the nubile forest nymph that the Disney Studio portrayed; its antithesis is the regal "Lady Rebecca," who was baptized a Christian, married John Rolfe, and met the king and queen of England.

Those two depictions of Pocahontas began their divergent routes through time with publication of John Smith's *Generall Historie* in 1624. From those pages, she emerged as both the bold and spirited girl of the rescue scene and as the dignified woman who visited the Court of St. James. Illustrations of those two antithetical characters also made their public debut in the *Generall Historie*. One is Simon Van de Passe's engraving of "Lady Rebecca" (Fig. 4.1); the other is Robert Vaughan's "Rescue of John Smith," which introduced Pocahontas as a half-nude child of nature (Fig. 4.2).

Van de Passe's "Lady Rebecca" has the greatest claim to authenticity of all representations of Pocahontas because he allegedly copied a portrait painted from life shortly after the Indian woman visited the royal family.[1] The print, which first appeared in the 1618

FIGURE 4.1   *Simon Van de Passe,* Matoaks als Rebecka *("Lady Rebecca"), engraving, 1616. Published in John Smith's* Generall Historie, *1624. Virginia Historical Society, Richmond, Va.*

FIGURE 4.2   *Robert Vaughan,* King Powhatan Comands C. Smith to be Slayne, His Daughter Pokahontas Beggs His Life ... *("Rescue of John Smith"), engraving, 1624. Published in John Smith's* Generall Historie, *1624. Virginia Historical Society, Richmond, Va.*

edition of the *Baziliologia: A Booke of Kings,* pictures Pocahontas staring at the viewer with large, dark eyes accented by heavy brows.[2] Her elongated, slightly darkened face and a cluster of feathers in her right hand hint of her native origins, but otherwise she looks European in her fashionable tall felt hat and brocade jacket topped by a stiff Elizabethan lace collar. Indeed, her pose and attire resemble that of any other seventeenth-century English gentlewoman—regal, sedate, and refined. The Dutch artist set his engraving in the same oval frame that he had used for the portrait of John Smith, as the frontispiece of the *Generall Historie* (Fig. 4.3).[3] Around the circumference of the Pocahontas portrait is a Latinate inscription, expanded in the legend below with this phrase: "*Mataoks als Rebecka, daughter to the mighty Prince Powhatan, Emperour of Attanougakomouch als Virginia converted and baptized in the Christian faith and wife to the wor* *Mr. John Rolff.*" Through its blend of Latin and English, interspersed with transliterations of native words, the inscription summarizes the legend Virginians loved to repeat. Her father was a "mighty Prince," she was baptized as a Christian, and she married John Rolfe. In those few phrases, she moved directly from her Indian name, Matoaka, to her Christian identity as Rebecca, with no mention of the nickname Pocahontas.[4]

Although Van de Passe's "Lady Rebecca" is a skilled example of precise draftsmanship, Vaughan's "Rescue of John Smith," which appeared in the *Generall Historie* as one of five vignettes surrounding a map of "Ould Virginia" (Fig. 4.4), is a crude and ill-proportioned pastiche. Huge figures are juxtaposed against smaller ones in a seemingly disconnected hodgepodge. And that was indeed the case, for Vaughan superimposed his renditions of Smith's adventures onto reproductions of John White's illustrations of coastal America.[5] In Vaughan's cut-and-paste vignettes, an oversized figure of Chief Powhatan presides over rows of dwarfed braves; the action takes place in a tunnel-shaped hut borrowed from a John White drawing. In the foreground, another giant—this one wearing a toga-style garment also adopted from White—is supervising three natives raising hatchets and leaning over a bearded man identified by the initials "C:S:" (Captain Smith). Kneeling in front of him is the small figure of Pocahontas. Her right arm extends over Smith's chest, her bare upper back implying that she wears nothing on her upper torso, although the viewer sees her only from behind. The inscription beneath the drawing reveals that "King Powhatan comands C. Smith to be slayne" while "his daughter Pokahontas beggs his life."[6] This Vaughan engraving was the first visual depiction of the famous rescue.

FIGURE 4.3   *Simon Van de Passe,* Captain John Smith, *engraving, 1616. Published in John Smith's* Generall Historie, *1624. Virginia Historical Society, Richmond, Va.*

FIGURE 4.4   *Robert Vaughan,* Map of Virginia, *engraving. Published in John Smith's* Generall Historie, *1624. Department of Prints and Photographs, Library of Congress, Washington, D.C.*

Buried in the pages of the *Generall Historie*, the divergent images of Lady Rebecca and the forest nymph attracted little notice until the book was republished in the early nineteenth century. Coupled with the release of a new engraving of Van de Passe's portrait in 1793, the *Generall Historie* inspired popular authors and printmakers–most of whom lived in the Northeast–to utilize the colorful stories that were laced through Smith's text.[7] Their favorite by far was the rescue scene. In that oft-quoted passage, the captain described how the Indians captured him and took him to Powhatan's headquarters, where his head was placed upon a stone; the chief then ordered his men to "beate out" Smith's "braines." Just as they were poised to strike, Smith wrote, "the King's dearest daughter" intervened by placing his "head in her armes" and laying "her owne upon his to save him from death," a maneuver that persuaded Powhatan to call off his warriors and release his captive. This dramatic moment would be replayed in literature and art for the rest of the nineteenth century.[8]

Other tales laced through the *Generall Historie* relate that Pocahontas provided food for the starving garrison, warned the Englishmen of planned Indian attacks, and served as an advocate for the Indians by pleading with the settlers to spare her captured tribesmen. Smith also described Pocahontas leading a coterie of thirty native women "naked out of the woods, onely covered behind and before with a few greene leaves, their bodies all painted." A wild orgy-like performance followed. The women dashed around singing and dancing in the "most excellent ill varietie . . . oft falling into their infernall passions." After their cavorting ended, the "Nymphes" invited Smith into their "lodgings" where they "tormented him . . . with crowding, pressing, and hanging about him, most tediously crying, Love you not me? love you not me?"[9] Not surprisingly, this passage has inspired a great many raucous literary and artistic interpretations.

Smith also described his visit with Pocahontas at Brentford in southern England. At first she refused to talk with him, he wrote, but in time she relented and hesitatingly admitted:

> You did promise Powhatan what was yours should bee his, and he the like to you; you called him father being in his land a stranger, and by the same reason so must I doe you. . . . Were you not afraid to come into my fathers Countrie, and caused feare in him and all his people (but mee) and feare you here I should call you father; I tell you then I will, and you shall call mee childe, and so I will bee for ever and ever your Countrieman. They did tell us alwaies you were dead, and I knew no other till I came to Plimoth; yet Powhatan did command Uttaamatomakkin to seeke you, and know the truth, because your Countriemen will lie much.[10]

This convoluted utterance has been interpreted as everything from a lover's reunion to a cultural misunderstanding. Some cite it as an example of Smith's endeavors to discredit his successors by implying that they tended to "lie much." Others have interpreted it as an indication that Powhatan had initiated Smith as his tribal "brother," thus Pocahontas considered him to be a kinsman.[11]

With these supposedly historical tales as background, authors derived a variety of suggestive fantasies.[12] The first notable corruption
came from a Frenchman, the Marquis de Chastellux, who visited the
Virginia plantation of Mrs. Robert Bolling Jr. in the 1780s. As the
French aristocrat wandered around her huge estate near Petersburg,
he was reminded that his hostess claimed Powhatan as an ancestor.
Well aware that Europeans loved to read about American Indians,
Chastellux amassed a mountain of material about the natives of Virginia and after his return to France wrote an account of his U.S. tour,
replete with a detailed recapitulation of the Pocahontas legend. *Travels in North-America in the Years 1780–81–82* was published in France
in 1787, and later that same year, the popular *Columbian Magazine*
supplied American readers with a translation of the marquis's story.[13]

Chastellux embellished the traditional narrative with a bit of
Gaelic earthiness. In Smith's book, Pocahontas saves his life by placing her head on top of his head to stave off the fatal blow. The Marquis, however, changed the emphasis by proclaiming that she "threw
herself upon his *body*" and "*clasped him in her arms*" (italics mine).[14] In
revamping a few phrases, Chastellux (or his translator) planted seeds
for future visual and literary embellishments. He went further afield
a few paragraphs later in his description of the encounter between
Smith and Pocahontas in Brentford, England, whereupon Smith
"was extremely happy to see her again, but dared not to treat her
with the same familiarity as at Jamestown." Even though Pocahontas
"threw herself" into his arms, he refused to return "her caresses with
equal warmth."[15] In the *Generall Historie,* Smith reported the incident
as a chaste reconciliation with no such suggestions of a tête-à-tête between former lovers. By turning Smith's text into fiction, Chastellux
discovered an unbeatable formula—the liaison between an "uncivilized" Indian woman and a lonely Englishman. And who could be
better models than Smith and Pocahontas?

The marquis's hints about a romance between Smith and Pocahontas proved to be more appealing than Smith's murky account designed to indict the Virginia Company. Subsequent authors embraced this spiced-up version of the Pocahontas story and
transformed the incident into a love affair between a gallant captain
and a sensual forest nymph. John Davis's *Travels of Four Years and a
Half in the United States of America,* published in 1803, was the most
popular of these flights of fancy, although the author alleged he was

transcribing a historical incident told him by Virginians. By combining the marquis's diary format and passages from Smith's *Generall Historie*, the English author converted the Pocahontas epic into an erotic romp. Indian women lusted to have sex with white males, Powhatan's wives fought "in convulsive throes" to be bedded by Smith, Pocahontas (filled with "every tenderness" and "soft emotions" of the "female bosom") hungered for Smith's attentions. Yet the captain spurned her "tumultuous extasy of love" and refused to agree to the marriage she so desired. Eventually convinced that Smith was dead, Pocahontas accepted Rolfe's proposal, partly because she was unable to resist "the ardour of his caresses." But even after her marriage, she never stopped yearning for the man she had rescued. Upon meeting him again in England, "the tender girl hung over Smith with tears" and died longing for his advances.[16]

Pocahontas emerged from the pages of Davis's book as an ideal male fantasy, a passionate girl of the forest totally unrestricted by European moral constraints. The tale that Davis wove into his *Travels* of 1803 was apparently so appealing that he embellished the narrative and reissued it as the admittedly fictional *Captain Smith and Princess Pocahontas*, published two years later. By amplifying the text with a detailed description of the Smith-Pocahontas-Rolfe triangle, the author transformed history into sensationalism.[17] Davis admitted as much in a correspondence with his publisher. "The character of the foundation of Jamestown," he wrote, "deserves to be known; and, if in tracing the progress of his [Smith's] Colonial establishment there be superadded the adventures he was involved in, History, without losing its dignity, will acquire new attractions."[18]

If "attractions" meant eroticism, he succeeded in embellishing the "adventures" considerably. On page after page, Davis described how Pocahontas's long black hair (which revealed her "coquetry") would "riot down her comely" back, shading "but not hiding the protuberance of her bosom." With few subtleties, the author frisked through numerous "passionate embraces" and "conjugal endearments" and went so far as to imply that Smith and Pocahontas enjoyed a sexual liaison while Powhatan held him in captivity. This was pretty steamy stuff for the early nineteenth century, as the popularity of the novel confirms. *Captain Smith and Princess Pocahontas* was, in fact, so successful that Davis immediately released an almost identical version entitled *The First Settlers of Virginia*. When

critics attacked the first novel for its "pedantry, vulgarity, affecta-
tion and conceit," Davis was so delighted that he instructed the
publisher to append the negative comments to the preface of *First
Settlers.*[19]

The same "passionate" Pocahontas appeared on stage for the first
time in James Nelson Barker's *The Indian Princess, or La Belle Sauvage*
of 1808. The playwright, a member of a prominent and politically
visible Philadelphia family, was in his early twenties when he wrote
the "operatic melo-drama." Although he was young, Barker had already produced several plays, an experience that had taught him
how to capture audiences by blending veiled sensuality, wholesome
humor, swashbuckling action, and unbridled patriotism. *The Indian
Princess* opened in Philadelphia but closed almost immediately because of controversies surrounding one of the actors. A year later,
however, it reopened to packed houses and complimentary reviews.[20] As one of the first plays in American theatrical history to
deal with an Indian theme, Barker's production predated by almost
two decades the raft of shows that entertained American audiences
during the 1830s and 1840s.[21]

Barker emulated Davis, not so much in the plot—which wanders
even further afield from Smith's history—but in the character of Pocahontas, who is lively, loving, and full of earthy passion.[22] Although
the playwright crafted much of his dialogue around Davis's love
scenes, including numerous heavings and throbbings of native bo-
soms, he dwelt less on the erotic than the intrepid. The complex plot
begins with the landing of Smith, Rolfe, and their party of British settlers on the shores of the "Powhatan River." Pocahontas, however,
does not appear until the beginning of Act 2. The scene is
Powhatan's "palace" at Werowocomoco, where the Indian chief sits
"in state" awaiting the execution of Smith. To a musical fanfare, composed by the British émigré John Bray, the Indians lead Smith into
the tent. Then the drama intensifies:

*The third signal is struck, the hatchets are lifted up: when the PRINCESS,
shrieking, runs distractedly to the block, and presses SMITH's head to her bosom.*

White man, thou shalt not die; or I will die with thee!

Music. She leads SMITH to the throne, and kneels.

My father, dost thou love thy daughter? listen to her voice; look upon her tears: they ask for mercy to the captive. Is thy child dear to thee, my father? Thy child will die with the white man.

Plaintive music. She bows her head to his feet. POWHATAN, after some delib-eration, looking on his daughter with tenderness, presents her with a string of white wampum. POCAHONTAS, with the wildest expression of joy, rushes forward with SMITH, presenting the beads of peace.

Captive! thou art free!—[23]

More music and a surge of effusive "joy" from the cast ended the first stage enactment of the famous rescue scene. It was a seminal event, es-pecially for those artists, illustrators, and, eventually, filmmakers who would later recreate that moment just as Barker had dramatized it.

Barker's characterization of Pocahontas may have come from Davis, but his depiction of Smith did not. The captain—generous, magnanimous, and appreciative of Pocahontas's bravery—did not re-semble the arrogant, self-centered scoundrel of Davis's prose. Nor did Barker allow any hints of romance to pass between Pocahontas and Smith, for all her passion was reserved for Rolfe. Their raptur-ous encounter in a wooded bower was the highlight of the perfor-mance. As he embraced her, he sighed:

But, ere the face of morn blush rosy red,
To see the dew-besprent, cold virgin ground
Stain'd by licentious step; O, long before
The foot of th' earliest furred forrester,
Do mark its imprint on morn's misty sheet,
With sweet good morrow will I wake my love.[24]

It was indeed the quintessence of romantic sensuality, suggestive but discreet, lifting what might otherwise have been labeled misce-genation to the level of melodrama.[25] Barker's play added a cast of characters that became stock players in future replays of the Poca-hontas story and in much of the romantic fiction that proliferated during the early nineteenth century. The Indians were lusty, child-like, and—with the exception of Pocahontas and her brother, Nan-taquas—weak and corruptible. This pair was distinctive because each accepted the values of the English settlers and expressed a desire to become respectable members of English society. Pocahontas, a girl of royal breeding, was not only a "good Indian" but a submissive and Anglicized one, her native "passions" controlled by her yearning to conform with the wishes of her "superiors." Such aspirations elevated the scarcely tamed child of the forest above her tribesmen.

Davis's publications and Barker's *Indian Princess* created a new heroine for the American public and spawned a host of popular Pocahontas romances that paid little attention to historical facts and often merged the characters of Smith and Rolfe. The interracial attraction remained central to the formula. So long as an English male received Pocahontas's affection, his identity was of secondary importance. She must be perceived as a nubile vixen, alluring and innocent, free from the constraints of European civilization. Objections to this sexy Pocahontas proved futile; so successfully had she captured the imaginations of early nineteenth-century Americans that she became an indelible strand in the evolution of the Virginia origin legend.

In 1845, South Carolina's premier man of letters, William Gilmore Simms, published an essay entitled "Pocahontas: A Subject for the Historical Painter," in which he chastised artists for not putting "to proper use by the pen or pencil" the story of John Smith's rescue. Those who had attempted to illustrate it, he complained, failed to capture "the struggle at its height, when face and form, and eye and muscle . . . are wrought upon by the extremity of action."[26] Simms was apparently responding to the numerous illustrations depicting Pocahontas rescuing Smith by cradling his head on her breast.

Beginning with the frontispiece of Davis's 1817 edition of *Captain Smith and Princess Pocahontas* and culminating in an illustration by Alonzo Chappel in J. A. Spencer's *History of the United States* (1866) (Fig. 4.5), these scenes repeat the iconography that Robert Vaughan had used two centuries earlier in his drawings for Smith's *Generall Historie*.[27] They picture a semiclothed Pocahontas; she kneels next to the tethered body of John Smith. In some prints, she cradles his head in her arms; in others, she throws her whole body onto his; in still others, she raises an arm to fend off the executioner. The male Indians are always menacing, their primitive costumes contrasting sharply with the neatly dressed Smith (Fig. 4.6). That juxtaposition of

FIGURE 4.5 *Alonzo Chappel,*
Pocahontas Saving the Life of Capt.
John Smith, *engraving, 1861.*
Published in J. A. Spencer, History of
the United States, 1866. *Author's
collection.*

FIGURE 4.6 *Thomas Sinclair,* Captain Smith Rescued by Pocahontas, *lithograph.*
Published in James Wimer's Events of Indian History, *1841. Divison of Prints and
Photographs, Library of Congress, Washington, D.C.*

raw masculine ferocity and female vulnerability had apparently become so thoroughly identified with the Pocahontas legend that the Italian sculptor Antonio Capellano duplicated it in his relief panel above the rotunda door in the U.S. Capitol (Fig. 3.5).

The half-dressed Native American woman had numerous visual antecedents, most notably the symbolic "America" found on everything from fountains to map cartouches. John White's early sketches showed native women with their breasts uncovered, and early visitors to the Jamestown settlement described the women as similarly attired. But intimate physical contact between a white male and an Indian female had few artistic precedents, thus rendering unique the depiction of John Smith with his head nestled against Pocahontas. That portrayal in nineteenth-century prints was all the more appealing because the twelve-year-old "princess" who had made her first appearance in Smith's *Generall Historie* had matured in two centuries to become a luscious woodland seductress.

Although the Indians and the English did dress quite differently in the early seventeenth century, rarely was there the marked contrast between partially nude Indians and fully clothed. English that artists and writers portrayed in the antebellum period. When the settlers first arrived, the East Coast Algonquians wore skins and furs in winter but soon negotiated with the British to exchange those coverings for woven blankets and, eventually, European clothing.[28] Nevertheless, the concept of the undressed Indian prevailed, especially in artwork picturing an armored or uniformed John Smith and a seminude Pocahontas (Fig. 4.7).

The English printmaker Edward-Henry Corbould, who hailed from a distinguished line of graphic artists, designed a popular engraving that was first printed in London about 1850 (Fig. 4.8). Set on the edge of a forest with a waterfall in the background, the dramatic composition might well have been inspired by Barker's *Indian Princess*. One can almost hear the music accompanying the melodrama as Pocahontas (turned sideways so that her breasts are visible) kneels to protect the victim from his assailant. Smith's hands are tied behind his back, fastened to a huge stone; his head is anchored to the boulder beneath his body. On the left is a chief holding a spear, and on the right, a ferocious brave (identified in a later version as the evil Opechancanough, perpetrator of the 1622 Jamestown raid) brandishes a pointed weapon. To learn about In-

FIGURE 4.7   *A. C. Warren,* Captain Smith Rescued by Pocahontas, *engraving, mid-nineteenth century. Author's collection.*

FIGURE 4.8   *Edward-Henry Corbould,* Smith Rescued by Pocahontas, *engraving by George Virtue, c. 1850. Division of Prints and Photographs, Library of Congress, Washington, D.C.*

dian markings, costumes, and artifacts, Corbould apparently studied
George Catlin's paintings of Plains Indians, exhibited at London's
Egyptian Hall in 1840–1841. However, the garments and weapons
in those works were nothing like those used by early seventeenth-
century Powhatans.[29] The artist's skewed attempt at authenticity,
however, did not hinder the print's popularity. Most likely it was the
swashbuckling drama and depiction of the partially exposed Pocahontas that promoted sales and induced frequent reproductions of
the image.

Most of these suggestive portrayals of Smith's rescue came from
Northern publishers of books and prints, an imbalance that was
widely recognized.[30] New England's domination of the press fostered
a spate of repetitive pictorial and visual images that antebellum
Southerners found demeaning. Attempts by Virginians to sustain a
counterimage of Pocahontas, one that eschewed sensuality in favor
of heroism and the nobility of Van de Passe's "Lady Rebecca," met
with formidable hurdles posed by both the anti-Southern bias operat-
ing within the major channels of communication and the seductive
appeal of sensationalism purveyed by the romanticized prints,
Barker's play, and Davis's novels.

Beginning early in the eighteenth century, the plantation elite were
determined to substantiate the aristocratic credentials of Pocahontas.
The historian Robert Beverley, for example, published a letter to
prove that Queen Anne had received Pocahontas during her sojourn
in England. The Indian "princess" was so admired as a "Lady," Beverley wrote, that she commanded "all imaginable Respect" from the
British nobility. He then further embellished the legend by declaring
that King James had frowned upon the marriage of the "Emperor"
Powhatan's daughter to a mere commoner.[31] Thirty years after Beverley published his history, William Stith described Pocahontas as a
British noblewoman who had been "well instructed in Christianity,"
always spoke "good and intelligible *English*," and conducted her affairs in a "very civil and ceremonious" manner "after the *English*
Fashion."[32]

These attempts to endow Pocahontas with a regal pedigree not
only removed the heroine from hints of Indian "savagery" but also

turned attention away from the mixed blood that flowed through many elite Old Dominion veins. The Marquis de Chastellux commented on that unusual heritage when describing his visit to the Virginia plantation of Mrs. Robert Bolling Jr. His hostess, he wrote, looked "quite European," though her "exterior beauty" was surely due to the native strain in her ancestry.[33] The marquis seemed fascinated by the blurring of racial distinctions that had prompted Robert Beverley to write in his 1705 history of Virginia that only by intermarrying with the Indians could the Jamestown settlers have avoided the "Rapines and Murders" that had so decimated the colony. "Likelihood, many, if not most, of the Indians would have been converted to Christianity by this Method," Beverley wrote, and "the Country would have been full of People, by the Preservation of the many Christians and Indians that fell in the Wars between them. Besides, there would have been a Continuance of all those Nations of Indians that are now dwindled away to nothing by their frequent Removals."[34] This early eighteenth-century advocacy of intermarriage to avoid racial extinction suggests that pureblooded Native Americans had vanished entirely, and the notion that racial mixing would end tribal warfare presented an early, albeit reasoned, argument for Indian survival through acceptance of Christianity. Yet despite these typical assumptions of the period, Beverley touched upon a blurring of racial distinctions that few of his contemporaries would have acknowledged.

A century later, William Wirt—a Maryland-born lawyer, politician, and author who lived most of his life in Virginia—elaborated upon Beverley's opinions. Swept to prominence as U.S. attorney general in James Monroe's administration, Wirt published a popular biography of Patrick Henry in 1818, defended the Cherokee tribes before the Supreme Court in the early 1830s, and ran for the presidency of the United States on the Anti-Masonic ticket in 1832.[35] One of his early publications, *Letters of the British Spy* (1803), provides revealing insights into the mindset of an enlightened follower of Jeffersonian republicanism. Structured as a correspondence between a visiting Englishman and a fictitious columnist, the book attempts to prove that the rescue of John Smith made possible the founding of the American republic. Had Pocahontas not intervened in the execution, Wirt wrote, "the anniversary cannon of the Fourth of July would never have resounded throughout the United States." Pocahontas had not only been wise enough to perceive "the superiority of the Europeans" but had been able to foresee "the probability of the subjugation of her countrymen." Her reason for marrying Rolfe, he continued, was to avoid further bloodshed and thus abolish "all distinction between Indians and white men." They would then become "one people, the children of the same great family."[36]

Wirt's position on racial mixing ran counter to Virginia law, for the state had strict legislation forbidding miscegenation, especially if the nonwhite was of African descent.[37] Progeny of the state's first families, in fact, drew a clear distinction between the "correct" marriage of the Rolfes and the "abhorrent" sexual liaisons between whites and blacks. They could afford to be more generous toward early seventeenth-century matings between the English and the Powhatans, because they believed the Indians had been thoroughly expunged from the area. That rationale allowed Virginians to ignore the assimilated Native Americans in their midst who had accepted the Anglo-American lifestyle and had therefore "vanished" into the general population.[38]

When Wirt published his *Letters of the British Spy,* Virginia's leaders not only controlled Congress and the White House but held such a firm grip on the lucrative tobacco trade that they were among the most prosperous landowners in the nation.[39] One such Tidewater heir was Edmund Randolph, who traced his lineage to Pocahontas. A prominent Virginia politician and state governor, he had been a delegate to the Continental Congress of 1776 and the Constitutional Convention of 1787; subsequently he served in George Washington's cabinet as attorney general and secretary of state. Upon retirement from public office in 1795, Randolph devoted the remainder of his life to writing a history of his home state. Although not published in its entirety until the twentieth century, the rambling account stands as a revealing example of the way elite Virginians chose to record their past.[40]

Like Wirt, Randolph coupled creation of the United States with the deeds of Pocahontas. The "Virginia patriot," he proclaimed, should "ascribe the preservation of Smith to that chain of grand events of which the settlement of Virginia was destined to be the foremost link, and which finally issued in the birth of our American Republic." For Randolph, the bravery and righteousness of Pocahontas transcended her native background and worked to overcome all possible tribal associations. Other Indians, he explained, "may be described as cool, cruel, sullen, suspicious, and designing," but Pocahontas belonged to "a better class." She was not only "beautiful, engaging and innocent" but "had a compassionate and susceptible heart." Most important, she admired Smith "as a second father, not as a companion for love."[41]

Another such disclaimer came from John Daly Burk, an Irish-born playwright living in the Old Dominion. In 1804, he published a detailed history of his adopted state in which he turned the Virginia origin legend into a thoughtful, yet lively, antidote to Davis's *Travels*, published a year earlier. For Burk, there was little question about the exemplary heroism of both Smith and Pocahontas. He was a man of "superior courage and genius," she the possessor of a "humane and feeling heart" and "an ardor and unshaken constancy in her attachments" that left her "almost, without a rival." To amplify her superlative qualities, Burk painted a verbal picture of the rescue scene in which a warm and gentle girl, "with her hair loose, and her eyes streaming with tears," begged "her enraged father" to spare the life of "his prostrate victim" whose head "he was about to crush . . . with a club." It was a situation, Burk concluded, "equal to the genius of Raphael."[42]

Without ever making specific references to current popular novels or plays, Burk reprimanded all who "consider the story of Pocahontas as an interesting romance" and treat it as "mere fiction." He insisted that authors who implied that she held an unrequited affection for Smith were merely venting "their spleen against the historian" because factual accounts kept insisting upon "marrying the princess of Powhatan to a Mr. Rolfe," despite "the expectations raised by the foregoing parts of the fable." Burk ended his section on Pocahontas by lauding the "virtues of mildness and humanity" evident in her illustrious progeny. But his reference to the prominent descendants was not just another tribute to genealogical superiority. In fact, Burk was quite direct when he determined that none of her line "has been conspicuous in arts or arms." And though he had not found "a single scion from the stock" to be anything other than "amiable and respectable" to "the highest degree," he felt their "want of the more showy and imposing qualifications" came from the "affluent circumstances of the family, which generally take away the motive to exertion and enterprize."[43]

In this dubious tribute to Powhatan's plantation heirs, Burk covertly touched upon another reason that aristocratic Virginians boasted of their racially mixed heritage. When the mantle of leadership passed from the native chief to his wealthy and influential offspring, power—once wielded by the club and bow—shifted from physical strength to material might. In Europe, royal lines often relinquished their leadership roles as generations passed, yet they maintained the elevated status afforded them by that tiny drop of regal blood. In short, Burk implied that descendants of Powhatan might lack "exertion and enterprize" but they redressed such failings by virtue of their impeccable noble heritage.

Historians were not the only Virginians defending the character of Pocahontas; several artists were also committed to perpetuating the dignity of Lady Rebecca. The first and most controversial was Robert Matthew Sully, nephew and protégé of the more famous artist Thomas Sully. Shortly after the younger Sully had settled in Richmond in 1830, his uncle asked him to copy a portrait of Pocahontas, rumored to have been painted when she visited England. After several inquiries, Robert Sully found the painting at Thomas Bolling's plantation near Petersburg, but he soon realized that it was so badly damaged that copying it would be impossible. Therefore, he decided to create a new portrait based on the deteriorating original, even though after viewing it, the artist had doubts about its alleged seventeenth-century origins.[44]

As Sully prepared to begin the project, word leaked to the press that he was planning to copy the so-called Turkey Island portrait, and suddenly members of the Bolling, Randolph, and Robinson families swung into action. Irate letters passed back and forth between these descendants of Rolfe and Pocahontas, some containing documentation to prove the authenticity of the Pocahontas portrait, others claiming that it was a fake. William Bolling, son of the owner, asserted that the artist had made the copy without authorization from the family. This opinion received the wholehearted backing of a few influential relatives. "I cannot consent, on my part," Linneaus Bolling wrote his cousin, "to acknowledge that Dowdy, Gross, course and homely picture, as the likeness of Pocahontas, who I have al-

ways believed, was a delicate slender and beautiful young Girl."
William Bolling echoed those protestations when he described the
subject of the painting as being "a large, fat, sallow" woman with
"dead white skin, enormously large breasts much exposed, brown
curly hair, with *blue* eyes, another fact which proves it was not the
portrait of an Indian."[45] Other members of the family, however, testi-
fied that the portrait was indeed Pocahontas.

Although the first version of Robert Sully's *Pocahontas* has been
lost, it survives through two sources, neither of which even remotely
resembles the "Lady Rebecca" image or the romanticized Pocahontas fictionalized by Davis and Barker. One is a widely circulated lithograph, first issued in 1842 and later published in Thomas McKenney and James Hall's *History of the Indian Tribes of North America* (Fig.
4.9). In it, Pocahontas is pictured as a heavyset woman with long,
curly hair, tawny skin, and a feather in her right hand. Her draped
costume corresponds with similar depictions in late seventeenth-
century English portraits, which is perhaps why certain members of
the Bolling family insisted that the woman in the original "Turkey Island" painting was someone other than Pocahontas. Matthew Sully's
portrait was also copied by his uncle in 1852 (Fig. 4.10).[46] Although
Thomas Sully titled his copy *Pocahontas*, he portrayed a woman wearing the scooped-neck gown, pearls, and brooch that were fashionable
during the antebellum period, a deliberate anachronism no doubt intended to link members of the Virginia gentry with their vaunted ancestor.[47]

A few years after completing his first portrait of Pocahontas,
Robert Sully began to have second thoughts. "It was difficult," he
conceded, "to associate the idea of the Indian girl of the Forest with
the stern & starched costume of the 17 Century." Still protesting that
he aimed to "preserve the likeness, contour, (and) features of . . . the
presumed original," he set about to transform "the civilized or rather
the *fashionable*, Princess," into "the beautiful forest girl, of more *pleasant associations*." After reading Beverley's *History and Present State of
Virginia* and Smith's *Generall Historie*, he decided that Pocahontas
should be "Crowned with wild Flowers" and wear "pearls from the
ear and on the neck" (italics are the artist's).[48] His first revision, probably done around 1850, is a synthesis of the idealized Pocahontas
and the "dowdy" and "gross" family portrait (Fig. 4.11). Pictured as
full-faced and full-figured, she lifts her eyes upward; her hair, now

FIGURE 4.9 Pocahontas, *after the Turkey Island portrait, lithograph. Published by Daniel Rice and James Clark for Thomas McKenney and James Hall's* Indian Tribes of North America, *1830s. Virginia Historical Society, Richmond, Va.*

FIGURE 4.10 *Thomas Sully,* Pocahontas, *oil on canvas, 1840s. Virginia Historical Society, Richmond, Va.*

FIGURE 4.11 *Robert Matthew Sully,* Pocahontas, *oil on canvas, early 1850s. The State Historical Society of Wisconsin, Madison, Wisc.*

FIGURE 4.12 *Robert Matthew Sully,* Pocahontas, *oil on canvas, early 1850s. Virginia Historical Society, Richmond, Va.*

unkempt, is topped by a large floral wreath. But still dissatisfied, the artist again revised the portrait. In two paintings completed shortly before his death in 1855, Robert Sully removed her double chins, trimmed her round face, and straightened her curls (Fig. 4.12). Now freed entirely from the family portrait, Pocahontas had become slender and elfin, a carefully blended synthesis of Lady Rebecca and the forest siren.

The evolution of Sully's *Pocahontas* signifies the persistence of the bifurcated image associated with Virginia's heroine. Even the descendants could not agree on which was the *real* Pocahontas. Because Robert Sully was attempting to reconcile that old dichotomy, he ended up producing a hybrid. Over the succeeding years, the same paradoxical views of the ephemeral native girl appeared and reappeared. Shirley Custalow McGowan, a late twentieth-century spokesperson for the Powhatans, is quite aware of how those garbled perceptions of Pocahontas not only distorted the legend but presented skewed visions of Native Americans. She commented in 1995 that the Disney film really did "have it accurate about the heart and soul" of her people. However, "They're not doing a film about the Powhatan Indians," she charged. "They're doing a film about Pocahontas," and even though the portrayal is historically incorrect, "kids are going to think it's true."[49]

McGowan has a valid point. For generations, children have heard conflicting stories about Pocahontas as historians vied with entertainers, neither able to obliterate the contradiction. "The history of Pocahontas is, in and of itself, a source of much controversy," commented Peter Schneider, president of the animation division of the Disney Studios. "Nobody knows the truth of her legend. We simply set out to make a beautiful movie about a Native American experience."[50] That rejoinder reveals a great deal. The "truth" of those long-ago events will remain forever shrouded in mystery. Whether a "beautiful movie" at the end of the twentieth century or a sensational melodrama of almost two hundred years earlier, the dilemma remains essentially the same. Amusement and historical accuracy have long coexisted in an implausible relationship. That delicate balance between two irreconcilable extremes perhaps explains the enduring attraction of Virginia's origin myth.

The Landing of
the Forefathers

$\mathcal{N}$ineteenth-century New Englanders were not plagued with any conflicts about their regional origins. They were certain that the first step onto Plymouth Rock constituted such a seminal event in world history that it determined the guiding principles of the future United States.

The coalescence of the Pilgrims' mission into a singular image of the Plymouth landing gave New Englanders a sense of unity and purpose lacking in the contradictory—and often frivolous—interpretations of the Pocahontas legend. Throughout the region, generation after generation experienced a spiritual lift each time they recited Felicia Hemans's "The Landing of the Fathers." From the mid-1820s, when it first reached America, until well into the twentieth century, this poem reigned as the most popular of all Pilgrim "hymns":

> *The breaking waves dash'd high,*
> *On a stern and rock-bound coast;*
> *And the woods, against a stormy sky*
> *Their giant branches tost;*
>
> *And the heavy night hung dark*
> *The hills and waters o'er,*
> *When a band of exiles moored their bark*
> *On the wild New England shore.*

Not as the conqueror comes,
They, the true-hearted came,
Not with the roll of stirring drums,
And the trumpet, that sings of fame; . . .

Ay, call it holy ground,
The soil, where they first trod!
They have left unstained what there they found—
Freedom to worship God! [1]

In these verses, Mrs. Hemans (as she signed her poems) captured the hazards of the Pilgrims' voyage, the hardships of their struggle to survive in the wilderness, and—most significant—the sacred character of their mission.

This was indeed a remarkable feat for an Englishwoman who lived in Ireland and had never set foot on American soil. She, in fact, admitted knowing nothing about the Pilgrims until one day when she happened to read a crumpled newspaper that wrapped a parcel, announcing "an address delivered at Plymouth on some anniversary." The oratory was so moving and the description of the landing "so beautiful," she later told the Reverend Charles Brooks, "I could not rest till I had thrown them into verse; I took off my bonnet, seized my pen . . . caught the fire from this transatlantic torch, and began to write." When Brooks informed her that "a thousand persons in the Old Pilgrim Church at Plymouth" sang "her exquisite hymn" every Forefathers' Day, her eyes filled with tears. And when the minister revealed that the worshipers' favorite lines were *"They left unstained what there they found / Freedom to worship God,"* she raised "her voice, her eye at the same moment beaming with religious enthusiasm" and exclaimed: "'It is the *truth* there which makes the poetry.'"[2] Hemans's response is worth noting, for her concept of "truth" mirrored the beliefs of most New Englanders. The humble Pilgrims brought freedom of religion to an "unstained" wilderness. One American editor commented that her exposition of "truth" will be understood "as long as the old Rock itself shall stand. . . . it was a truth stronger than fiction ever was, and which fiction could but degrade."[3]

Felicia Dorothea Browne Hemans epitomized the popular nineteenth-century concept of a romantic bohemian. Born into the household of a Liverpool merchant and his Venetian wife, she began writing poetry as a child and continued to do so obsessively through-out her life. At eighteen, she married Captain Alfred Hemans and rapidly produced five sons. Then her husband fled to Italy. After his departure, Felicia moved in with her mother and sisters; they tended the children while she wrote poetry about faraway places and imagi-nary worlds. Her one attempt at playwrighting, *The Vespers of Palermo,* received such negative criticism that it closed after only one perfor-mance.[4] Following this disappointment, the once delicate beauty be-came an eccentric recluse, reputed to wear the same clothes for days and bathe only on rare occasions. She moved her household con-stantly, first to Wales and later to Ireland, where she died in 1835, a lonely and broken woman of forty-two.[5]

Although Hemans enjoyed only moderate success in Britain, she was widely acclaimed in Massachusetts, perhaps because her uncon-ventional lifestyle and excessive sentimentality was antithetical to the regional code of behavior.[6] Prominent Bostonians—among them William Ellery Channing, George Bancroft, and Andrews Norton—often sought her out during their European tours. With each of these men she carried on lengthy correspondences and exchanged books; in turn, they helped her procure American publishers. Hemans was so successful in selling her works in Massachusetts that once she seri-ously considered moving to Boston.[7]

New England's enchantment with Hemans's "Landing of the Fa-thers" is easy to understand. Her Pilgrims were courageous fighters conquering the ravages of nature to gain religious freedom. Such phrases as "stern and rock-bound coast" and "holy ground" captured the mystique of the Pilgrim legend treasured by most nineteenth-century New Englanders.[8] By the time her poem appeared, the land-ing had acquired a palimpsest of metaphorical layers. For many, it connoted transmission of the Protestant religion, British culture, and Puritan values throughout the United States. For others, evocation of the anchoring on Plymouth Rock provided an appealing image for persuading voters. For most New Englanders, however, musings about the landing inspired a sense of security and pride in the ac-complishments of their legendary regional ancestors. Each of these perceptions developed during the first quarter of the nineteenth cen-tury, thus Hemans's poem marked a culmination and consolidation of the landing metaphor that had been evolving for more than three decades.

Bradford's description of the *Mayflower*'s landing at Plymouth has become a cornerstone of the New England origin myth:

> Being thus arived in a good harbor and brought safe to land, they fell upon their knees & blessed the God of heaven, who had brought them over the vast and furious ocean, and delivered them from all the periles and miseries thereof, againe to set their feete on the firme and stable earth, their proper elemente. . . . Being thus passed the vast ocean, and a sea of troubles before in their preparation . . . they had now no friends to wellcome them, nor inns to entertaine or refresh their weatherbeaten bodys, no houses or much less townes to repaire too, to seeke for succoure . . . And for the season it was winter, and they that know the winters of that cuntrie know them to be sharp and violent, and subjecte to cruell and feirce storms, deangerous to travill to known places, much more to serch an unknown coast. Besides, what could they see but a hidious and desolate wildernes, full of wild beasts & willd men?[9]

With this description unknown—or misquoted—until the late 1850s, interpreters related the landing on Plymouth Rock in any manner they saw fit. The settlers of Plymouth, Judge John Davis told a Forefathers' Day audience in 1800, held "a firm and consoling belief" that they "were destined by the Almighty to be instruments of great good to mankind."[10] Such sentiments resounded often in Forefathers' Day oratory throughout the early nineteenth century as New Englanders held fast to the belief that the emigrants from Leyden had crossed the Atlantic with a mission. Although interregional conflict and cultural disparities might produce differences of opinion on the exact nature of that mission, most New Englanders believed that the *Mayflower*'s landing represented the beginning of a new era. To some, it suggested a prior fulfillment of Bishop George Berkeley's prediction that the course of empire would advance from east to west.[11] John Adams once recalled: "There is nothing . . . more ancient in my memory than the observation that arts, sciences, and empire had travelled westward; and in conversation it was always added, since I was a child, that their next leap would be over the Atlantic into America." Adams's brother-in-law, Richard Cranch, recalled the opening lines of a poem attributed to Berkeley ("The eastern nations sink, their glory ends, / And empire rises where the sun descends"), which old-timers believed to have been etched into Plymouth Rock by the *Mayflower* passengers.[12]

The impulse to attach momentous significance to the Pilgrims' arrival—even though no testamentary evidence documented the actual stepping ashore—sparked a number of apocryphal tales during the early national period. For example, a continuing debate between the descendants of John Alden and offspring of Mary Chilton enlivened newspaper columns, each side claiming that its ancestor had been the first to leap onto Plymouth Rock.[13] It seemed for a time that even the date of that first step ashore would be disputed. Bradford had recorded December 11 as the landing date according to the Julian calendar then in use. However, in 1752, England adopted the Gregorian calendar, which pushed up the date by eleven days. In the long run, the Old Colony Club settled matters in 1769 when it pronounced December 22 to be Forefathers' Day, and with few exceptions, New Englanders continued to celebrate the *Mayflower*'s landing on that date.[14]

By the early nineteenth century, pictures of that first step onto American soil had become an accepted venue for illustrating European civilization's westward migration. Although the Pilgrims did not figure exclusively in such portrayals, the iconography for characterizing the landings was remarkably similar. Vanderlyn's *Landing of Christopher Columbus* in the U.S. Capitol (Fig. 3.3), for example, shows a submissive band of natives seemingly startled that their territory had been "discovered" by a band of white Europeans.[15] With slight variation, the debarkation at Plymouth fit into that mold. One of the earliest such representations appeared as a cartouche on a New England map of 1774 (Fig. 5.1). That illustration by the British artist Thomas Jefferys depicts a band of Europeans confronting an Indian. The native bows to the British settlers, while the goddess Liberty—holding her customary pole topped by a cap—stands at his side. Pine trees and palm trees dot the background, and a crewman unloads cargo from a waiting ship. A similar vignette on a map of Latin America might picture the landing of Columbus; a map of Pennsylvania, William Penn; and one of New York, Henry Hudson.[16] To anchor this scene to Massachusetts, Jefferys included a rock inscribed "PLYMOUTH MDCXX" and placed fish in a net at its base. As G.N.G. Clarke observes, the date "1620 is at once historical fact and contract—an inference of a signed affidavit, so to speak, between the

FIGURE 5.1   *Detail of cartouche by Thomas Jefferys,* A Map of the Most Inhabited Part of New England . . . , *engraving, 1774. Colonial Williamsburg Foundation, Williamsburg, Va.*

arrival of the figures and the land on which they now write their history." In other words, possession of the territory was affirmed by the illustration of English men and women stepping ashore.[17]

Maps are linear abstractions of a three-dimensional reality, and their accompanying cartouches usually identify the location in an emblematic language; different types of communication, however, require more specified forms of visual identification. For example, when Samuel Hill designed an invitation for Boston's annual Forefathers' Day celebration toward the end of the eighteenth century, he employed another contemporary model, the landscape view or prospect. These horizontal chartings of port cities provided a readable system for designating landmarks and labeling the important vessels docked at water's edge.[18] Following this model for his illustration, Hill pictured a rowboat jammed with men approaching a jagged rock bearing the date "Dec. 22, 1620" (Fig. 5.2). Atop the

FIGURE 5.2   *Samuel Hill,* Invitation to Forefather's Day Dinner, *engraving, c.*
1798. Courtesy Massachusetts Historical Society, Boston, Mass.

boulder, a sailor stands ready to pull the passengers ashore, two natives view the arrival from a craggy precipice on the right, and barely
visible along the horizon loom the triple masts of the *Mayflower.* It is
a stark landscape, relieved only by the actions of the landing party
and a flurry of birds in the background. This representation of the
Pilgrims' landing is curiously anachronistic. The rugged coast hardly
resembles the placid inlet of Plymouth Bay, and the rowboat crew
wears costumes of the late eighteenth century instead of the Ja-
cobean clothing of the Pilgrims' own time. Nevertheless, those subtle
touches conveyed a specific message to recipients of the invitation.
The rockbound landscape had come to symbolize the hardships endured by the forefathers as well as the heritage of austerity and dili-
gence perpetuated by heirs of the Pilgrim tradition. Similarly, the
contemporary clothing worn by men in the rowboat associated
Bostonians attending the Forefathers' Day celebration with the people they were commemorating. Hill's illustration was apparently so
successful that it continued to adorn Boston's Forefathers' Day invita-
tions for several decades and was reproduced on objects that ranged
from glass paintings to Staffordshire china.[19]

The Italian immigrant Michele Felice Corné used a format almost identical to Hill's for his *Landing of the Pilgrims*, painted at least five times in the first decade of the nineteenth century (Figs. 5.3 and 5.4).[20] Although in principle Corné followed the same formula of a small boat mooring on Plymouth Rock, the addition of color and a greatly expanded scope endowed his large paintings with a dramatic quality impossible to convey in a small illustration. Each snowy landscape pictured a rowboat entering from the left filled with passengers wearing early nineteenth-century costumes, a crew member near the center tying the vessel to the rock, and natives viewing the spectacle from a raised promontory on the right.

Corné, however, expanded the contemporary relevance of the scene by introducing several idiosyncratic elements that may reflect his own preoccupations. Having recently immigrated to Salem, Massachusetts, the flamboyant artist often boasted of his flight from Naples to elude Napoleon's recruiters.[21] In one depiction of the Plymouth landing, he included in the approaching rowboat a British redcoat, an officer in a blue uniform holding a white flag, and men wearing the broad-brimmed black hats and tight-fitting waistcoats of the artist's mercantile contemporaries. With no documentary evidence to explain the inclusion of such figures, one can only speculate whether it suggests Corné's own experiences or specific wishes of his patrons. But regardless of the reasons he included these figures, there is little doubt that Corné intended to conflate the landing of the Pilgrims with more recent events, possibly the American and French Revolutions and the wealthy merchants of Boston or Salem.

That unlikely merger of past and present was not merely an accidental caprice on Corné's part but rather a conscious deployment of conventional imagery with proven popular appeal. Perhaps blending the Boston merchants with their Puritan forebears is not so much an anachronism as a logical working out of history that recalled Forefathers' Day rhetoric linking the Pilgrims with formation of the United States. The very fact that Corné painted multiple versions of the landing, each with slight alterations, suggests he had hit on a successful format. Although the landing on Plymouth Rock remains constant in each canvas, the various versions differ markedly in their details. Corné moved the Indians, altered the men in the boat, and

FIGURE 5.3   *Michele Felice Corné,* Landing of the Pilgrims, *oil on canvas,*
1800–1810. Photograph courtesy of the Vose Gallery, Boston, Mass.

FIGURE 5.4   *Michele Felice Corné,* Landing of the Pilgrims, *oil on canvas,*
1800–1810. Courtesy of the Pilgrim Society, Plymouth, Mass.

reconfigured the landscape. Whether the emendations were his own idea or were suggested by his patrons must remain a mystery because no records of the purchasers exist. The most important feature in Corné's varied landings is his contemporizing of the myth. If a single artist could twist that overarching subject to suggest different—and perhaps conflicting—affiliations, then the metaphorical "stepping ashore" had grown from being merely one element of the origin legend to constituting a composite allegory all by itself. And indeed, that was precisely what had happened. Until the 1860s, the ubiquitous image of the Pilgrims' stepping ashore would grace artwork, literature, and oratory to justify everything from political convictions to religious beliefs.

Printmakers of the antebellum period were responsible for promulgating that image through an array of subscription prints and book illustrations. The remarkable thing about this display of graphic art is the similarity of the "plot" being reenacted. With slight variations and fluctuating degrees of skill, each artist pictured an icy shoreline with passengers disembarking from the *Mayflower*, often shown as a tiny speck on the background horizon. All of these "landing of the Pilgrims" prints feature a group of men and women, usually wearing early nineteenth-century clothing, encamped on the edge of the sea in a makeshift settlement. One version, which had various reincarnations, follows the landscape setting of the Hill engraving and Corné paintings (Fig. 5.5). It depicts a wintry landscape with passengers carrying burdens up a hill from the harbor; a group of men surrounding a blazing campfire with an iron pot suspended above it; and an Indian crouching behind a large rock or tree to remind viewers that danger lurks in the wilderness. Another rendition of the same scenario presents a more intimate view of the settlers in their first encampment (Fig. 5.6). This variety usually focuses on a group of people near the shore, some arriving in a rowboat, others gathered around a campfire; in almost all of these, a wood-gatherer in the foreground peers warily at the ubiquitous Indian presumably waiting to pounce.[22]

By midcentury, most prints of the Pilgrims' landing had been reduced to such a recognizable formula that they became a visual shorthand for the entire Pilgrim legend. Typical was an illustration in the *History and Antiquities of New England, New York, and New Jer-*

FIGURE 5.5 *Anonymous,* Landing of the Pilgrims at Plymouth, Dec. 22nd, 1620, *engraving, c. 1840. Division of Prints and Photographs, Library of Congress, Washington, D.C.*

FIGURE 5.6 *H. Carmienecke,* Landing of the Pilgrims at Plymouth, December, 1620, *heliotype, 1856. Courtesy Massachusetts Historical Society, Boston, Mass.*

sey, published in Boston in 1841 (Fig. 5.7). Although the scene bears
no identifying attributes, readers would have understood readily
that the snowy setting and pious assembly were meant to represent
the landing at Plymouth. That same kind of graphic shorthand appears in the frontispiece for *Historical, Poetical and Pictorial American
Scenes*, published in New Haven in 1851 (Fig. 5.8). This scaled-
down and modernized version of Jeffreys's map cartouche reduces
the formula to its simplest components—a winter landscape with
four figures emerging from a rowboat, while a sailing ship rests on
the horizon—suggesting that the landing had become such an integral part of the region's visual lexicon that it required no identifying text.

Nathaniel Currier published a popular landing print around
1850 (Fig. 5.9). The familiar mixture of clergy and laymen gather
around the fire, their costumes updated to resemble provincial
New Englanders of the early nineteenth century. The settlement resembles a contemporary New England village instead of a wilderness outpost, and the man gathering wood in the foreground
appears to glance toward the native intruder with a relaxed expression of bemused curiosity. The immigrants, under the supervision
of a minister, look as if they are cheerfully cooperating to build a
Protestant community based upon rules of law and order. Unlike
the earlier prints, this rendition conveys an atmosphere of folksy
hospitality and security, with no sense of impending dangers. The
Currier lithograph thus caps off four decades of prints depicting
the landing at Plymouth. During the preceding years, artists had
been updating the legend by altering the costumes and reflecting
differing moods to correspond with changing styles; most of them
no doubt realized that the audience (whether purchasers of books
or subscribers of prints) cared little about historical verisimilitude
and preferred to view the Pilgrim legend in the context of their
own daily lives.

These prints depicting the landing of the Pilgrims convey an opposite message from those picturing the rescue of John Smith, also
popular during the same years. Although both tell of English survival in America, the Plymouth scenario stresses the mutual cooperation of a large group, whereas the "rescue of John Smith" prints
feature the deed of a single girl (or woman). During the 1840s and

FIGURE 5.7 *S. E. Brown,* Landing of the Pilgrim Fathers. *Engraving published in John W. Barber,* History and Antiquities of New England, *New York, and New Jersey, 1841. Courtesy of American Antiquarian Society, Worcester, Mass.*

FIGURE 5.8 *Anonymous, engraving, 1851. Frontispiece in John W. and Elizabeth Barber,* Historical, Poetical, and Pictorial American Scenes. *Courtesy of American Antiquarian Society, Worcester, Mass.*

FIGURE 5.9   *Nathaniel Currier,* Landing of the Pilgrims at Plymouth 11th Dec.
1620, *lithograph, c. 1850. Division of Prints and Photographs, Library of Congress,
Washington, D.C.*

1850s, as hostility between North and South intensified, more and
more reproductions of the landing of the Pilgrims and the rescue of
John Smith circulated. Almost all such prints rolled off Northern
presses, and the Pilgrims in their nineteenth-century clothing therefore appeared to be industrious protagonists triumphing over adversity and spreading Christianity. In contrast, the celebrated
"founder" of Virginia is reduced to the humiliating shame of dependence on a half-clothed (and thus uncivilized) Indian to save his
life.

In these illustrations of the origin myths, Native Americans played
a significant role. Even with scant clothing, Pocahontas always came
across as a "good Indian," while her tribesmen, poised to lower their
axes, were pictured as villains. Similarly, the natives peacefully observing the Pilgrims' arrival in the Hill and Corné landscapes are
friendly welcomers, while the Indian behind the tree in the earliest
Pilgrim-landing prints personified the murderous monster described
in popular captivity narratives.[23] Attitudes toward Indians had
changed, however, by the time Currier designed his lithograph at

midcentury. Natives were no longer perceived as a threat in Massachusetts, and the Indian removal policies of the Jackson administration led many New Englanders to question whether the real villains lived in the wilderness or in Washington. Consequently, midcentury artists felt free to depict the native behind the tree as a benign member of a vanished race. Changing perceptions did not, however, prompt artists to remove the Indian from the formulaic landing scenario. By 1850, he had become a familiar emblem, if not to represent evil, then to signify the pagan "other" waiting to be civilized by Pilgrim saviors. Together, these landing prints create a composite picture of sacrifice, missionary zeal, communal harmony, and courage against man and the elements, an image that tied the stepping ashore on Plymouth Rock to a variety of issues then confronting New Englanders.

One point of contention in early nineteenth-century Massachusetts was the religion that had purportedly brought the Plymouth settlers to America in the first place. By the 1820s, a variety of New England Protestants were claiming spiritual descent from the Pilgrims, a heritage that found its way into a pervasive religious controversy. Ever since the mid-eighteenth-century wave of evangelical fervor known as the Great Awakening, scores of frustrated Congregationalists—unable to accept the burden of original sin, predestination, public confessions, and other doctrines of orthodox Calvinism—had been leaving the established church to follow John Wesley, George Whitefield, and other charismatic evangelicals then touring the Eastern seaboard. Their well-attended revival meetings provoked a variety of doctrinal disputes within New England's old Puritan churches, and by the early nineteenth century, deep divisions between the orthodox clergy and the reformers (often called Arminians) threatened to undermine the commanding position Congregational ministers then enjoyed.[24]

The schism that divided Plymouth during those years typified similar divisions throughout the region, but it acquired heightened significance because the First Plymouth Church boasted of being the parish founded by the *Mayflower* passengers. Originally independent from the more dominant Massachusetts Puritans, this most visible

congregation became a bellwether for what was to transpire throughout New England in subsequent years. During the 1740s, the Reverend Nathaniel Leonard of the First Church, fearful of further losses
from his already diminishing flock, took the desperate measure of
inviting evangelicals to preach from his pulpit. This unorthodox attempt to stem attrition so angered the more traditional members of
his congregation that many left to form the Third Plymouth Church.
The erstwhile malcontents, however, rejoined the fold after 1783,
when the new pastor, Chandler Robbins, turned back toward orthodoxy. That reconciliation lasted less than two decades. Around 1801,
when Robbins's successor, James Kendall, loosened the restrictions
instituted by his predecessor, the conservatives again bolted. This
time the rupture was permanent. Eventually, the First Church became formally affiliated with the Unitarians, but the Third Church
retained its Congregational designation.[25]

Because descendants of the Pilgrims filled both congregations,
each church insisted it was perpetuating the religion of the forefathers. The renegades claimed that the Pilgrims themselves had broken away from both the Anglicans and the Puritans, while the conservative establishment insisted that the *Mayflower* passengers were
merely a segment of mainstream Puritanism. Those contrasting interpretations indicate that the Pilgrim heritage, like the gospels themselves, were often cited to substantiate all points of view, and the
landing at Plymouth—which signified a period of religious unity and
communal harmony—served as a touchstone for both doctrinal extremes.[26]

The "new lights" summoned the Pilgrims to suggest defiance of religious orthodoxy, while their opposites (often called "old lights") reminded parishioners that their ancestors had submitted to the authority of the Puritan elect. For example, the reformist John Allyn
told a Forefathers' Day congregation of 1801 that he called upon "the
rock of the pilgrims, and every vestige of antient times" to remind
the parishioners that the "profane world" had discriminated against
their ancestors; he further implied that the doctrinaire Calvinists
were similarly intolerant of dissenting ideas expressed by the Pilgrims' descendants.[27] On the same occasion five years later, the conservative Abiel Holmes—father of the physician-writer Oliver Wendell Holmes and grandfather of the Supreme Court justice of that
same name—summoned the authority of the forefathers to prove the

opposite point, denouncing the religious renegades and proclaiming that "the Puritan Reformers" were opposed to "innovation" and had severed ties with the English Puritans in order to pursue the "pious desire" of returning "to the original form and usages of the Christian church."[28] Long after the Unitarians formally broke away in 1824, New England clergymen of all persuasions continued to invoke the Pilgrims in support of their positions. When faced by such fiery democratic evangelists as Charles Grandison Finney and Lorenzo Dow, both sides of the Congregational divide felt comfortable recalling a homogeneous band of Englishmen whose rational and pious cohesiveness inspired harmony among parishioners.[29]

Until 1833, the established church controlled the Massachusetts legislative and judicial systems. Despite the separation of church and state mandated by the U.S. Bill of Rights, the clergy effectively ruled on matters ranging from taxes to public education.[30] This unique extension of clerical domination intensified the struggle between the old and new lights. A bevy of Yale-trained Calvinist evangelicals—including such notables as Jedidiah Morse, Abiel Holmes, Samuel Austin, and Joseph Lyman—spearheaded a counterreformation, often called the Second Great Awakening. Its purpose was to destroy the Arminian dissidents and counteract the democratic evangelists by reviving the religious conformity of the early Puritans.

Although reformers and orthodox Calvinists could be found in both the Republican and Federalist Parties, most conservative clergymen in the Boston area preached the Federalist canon. In fact, when the clerical orthodoxy cooperated with prominent Bostonians to preside over the 1798 Forefathers' Day dinner, the event became a loosely disguised Federalist rally.[31] Toasts lauded the presidential administration of Massachusetts's own John Adams, especially his sanction of the "Alien and Sedition Laws" aimed at limiting the number of French revolutionaries entering the United States. One guest in 1797 saluted the "strong arm of government . . . May it be felt by intrigaing [intriguing] aliens, and seditious citizens."[32]

After Thomas Jefferson defeated Adams in 1800, the confrontational tenor of Forefathers' Day rhetoric in Boston increased. Although portraits of *Mayflower* passengers hung around the hall and participants drank toasts to Massachusetts founders, these tributes were merely preliminaries to promoting prominent Federalist officials and denouncing the Republicans. During the Jefferson adminis-

tration, a Forefathers' Day toast proclaimed: "May the ghosts of our
pious forefathers walk during the approaching reign of infidelity, and
deter the daring philosophists from attacking the sacred temple of religion."[33] By calling upon the ghosts of Brewster, Standish, and
Carver to haunt the new administration, Boston politicians and their
ministerial colleagues firmly aligned the goals of the Federalist Party
with the ideals that the Pilgrims ostensibly transported to New England's shores.

Among orthodox ministers in the Boston area, Jedidiah Morse was
the most outspoken. From his pulpit in the First Congregational
Church in Charlestown, he ranted against Arminians, Unitarians,
Baptists, Anglicans, "Papists," and all other perceived threats to the
New England establishment.[34] Steeped from youth in New England
bias, Morse often wrote and lectured about the virtues of the original
Plymouth settlers, exhibiting few sympathies for other sections of the
country. In the late 1780s, he traveled through Virginia en route to a
temporary ministerial post in Midway, Georgia, a journey that gave
the newly ordained minister an opportunity to observe Southern customs and mores for the geography books he was planning to write.
The combination of slavery and warm weather in Virginia, he concluded, produced a society predicated on idleness, irreligion, and
gambling, an intolerable mixture that confirmed his convictions
about New England's ethnic purity and moral superiority.[35]

Morse published these conclusions in his *American Geography* (1789)
and repeated them four years later in *American Universal Geography*.
As might be expected, Virginians were enraged. "Heavens, what a
picture!" exclaimed William and Mary law professor and judge St.
George Tucker in a published response to Morse's attack. "A few
more touches of the reverend Geographer's pen would have exhibited to us Sodom, or Gomorrah, on the eve of eternal wrath." Tucker
augmented his reproof by declaring: "Had this teacher of the gospel
of Christ participated of that charity which his divine master taught
was the first of virtues," he would have discovered among Williamsburg's residents three ministers, a bishop, and numerous other "distinguished characters."[36] This upbraiding scarcely deterred Morse
from exhibiting even stronger regional chauvinism in the *Compen-*

dious History of New England (1804), coauthored with the Reverend Elijah Parish. That volume, more than any other, furthered the notion that New Englanders had been chosen by providence to spread God's word throughout the nation.[37]

Jedidiah Morse's reinterpretation of the Puritan past was part of an unremitting battle waged against anything that seemed to threaten his Calvinist orthodoxy. After the liberal minister Henry Ware assumed the Hollis Professorship of Divinity at Harvard and a second reformist, Samuel Webber, became president of the college in 1804, Morse mounted a vigorous and noisy attack against them and spearheaded a campaign among like-minded clergymen to reinstate Calvinist dominance over the institution founded by their Puritan forebears.[38] A decade earlier, he had lashed out against the "Bavarian Illuminati," a radical wing of the Masonic order that he believed to be undermining the Christian foundations of American society.[39] Ever suspicious of encroaching conspiracies, he perceived liberalism in the church as part of a concerted effort to undermine New England traditions, the threat of which became all the more terrifying once Jeffersonians began to dominate national affairs.

Around 1811, the strong views of Jedidiah Morse intersected tangibly with the career of his son, Samuel Finley Breese Morse.[40] Then barely twenty and recently graduated from Yale, Samuel produced a large painting entitled *Landing of the Forefathers* (Fig. 5.10). It pictures a male scouting party cruising along the New England coast just prior to sighting land. By presenting a close-up view of distinctive individuals, the young artist was departing from the Hill and Corné model, with its tiny figures within a larger seascape. Morse thus created a more intimate interpretation of the landing, and by dressing his men in what he perceived as historically correct costumes, he was aiming at an accuracy his predecessors had deliberately spurned.

Jedidiah had indoctrinated his three sons with his missionary compulsion to reshape society according to standards of an earlier New England, and therefore the aspiring painter probably selected the Pilgrim topic to convince his father that a career in art could serve a higher purpose.[41] Paul Stati observed that by "reinvoking in his first history painting the inception of colonial New England theocracy, Morse was entering orthodoxy's contemporary argument against the growing secularization of post-Revolutionary America."[42] There might be an even more direct link between Samuel Morse's first

FIGURE 5.10   *Samuel F. B. Morse,* Landing of the Forefathers, *oil on canvas, 1811.*
Courtesy of the Trustees of the Boston Public Library, Charlestown Branch, Charlestown, Mass.

grand-style history painting and his father's instruction. Appended to
Morse and Parish's *Compendious History of New England* was John
Davis's Forefathers' Day address of 1800, which contained the following description of the landing: "We see the approaching shallop,
with its precious charge, struggling in the boisterous sea; their garments are stiffened with ice, their limbs benumbed with cold; the
rudder breaks; the storm rises; the night advances; we hear the pi-
lot's despairing cry, Lord have mercy on us."[43] This is the dramatic
scene that young Morse was attempting to recreate.

   Although his later interests (like Jedidiah's) careened off in several
directions, the teachings of his dynamic and forceful father concerning the potency of the Pilgrim legend remained an overwhelming
preoccupation.[44] From 1811, when he painted *Landing of the Forefathers,* until the late 1830s, when he abandoned art altogether, Samuel
F. B. Morse repeatedly expressed his yearning to paint the Massachusetts origin myth—as though he were driven to show his irrepressible

father that he would carry on the fight to spread Puritan doctrines throughout the land.

The Pilgrims' landing at Plymouth overshadowed another prominent Massachusetts family, that of Robert Treat Paine Jr. In this case, the burden of patriarchal domination did not enhance respect for past generations; rather, it divided father from son. Robert Treat Paine Sr., a well-respected patriot and statesman who had signed the Declaration of Independence, served as Massachusetts attorney general and sat on the state Supreme Court. Although he abandoned Congregationalism and became a Unitarian, he continued to believe in the decorum and austerity of the Puritan tradition. That conservative bent soon outweighed his youthful enthusiasm for revolution and, like many of his generation, he settled down to become a cautious Federalist.[45] Robert Treat Paine Jr.–like Samuel F. B. Morse–remained haunted by the imposing shadow of his parent, though unlike Morse, he spent his entire life trying to escape from it.

The story of the rebellious younger Paine is all the more intriguing because on each Forefathers' Day throughout the nineteenth century, heirs of the Pilgrims sang his verses. One of the best loved, "Rule New England," written in 1802 to the tune of "Rule Britannia," ends with the lines: "Rule New England! New England rules and saves! / Columbians never, never shall be slaves."[46] The Pilgrim heirs who chanted Paine's verses each December may not have realized that the "hymn" had been composed by one of Boston's most troublesome insurgents. Robert Treat Paine Jr.–originally christened Thomas and called that until he changed his name later in life–had always been a renegade; he seemed to be deliberately following the rebellious path blazed by a more notorious Thomas Paine, the inflammatory English pamphleteer. The young Bostonian's keen wit and flamboyant behavior provoked incessant clashes with his parents and with school authorities. That rebellion reached a climax during the 1790s while he was studying law at Harvard, for it was then that Paine began hanging around the new Boston Theatre, where he soon landed a job writing prologues. Although Boston was slowly relaxing its Puritan bans on entertainment, most local authorities still considered the stage disreputable. Thomas further shocked his family by founding a Jacobin newspaper, the *Federal Orrery*, to broadcast his liberal political opinions, and his editorials supporting the French revolutionaries proved so disturbing to Federalist Boston that a mob attacked his house. In retribution, young Paine further defied his parents by marrying an English actress and agreeing to be master of ceremonies at the Boston Theatre. That was more than the prominent Paines could stomach, and shortly after the marriage, Robert Treat Paine Sr. disowned his son.[47]

His father's rebuff caused the mercurial Thomas Paine to spring into action. Upon receiving his law degree in 1795, he offended the authorities by reading a Jacobin poem at the Harvard commencement. For three years thereafter, he pursued his revolt by spending even more time at the theater and drinking heavily, but eventually he was forced to recant. His newspaper's financial straits forced him to sell it at a loss in 1796; then in early 1798, the theater burned. But the greatest blow came when his older brother, Robert Treat Paine Jr., died of yellow fever, a tragedy that fostered a dramatic (if temporary) change in Thomas's life. Within three years, he had renounced the sins of his past and had legally assumed his brother's name. By so doing, the erstwhile Thomas Paine disassociated himself from the rabble-rousing English pamphleteer and absorbed the respectable persona of his late brother.[48]

As part of his conversion, the reformed, newly christened Robert Treat Paine Jr. began practicing law with Theophilus Parsons—then chief justice of the Massachusetts Supreme Court—and turned his literary talents toward composing patriotic ballads. Among these was "Adams and Liberty," written in 1798 for the Massachusetts Charitable Society.[49] It was an immediate hit, netting the author an unprecedented $750 in sales. "There was scarcely in New England a singer that could not sing this song," Paine's friend Charles Prentiss wrote. "It was sung at theatres, and on public and private occasions, throughout the United States; and republished and applauded in Great Britain."[50] Three years later, Paine composed "Jefferson and Liberty," an anthem written for the Republicans of Wallingford, Connecticut, to celebrate the inauguration of the nation's first Republican president. Like its Federalist predecessor, "Jefferson and Liberty" became a standard, not only for the Republican Party during the early national period but for its heir—the Democratic Party—which was formed two decades later.[51] This gave Robert Treat Paine Jr. the curious distinction of composing campaign songs for opposing political parties.

Perhaps it was Paine's knack for pleasing all contenders that prompted the Old Colony Club to commission a ballad for Plymouth's Forefathers' Day celebration of 1800. It rapidly became a stock item, reprinted year after year in pamphlets and song sheets distributed by the Pilgrim Society.[52] With its full array of biblical analogies, Paine's "Ode" united church and state with a chauvinistic fervor equal to that of any orthodox Calvinist. The rousing ballad included these jingoistic stanzas:

> *Round the consecrated rock,*
> *Convened the patriarchal flock,*
> *And there, while every lifted hand*
> *Affirmed the charter of the land,*
> *The storm was hushed, and round the zone*
> *Of Heaven, the mystick meteor shone,*
> *Which, like the rainbow, seen of yore,*
> *Proclaimed that Slavery's flood was o'er,*
> *That pilgrim man, so long oppressed,*
> *Had found his promised place of rest.*

> *CHORUS*
> *Sons of Glory, patriot band,*
> *Welcome to my chosen land!*
> *To your children leave it free,*
> *Or a desert let it be.*

> *Heirs of pilgrims, now renew*
> *The oath your fathers swore for you,*
> *When first around the social board,*
> *Enriched from Nature's frugal hoard,*
> *The ardent vow to Heaven they breathed,*
> *To shield the rights their Sires bequeathed!*
> *Manes of Carver! Standish! hear!*
> *To love the soil, you gave, we swear;*
> *And midst the storms of state be true*
> *To God, our country, and to you.*
> *Sons of Glory, &c.*[53]

With this "Ode" of 1800, Paine proved he had mastered the art of compressing popular beliefs into ten-line stanzas. His verses described the first settlers of Plymouth as both wise men from the East pursuing a "mystick meteor" and "slaves" fleeing from oppression to convert New England's metaphorical desert into a "chosen land." By blending Old and New Testament imagery, Paine endowed the act of stepping onto the "consecrated rock" with heightened religious significance. He then implanted a political message: "Heirs of pilgrims" had an obligation to "shield the rights their Sires bequeathed" and guard that bequest against the "storms of state" inflicted by the Jeffersonians then in control of the federal government. The combination of political innuendo and religious analogy guaranteed that Paine's "Ode" would become an enduring Forefathers' Day hymn.

By 1805, Robert Treat Paine Jr. was lapsing into the old pattern of excessive drink, reducing him to a life of illness and poverty. After his law practice faltered in 1809, his aging father reprimanded him for his "irregularities" and his degenerate existence.[54] Oppressed by such judgments from his parent, Paine Jr. succumbed to debauchery and died in 1811 at age thirty-eight.[55] For decades to come, pious and conservative New Englanders would chant his "Ode" each Forefathers' Day. What irony that a man incapable of living up to the Puritan virtues his verses celebrated should compose the very hymns that future generations of less-gifted songsters would imitate.

The unrelenting piety exemplified by the verses of Hemans and Paine was bound to trigger a backlash, and it is hardly surprising that it should come from the most besieged profession in Massachusetts—playwriting. In 1802, Joseph Croswell submitted his play *A New World Planted; or, The Adventures of the Forefathers of New England Who Landed in Plymouth, December, 1620* to the Boston Theatre. Managers of the playhouse (perhaps then including Robert Treat Paine Jr.) rejected the slightly irreverent and highly politicized recapitulation of the Pilgrim myth, Croswell later wrote, because it was too "tinctur'd with Republicanism."[56] It was published, however, and thus has enjoyed the admiration of succeeding generations.[57]

In Federalist and Calvinist Boston, where even the most inoffensive plays were suspect, it is easy to understand why Croswell had difficulty convincing theaters to produce *A New World Planted.* The dramatist not only wove political messages into the dialogue but also pointed a cynical finger at the fractured Congregational Church. He was clearly ridiculing the current state of affairs in Massachusetts as well as addressing his own misfortunes. The only known record of Croswell's life comes from a letter written to Jefferson's treasury secretary, Albert Gallatin, in 1801. In that correspondence, Croswell explained that shortly before the Revolution, he had settled in Plymouth and joined the patriots in opposing the loyalists. When peace came he remained there, working in the "fishing business" and voicing his opposition, first to the Tories and later to the Federalists.[58]

Around 1780, Croswell ran afoul of a number of Plymouth merchants and shippers engaged in a smuggling scheme that involved local customs officials. Boycotted by these same merchants after he attempted to expose them, Croswell ended up in such dire financial straits that he was reduced to soliciting Gallatin for a job as tax collector. His ardent support for the Republican Party, he explained, had prompted his friends to propose him as a candidate for Congress. They withdrew the offer, however, because he had published such inflammatory political articles in the *Boston Chronicle.* Similar adversity, he added, surrounded his "dramatic piece founded on the landing of our forefathers," which was then "under the imposition of the proprietors of the Boston Theatre."[59]

In *A New World Planted,* the satirical plot does not unfold until the second act, when John Lyford and John Oldham—whom Croswell portrayed as conservative Catholics—scheme to overthrow the colony of "Independents." These villains admitted that they wanted to obliterate all individual freedoms, place Plymouth under strict royal control, and supplant separatism with the "real doctrines of the Church of Rome." During the course of the play, Bradford and his colleagues uncover the "popish" plot and defeat the insurgents in battle; in the end, a Plymouth court votes to banish the villains forever. By turning the Pilgrim legend upside down and making Lyford and Oldham into Catholics instead of Protestants, Croswell was parodying the intransigence and petty jealousies of the Congregational ministers.[60] The threat to liberty, he implied, came not from the values or institutions of the original Plymouth Separatists but from theocratic outsiders (Puritans) who destroyed the egalitarian and benevolent society of the Plymouth fathers. In further portraying the insurgents as royalists intent on bringing the colony under the dominance of James I, he was leveling a veiled criticism at the "monarchist" policies of recent Federalist administrations.

Croswell addressed the rivalry between Massachusetts and Virginia by introducing a romance between a colonist called Hampden and Pocahonte, the young, beautiful daughter of Chief Massasoit. This clever reversal of regional histories, which transformed the hallowed ancestor of the Old Dominion into a New England heroine, mocked the denunciations of Jefferson's administration heard each Forefathers' Day; it furthermore implied that a "marriage" between New England and Virginia would rescue Massachusetts from the clutches of latter-day Puritans. Croswell repeated this political message in the epilogue, intended to bring down the final curtain:

> For now, the nineteenth centry's come in view,
> And blessings on our country rise anew:
> Philosophers and Statesmen I survey,
> Guiding the Councils of America;
> Such luminaries in our hemisphere,
> Portend the great millennium is near;
> But the tri'd optic's of the mind oppress'd,
> With these refulgent scenes, retires to rest.[61]

The prediction of an approaching "great millennium" under Republican rule was no doubt too controversial for proprietors of the Boston Theatre. Production of *A New World Planted* surely would have outraged Federalist politicians and orthodox clergymen, both then invoking the hallowed forefathers as originators of their conservative policies. However, rejection of Croswell's play by theater managers deprived Bostonians from seeing one of the era's most entertaining satires.[62]

Around the time Croswell was parodying the Pilgrims' arrival, Henry Sargent was preparing to extol that same event with a huge and ambitious history painting.[63] His *Landing of the Fathers* (Fig. 5.11), first publicly exhibited in 1815, depicts an array of armored and helmeted men, accompanied by women and children, grouped horizon-

FIGURE 5.11   *Henry Sargent,* Landing of the Fathers, *oil on canvas, 1815–1824. Courtesy of the Pilgrim Society, Plymouth, Mass.*

tally across an icy shore; in the foreground, the Indian Samoset, loosely clad in a toga-style animal skin, bows submissively to the European strangers. The slashing diagonals of the men's lancets and muskets, their steely gray armor, the metal plating of their crested helmets, and the severity of their attire combine to create a frosty and rather ominous atmosphere, relieved only by a few blotches of subdued color.[64] Contributing to the mood of desolation are the jagged rocks and barren trees that recall the wintry landscapes of Samuel Hill and Michele Corné.[65] Sargent, like other artists of his day, deliberately "quoted" those works and borrowed the closely packed crowd and Samoset's subservient pose from Thomas Jefferys's well-known New England map cartouche of 1774 (Fig. 5.1). Although critics commended the artist for depicting each member of the landing party as a distinct individual, the male faces—with their

FIGURE 5.12
Unknown artist,
Edward Winslow, *oil*
on canvas, c. 1650.
Courtesy of the Pilgrim
Society, Plymouth, Mass.

trim beards, pointed noses, and square jaws—all look alike. Sargent probably copied these features from the portrait of Edward Winslow (Fig. 5.12), the only known likeness of a *Mayflower* passenger.[66] The presence of the Indian suggests that the malleable Massachusetts natives welcomed the "civilizing influence" of British rule and Protestant dominance.

The artist possessed the proper credentials for addressing the Pilgrim legend so vigorously. Born in 1770 into a well-respected Gloucester mercantile family, Henry Sargent could trace his heritage back to the early settlers.[67] While he was still young, the family moved to Boston, where they hobnobbed with the city's social elite. After trying his hand in business, Sargent decided to pursue a career in art, and in 1793, embarked for London to study with the American expatriate Benjamin West. However, unlike most other Americans given the opportunity to apprentice in the studio of the illustrious West, Sargent devoted little time to painting. Can "you make nothing by your Brush?" his father scolded on several occasions. Henry usually answered such queries with excuses. There were too many visitors from home, the lure of Paris was too tempting, the activities of London too time-consuming. In this dilatory fashion, he spent six leisurely years occasionally copying old masters and attending exhibitions—until 1799, when he ran out of money and had to return home.[68]

After settling in Boston, Sargent joined the newly formed national army under the command of Alexander Hamilton, and after completing his term of service, he remained in the Boston Light Infantry, eventually achieving the rank of colonel. During this time, he painted only sporadically; so in 1833, when William Dunlap came seeking material for his history of American painting, Sargent apologized for having "long since neglected to paint" except for "his own amusement." Even though his "love for the art has not abated," he explained, he had "so little practice" that he could "hardly claim to be more than an amateur artist."[69] But despite the random nature of his career, Henry Sargent managed to create some remarkable paintings, including *The Dinner Party* and *The Tea Party*, often praised for providing a sensitive and unique glimpse into the closed world of Boston Brahmin society.[70]

Landing of the Fathers, the largest of his known works, is clearly a theatrical tour de force. "An historical painting ... is a species of drama presented to the eye," wrote a columnist for the Federalist Boston *Palladium*, when first viewing Sargent's huge painting in 1815. Theater was uppermost in the mind of another reporter who insisted that "drums, trumpets, fiddles and clarinets" would be a worthy accompaniment to the exhibition. A writer for Plymouth's *Old Colony Memorial* elaborated even further upon the painting's dramatic effect. "We cannot look upon the painted scenery and the moral scene of the landing without emotion. . . . The event of which the Picture so forcibly speaks, that the story it so eloquently tells, is one of the grandest, the sublimest in history."[71] Many others commented about how moved they had been by the overwhelming presence of the life-size representations of the Pilgrims. Sargent, indeed, seemed to be recreating the atmosphere that Joseph Warren Brackett evoked in his Forefathers' Day "hymn" of 1807:

> *In Plymouth they land*
> *On the bleak barren strand,*
> *Yet they're strong in their shield—an omnipotent band:*
> *For there, to their wand'rings, a period they find,*
> *And their brows with the laurels of freedom first bind.*[72]

Familiar with the celebrations each December, Sargent may have conceived the "omnipotent band" in his *Landing* as a visual equivalent to Brackett's hymn and certainly as a theatrical reenactment of the Pilgrim myth that was then inspiring so much overblown and fiery rhetoric.

By dressing his Pilgrims in armor and battle helmets, Sargent was endowing the "omnipotent band" with the accoutrements of war. And indeed, when he exhibited his work in 1815, the War of 1812 had just ended. New Englanders had been uneasy about that confrontation from the outset because they saw it as yet another blow from the so-called Virginia Dynasty then controlling the federal government. Ever since the election of Jefferson in 1800, the Federalists contended that the Virginians in power were deliberately trying to cripple New England's mercantile economy.[73] That dissatisfaction boiled over when Jefferson's successor, James Madison, declared war on Britain in 1812, and when the exigencies of wartime halted Atlantic commerce, the New England Federalists became so furious that they began to whisper the word "secession."[74] In December 1814, some of the more heated New Englanders gathered in Hartford to lodge a formal complaint against Madison and his policies. Although the Hartford Convention did not vote for outright secession, it did produce a set of resolutions chastising the Virginia Dynasty for its conduct of the war. But before their complaints reached Washington, a peace treaty was in the making and their charges became moot.[75]

In May 1815, a few months after those events, the artist exhibited his *Landing of the Fathers* in Boston. It was perfect timing, as William Dunlap realized when he noted that Sargent "had genius enough to seize the thought and make the best of it."[76] By portraying the forefathers as Oliver Cromwell's Roundheads dressed to battle the Stuart Cavaliers, the artist seemed to be adroitly capturing the spirit of belligerence that Bay Staters felt toward Virginians. Upon seeing the painting, a columnist for the *Old Colony Memorial* wrote: "They fought the good fight of faith. Righteousness was their breastplate, faith their shield, and for [a]helmet they had the good hope of salvation."[77] Planting their boots on the desolate shore, the proud and purposeful forefathers exuded a positive sense of mission. They appeared to control their own destinies and would spread their ideals—by force if necessary—not only to the New World but to the Old World as well.

It was a message residents of Massachusetts welcomed. One Bostonian wrote in 1815: "We feel a mingled sensation of pride and pleasure that this performance is the effort of a native artist" and hope that the painting will remain in the Boston area where it will not only "perpetuate the reputation of the artist" but "add lustre to our national fame." A decade later, another Boston writer expanded that concept of "lustre" when he described the painting as "a heart-moving representation of the Patriarchs of our own blessed Tribe, now spread and spreading throughout this vast land of promise."[78] For Bay Staters, Sargent had created a theatrical representation of their determination to reclaim national prominence and thus place their own stamp of "civilization" on the land. Every facet of Massachusetts society yearned for that positive affront. From the angry merchants anxious to recoup their lost fortunes to the orthodox Calvinists under the threat of a potential schism in the established church, all needed the venerated forefathers to fight their battles and help restore the region's depleted economy and recover its dwindling political hegemony. Thus, Sargent's Massachusetts neighbors readily applauded his *Landing* as a grandiose embodiment of an ancestral army sacrificing Old World comforts to preserve traditional values.

Five years after Sargent exhibited his *Landing of the Fathers* in Boston, Daniel Webster used the painting to enhance his own political agenda. The occasion was the bicentenary celebration of the Pilgrims' landing, at which Webster was the featured speaker. Having recently completed a four-year stint in the House of Representatives, the charismatic lawyer, dressed in flowing black robes, strode to the front of the First Plymouth Church and surprised the audience by walking past the pulpit to position himself at the deacon's seat. For the next hour and a half, he held the congregation spellbound.[79]

"We have come to this Rock," he began, "to record here our homage for our Pilgrim Fathers. . . . And we would leave here, also, for the generations which are rising up rapidly to fill our places, some proof that we have endeavored to transmit the great inheritance unimpaired." Then focusing on Sargent's painting, which the artist had transported to Plymouth for the bicentenary, Webster intoned:

> We seem even to behold the Forefathers as they struggle with the ele-
> ments, and, with toilsome efforts, gain the shore ... and we see ...
> chilled and shivering childhood, houseless, but for a mother's arms,
> couchless, but for a mother's breast, till our own blood almost freezes.
> The mild dignity of CARVER and of BRADFORD; the decisive and
> soldier-like air and manner of STANDISH; the devout BREWSTER;
> the enterprising ALLERTON; the general firmness and thoughtfulness
> of the whole band; their conscious joy for dangers escaped; their deep
> solicitude about dangers to come; their trust in Heaven; their high reli-
> gious faith, full of confidence and anticipation; all of these seem to be-
> long to this place, and to be present upon this occasion, to fill us with
> reverence and admiration.[80]

Webster's tribute reveals not only how adroitly Henry Sargent had
reproduced the Massachusetts vision of the Plymouth landing but
also amplifies the spiritual mission of the Pilgrims in phrases that
heightened the painting's theatricality. Webster devoted the remainder of his lengthy oration to linking the Plymouth founders with the
destiny of the United States and enumerating why descendants of the
Pilgrims were duty bound to endow future generations with the heritage of free education, universal suffrage, and an administrative system based upon "morality and religious sentiment."

Toward the end of his talk, the future senator made a bold move;
he tied the Pilgrim heritage to denunciation of the slave trade:

> In the sight of our law, the African slave-trader is a pirate and a felon;
> and in the sight of Heaven, an offender far beyond the ordinary depth
> of human guilt. .... I would call on all the true sons of New England to
> cooperate with the laws of man, and the justice of Heaven. If there be,
> within the extent of our knowledge or influence, any participation in
> this traffic, let us pledge ourselves here, upon the rock of Plymouth to
> extirpate and destroy it. It is not fit that the land of the Pilgrims should
> bear the shame longer.[81]

At that time, Webster was making a name for himself by successfully
arguing two important cases—*McCulloch v. Maryland* and *Trustees of
Dartmouth College v. Woodward*—before the Supreme Court, and because he was anticipating another run for Congress, he needed the
backing of local antislavery forces.

In debates earlier that year over the Missouri Compromise, which
established a dividing line between slave and free states, Webster had

been outspoken in his condemnation of the South's efforts to spread its "peculiar institution" into newly acquired Western lands.[82] Webster's deliberate attempt to ally the Pilgrim Fathers and New England against Southern interests shifted the emphasis of Forefathers' Day from past to present and not only united the ghosts of the regional ancestors with the political fortunes of nineteenth-century America but cleverly mingled historical mythology with his own ambition. That fusion of history and politics worked for Webster. Publication of an expanded version of his Plymouth oration broadcast his talents, and three years after delivering the speech, he won reelection to the House of Representatives, moving over to the Senate four years later.[83]

By mixing politics with the Pilgrims' landing, Webster established a precedent that other Forefathers' Day speakers would emulate. Edward Everett–who had been recently elected to the House of Representatives–took advantage of an invitation to speak at the formal opening of Pilgrim Hall on December 22, 1824, to air his own political agenda. In hopes of rivaling Webster's prior performance, the former Congregational minister, Harvard professor, and editor of the *North American Review* also titled his speech "First Settlement of New England." But Everett exceeded his predecessor in allying the Pilgrims with the fortunes of both region and nation. He demonstrated first how that step onto Plymouth Rock influenced transatlantic navigation, continental expansion, and even manufacturing. Then he moved on to foreign policy, thus extending the Pilgrims' mission even further into American politics. The Pilgrims had emigrated, Everett explained, to separate themselves from Europe and "all foreign institutions . . . behind the mighty veil of waters," and that seclusion must now continue because next to "UNION AT HOME . . . separation from all other countries in policy, spirit, and character is the great principle by which we are to prosper." Everett illustrated his point by showing how European interference had promoted "the most frightful systems of despotism" throughout South America.[84] It would not have escaped the audience in Pilgrim Hall that these opinions corresponded with those of native son John Quincy Adams, author of the Monroe Doctrine and supporter of independence for Latin American nations. Those issues were especially relevant because at that very moment Adams was awaiting a decision that would determine whether he had won a very close presidential race.[85] From the vantage point of a freshman congressman, Everett was cautiously casting his lot with Adams, yet covering his tracks by evoking the Pilgrim legend so as not to offend the weakened, but still influential, Massachusetts Federalists.

As Everett was speaking, the audience was looking at Sargent's large *Landing of the Fathers*, which provided visual reinforcement to the congressman's assertions about the seminal importance of the Pilgrims' arrival. To commemorate the 1824 opening of Pilgrim Hall, the artist had installed his painting on the wall of the second-floor gallery, a spot that the architect Alexander Parris had designed for just that purpose (Fig. 5.13). However members of the Pilgrim Society were in a quandary because—even though they had instructed Parris to provide space for the painting in his plans—they were unable to come up with the $3,000 Sargent requested.[86] Nevertheless, the painting remained in Pilgrim Hall for over a decade while the society's leaders tried in vain to obtain the requisite funds; finally in 1835, Sargent reluctantly agreed to donate the canvas.[87]

Visitors to Pilgrim hall today will find the painting hanging just where Sargent placed it in 1824 but are not likely to be moved, as earlier visitors were, by the "blessed Tribe" of biblical-style warriors in Roundhead gear.[88] Beyond the fact that Sargent's awkward depiction lacks that spark of genius that allows a few masterpieces to transcend their time, the message that seemed so relevant in the 1820s eludes viewers today. Yet, if for no other reason than its enormous size, Sargent's *Landing* cannot be ignored; it reigns in Plymouth as an imposing relic of the self-image that Massachusetts wanted to perpetuate during the opening years of the nineteenth century.

Sargent's painting—like the speeches by Webster and Everett—illustrates how thoroughly the landing at Plymouth had entered regional mythology to convey a bundle of ideals believed to have been carried across the Atlantic on the *Mayflower*. The act of stepping ashore represented transmission of culture and religion and spoke of new beginnings. Abiel Holmes, John Quincy Adams, Washington Allston, William Cullen Bryant, and numerous other dignitaries wrote poems and "hymns" that repeated that belief; and every Forefathers' Day, speakers holding diverse opinions cemented that link between the Pilgrims' landing and the future of the United States.[89] George Bancroft summed it up in his *History of the United States* (1834):

FIGURE 5.13   *Sargent's* Landing of the Fathers *in Pilgrim Hall, Plymouth, photograph, c. 1870. Division of Prints and Photographs, Library of Congress, Washington, D.C.*

A grateful posterity has marked the rock which first received their footsteps. The consequences of that day are constantly unfolding themselves, as time advances. It was the origin of New England; it was the planting of the New England institutions. . . . The system of civil government had been established by common agreement; the character of the church had for many years been fixed by a sacred covenant. As the Pilgrims landed, their institutions were already perfected. Democratic liberty and independent Christian worship at once existed in America.[90]

This explanation of the landing reflects lessons Bancroft absorbed during his boyhood in Worcester, Massachusetts.[91] The Pilgrims, he told his readers, deserved the adulation of succeeding generations because their "perfected" institutions introduced "democratic liberty" and "independent Christian worship" to an otherwise pagan land. However, by the time Bancroft published the first volume of his history, New Englanders were beginning to reevaluate their regional origins to accommodate the frontier culture associated with Jacksonian democracy. The Indian Removal Act, the mounting number of immigrants coming to Massachusetts, and the expanded reformist movement all came together to reconfigure the Pilgrim myth for a new generation.

6

Vanishing Indians and Noble Women

Pocahontas, or The Settlers of Virginia by George Washington Parke Custis, step-grandson and adopted heir of the nation's first president, played successfully in Philadelphia and New York during 1830. The drama brought together the erratic playwright's loyalty to the Old Dominion, reverence for Andrew Jackson, and ambivalent feelings about American Indians, thus producing a curious mixture of pathos and melodrama that became a bellwether for artistic treatment of the legend during the next two decades.[1] Known for delivering endless orations and making frequent appearances in parades and at rallies, Custis seemed to leap from one exuberant outburst to another, often reversing in midair. Having begun as a Federalist, he transformed himself into an avid Jacksonian, then did an about-face and joined the Whigs. As a young man, he had tried military service and local politics, then opted to devote his days to farming, writing, and especially to perpetuating the legacy of his step-grandfather, George Washington. Toward that end, he turned his home, Arlington House (today known as the Custis-Lee Mansion), into a memorial for his surrogate ancestor. Positioned at the dramatic crest of a hill across the Potomac from Washington, the estate's auspicious panorama intrigued visitors as they talked with the owner and viewed Washingtonian relics.[2]

Though hardly typical, Custis was a product of his times; even his eccentricities seemed in tune with the turbulence that accompanied

Jackson to the White House in 1829. In fact, his play *Pocahontas* en-
capsulated many of the contradictions that pervaded that age of national growth and political ambiguity. Audiences applauding Custis's
drama in the year after Jackson's inauguration were well aware of the
so-called "Indian question," a euphemism that applied to the displacement of Eastern tribes from their ancestral lands as well as to
the debate about where and how to relocate them. By the time Andrew Jackson became president, the situation had reached a crisis.
Prospectors had recently discovered gold in the Cherokee nation situated in northern Georgia. The ensuing gold rush convinced Jackson
that he should honor his campaign promise and force the Cherokees
to relinquish their lands.[3] Ironically, the tribe had been gradually
adopting the tenets of U.S. culture and society in hopes of appearing
"civilized" enough to retain their territory. They wrote a constitution,
built schoolhouses, published newspapers in their own language, and
utilized modern methods of farming; wealthy Cherokee landowners
even lived on plantations and owned black slaves. Such attempts to
imitate white society not only failed to impress Georgia legislators
but seemed rather to spur them to intensify their efforts for expul-
sion. With the full support of President Jackson, Georgia governor
George Gilmer announced that the "ignorant, intractable, and savage people" must be "induced without bloodshed to yield up what
civilized people had the right to possess by virtue of that command
of the Creator delivered to man upon his formation—be fruitful, mul-
tiply, and replenish the earth, and subdue it."[4] Such was the convoluted logic behind Indian removal.

The Cherokees refuted the accusation by adopting the stratagems
of white society and taking legal action. Within a relatively short
time, the precedent-breaking *Cherokee Nation v. Georgia* moved all the
way up to the Supreme Court. Representing the Cherokees was
William Wirt, the man who two decades earlier in his *Letters of the
British Spy* had written a tribute to Pocahontas and advocated the intermarriage of the English with Indians.[5] Wirt based his logic on the
incongruity between official demands for the Indians to integrate
into American society and the realities of Cherokee accomplishments.[6] Attorneys representing Georgia cited the illegality of an independent nation existing within the boundaries of the United States,
an argument that ultimately led the court to rule against the Cherokees. The next year, the tribunal reversed that decision in *Worcester v.*

Georgia and concluded that the state had no sovereignty over Indian territory. But by that time Congress was in the process of passing legislation to legalize state seizure of tribal lands and forcing relocation of Native Americans west of the Mississippi. The "original dwellers of our land," said Jackson in his last message to Congress, "are now placed in a situation where we may well hope that they will share in the blessings of civilization and be saved from the degradation and destruction to which they are rapidly hastening while they remained in the states."[7] Under this dubious cloak of "protection," General Winfield Scott rounded up the remaining Creeks, Cherokees, Seminoles, and Choctaws, and by 1838, most had been herded to Oklahoma during the infamous Trail of Tears.[8]

One year before *Cherokee Nation v. Georgia* reached the Supreme Court, Custis produced *Pocahontas.* The play turned the familiar rescue of John Smith—which Custis reserved for the last scene—into an allegorical reenactment of the real Cherokee drama then unfolding. The playwright characterized Smith as an idealized Andrew Jackson, reluctantly forced to defeat the "savages" even though he expressed a patient sympathy for their irreversible plight.[9] Like Jackson, Custis's John Smith accused the Indians of bringing about their own eradication because they refused to give up their administrative and cultural autonomy. With repeated insinuations that the Indians' downfall was self-imposed, Custis endowed the rescue scene with the fatalism of a Greek drama, but in this case it was tribal, rather than individual, hubris that brought down the wrath of the gods and destruction of a people.

To conform with current ideas of female virtue—and to please fellow Virginians who claimed her as an ancestor—Custis characterized Pocahontas as a paragon of dignity and charm, the antithesis of the salacious siren who two decades earlier had romanced her way through Barker's play and Davis's novels. Her decisive preference for all things British draws her to Rolfe early in the drama, and in response to her affection, Rolfe (whom she calls "Sir Cavalier") proclaims that the "gentle fawn of Virginia" need not fear because "the lion of England doth guard her on her way."[10] The pair's mutual devotion—with no hint of sensuality—acquits Virginia's fine lady of all charges of wantonness.

In Custis's recasting of Virginia's origin myth, Pocahontas's baptism becomes a central theme. She supposedly converted long before either Smith or Rolfe came to Virginia, a patent absurdity since Christianity was unknown in Virginia before the English arrived. Nevertheless, the playwright emphasized the heroine's Christian devotion to prove that the Indians must accept Christianity in order to survive. In the first act, Pocahontas proclaims, "I have learn'd that mercy is one of the attributes of the divinity I now adore." Her faith impels her to challenge her father, whom she refers to as "cruel king." Pleading with Powhatan to stop Smith's execution, she forswears her people's "sanguinary religion" and informs her father that she is denouncing his "senseless gods" in favor of the "Supreme Being, the true Manitou, and the Father of the Universe."[11]

More important than its efficacy in the salvation of her own soul or even that of her people, Pocahontas's conversion facilitated her marriage to John Rolfe. Combined with her baptism, their union signifies her capitulation to the English way of life. In the nineteenth century, a woman was expected to be the subservient partner, thus by acquiescing to the marriage vows, Pocahontas denounced her native identity and entered Rolfe's world. Custis thereby posed total submission to English culture as the only possible solution to the troublesome "Indian question." The playwright delivered that message in Powhatan's ringing endorsement of his daughter's wedding that brings down the final curtain:

> And may the fruits of this union of virtue and honour be a long line of descendants, inheriting those principles, gifted with rare talents, and the most exalted patriotism. Now it only remains for us to say, that looking thro' a long vista of futurity, to the time when these wild regions shall become the ancient and honour'd part of a great and glorious American Empire, may we hope that when the tales of early days are told from the nursery, the library, or the stage, that kindly will be received the national story of POCAHONTAS, OR THE SETTLEMENT OF VIRGINIA.[12]

With this closing speech, Custis established the descendants of Pocahontas as founders of a "glorious American Empire." As a loyal son of Virginia and self-styled champion of the Old Dominion heritage, the eccentric playwright produced a manifesto of regional patriotism reinterpreted to encompass the "Indian question" that had become so central to Jackson's administrative policies.

Custis was not the first playwright to address that issue. A year earlier, John Augustus Stone's *Metamora; or, the Last of the Wampanoags* had opened in New York with the famed Edwin Forrest in the lead role; the drama centered around the plight of the Massachusetts chief, vanquished during King Philip's War.[13] The overwhelming success of that play no doubt challenged Custis to demonstrate that Virginia's native heroine could invoke the Indian issue with just as much melodrama and pathos. Responding to the popularity of *Metamora*, he included a character named Matacoran (a combination of the play's hero and King Philip's tribal designation, "Metacom") and cast him as a brave who expected to marry Pocahontas. This character symbolized the proud but defiant male "savage" preferring to "follow the western wave" and remain "wild and free" rather than submit to "the usurpers," who drove his people to "the utmost verge of the land."[14] By covering Matacoran with the tragic mantle of the doomed Metamora, Custis was suggesting that Virginians had treated the Indians more humanely than their counterparts in New England, for by incorporating them into their world, they rescued the natives from certain extinction.

Pocahontas conveyed a dual commentary on issues of 1830. On the local level, it was a Virginian's dignified and reverential recapitulation of the origin legend as a "national story." With the fate of the Eastern tribes pending in the courts and hoards of settlers poised to move into former Indian territory, it also explored contemporary concerns. Like most white Americans, Custis wanted to see the Western territories settled by Europeans, an "inevitable" process that the Indians stubbornly refused to accept. To reinforce that point, he framed his Native American characters to conform with current stereotypes. Powhatan and Matacoran personify the "noble savage," an eighteenth-century concept of the defeated but honorable hero; their predicament embodies the nineteenth-century notion of the "vanishing Indian," an epithet that implied racial extinction to enable the advance of Anglo-American "civilization." Pocahontas, by contrast, was a native Joan of Arc, sacrificing herself to assure the development of a Protestant, nonpagan America.[15] These archetypal portrayals would populate American drama for the next twenty-five years.

❧

Another Virginian, John Gadsby Chapman, also sought to use the Jamestown legend as a paradigm of the confrontation between English settlers and Native Americans. His *Baptism of Pocahontas* (Fig. 6.1), installed in the U.S. Capitol rotunda in 1840, combined historical mythmaking, concerns about the fate of the "noble savage," and respect for the Virginia heritage. Like Custis, the artist had deep roots in the Virginia soil; his father, Charles, came from an old Prince William County family; his maternal grandfather, John Gadsby, owned the famous Alexandria tavern that is now a Virginia landmark.[16] Born near there in 1808, Chapman grew up with Mount Vernon and its powerful Washington legacy a few miles to the south and the newly constructed federal city taking shape upriver on the Potomac. Both were to have a profound effect on his future ambitions. During a brief and futile attempt to study law in Winchester, Virginia, he formed a close friendship with future Virginia congressman and governor Henry Alexander Wise.[17] In 1828, the young artist toured Europe, there enriching his artistic education while making friends with such notables as James Fenimore Cooper, Samuel F.B. Morse, and the sculptor Horatio Greenough.

Chapman might have taken advantage of such influential friends to help him launch his career in New York upon his return in 1831. Instead he chose to settle in Virginia, where he eked out a scant living painting portraits.[18] During his youth, Chapman had witnessed the rebuilding of the Capitol after its destruction during the War of 1812 and had later watched John Trumbull install his four Revolutionary War paintings in the rotunda. Hoping one day to create a similar "national picture" for the Capitol, he began to contact influential politicians and exhibit his paintings around the District of Columbia.[19] In 1836, six days after Congress announced the competition for murals in the rotunda, Chapman wrote to his friend Henry Wise, then a freshman congressman. He acknowledged that several of his "brethren of the brush" had "moved eagerly" to obtain the commission, but his "incapacity to electioneer" or push his "humble pretensions" meant he would have to "rest upon the exertions" of his friends. "How fondly I have dreamed over this event in years of anticipation," he exclaimed. "It has cheered the loneliness of an arduous rotine of study in a foreign land and cast a glow over the coldest neglect that has sometimes been my lot to feel since my return." He asked Wise to remind his "Virginia

FIGURE 6.1 *John Gadsby Chapman,* Baptism of Pocahontas, *oil on canvas, 1837–1840. Architect of the Capitol, U.S. Capitol, Washington, D.C.*

and southern friends" that he wanted the commission, and in response, several influential people petitioned on his behalf.[20]

Upon learning that Congress had chosen him as one of the four artists, Chapman initially considered painting John Paul Jones's capture of the British ship *Serapis,* but he was soon persuaded that the Jamestown legend was a more appropriate subject for Congress's representative Southern artist.[21] Very likely, he received help in reaching that conclusion from George Washington Parke Custis when he visited Arlington House in preparation for his most ambitious project to date, illustrating James Kirke Paulding's *Life of George Washington.* While studying Washington family artifacts and copying Charles Willson Peale's portrait of the first president in Custis's collection, Chapman no doubt listened to the loquacious playwright's accounting of the recent production of *Pocahontas* and heard stories about the adventures of Virginia's heroine.[22]

By this time, Chapman had moved to New York City, where he was establishing a creditable reputation as a printmaker and illustrator. As soon as he returned home, the artist began painting episodes from the Pocahontas saga, the first being two small canvases–*The Coronation of Powhatan* (Fig. 6.2) and *The Warning of Pocahontas* (Fig. 6.3)–which he exhibited at the National Academy of Design in 1836. In 1837, he composed his own version of the famous rescue scene, *Pocahontas Saving the Life of Captain John Smith* (Fig. 6.4), and between 1839 and 1841, he painted *Good Times in the New World*, originally titled *The Landing at Jamestown* (or *The Hope of Jamestown*) (Fig. 6.5).[23] It was by way of these compositions, each interpreting an aspect of the Jamestown saga, that Chapman prepared himself to undertake his defining treatment of the tale, *The Baptism of Pocahontas*, destined for the walls of the U.S. Capitol. The Pocahontas paintings comprise a unique pictorial series and offer a rare glimpse into the process of visualizing the region's origin myth as conceived by a native son steeped in the state's culture and lore.

Chapman took his cue for *The Coronation of Powhatan* (Fig. 6.2) from an episode in the *Generall Historie,* in which Smith describes the arrival of Captain Christopher Newport at Jamestown with a copper crown sent by James I to be placed upon Powhatan's head in a formal coronation ceremony. According to Smith, the chief not only refused to kneel for the customary investiture but balked at the whole idea of accepting the white man's bribe. Nevertheless, Smith, Newport, and a party of English settlers trooped out to Powhatan's village in hopes that a shower of gifts would persuade the chief to accept the dubious honor. Smith apparently viewed the entire maneuver as another blunder by English authorities.[24] Chapman picked up on that distaste. To emphasize the pathos of that encounter, he divided the composition in half to separate the fully dressed English from Powhatan's partially clothed tribe lounging in the leafy shade. He showed Captain Newport lifting his arms, encased in long embroidered sleeves, to present a jeweled crown to the elderly Powhatan, who wears only a feathered skirt, headdress, and moccasins.[25]

In every sense, British superiority dominates the composition. The English lance eclipses Powhatan's bow, the ornate crown outweighs the chief's feathered headdress, and the ordered assembly of settlers outnumbers the disparate band of natives. Although Virginia's first families often boasted that they were descendants of native "royalty," regal grandeur is absent in Chapman's hollow ceremony, which hints of a proud people's humiliation at being cajoled into accepting

FIGURE 6.2 *John Gadsby Chapman,* The Coronation of Powhatan, *oil on canvas, 1836. Greenville County Museum of Art, Greenville, S.C., museum purchase with funds donated by the Arthur and Holly Magill Foundation.*

FIGURE 6.3 *John Gadsby Chapman,* The Warning of Pocahontas, *oil on canvas, 1836. Private collection, photograph courtesy of Gerald Peters Gallery, Sante Fe, N. M.*

FIGURE 6.4 *John Gadsby Chapman,* Pocahontas Saving the Life of Captain John Smith, *oil on canvas, 1836. Collection of New York Historical Society, New York, N.Y.*

FIGURE 6.5 *John Gadsby Chapman,* Good Times in the New World (*or* The Hope of Jamestown), *oil on panel, 1841. Virginia Museum of Fine Arts, Richmond, Va., Paul Mellon Collection.*

a token of the white man's triumph. In light of the recent Trail of Tears and in keeping with the last scene in Custis's *Pocahontas,* Chapman captured the stereotypical "vanishing Indian," a beaten but proud man who reluctantly submits to English superiority.

The *Warning of Pocahontas* (Fig. 6.3), like its pendant, *The Coronation of Powhatan,* also investigates an interaction between two cultures. In the *Generall Historie,* Smith described the way Pocahontas stole away in the "darke night and came through the irksome woods" to warn the English that her father was planning an attack. Chapman's composition pictures Pocahontas approaching Smith in the lantern light of a darkened tent, where the captain's men lie sleeping in the shadows. The *Warning* opposes the regimentation of the *Coronation;* one painting is set in sunlight, the other in darkness; in one, whites are active and the Indians passive, the other reverses the situation. Pocahontas's visit to John Smith's tent temporarily staves off potential violence while the British conceived Powhatan's coronation as a peaceful overture. Both incidents resulted in only temporary alliances, for the Indians *did* soon devastate Jamestown and the English settlers *did* eventually displace the Powhatan nation. Viewed as a pair, therefore, Chapman's *Coronation* and *Warning* compare the noblesse oblige of white settlers with the magnanimity of Christianized Indians, and together they point to the tragic outcome that each produced.

Pocahontas Saving the Life of John Smith (Fig. 6.4) augments this confrontation between the English conquerors and their hapless victims. At first glance, the painting appears to be yet one more version of the rescue scene with all of the customary stereotypes. But closer examination reveals that the "savages" wielding axes and clubs seem hesitant about the deed they are about to perform, and some of their brethren stare into the campfire, lost in pensive meditation. Not only is Pocahontas's nudity cloaked by both a shawl and her long black hair, which cover her upper torso, but Smith's head rests on a stone next to her knees rather than on her bosom. By dignifying Pocahontas and minimizing the brutality of Smith's assailants, Chapman's depiction of the rescue counteracted the sensuality implicit in such popular prints as Corbould's *Smith Rescued by Pocahontas* (Fig. 4.8).[26]

Whereas the *Coronation,* the *Warning,* and *Pocahontas Saving the Life of John Smith* comment on the encounter between Native Americans and Europeans, Chapman's *Good Times in the New World* (Fig. 6.5) addresses the respectability of Virginia's early settlers. The scene takes place along the riverfront as a group of men and women eagerly await the arrival of an approaching boat, launched from a ship at anchor in the distance.[27] Three Indians camped near a beached rowboat inscribed "Hope of Jamestown" seem detached from the action. *Good Times* originated as an illustration for James Kirke Paulding's story, "Cradle of the New World," which centers upon the arrival of a new shipload of English ladies and gentlemen to increase the upper echelon of respectable residents in the Jamestown colony.[28] In portraying the colonists in costumes that ranged from clerical respectability to Elizabethan splendor, Chapman followed the author's lead in denying that the Jamestown inhabitants were criminals and wastrels, a characterization frequently emanating from New Englanders.[29]

Seen as a whole, Chapman's Jamestown series sought to establish both the respectability of the colonists and the dignity and honor of its native inhabitants. The artist's loyalty to Virginia survived his residence in New York and even his eventual relocation in Italy; he expressed that regional pride by treating its origin legend with the seriousness he believed a seminal moment in American history deserved. Undoubtedly sensitive toward the contemporaneous theatrical and artistic depictions of Indians as either "noble savages" or ferocious brutes, Chapman sought to rise above the stereotypes by taking a middle course and rendering Pocahontas and the other Powhatans as respectable, if somewhat romanticized, individuals.

The artist's earnest endeavor to dignify his state's genesis legend came to full fruition with his painting for the Capitol. The baptism he ultimately selected turned out to be the least documented and most apocryphal segment of Virginia's historical legacy. Although Smith's *Generall Historie* and other records of the early colony mentioned that Pocahontas had become a Christian before she married Rolfe, there are no written records to substantiate an actual baptism ceremony. In search of more information and possible artifacts left by Pocahontas and Rolfe during their English sojourn, Chapman traveled to Britain in 1837. To his chagrin, he uncovered no hidden documentation, artifacts, or portraits and thus returned home knowing little more than when he left.[30] He thus worried that he would have to rely upon either Sully's copy of the Bolling family portrait (Figs. 4.11 and 4.12) or the seventeenth-century Van de Passe print (Fig. 4.1) for the likeness of Pocahontas. Anticipating that choice, he consulted William Bolling, who assured him that he was under no "obligation" to duplicate the "coarse" and "unpoetical dimensions" of the "spurious" family portrait. In hopes of preserving "the romance of the story" Chapman told Bolling that he had decided to model his figure of Pocahontas on Van de Passe's "Lady Rebecca." It was a "sore temptation," the artist confessed, to place John Smith in the composition, but he abandoned the idea because Smith was back in England at the time of Pocahontas's baptism and it would be inaccurate to include him.[31] Determined to maintain historical verisimilitude at all costs, Chapman combed the area to find models among residents of the region; or as he phrased it, he would employ "the fair daughters" and "young cavaliers" of contemporary Virginia to pose as Jamestown ancestors.[32]

To facilitate work on what he called "the big painting," Chapman moved his wife and children from New York to Washington in the fall of 1838. Within weeks of his resettlement, he was confessing to disillusionment with the commission he had tried so assiduously to obtain. He complained that his household expenses far exceeded the annual $2,000 stipend allowed by Congress, and official Washington's indifference was forcing him to struggle through "much more trouble and annoyance with mechanics" than he had anticipated. Worst of all, he seemed to have difficulty channeling his energies into the task at hand. He told his friend William Kemble that the "buoyancy of spirit and glow" that had once directed his efforts had vanished. Working in fits and starts amid intermittent illnesses, family problems, and continuous financial distress, Chapman was not able to complete his painting until late November 1840. By that time, he was physically, financially, and emotionally stretched to the breaking point.[33]

On the evening of the formal unveiling in the rotunda, he wrote Kemble to vent his anxieties, remarking with wry resignation:

Tomorrow night I shall take off my hat to Pocahontas, and next week present her to the "enlightened public"! The picture has been in its place for a week, and I have retouched it in the light it is to remain in. The trial is yet to be made of its success—but I have done my best—I have acquitted my conscience—and should it fail to realize the expectations of my friends, however acutely I may feel my misfortune, I have no willing fault to accuse myself of—setting all egotism aside—I do not think the picture a failure, and however it may be assailed time will do it justice though I be not "there to see."[34]

A few weeks after Chapman installed his painting in the Capitol, a reporter for Washington's *Daily National Intelligencer* remarked that the "subject appears . . . to have been an unfortunate one for an historical painting, being more local and individual than national."[35] This was a revealing commentary on the differing degrees of acceptance accorded the Virginia and Massachusetts legends, for no such observations would be made about R. W. Weir's *Embarkation of the Pilgrims* when it was placed in the same hall four years later. Chapman apparently anticipated that kind of criticism, because a brochure printed for the unveiling explained that Pocahontas was "deemed a fit subject for a National Picture painted by order of Congress" because she "appeals to our religious as well as our patriotic sympathies, and is equally associated with the rise and progress of the Christian church, as with the political destinies of the United States." She was not only "a spotless virgin" who "joined a sagacity of mind, a firmness of spirit, and an adventurous daring" but "stands foremost in the train of those wandering children of the forest who have . . . been snatched from the fangs of a barbarous idolatry, to become lambs in the fold of the Divine Shepherd."[36]

Chapman also justified the relevance of his subject by insisting it would right "the erroneous impression" created by "careless, indifferent compilers of History" who failed to mention the actual baptism in their writings.[37] That correction apparently meant dignifying Virginia's origin legend in light of what Chapman considered to be recent distortions. The brochure stated that Virginia's first settlers were not "daring and desperate adventurers, who left their home and native land for no other purpose than to exterminate the ancient proprietors of the soil, and usurp their possessions."[38] To emphasize the propriety of the heroine and the sobriety of the baptism, Chapman attempted to impart an aura of reverence. A preliminary oil sketch (Fig. 6.6) shows the central figures—Pocahontas and Reverend Alexander Whitaker—in a more relaxed pose, with the minister taking Pocahontas's hand. Chapman must have abandoned the intimacy of that configuration to make Whitaker appear more pontifical and Pocahontas more suppliant.[39]

He made other significant alterations between the oil sketch and the final mural, most notably in his treatment of the Indians, who are shadowy figures merging into the periphery of the composition in the sketch. A key printed to accompany the painting (Fig. 6.7) identi-

FIGURE 6.6   *John Gadsby Chapman*, Baptism of Pocahontas, *oil sketch. Jamestown-Yorktown Educational Trust, Williamsburg, Va.*

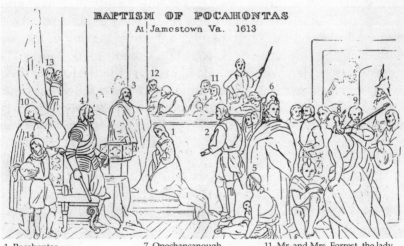

1. Pocahontas
2. John Rolfe
3. Alexander Whiteaker
4. Sir Thomas Dale
5. Sister of Pocahontas
6. Nantequaus, brother of Pocahontas

7. Opechancanough
8. Opachisco, uncle of Pocahontas
9. Richard Wyffin
10. Standard bearer

11. Mr. and Mrs. Forrest, the lady being the first gentlewoman to arrive in the colony
12. Henry Spilman
13. John and Anne Laydon, the first persons married in the colony
14. The page

FIGURE 6.7   *John Gadsby Chapman, key to the* Baptism of Pocahontas, *engraving, c. 1840. Architect of the Capitol, U.S. Capitol, Washington, D.C.*

fies the natives as Pocahontas's brother Nantequas (standing with his head turned to the right); her uncle, the villainous Opechancanough (sitting on the floor); another uncle, Opachisco (bursting in from the far right); and an unnamed sister holding a baby (in the central foreground).[40] They are a curious lot, some attired for battle, others swathed in flowing classical drapery. Thus, they pose a pagan contrast to the Christian rite taking place; two of them turn away from the altar, the other thrusts himself angrily into the chapel.[41] Their combined disdain and hostility suggest the way Native Americans had resisted capitulation to the dictates of American authorities, an act of defiance that prompted the long trek to Oklahoma.

The brochure actually attempts to sidestep the Indian question by avowing that the founders of Jamestown had "a sincere and fervent desire to propagate the blessings of Christianity among the Heathen savages ... however we may deplore the means adopted to attain their object and the consequences which followed."[42] This stumbling defense of the Jamestown settlers suggests that Chapman was caught between praising the Englishmen as Christian saviors and censuring them as conquerors. He seems to have been affected by the Trail of Tears, which had occurred two years before he installed his mural in the Capitol. The reality of that tragic march may explain why he featured the Indians more prominently in the final version of the painting than in the preliminary sketch. The woman identified as Pocahontas's sister (an apocryphal figure) is the heroine's pagan antithesis. Her moccasin, which almost touches the flowing train of Pocahontas's gown, forms a diagonal that in one sense connects and in another separates the chaste heroine from her heathen sibling. John Rolfe, who stands between the two sisters, connotes the couple's impending wedding, thus his presence represents the merger of two Christian sacraments, baptism and marriage.[43] By so depicting the symbolic baptism, Chapman was interpreting the ancestress of Virginia not just as a fearless heroine or as John Smith's "only Nonpareil of the land" but as an American heroine who rescued the English settlement from the ravages of brutality and saved Protestantism from "the fangs of barbarous idolatry."

In "Pocahontas: A Subject for the Historical Painter" (1845), William Gilmore Simms lauded Chapman's artistic abilities but reprimanded him for passing over the rescue of Smith—the "nobler event"—in favor of the baptism for the Capitol painting.[44] Simms missed the point. Chapman had in fact rejected his own *Pocahontas Saving the Life of John Smith* in favor of the more complex *Baptism.* That subject not only presented a new approach to the ancient legend but also told a composite story with a direct bearing on Virginia's position in contemporary society.

Perhaps only Virginians understood Chapman's real intentions. Mary Webster (a Pocahontas-Rolfe descendant) wrote a long epic poem entitled *Pocahontas: A Legend* and published it in 1840 just as Chapman was preparing to install the *Baptism* in the Capitol. In the introduction, Webster explained that her purpose was twofold. Primarily, she hoped to "snatch a fast-fading relic of other days from the mysteries which envelop that interesting race of beings, the free sons of the forest," who were "undisturbed by the restraints of civilization and unsubdued by the yoke of the oppressor." And because Webster identified herself as a "seventh remove in lineal descent" from Pocahontas, she inveighed her "fair countrywomen" to "raise a shrine" to Virginia's noteworthy ancestor. She must have seen Chapman's painting before he installed it in the rotunda, because her description of the baptism matches his portrayal of the event:

> *While lowly bending at the altar-stone*
> *Alone in seeming, not in heart alone,*
> *The bright girl knelt, bathed in repentant tears—*
> *Connecting link between two hemispheres. . . .*
>
> *Sublime in youth and hope the aspirant stood,*
> *Nature's untutored child, late tenant of the wood;*
> *Her dark hair floating on the summer wind,*
> *And loose her robe no art had taught to bind.*
>
> *But who is that with eye and brow serene,*
> *Of swarter [swarthier] visage than the forest Queen?*
> *Does heavenly grace its holy light reveal,*
> *Or bears his bosom but the stoic's zeal?*
> *Pride of his race where lofty courage stands;*
> *The test of virtue in his own bright lands? . . .* [45]

In these lines Webster credited Pocahontas's baptism and subsequent marriage as being the "connecting link" between Europe and

America a full decade before the Pilgrims reached Plymouth. With that ceremony in the Jamestown chapel, Pocahontas moved from "Matoaka" to "Lady Rebecca," a transformation that legitimized the blood lines of her progeny and underscored Virginia's rightful place among the nation's leaders. Pocahontas accepts "heavenly grace," while her kinsmen "of swarter visage" reject "those elements sublime" in the Christian rite that might have saved their race from inevitable doom. The biracial audience in the chapel (which Webster described as a mixture of knights "in blazonry of pomp and power," squires, and "swart denizens of forest shade") signified a monumental cultural confrontation. It provided a fatalistic commentary on Indian removal and, like Custis's play, described the displacement of thousands as a self-imposed exile that only compliance with the dominant culture could have prevented.

Seen in this context, Chapman's *Baptism* celebrates the triumph of enlightened Christianity over primitive paganism. By the time the painting was firmly attached to the wall of the U.S. Capitol, tribal relocation was a fait accompli. Following close on the heels of the long march to Oklahoma, installation of Chapman's rotunda painting marked a watershed in the revision of the Pocahontas legend to conform with contemporary issues. Custis, Chapman, and Mary Webster, Virginians all, were bent on emphasizing the saintly presence of their regional ancestor and presenting tribal relocation as a tragic but necessary stratagem. As will be noted shortly, Northerners and foreigners would treat the story differently, especially after the federal government had successfully vanquished the Eastern tribes and moved their crippled nations and "pagan rituals" beyond the borders of the then existing United States.

As Chapman was applying the finishing touches to *The Baptism of Pocahontas* in July 1840, a reproduction of Van de Passe's "Lady Rebecca" appeared next to the lead article of the *New-York Mirror*. The text was a paean to true womanhood.[46] The "woman's heart" of Pocahontas "melted," the author wrote, when she saw Smith "stretched on the stone of sacrifice." Her compassion "rose with the emergency" because "the heart of a woman is ever highest when the feelings of nature are outraged." The author then observed that "the difference between Pocahontas and Powhatan" was a conflict "between man and woman," because her reasons for intervening to save Smith were purely humanitarian but her father's were based on "profit."[47]

These opinions marked an emerging trend. After the Trail of Tears virtually ended public debate over Indian relocation, the heroine's femininity emerged as a dominant theme in Pocahontas literature. Typical was the tribute offered by William Waldron. In the introduction to a long poem about Pocahontas, he wrote that she "serves as a beacon to light us on our way, instruct us in our duty, and show us what the human mind is capable of performing when abandoned to its own operations." To Waldron, she represented the "simple child of nature, prompted by her own native virtues alone." She loves "her enemies" and performs good deeds for "those who despitefully used and persecuted her"; she existed on earth, said Waldron, as "'a teacher come from God.'"[48] A columnist for the *Southern Literary Messenger* made essentially the same judgment about the virtues and sufferings" of the "Princess Pocahontas" in 1838 and then posed a question: "Who gave to this dark daughter of the red man, nurtured in the wigwam of the savage, and familiar with blood, those gentle emotions, those generous feelings, that delicate sensibility that maidenly decorum . . . which have ranked this Indian girl among the loftiest of her sex in any age or clime?"[49]

The question echoes the biases and fears that pervade most American attitudes toward Indians and points to another literary consequence of the Trail of Tears. In the plays and poems about Pocahontas, the emphasis shifted from converting and Anglicizing the natives to considerations of the differences between good Indians and bad ones. It usually boiled down to gender. Many writers implied that male braves and chieftains were inherently treacherous, whereas the peace-loving and Christian Pocahontas was a paragon of virtue whom other members of her "doomed race" should emulate. Although Robert Dale Owen, Seba Smith, and other more thoughtful authors commented on the contradictory nature of such logic, most commentators readily admired the courageous (but feminine) Pocahontas and condemned her violent, uncompromising male counterparts. These opposing characterizations of Indians—one masculine, thus destructive; one feminine, therefore salutary—revealed yet another paradox embedded in the Virginia origin myth.

In a cultural climate that fostered numerous Indian poems, plays, and novels, authors construed the Jamestown legend as a tragic but unavoidable clash of cultural values.[50] Literary works of the 1830s and 1840s implied that only Pocahontas recognized the advantages of peaceful submission to the more powerful English, while male Indians, blinded by pride and native brutality, rejected white civilization and thereby brought about their own extinction. Some authors treated this contrast as a metaphor of a social system gone awry; some interpreted it as a romantic tragedy; still others perceived it as a consequence of a woman's decisive but gentle intervention.

One of the first to address the gender differences explicitly was South Carolinian William Gilmore Simms, who published the poem "Forest Maiden" in 1833. In an introductory paragraph, Simms defined the rescue of John Smith as a pathetic confrontation between male energy and female docility and announced that he planned to place "the amiable spirit of Pocahontas" in a "stronger light" and emphasize the "great sacrifice" Powhatan made when forced to disregard his "native impulse" and succumb to his daughter's "entreaties."[51] Simms's Powhatan is an angry, fallen warrior driven to seek "sweet revenge" on the white settlers for the death of his son. In contrast, Pocahontas is "free from all taint of thought or deed," the epitome of the "woman's mood" and "human heart" whose "soothing" temperament served as a counterpoint to her father's belligerence. In the poem's conclusion, Simms expressed the potential tragedy inherent in Powhatan's capitulation to the supplications of Pocahontas.

> *How could that dark old king forbear,*
> *Though writhing with his own despair,*
> *To still her plaint—to grant her pray'r!*
> *How could he check the angel grace*
> *That gave such beauty to her face,—*
> *How stay the more than sweet control,*
> *That, to the savage could impart,*
> *Tho' all untaught, the Christian soul,*
> *The woman's mood, the human heart!*[52]

When feminine tenderness triumphs over masculine pride, this passage implies, the resulting humiliation portends certain defeat for

Powhatan and his entire race. Where Custis found redemption in the triumph of a virtuous woman, Simms saw only emasculation. As a dedicated Jacksonian, Simms followed Custis in making Smith a forerunner of the president, thus establishing a scenario that cast his Indians as counterparts of contemporary political forces. In one sense, they represented nullifiers defying Jackson's benign authority; in another, they were the recalcitrant tribal chiefs resisting relocation. Simms conjured up that specter of a complex and seemingly unresolvable conflict of wills, a bleak vision that was to haunt him for many years to come.[53]

Robert Dale Owen, son of the English reformer Robert Owen, also chose to rewrite the Jamestown legend to address current political and social issues. He had come to the United States in 1825 to help his father and brothers found an experimental cooperative in New Harmony, Indiana. While there, he met the outspoken Frances Wright whose ideas on birth control and the "emancipation" of women shaped his opinions. After the New Harmony colony failed, the younger Owen traveled through Europe and America attempting to reform industrial conditions and bring about a more equitable distribution of wealth. In 1836, he entered politics, first as a member of the Indiana legislature and later as a Democratic representative in Congress. His political involvement and social conscience had a bearing on his play, *Pocahontas: A Historical Drama,* which was performed briefly at New York's Park Theater in February 1838 before touring Indiana the following year. Critics assailed the turgid blank verse and chided the author for his somber message.[54] The play received better treatment, however, when it appeared in print in 1837 under the pseudonymous authorship of "A Citizen of the West."

In the introduction, Owen made the standard claim that his principal goal was to expose "the fates of a noble race, which is fast fading away from the earth. . . . a race, the savage magnificence of whose character appears to me indifferently well adapted to dramatic effect."[55] Actually, the reformer was using Virginia's origin legend to convey his own theories about the negative effects of capitalism, the exploitation of women, and the evil influence of colonialism.[56] The real villains of the play are the English, or "Yengeese," who took advantage of the Indian's hospitality, profited by their agricultural expertise, pillaged their storehouses, decimated their population, and then acted "as if the Mighty Spirit had given this land to them."[57]

Like Simms and Custis, Owen endowed John Smith with Andrew Jackson's virility and courage, although he characterized the captain as an introspective individual tempted by self-interest and burdened by indecision. Rolfe, by contrast, shines as an honest—if often naive—admirer of the "worthy" and "venerable" natives. He reprimands Smith for speaking ill of Powhatan, whose "high, dark brow and noble Roman features bear impress, not of craft but dignity." In the long run, Smith opts to defend and protect the Indians because his hatred of privileged Englishmen outweighs his distrust of the natives, especially after John Ratcliffe and his band of "ice-hearted, faithless villains" expropriate leadership of the colony.[58]

In Owen's rendering of the Jamestown story, the heroine and all other characters emerge as symbolic representatives of the author's reformism. For example, he found John Smith's criticism of the materialistic Virginia Company to be compatible with his own misgivings about capitalism. His strongest indictment of entrepreneurial expansion comes toward the end of the play, when Smith delivers a lengthy monologue about how Englishmen "bring home gold, and leave behind them a desert, strewed with bones, and soaked with blood." Pocahontas, a composite of native nobility and courageous independence, joins the English primarily to assure survival of her people. Owen also casts her as an advocate of women's rights, who tells her sister that she had been "born to aid but not to slave; to stand beside not crouch behind" her husband.[59] The social activist demonstrated his conviction that women should have a larger role in determining their fate. As was customary in his day, however, he advocated that their independence take place within the traditional confines of marriage and motherhood.[60] Owen's play nevertheless contributed a new note to the growing library of Pocahontas literature by using that historical episode as a vehicle to proselytize for social and political reform.

During the early 1840s, a number of writers—most with ties to New England—followed Owen's lead by using the Virginia origin myth to plead their cases. Some evaluated Pocahontas's decisive actions as a curse that precipitated the Indians' eventual conquest; others viewed her bravery and determination as a positive virtue. The Maine native Seba Smith took the first route in his poem, *Powhatan: A Metric Romance* (1841). Best known for his humorous "Jack Downing" columns, which ridiculed everything from local politics to Jacksonian values, Smith used the Jamestown legend to make wry observations about human frailties, to satirize the irony of contemporaneous Indian policies, and to lament the capitulation of Powhatan to the wiles of his persuasive daughter. Oddly, commentators on Seba Smith's work have typically overlooked the poem's satiric overtones and have treated *Powhatan* as one of the humorist's rare serious performances.[61]

One reason for that oversight is the failure to connect this poem with Seba Smith's humorous volume entitled *John Smith's Letters with 'Picters' to Match*, published three years earlier. Written in the form of his Jack Downing letters, this book lampooned life and politics in a fictional Maine town called "Smithville," where most inhabitants shared a common ancestry and the name "John Smith." Their heritage descended in a somewhat "crooked" line to the sixteenth-century captain "that first settled in old Virginny." A "braver man than he was never lived," wrote the fictitious author, who claimed to have John Smith's original coat of arms "made up in a picter, hanging up in our fore room."[62] The book not only poked fun at Virginia's legendary founder, whose last name Seba Smith shared, but ridiculed the entire practice of ancestor veneration.

In the poem *Powhatan*, Seba Smith addressed two main issues—the plight of the "vanishing Indian" and the role of women in nineteenth-century America. Smith had more than a casual interest in the latter subject. A year before he published *Powhatan*, his wife, Elizabeth, an early advocate of women's rights, had contributed a column to the *Southern Literary Messenger* on the subject of John Smith and Pocahontas. The short article passed quickly over the captain's "valor, skill and judgment" to wax poetic about Pocahontas, whom she called "the beautiful personation of all that is loveliest in woman—the meek, loving child of the forest, whose history seems like a tale of romance, with its sad melancholy close." Her personality, she wrote, "beams forth in those dark and perilous times, like some kindly spirit, hushing the tempest of savage passion, dispensing comfort and succor to the disheartened exile, and with her own gentle bosom warding off all the evils that threaten the infant colony of Jamestown."[63]

Seba Smith's *Powhatan* subtly subverted his wife's tribute to Pocahontas's nurturing qualities by suggesting that those very wiles were often used to manipulate men. He wrote of "Metoka" (a corruption of Matoaka), who with "tearful eyes upturn'd," prevented her father from executing Smith ("Sir John"), while the "soft contagion" of her heavenly influence spread to Powhatan's "warrior men" so that their hearts were "touch'd and passions hushed." But Metoka lacks the depth or complexity that were qualities Seba Smith reserved for the poem's male personae. He followed his predecessors by transforming John Smith into a surrogate Andrew Jackson, but in his characterization, Virginia's hero becomes a wily and fearless diplomat taking advantage of every opportunity to promote himself. In contrast to John Smith's intrepidity and bluster, Powhatan's indecisiveness stands out; and he emerges as a beaten chieftain, perplexed about his inability to stem the tide of history. His "iron knee" refused to bend to the English, the author wrote. In fact "he stood upright in native dignity, like an old oak of the wood" when Newport offered him King James's crown but in the end, he succumbed to the demands of the insistent English.[64]

Although in Seba Smith's *Powhatan* the final battle between the English and their native adversaries ends in a standoff, the once mighty chief recognizes the superior strength of his enemy and concedes defeat. After realizing that his "warriors all were dead" and loved ones gone, he dolefully opts to go west. Describing this retreat, Smith wrote:

> *And casting one long, painful look*
> *On his lost land and home*
> *Ere through the western wilds afar*
> *A pilgrim he should roam,*
> *He took his war-club for a staff,*
> *And footsteps westward turn'd,*
> *And sought for rest in the far-off land,*
> *Where the ruddy sunset burn'd.*[65]

In wake of recent tribal relocation, this repetition of the "vanishing Indian" theme carried a tragic message of fatalism and resignation in which the proud Powhatan—caught in a three-way bind between his brother Opechancanough's ferocity, the magnitude of the "paleface" threat, and the persuasiveness of his daughter's compassion—finds his own strength sapped. He therefore suffered a loss of face occasioned by fleeing from his own manly instincts and derived not merely from a reluctant acceptance of fate but from a humiliating submission to the entreaties of a woman.[66] Through this characterization, Seba Smith turned on its head the standard mid-nineteenth-century interpretation of Pocahontas's heroism and implied that her well-intentioned determination to protect the English ultimately condemned her father and all of her former tribesmen to a future of shame and displacement. Read as such, Seba Smith's "metrical romance" becomes a negative commentary on emasculation caused by a woman's interference and therefore jabs at the very core of the Pocahontas myth.

Virginians, however, apparently failed to reach that conclusion. A reviewer in the *Southern Literary Messenger* not only applauded the poem but wrote:

> The subject is one of the most interesting in the annals of Indian life. It is emphatically a national theme. Mr. Smith deserves great credit for having boldly seized a local topic and familiar tradition. It was foreign to his purpose to decorate such a story with high-wrought diction and splendid imagery. He has adhered rather with an historian's fidelity to fact.[67]

Fact, it seems, was in the eye of the beholder. If Virginians wanted to read the poem as a truthful appraisal of their origin legend and relate it to the national Indian tragedy, so much the better. It provided just the ironic twist that the wry New Englander may have anticipated.

Like Seba Smith, Lydia Huntley Sigourney was a New Englander who used the Jamestown legend to comment upon current issues. But unlike Smith, she viewed it from a woman's perspective and therefore shifted the emphasis from Powhatan's failure to his daughter's heroism. Although Sigourney's poem "Pocahontas" of 1841 contributed a feminine perspective to the predominantly male collection of Pocahontas literature, it did so by borrowing heavily from Sigourney's own masculine predecessors. Her tragic heroine combined Chapman's virginal paragon and Owen's advocate of woman's rights to become a female counterpart of Seba Smith's tragic Powhatan. But Sigourney's Pocahontas also corresponded with Virginia's noble "Lady Rebecca" and thus was the antithesis of the ubiquitous forest siren then being reproduced in lithographs and etchings. This resolute yet delicate Indian maiden is served up as the quintessential victim. She not only unwittingly embraces the white aggressor and thus condemns her people to extinction but also sacrifices her own short life to become a pawn of the Englishmen's wishes.

For Sigourney, the "new joy" of Pocahontas's Christianity induced her to "choose the narrow path that worldlings scorn" and prompted her to accept the "heritage sublime—a mansion in the sky."[68] Sentimental religiosity was a key ingredient in the work of this ex-schoolmistress and Hartford housewife, whom Edgar Allan Poe had disparagingly dubbed "the American Hemans." Sigourney propounded the view that acceptance of Christ saved Pocahontas and would have redeemed her people if only they had followed her to the baptismal font, a predictable conclusion for a writer who in an 1822 publication—*Traits of the Aborigines of America*—had compared Pocahontas's rescue of Smith with the finding of Moses by Pharaoh's daughter.[69]

Sigourney's virtuous Pocahontas was the antithesis of the villainous Jamestown settlers, whom she described as scoundrels brutalizing the helpless Indians. Future historians, she charged, must not blame "those erring, red-brow'd men," for even though they had been "nurs'd in wiles," the real transgressors were "the white-lipp'd" settlers who caused so much destruction. The Jamestown colony was populated by "dejected men, with disappointed frown . . . spoil'd youths," and "keen gold-gatherers."[70] The poet clearly saw these first Virginians with a New Englander's prejudiced eye. They erred, she insisted, because they never extended a "brother's arm," nor did they lead the Indians, "sad of heart, to the blest Lamb of God."[71] If John Smith and company had imitated New Englanders, she implied, they would have persuaded the natives to follow Pocahontas's example. Through conversion, they would not only have rescued individual Indian souls but would have saved the entire race from extinction.

Another woman, the English actress-playwright Charlotte Barnes, duplicated Sigourney's poetic excesses in *The Forest Princess, or Two Centuries Ago*, produced in the United States in 1848. The play combined current views with the sentimentality found in Pocahontas literature from the previous decade. Barnes, like Sigourney, chose to span the full spectrum of Pocahontas's life from the innocence of her forest childhood in Virginia to the tragedy of her untimely death in England. The legend had a special affinity for Barnes, whose mother, Mary, had starred in Custis's *Pocahontas* during its 1830 run. In

Barnes's estimation, the saintly heroine exemplified "mercy, peace, unselfishness and truth" because her life was "pure, active and affectionate." But she also harbored a "warrior's Spirit in a woman's form."[72] Rescuing Smith was only a prelude for her many daring deeds aimed at staving off the "red man's hand." In addition to protecting the colony from "famine" and "death," Pocahontas uncovered a conspiracy to undermine British rule and execute John Rolfe.

Barnes treated Powhatan in a stereotypical fashion. He is kindly, sage, and courageous, but fated to certain extinction. He reluctantly submits to the bidding of the "Great father" and allows the English to occupy his property, though not before asking why there were not lands enough for the paleface "across the waters" and pointing out that America was reserved for the Great Spirit's "red children." Adding to the cloying sentimentality of Barnes's play is the mawkishness of Indian stage-talk, especially marked when Rolfe visits Powhatan to ask for his daughter's hand. Pocahontas explains to her father that their marriage would "blunt" the white man's "tomahawk," and that promise of peace convinces Powhatan that he must accept "the young brave" and treat him like a son. Pocahontas then turns to her future husband and tells him that "whene'er a forest-maiden gives her heart" to the "husband of her soul," she remains faithful forever and "from her sight shuts out all other men."

Surely Virginians claiming descent from that union must have applauded those sentiments and shed a tear or two as the pair knelt before the elderly chief to demonstrate their respect and mutual devotion, while trumpets sounded and the curtain descended. For Barnes, the Indian vanished not because of the settlers' cruelty but because the English were so superior that they merely absorbed the natives into their fold.[73] The marriage of Pocahontas and Rolfe, in fact, shone as a supreme example of cultural rapprochement, a deed that united "in peace and love the Old World and the New."[74]

The outcome of this accord was a future empire marred only by the gradual disappearance of Indians from within its borders. The stage instructions indicate that Pocahontas herself envisions this glorious future as she languishes on her deathbed:

A strain of invisible music is heard, and thin clouds obscure the view from the casement. The clouds gradually disperse and . . . through them a figure of Time passes, beckoning Peace who follows. The clouds partially disperse, and disclose in the distance, the form of Washington.—The Genius of Columbia stands near him. Time hovers near, and Peace encircles with her arms the Lion and the Eagle. A mist then conceals the allegorical group, and again dispersing, discovers the view of Gravesend, at sunset. . . . The music dies away.

Suddenly, Pocahontas opens her eyes and realizes she is not dreaming, and at that moment, the melodrama intensifies. "The Father of his Country!" shall be the new "noble chief," she proclaims, and "Time" will lead "Peace" bound by "ties of love and language" as the "Island-Mother and her Giant Child" grasp arms across the "narrowing seas." Shortly thereafter, the heroine draws her loved ones near and announces: "My eyes behold Virginia's grassy turf–I hear my father–Husband fare thee well. We part–but we shall meet above!" Her hand, which was pointing upward, falls to her side and she dies in Rolfe's arms with John Smith a silent witness.[75]

In 1848, the same year that the *Forest Princess* had its American debut, the artist Junius Brutus Stearns exhibited a painting entitled *The Death of Pocahontas* at the American Art Union.[76] In keeping with the artistic trends of the era, Stearns captured the pathos of the play's closing act by displaying its cast of characters, all of whom recall some phase of Pocahontas's life. The dying heroine lies in a spotlighted bed; an Indian woman leans over her; two braves watch sorrowfully; and a grieving Rolfe hugs his son. Among the well-dressed English men and women who surround the deathbed is a Cavalier with a pointed beard, apparently meant to be John Smith.

Barnes's *Indian Princess* marked the grand finale for sentimental dramatizations of the Pocahontas story. It also proved to be the American stage's fond farewell to portrayals of the "vanishing Indian." Performed in the northeastern United States just as the nation was moving to acquire vast Western lands at the conclusion of the Mexican War, the drama extolled the concept of a future American empire. Acquisition of lands formerly belonging to Mexico set in motion a series of events that would soon render the concept of disappearing Indians passé. Settlement of the new territories brought Anglo-Americans once more face to face with tribal leaders, and fighting over territory again became a reality. Met with fierce resistance on the part of the Western tribes, the push into the new territory inspired images of brutality and menace that soon subsumed the melodramatic "vanishing Indian." Hence, within a few decades, paintings, poems, and theater would laud brave cowboys eradicating menacing "savages." Consequently, the only thing that vanished was compassion for the Indians.

The Forest Princess also brought down the curtain on endeavors to carry Virginia's origin legend to other parts of the nation and the world. After 1850, the story of Pocahontas became a scapegoat for New Englanders, and as the slavery issue began to dominate all cultural endeavors, few tears would be shed over the fate of Pocahontas. The United States was on the brink of an internal upheaval that would divide the descendants of Jamestown from those of Plymouth. Soon, both the Indian question and the nascent drive for women's equality would be overshadowed and indeed replaced by sectional bitterness. Only the Old Dominion would remember Pocahontas's daring deeds, but those stories would soon be directed toward preserving the Southern way of life. Her devotion to Christianity and Rolfe and her daring intrepidity would soon be used to substantiate the decent and noble heritage of Virginia's first families. In Massachusetts, the Virginia legend would eventually elicit skepticism and scorn. But before that occurred, New Englanders reconsidered the Pilgrim legend and began revising it to address and justify concerns of their own.

7

Compact with Destiny

$\mathcal{A}$ delegation of congressmen and other dignitaries assembled in the Supreme Court chambers on May 24, 1844, to see whether Samuel F.B. Morse's telegraph machine would work or whether, as many thought likely, the erratic artist had squandered the substantial amount of public and private funding invested in the experiment. Cautiously, the inventor tapped "What has God wrought!" to Alfred Vail, waiting in Baltimore. Within minutes, the wires began clicking, and slowly the code of dots and dashes returned Morse's message. The room filled with cheers. A new era of rapid communications had begun.[1] The profound spiritual implications of the words that launched the telegraph would surely have made old Jedidiah Morse proud. And for his son, who had been striving for fifty-three years to satisfy the ghost of his domineering parent, those words signaled a moment of personal triumph.

Five months earlier, shortly before Christmas of 1843, another crowd had gathered on Capitol Hill; this time, the event was the unveiling of Robert Walter Weir's *Embarkation of the Pilgrims* in the Capitol rotunda. Although it attracted less public notice than the successful introduction of the telegraph, the installation of Weir's mural was devastating to Samuel F.B. Morse, who had been lobbying for decades to place his own Pilgrim painting in the rotunda. Ever since he had created the *Landing of the Forefathers* in 1811, Morse had been longing to again pay homage to the founders of Massachusetts, but now he wanted to illustrate what he considered to be a more meaningful subject—the signing of the Mayflower Compact.[2] That subject was immensely important for New England in the 1840s. Just as the "landing on Plymouth Rock" had spoken to an earlier generation, the Mayflower Compact signified the Pilgrims' mission to disseminate their ideals to the nation.

When the House of Representatives made the choice of artists in 1836, Morse had every reason to believe that he would be one of those selected. At the time, he was a leading member of New York's cultural establishment and was serving as the first president of the National Academy of Design, an art school and exhibition salon that he had helped organize. Certain that his prominence would give him preference for the congressional project, he began petitioning friends in high places before embarking on a three-year tour of Europe to conduct research for the project.[3] As he later recalled, he "felt a consciousness of ability to execute a Historical picture honorable to my country." He informed his friends, his congressional contacts, and the press that his topic, "Signing of the Mayflower Contract," was a "New England Subject," that represented the "germ of the Republick."[4]

Morse probably would have succeeded in obtaining that coveted commission had he not expressed such a rabid hatred of Roman Catholics, a prejudice he had inherited from his opinionated father. The first vehicle for such rantings was a series of letters signed "Brutus" that ran during 1834 in the *New York Observer,* a conservative paper founded by his brother Sidney. Later that year, the columns were published in book form.[5] Morse's prime targets were the Jesuits and the Austrian-sponsored Leopold Association, which he claimed was engineering a large-scale infiltration of American society during a time when Catholics from Germany, Italy, France, and Ireland were moving into cities of the Eastern seaboard, leading Morse to advocate curbing immigration as a means of averting displacement of Protestantism in the United States.

Before the 1830s, most Americans viewed European immigrants as beneficial to the welfare of the nation, but attitudes changed as more poor, nonskilled, and uneducated people began to arrive.[6] Although statistics were often exaggerated, there was no denying the dramatically altered demographics of the major cities.[7] Boston was especially hard hit by the influx of foreigners during the 1830s and 1840s. The number of Irish entering the port jumped from 2,361 in 1831 to 10,157 in 1841 and then to 65,556 in 1846, the year after the potato blight hit. But long before famine had decimated the countryside, excessive taxation and stringent English eviction laws drove a steady stream of Irish farmers to emigrate. As the economic and physical configurations of Northeastern cities shifted to accommodate these immigrants, unbridled prejudice and hostility mounted.[8]

Morse, who played on widespread apprehension about new immigrants, often implied in his writings that the Pilgrims came to America to escape from Catholic oppression, or "Popery," and "to wrest from Popish usurpation those invaluable rights, civil and religious." By plotting to give Catholicism a "foothold among the descendants of the persecuted Puritans," Morse continued, the Church of Rome connived to deceive the population into thinking that "Popery" was not a "monster" but rather a subterfuge for lulling people into assuming that the Roman "tyrant had grown mild and tolerant."[9]

Such harangues elicited so much attention among anti-Catholics that the New York Nativist (or antiforeign) Party asked Morse to run for mayor in 1836, the very year that Congress chose artists for the rotunda project. The son of Jedidiah Morse was clearly driven to make a big splash, if not through art then through politics. However, his erratic behavior and venomous prejudices led to certain defeat in both contests. Conservative New York voters were apparently angry that he had backed the Democratic presidential candidate, Martin Van Buren, while legislators in Washington were reluctant to have their names attached to an outspoken opponent of immigration when naturalized citizens were beginning to make a serious impact on election returns.[10]

Morse did not go down easily, however. In fact, he kept insisting that Congress would eventually commission his painting and remained hopeful even after the Library Committee asked seven other artists to submit sketches for possible murals. When the House formally announced that Chapman, Weir, Vanderlyn, and Inman had been selected for the job, his guarded optimism continued. "Tantalizing rumors" were keeping his hopes alive, he claimed.[11] When those failed to produce the desired results, Morse's spirits plummeted. The final blow came in March 1837 when Weir called on him to say he wanted to paint the signing of the Mayflower Compact for his assigned rotunda panel. Morse exploded in a fit of rage and made Weir promise never to paint the subject. After that conversation, Morse retreated to his bed, where he remained for several days, submerged in a deep and debilitating depression.[12]

He rallied, however, when friends from the art and literary world pledged $50 apiece (with the projected goal of raising $3,000) to facilitate his painting the "Germ of the Republick" in the twelve-by-eighteen-foot format of the rotunda panels. It was a humanitarian gesture designed to lift Morse's spirits, though neither the recipient nor the donors were thoroughly convinced that Congress would hang the painting when it was completed. Nevertheless, Morse dove into the project with a burst of enthusiasm. His "energies roused to the subject," he wrote the artist Washington Allston, for he was eager to illustrate that "first written Constitution" that formed the "nucleus or germ of our government."[13] During summer 1837, Morse obtained a large canvas and then toured Massachusetts (Boston, Plymouth, Provincetown, and Worcester) to gather information and make preliminary sketches. He even began soliciting models for "the family circle of those noble pilgrim fathers who laid the foundations of our government on the deck of the *Mayflower.*"[14]

But after his initial burst of energy, Morse lost interest in the project, as his electromagnetic experiments began occupying most of his time. In 1838, after demonstrating his first telegraph, he issued a formal statement requesting that subscribers to his painting delay further payments until after he finished testing his invention. He then traveled around Europe and the United States to secure funding for the proposed telegraph, successfully enticing wealthy men to back his invention and eventually procuring $30,000 from Congress to place wires between Washington and Baltimore. As chances for success with his scientific endeavors rose, Morse's interest in the Pilgrim painting waned. Suspecting that he would soon abandon art altogether, friends deluged him with letters of encouragement in hopes of reviving his excitement, but by then he had become totally consumed by the telegraph.[15]

In October 1841, a brief article appeared in the *New-York Mirror* asking "what had become" of Morse's "Cabin of the *Mayflower.*" The paper, which had pledged its own $50, was baffled by the secrecy that seemed to shroud the artist's progress. It has been "upwards of a year," the writer complained, and no one has heard a word about the painting; therefore the *Mirror* decided to put the question "to Mr. Morse himself."[16] The published inquiry goaded Morse into responding with defensive furor. He drafted an irate letter summarizing the "history of the transaction" from his first endeavors to attain the rotunda commission through his travels to promote the telegraph. Although that letter was apparently never mailed, the *New-York Mirror* column so stirred his conscience that within the next few weeks, he gradually began repaying his supporters and hinting about abandoning painting and dedicating his life to science.[17]

Morse's obsessive determination to illustrate the Mayflower Compact related directly to his anti-Catholic diatribes. At the same time that immigrants were pouring into the Northeast, heirs of the Puritans were experiencing an erosion of their former religious and political hegemony. The sense of displacement brought by these demographic and ecclesiastical changes manifested itself in two interrelated strains: One was a virulent anti-Catholicism that would eventually explode in the Know-Nothing movement of the 1850s; the other was a mission to spread Protestantism into the new Western territories. The Pilgrims figured into both crusades, as did faith in the republican "germ" that Morse and many others believed had spread from the decks of the *Mayflower* to the halls of Congress.

The ardent nativism of Samuel F.B. Morse and his obsession with the Mayflower Compact are parallel vestiges of his strict Calvinist upbringing and an extreme manifestation of the New England outlook that shaped his character. He knew full well when he allied the region's origin legend with fears of immigrants that he had a receptive audience back home. Much of Massachusetts shared Morse's belief that individual liberty would be directly threatened if the Catholic Church were to gain strength in the United States; orators and ministers were forever summoning the Pilgrim legend to rally resistance to a suspected "Popish" incursion. Catholicism loomed as a convenient scapegoat for the diminishing power of New England's Congregational orthodoxy.[18]

Lyman Beecher equaled Morse in virulent anti-Catholic rhetoric. During the late 1820s and early 1830s, the fiery minister wielded tremendous power in the Boston area, thus filling a conservative niche once occupied by Jedidiah Morse. Their backgrounds and missions were remarkably similar. Both had been reared in rural Connecticut and educated at Yale to preach the doctrines of orthodox Calvinism; like Jedidiah Morse, Beecher had tremendous influence on the lives of his illustrious offspring, who included the author Harriet Beecher Stowe and minister Henry Ward Beecher. From the pulpit of Boston's new Park Street Church, which he took over in 1826, Lyman Beecher ranted against the evil influences of Unitarians, Catholics, and infidels.[19] "The Protestant clergy," he wrote in 1835, "are congenial with liberty . . . chosen by the people who have been educated as freemen . . . dependent on them for patronage and support." But the "Catholic system is adverse to liberty, and the clergy to a great extent are dependent on foreigners opposed to the principles of our government, for patronage and support."[20]

The theories of Morse and Beecher were rooted in Puritan fundamentalism, for Catholics had always been considered anathema in New England. During the colonial period, Bostonians had burned the pope in effigy every November 5 as a means of commemorating Britain's Guy Fawkes Day. Such ingrained bigotry presaged a chilly reception for the Catholics of Boston, who had become numerous enough by 1803 to erect the Church of the Holy Cross (designed by Charles Bulfinch) and to have Jean Lefebre de Cheverus appointed as Boston's first Catholic bishop in 1808. However, only when the Irish entered the scene in the 1820s did the old repugnance escalate into venomous hatred. Federalists—and eventually Whigs—feared the lower-class Irish, not merely for their religious affiliation but also for their propensity to vote the Democratic ticket en masse.[21]

Boston's prejudices spilled over into the streets in the early 1830s, when Protestant gangs marched to protest encroaching "Papism." Nasty anti-Catholic books and pamphlets circulated, some accusing nuns and priests of sexual and ritualistic perversities. In 1834—influenced by rumors that nuns had kidnapped and tortured students attending an Ursuline Convent in neighboring Charlestown—a gang of working-class Bostonians set the convent on fire. The Irish Catholics responded by openly opposing the Protestant establishment and defying authorities at every turn, thus ensuring that hostilities between the two sides would remain at a fever pitch.[22] "Has it come to this?" asked Beecher, "that the capital of New England has been thrown into consternation by the threats of a Catholic mob, and that her temples and mansions stand only through the forbearance of a Catholic bishop?"[23]

With Irishmen retaliating by fighting in the streets, descendants of many old Boston families began to believe they were the last bastions of Protestant probity. Beecher readily exacerbated these fears by conjuring up Papist hoards invading the nation. The growing number of poor immigrants, he ranted, paid "an oppressive taxation" to the church that went to support the clergy, the "cathedrals of royal splendor," the "nunneries," and the "cheap schools"—all of which were beholden to "European patronage."[24] Jacob Abbott expressed similar apprehensions during 1835. "More than once have our large cities been disgraced by the tumult of an Irish mob, sweeping through the streets," he wrote. "The influence of the Catholic priest over the[se] Irish emigrants is very peculiar and powerful . . . no one can doubt that on the whole it is infinitely disastrous."[25] They arrive "in our sea-ports wholly destitute of property," proclaimed a writer for the *North American Review* the same year; they find "themselves in our principal cities, without personal resources or friends, and in many instances with very erroneous impressions of the nature of our political and municipal regulations."[26]

As the numbers of incoming immigrants climbed, New Englanders began to contrast the destitute and uneducated newcomers fleeing from economic deprivation with their pious and dignified ancestors, who purportedly came only to escape religious discrimination. Daniel Webster told his Plymouth audience in 1820 that the Pilgrims had embarked for the "chosen land" solely to escape religious intolerance; other bicentennial orators repeated the same message. James Sabine, at the Plymouth Pilgrim Church on December 22, 1820, insisted: "Was it not RELIGION? RELIGION ALONE? RELIGIOUS INDEPENDENCE OF EVERY THING BESIDES ITSELF?" that was the "single object which called your Fathers to this land." They were not "cast offs," he said, but victims of "bigotry," not motivated by "false zeal" but intent on "planting in this wilderness . . . *a pure gospel Church*."[27] In 1822, P. M. Whelpley, pastor of the First Presbyterian Church of New York, enlarged the message by telling a meeting of the New England Society that unlike the Spanish who sought gold in Mexico, the "chosen and heaven-directed" Pilgrims were "not the refuse of society, but men of strong intelligence, and proved integrity, who understood well, and were determined, at the hazard of Martyrdom, or burial in the ocean to maintain the rights of conscience and the religion of Jesus Christ."[28]

One method of contrasting the flawless Pilgrims with impoverished Catholics was to describe the Plymouth settlers as a master

race. When addressing the Pilgrim Society of Plymouth on Forefathers' Day 1835, the Honorable Pelig Sprague claimed that all Caucasians were "eminently distinguished" because of their "intellectual
superiority." And among Caucasians, the Teutonics were "preemi-
nent for all higher endowments," especially those "remarkable" folk
from Saxon England, of whom "the Puritans were a peculiar and selected few; and into the indomitable, severe Saxon blood was in-
fused by them another ingredient . . . religious principle . . . giving
new strength and firmness to a before strong and well compacted
moral texture." And the Puritan blood that "flows everywhere,
swelling every vein of the great republic" is "least contaminated by
foreign intermixture" in the Old Colony. Unlike the "murky regions
of heathenism" that mark the rest of the United States, Sprague continued, the Massachusetts society "rests, not only on the rock of Plymouth, but the Rock of Ages. When the Pilgrims here planted their
feet, it was with the Bible in their hands and its precepts in their
heads."[29]

It is no "mere lucky accident that this Atlantic seaboard was settled
by colonies of the Anglo-Saxon race," Robert Winthrop—a direct descendant of John Winthrop, founder of the Massachusetts Bay
Colony—said in a Forefathers' Day speech of 1839. The miracle of
Plymouth was due to "Divine intervention" of a "Power which was
over the Pilgrims in their humble but heroic enterprise."[30] This vision
of spiritual, moral, cultural, and racially superior Pilgrims posed an
antithesis to the imagined peril of debased, poverty-stricken, brutal,
and superstitious Irish overtaking their cities. Having been standard
fare of annual Forefathers' Day orations for decades, the refined and
pious Anglo-Saxons of Plymouth would soon migrate from the podi-
ums of New England to the walls of the national Capitol.

The fears associated with increased immigration and the vicious anti-
Catholicism it spawned were an inescapable part of New England
life at the time Robert Walter Weir began to paint the *Embarkation of
the Pilgrims* for the Capitol rotunda (Fig. 7.1). Unlike Morse, Weir had
no direct ties to Massachusetts. Born in the heart of New York City,
he considered himself a Knickerbocker through and through. When
selected by Congress in 1836, he was thirty-three years old and just

FIGURE 7.1   *Robert Walter Weir,* Embarkation of the Pilgrims, *oil on canvas, 1837–1844. Architect of the Capitol, U.S. Capitol, Washington, D.C.*

experiencing the first flush of success as an artist and illustrator. In the still-small New York cultural community, he had become part of the coterie that formed the Sketch Club and the National Academy of Design, then under Morse's leadership. In 1834, influential friends from these organizations recommended Weir for the post of drawing instructor at the U.S. Military Academy.[31] For the next forty-two years, he remained at West Point, teaching cadets the proper techniques for accurately sketching terrain and battle plans; and he also raised a large family, among them the future artists John Ferguson Weir and Julian Alden Weir. His teaching duties were light enough to enable him to produce a sizable number of historical and religious paintings.[32] That creative outpouring–coupled with his successful start at the military academy–convinced members of Congress that the artist was a humble and temperate man with proven abilities to work well within a bureaucracy; and like Chapman, he had friends in high places.[33]

Although the formal commission issued by the House of Representatives did not specify subject matter, the artist understood from the outset that Congress expected him to depict a scene from the history of the "Eastern states."[34] Weir found himself in a quandary, however, for shortly after winning the congressional competition, he had promised Morse that he would not paint the signing of the Mayflower Compact. But when he could find no suitable alternative, he wrote his friend and supporter, Gulian Verplanck, hoping either he or William Cullen Bryant could "spirit" him by suggesting another subject. "I don't like the idea of going farther back than the landing of the Pilgrims," he told Verplanck, and more recent events lacked both the mythic resonance or political relevance of the Pilgrim story.[35] With the Mayflower Compact seemingly the only viable option, Weir once again approached Morse, this time to beg release from his earlier promise. But Morse still stubbornly refused to bend and even demanded that the matter be brought before an arbitration board. Not wishing to take on the powerful president of the National Academy, Weir began his search for a different Pilgrim topic.[36]

Toward that end, he contacted Eliza Robbins, a Boston author of historical texts and children's books. She responded with a long and sympathetic letter that conveyed her annoyance with the arrogant Morse. Most "men in your circumstance," she fumed, "would not have consulted Morse's feelings at all." But realizing that Weir wanted no more confrontations with his senior colleague, Robbins suggested that he consider the passage from Mather's *Magnalia* that described "a number of devout Christians of the English nation . . . parting from their brethren" at Leyden. The scene had many visual possibilities, she continued, especially the description of the "excellent pastor" bidding "adieu" to the "pilgrims and strangers" migrating to America.[37]

With relief, Weir seized upon this suggestion and informed Senator William C. Preston, chairman of the congressional Library Committee, that although it was "painful" to "relinquish a favorite subject," he now wished to paint the departure of the Pilgrims for the New World. The artist had hoped to visit Holland to gain firsthand information about the actual sites, but his family and teaching responsibilities prevented him from leaving America. He would therefore rely on friends abroad for information about Puritan dress and accoutrements and would limit his own research to collecting data in and around Plymouth. As it turned out, he found himself following Morse through Massachusetts, the would-be inventor still seeking data for "The Germ of the Republick," with Weir close on his heels investigating the same material for his *Embarkation of the Pilgrims.*[38]

Weir completed several finished studies before settling on the final composition, which depicts the pastor John Robinson kneeling, surrounded by a semicircle of men, women, and children; at his right, in the center of the gathering, ruling elder William Brewster holds a bible opened to the beginning of the New Testament.[39] Adjacent to these principal figures are John Winslow, William Bradford, Miles Standish, and their wives. In an attempt to remain historically accurate and demonstrate his extensive research, Weir included numerous details. The lettering on the deck, for example, identifies the ship as the *Speedwell,* and among the cast of characters are such minor players as the parents of Peregrine White (the first English child born in Massachusetts), Brewster's son, who died during the voyage, and a Mrs. Fuller, who stayed behind (Fig. 7.2).[40]

Perhaps to recall the protagonists in Henry Sargent's *Landing of the Fathers* (Fig. 5.11), Weir placed a suit of armor in the central foreground. But this acknowledgment of his predecessor is the only link between the two men, for in both conception and execution their paintings are products of different eras. Sargent's heavily armed warriors stretched across a harsh coastal landscape tell of a time when New Englanders were angry with the so-called Virginia Dynasty for waging war against Britain. But by the 1840s, heirs of the Pilgrims were envisioning the regional ancestors as missionaries of Christ's doctrine, and therefore Weir pictured fashionably dressed aristocrats kneeling in prayer beneath a softly draped sail; only the tilted deck, waiting armor, and exaggerated shadows suggest that future hardships await the Pilgrims upon their arrival in America. That same contrast of security and danger separates the upper quarter of the composition—occupied by the voluptuous sail that resembles a nomad's tent or theatrical curtain—from the bare wooden boards of the rigid deck below. In between these two tactile extremes, the emigrants partake in an orderly, rational, and dignified religious ceremony.[41]

Before installing the *Embarkation* in the Capitol, Weir exhibited it in Boston, New York, and Philadelphia. Crowds viewing the painting were large and enthusiastic, especially in Massachusetts, where the many *Mayflower* descendants wanted to believe that their ancestors were well-bred, refined, and pious. "There are few sons of New En-

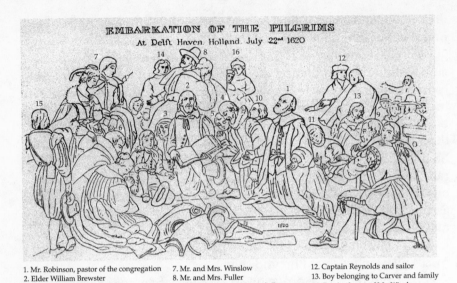

EMBARKATION OF THE PILGRIMS
At Delft Haven, Holland. July 22ᵈ 1620

1. Mr. Robinson, pastor of the congregation
2. Elder William Brewster
3. Mrs. Brewster and sick child
4. Governor Carver
5. William Bradford
6. Mr. and Mrs. White

7. Mr. and Mrs. Winslow
8. Mr. and Mrs. Fuller
9. Miles Standish and his wife Rose
10. Mrs. Bradford; she fell overboard
    the day the vessel came to anchor
11. Mrs. Carver and child

12. Captain Reynolds and sailor
13. Boy belonging to Carver and family
14. Boy in charge of Mr. Winslow
15. Boy belonging to Mr. Winslow's family
16. A nurse and child

FIGURE 7.2   *Robert Walter Weir, key to* Embarkation of the Pilgrims, *engraving, c. 1844. Architect of the U. S. Capitol, Washington, D.C.*

gland sires" exclaimed a columnist for the Boston *Critic,* "who can look upon this picture without emotion–or who can afterwards leave the Hall without feeling a stronger sense of his duties as a patriot, citizen and a Christian." A writer for the Boston *Transcript* explained that Bostonians should be moved by Weir's painting because it captured "the character of that body of men and women, who for the liberty of faith alone, resolutely and deliberately exchanged the delights of home and the comforts of civilized life, for toil and danger." A notice in the newspaper *Plymouth Rock* advised "all the descendants of the Pilgrims, in particular, and everybody else, to go and see this picture" for in that "momentous" episode "came the germ of our Republic."[42] Weir had clearly stolen Morse's thunder.

As the painting toured the Eastern seaboard, reviewers repeatedly commented that the composition illustrated the Pilgrims' voyage to America as a spiritual exodus undertaken by pious English men and women leaving the security of a well-to-do family in search of religious freedom.[43] Speaking in New York on Forefathers' Day 1843,

Massachusetts lawyer and public figure Rufus Choate praised Weir's *Embarkation* because it inspired "a thirst for freedom . . . the spirit of liberty . . . and a sense of religious duty."[44] The staple image of well-groomed "Teutonics" seeking religious freedom now had a focal point in Weir's Capitol mural.

The *Embarkation of the Pilgrims* inspired an outpouring of poetic emotion that emphasized the forefathers' piety.[45] For example, a poem in the *Knickerbocker* explained that Weir's *Embarkation* told a "noble theme of other days" about "men who strove in vain to break the stern oppressor's rod" for "the right to worship God." The lengthy description of the painting, the artist, and his principal subjects that followed ended with a tribute to the religious mission that had motivated the Pilgrims:

> *Tell ye, O mute, yet speaking forms, creations of his skill*
> *How trust in GOD, and lofty hope and firm unconquered will,*
> *Sustained and soothed each aching heart among that little band,*
> *Who bore with them across the sea the freedom of our land!*
>
> *Thank GOD, my country, that the seed, in doubt and meekness sown,*
> *To such a spreading lordly tree in later times hath grown:*
> *A pilgrim sire's beloved name a noble boast should be;*
> *A pilgrim's grave a holy trust, oh, Children of the Free!* [46]

One of the most revealing tributes to Weir's painting was that delivered in Washington's Unitarian Church by the Reverend S. G. Bulfinch, son of Charles Bulfinch, the Capitol's principal architect. The painting, he said, should inspire patriotic and holy Christian feelings for the sacrifices made by the Pilgrims. After summarizing the legend of the forefathers, the minister proceeded to explicate the other rotunda paintings on the basis of their religious import. The "kneeling Puritans" of Weir's *Embarkation,* Bulfinch explained, portray the Puritan foundations of New England and therefore complement Chapman's *Baptism,* "which exhibits the priestly vestments of Episcopalian worship." The relief sculpture of *Penn's Treaty with the Indians* depicts the Quakers, and Vanderlyn's still-unfinished *Landing of Columbus* represents "the symbols of the Roman Catholic belief." It is appropriate, he added, "that these varying denominations should thus meet . . . in the Legislative palace of our Union," and although no one denomination is superior to another, Bulfinch insisted, the orderly Pilgrims had a special mission. Their "love of freedom was not the unthinking, unrestrained transport of the wild enthusiast"; their "indignation against oppression" did not prompt them "to lay the axe to the root of social order, and to involve in common destruction all time-worn abuses and all time honored institutions." On the contrary, the Pilgrims "were friends of social order, friends of law, and prepared, as that should direct them, to discharge the duty of magistrates with mild dignity, or that of private citizens with orderly, though not servile obedience."[47]

These idealized "saints" of Bulfinch's sermon and Weir's *Embarkation* were pious, educated, dignified Anglo-Saxon Protestants united in their quest to pursue their religion in an orderly social and legal environment. Weir envisioned the departing Pilgrims as strong, fair "Teutonics," dressed in satins and endowed with the dignity and composure of a well-ordered Protestant congregation; his Pilgrims appeared to be elevated far above the unkempt, poor Catholics then filling Boston's slums. And with this subtle communication of a prevailing regional concern, Weir moved Pilgrim imagery away from the narrow focus of the landing at Plymouth to a broader investigation of how the *Mayflower* passengers shaped the homogeneous society that recent immigrants were threatening to destroy.

By the 1840s, several factors in addition to immigration were worrying more traditional New Englanders. Unitarians were threatening religious and ethnic coherence by siphoning off thousands of the most prominent Puritan heirs, while the rising tide of evangelical Baptists, Methodists, and missionary Catholics were winning the allegiance of settlers and Indians in the West. The spread of slavery into the newly opened territories—and its corollary, the power of Southerners in Congress—posed yet another threat to New England's ascendancy. In hopes of preserving the power and prestige of the Puritan heritage, an army of Congregationalist missionaries moved westward with the goal of shaping the residents' religious views and influencing their anti-Southern political orientation.

Ever fearful that a clandestine campaign to "convert Protestant children to the Catholic faith" lurked all around, Lyman Beecher moved his base of operation from Boston to Cincinnati in 1832. From his bully pulpit at the newly formed Lane Theological Seminary, as president and professor of theology, Beecher mounted an intense proselytizing campaign. In his *Plea for the West* (1835), he cautioned against abandoning the mission God had given the forefathers and warned that the "danger from [an] uneducated mind is augmenting daily by the rapid influx of foreign emigrants, the greater part unacquainted with our institutions, unaccustomed to self-government, inaccessible to education," predisposed "to credulity, and intrigue" and easily "wielded by sinister design."[48] With these goals foremost, Beecher directed his Protestant counterattack toward the receptive and vulnerable West.

While Beecher was pursuing his "errand into the wilderness" of Ohio, clergymen back home carried on his mission with renewed vigor. To those gathered in Boston's Church of the Disciples on Forefathers' Day 1842, James F. Clarke recited the following lines:

> *Let us, remembering the Pilgrims, say*
> *That we will seek for Light as they have sought,*
> *And if, where'er New-England's children go,*
> *Where'er her tides of emigration flow,*
> *To places low or high, they carry still*
> *Their Fathers' faith, their Fathers' manly will.*
> *That Pilgrim spirit shall forever be*
> *The land's best glory and security.*[49]

Eight years later, the Reverend Samuel W. Worcester told a Plymouth Forefathers' Day audience that "of all the people in the world," New Englanders "are under the highest obligations to support munificently, and communicate to the ends of the earth, the knowledge and the institutions of the 'everlasting gospel.'"[50] Newspapers, too, were touting that mission. "As the train of civilization rolls Westward or Southward the Pilgrim son is there," wrote a columnist for Plymouth's *Old Colony Memorial.* "From the very rock where they landed their children have embarked to carry with them toward the setting sun, their lineage; and we hope their principles and virtues."[51]

In this same vein, Lydia Sigourney's poem "The Pilgrims" describes history and current events coming together to define the missionary obligation of New Englanders:

> *And can ye deem it strange*
> *That from their planting such a branch should bloom*
> *As nations envy? Would a germ, embalmed*
> *With prayer's pure tear-drops, strike no deeper root*
> *Than that which mad ambition's hand doth strew*
> *Upon the winds to reap the winds again?. . . .*
>
> *Make faint the Christian purpose in your soul,*
> *Turn ye to Plymouth's beach,—and on that rock*
> *Kneel in their foot-prints, and renew the vow*
> *They breathed to God.*[52]

Sigourney's "Christian purpose" blends Beecher's missionary rhetoric with the dire predictions leveled by seventeenth- and eighteenth-century Puritan divines. Like her clerical predecessors, she exhorted other New Englanders to spread the religion and customs of the forefathers into territories inhabited by heathens.

Daniel Webster picked up on that theme in an address of 1850. "New England is a ship, staunch, strong, well-built, and particularly well-manned," he proclaimed, but until their own day "that little vessel" has "crept along the shore." But now it "has crossed the continent. It has not only transcended the Alleghany, but has capped the Rocky Mountains. It is now upon the shores of the Pacific"; and soon "descendants of New England will there celebrate the landing." A voice in the audience interrupted Webster's speech to announce that this very day New Englanders were celebrating Forefathers' Day on the West Coast. "God bless them!" Webster retorted. "Here's to the health and success of the California Society of Pilgrims assembled on the shores of the Pacific." The prolonged applause that roared through the hall stirred Webster to raise his audience even higher. He would not be surprised, he avowed, "if the three hundred millions of people of China—if they are intelligent enough to understand any thing—shall not one day hear and know something of the Rock of Plymouth too!"[53]

Although Protestant missionaries were in the process of spreading their beliefs to China, Webster's biased chauvinism was merely a reflection of how ambitious the New England missionaries had become. At midcentury, as Webster observed, Protestant schools and churches dotted the prairies; they stretched across the Rockies; and they challenged the entrenched Spanish in California. A columnist writing in Plymouth's *Old Colony Memorial* provided a rationale: New England's "power in the councils of the nation has unavoidably in a great measure passed away and forever. The great West has outran the East, and its boundless and luxuriant territory has been more than a match for the intelligence and enterprise of the older states."[54] And as the old New England elite saw its national clout rapidly eroding under the triple threat of immigration, expansion, and "Papism," it focused its missionary efforts in two directions—westward to fight alien influences and eastward to combat the foreign interlopers at home.

The anti-Catholic animosity that had been smoldering in Massachusetts for two decades intensified after the potato famine of 1848 sent thousands of Irish refugees to Boston. The response was an outcry of Anglo-American indignation. "When I call to mind the world-wide difference which exists between our native born American population and the Roman Catholic emigrants to these shores," wrote an anonymous pamphleteer in 1854, "I almost wonder that they can breathe our atmosphere and live. It is a difference, not only of nation and of creed, but of thought, feeling, action, principle, of all that makes free men what *they ought to be.*"[55] Fear and bigotry fostered a policy of resentment that in the mid-1850s was channeled into formation of the American (or "Know-Nothing") Party. Begun in New York a few years earlier, the movement grew rapidly through a network of clandestine cells that admitted members under the code name "Sam." These Know-Nothings—so named because of their secrecy—attracted Nativists along with a large number of disillusioned Whigs and Democrats, most of them angry about jobs lost to immigrants and impatient because local leadership did nothing to help them find work.[56]

Although the American Party boasted of members in both Northern and Southern states, its greatest strength was in the Northeast, especially in New England. In 1854, Know-Nothings swept the Massachusetts elections by winning all forty seats in the state Senate, all but
three seats in the state's 379-man lower House, and the entire delegation to the U.S. House of Representatives. In addition, the American
Party candidate, Henry J. Gardner, took over the Massachusetts gov-
ernorship, and Henry Wilson, a former Free-Soiler, was elected on
the American Party ticket to represent the state in the U.S. Senate.
Plymouth's moderate Whig paper, the *Old Colony Messenger*, warily
acknowledged that the Know-Nothings spoke "the sentiment of the
masses who have long watched in jealous silence or in but lowly
murmured complaint, the growing influence of foreigners in all our
public affairs, and the rapidly invading power they have exercised
over us as a nation." But, the columnist predicted, the party's "hour
of influence" will be brief and will "perish from the same inherent,
internal causes of weakness which have swept so many parties
away."[57] He was right. In less than two years, the Know-Nothing phenomenon crashed as suddenly as it had risen. The overt bigotry in
the party's platform soon disgusted moderates, while the newly organized Republicans were siphoning off large numbers of disenchanted
voters.

During their meteoric rise and short domination of Massachusetts
politics, the Know-Nothings succeeded in inflaming simmering anti-
Catholic prejudices, sometimes enlisting the Puritan legend to further its campaign of hatred and mistrust. Professions of loyalty to region and nation persuaded the Massachusetts branch of the
American Party to inscribe its secret rituals on a stone tablet purportedly cut from Plymouth Rock. Large segments of the gift books issued by the Know-Nothings lauded the Pilgrim fathers. *The Wide-
Awake Gift*, for example, intermingled its anti-Catholic and
antiforeign diatribes with stories about the Pilgrims, Hemans's
"Landing of the Fathers," and excerpts about the Plymouth colony
from writings and speeches of Edward Everett and Lyman Beecher.
Similarly, *Our Country*, a gift book published in Boston around the
same time, featured a story about a young Englishwoman who left
home to embrace her Puritan husband's religious beliefs and follow
him aboard the *Mayflower*.[58] Its opening essay by the Reverend T.
Whittemore explained that although the Pilgrims emigrated to estab-

lish "a pure worship," their sons failed to "understand this principle in its fullest application. . . . Thousands and tens of thousands of foreigners are landing upon our shores," Whittemore warned, and all will be "bringing principles hostile to the genius of our institutions." The greatest "lurking danger," in his estimation, was the Catholics' plotting to take over the public schools.[59]

For Know-Nothings like Whittemore, the "Arch Fiend" was New York's archbishop, John Hughes. The *American and Foreign Christian Union* angrily attacked the prelate because of his campaign to remove Protestant bibles from public school classrooms and assured its readers that Protestants would fight to keep their gospels in the schools "so long as a piece of Plymouth Rock remains big enough to make a gun flint out of."[60] As if fulfilling the dire prophesies of Morse and Beecher, Archbishop Hughes launched a counterattack aimed directly at the Puritan legacy. The first settlers of Virginia, he told a Boston Catholic audience, were "highminded, chivalrous—disposed to cultivate and realize their ideal of English gentlemen, even in the wilderness." Yet "very different" were "the Pilgrim Fathers of Plymouth," who "had no objection that others should enjoy liberty of conscience," so long as it was not in their colony. In fact, Hughes said, they decided that if others wished "liberty of conscience," they should find "a Plymouth rock in some other bay." On the school issue, the archbishop praised New England's debt "to their Pilgrim ancestors," but, he added, "it never occurred to the founders" that by "shutting out sectarianism, Christianity itself should be excluded from popular education."[61] Hughes's challenge proved that the Pilgrim myth had become so thoroughly integrated into the prevailing discourse that it could set the terms of debate over the Protestant-dominated school system. Whether lauding their example or taking issue with it, both sides acknowledged that the specter of the Plymouth settlers still had persuasive power.

If there was one thing upon which New England missionaries agreed, it was that the document known as the Mayflower Compact shaped American republicanism. According to their version of the event, the Pilgrim fathers devised the pact as a republican constitution and submitted it to all *Mayflower* passengers for approval by mutual consent prior to the landing on Plymouth Rock. As Morse's obsession with the subject indicates, New England's apostles were bent on convincing the entire nation that the Mayflower Compact contained the "germ of the republic." In actuality, the agreement was far less comprehensive than its mythologizers professed. Bradford recorded it as follows:

> In the name of God, Amen. We whose names are underwriten, the loyall subjects of our dread soveraigne Lord, King James, by the grace of God, of Great Britaine, Franc, and Ireland king, defender of the faith, etc. Having undertaken, for the glorie of God, and advancemente of the Christian faith, and honour of our king and countrie, a voyage to plant the first colonie in the Northerne parts of Virginia, doe by these presents solemnly and mutualy in the presence of God, and one of another, covenant and combine our selves togeather into a civill body politick, for our better ordering and preservation and furtherance of the ends aforesaid; and by vertue hearof to enacte, constitute, and frame shuch just and equall lawes, ordinances, acts, constitutions and offices, from time to time, as shall be thought most meete and convenient for the generall good of the Colonie.[62]

The various interpretations of Bradford's journal that found their way into print before publication of the original in 1856 minimized the part that spoke of "submission and obedience" to the dictates of King James and emphasized the portion that empowered the settlers to frame just and equal laws for the good of the colony. In its original form, the Mayflower Compact was a loyalty oath that certified Great Britain as the suzerain of the new Plymouth colony. Bradford himself admitted that "the discontented and mutinous speeches that some of the strangers amongst them had let fall from them in the ship" necessitated reaching an understanding because the "Patente" was "for Virginia, and not for New england, which belonged to an other Government, with which the Virginia Company had nothing to doe." The Leyden immigrants, he wrote, feared that because of that geographical discrepancy, the "strangers . . . would use their owne libertie" in a land where "none had power to command them."[63] As this indicates, the compact was actually a means of ensuring that the Separatist leaders would maintain control of their flock while forestalling the intervention of nonbelievers; in addition, the emigrants from Leyden were concerned that their agreement with their London financiers would be null and void if they settled outside of the Virginia Company's jurisdiction.[64] Evidence, therefore, suggests that the compact was not a prototypical constitution; rather, it legitimized the authority of the Separatist minority over a recalcitrant mélange of "strangers" in a territory outside the reach of the Virginia Company's purview.

Before the 1830s, few historians or orators mentioned the Mayflower Compact, even though it had been long known through *Mourt's Relation.* When ministers and others did talk of the document, they used the word "covenant" instead of "compact" to give the agreement quasi-religious overtones. That changed during the early years of the nineteenth century, when it became a tool of politicians, most notably John Quincy Adams, who (in concert with the legal scholar James Wilson) referred to the Mayflower Compact as a precedent for legitimizing the separation from Britain and creating an independent American nation. In using this argument, Adams and his colleague conveniently ignored those clauses that swore allegiance to James I.[65] Following this lead, New Englanders from 1820 onward claimed that the Mayflower Compact was the bedrock upon which both the U.S. Constitution and New England's legal, social, and religious structure rested. In his 1820 address, Webster said that "at the moment of their landing," the Pilgrims "possessed institutions of government, and institutions of religion" that became the guiding principles of the first Massachusetts settlement.[66] Thirty years later, the venerated senator expanded this interpretation of the Mayflower Compact to include the concept of obedience to a written constitution. That submission to law, he said, "is the very ligament, the very tie, which connects man to man in the social system."[67] For Webster and other Whigs, "obedience" to a tradition begun by the Mayflower Compact extended not only to formation of the Constitution but reached further to demand a steadfast allegiance to the nation that embodied the principles the Pilgrims had initiated.

In his Forefathers' Day address of 1843, Rufus Choate also emphasized the significance the Mayflower Compact: The pact had not only brought "representative republican government" to America but had inspired the "congenial institutions and sentiments" of the entire nation. Most important, the compact was the fountainhead for the "germs of progress" that spurred the economy and, in Choate's reading, it contained "the grand doctrine, that all men are born equal and born free, that they are born to the same inheritance exactly of chances and of hope," and that "every child" had the right "to strive for the happiest life, the largest future, the most conspicuous virtue, the fullest mind, the brightest wreath."[68] Whereas Choate, a moderate Whig, credited the Mayflower Compact with promising "that all men are born equal and born free" as prescribed by the Declaration of Independence, Bancroft—an avowed Jacksonian—stretched the egalitarian premise even further. The compact, he declared in the first volume of his *History*, composed "the birth of popular constitutional liberty through which humanity recovered its rights, and instituted government on the basis of 'equal laws' for the 'general good.'"[69]

Samuel F.B. Morse's aborted painting of the "Germ of the Republick" was intended to advance the mission of the Mayflower Compact by exerting a "great moral influence on the country and the world," the very prospect of which stirred Morse's "sectional pride" and "ambition."[70] But by the time that uplifting subject surfaced, it did so as a semicommercial venture. Tompkins H. Matteson, an artist working in upstate New York who specialized in history paintings for the popular-print market, decided to tackle the topic despite the unwritten ban proscribed by Morse. The artist had already appropriated parts of the Pilgrim legend for this purpose in previous works and in 1850 added *Signing of the Mayflower Compact* to his repertory (Fig. 7.3).[71]

Survival in the print market depended on conveying a familiar message within a reliable context, thus Matteson decided to base his composition on the semicircular configuration of Weir's *Embarkation of the Pilgrims*. Following Weir's format, he placed the bearded figure of William Brewster in the center of a crescent-shaped grouping and surrounded him with fashionably dressed English men and women. To emphasize the link between the compact and the U.S. Constitution, Matteson placed a quill pen in one of Brewster's hands and had him gesture with the other toward the Mayflower Compact resting on a table nearby. Whereas Weir's Capitol mural stressed the Protestant foundation of the United States, Matteson used the same setting to emphasize the legal framework purportedly transported to America aboard the *Mayflower*. That differing focus underscores a significant shift in national concerns. In 1844, when Weir installed his painting in the rotunda, heirs of the Pilgrims were worried about a

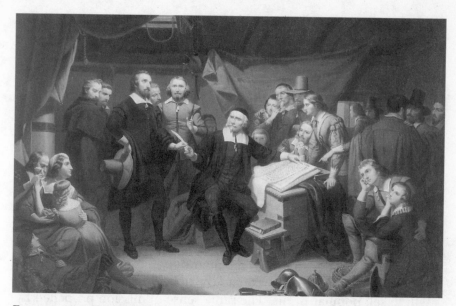

FIGURE 7.3 *Tompkins H. Matteson,* Signing of the Mayflower Compact, *oil on canvas, c. 1850. Private collection.*

possible peril augured by an unwanted foreign incursion, but by 1850, when Matteson was painting the *Mayflower Compact,* Southern secession posed a greater potential danger. For years, New Englanders had been touting the direct connection between the document written aboard the *Mayflower* and the U.S. Constitution. With this linkage now an integral part of most Northerners' cultural background, it became easy to read Matteson's painting as a commentary on preserving the unified nation that began with a "germ" that the Plymouth immigrants implanted.

A few years earlier, Matteson had painted *The First Sabbath of the Pilgrims,* which shows the Pilgrims praying in a wilderness setting. A critic praised the work for the artist's "execution and choice of subject." Matteson's aim, wrote the reviewer, was to embody "the religious and severe devotional zeal which so strongly characterize the 'Pilgrim Fathers,'" a "sentiment" that pervades the whole composition.[72] As this comment indicates, the "errand" placed literally in the wilderness was seen to be a religious counterpart to the *Mayflower*

Compact, thus the two paintings were often listed as companion pieces, complementary versions of the twin Pilgrim benefaction—one secular, the other sacred—upon which the foundations of the United States rested. By envisioning the Plymouth settlers as serious, dignified gentlefolk, Matteson supplied heirs of the Pilgrims with a visualization that reconfigured their origin myth to correspond with the region's missionary goals.

Matteson's *Mayflower Compact* and *First Sabbath* were part of an ever-expanding portfolio of mythmaking imagery that revamped the Pilgrim legend to conform with issues of the 1830s and 1840s. Widely reproduced as prints, they spread the essence of New England's missionary goals across the nation. That missionary impulse had driven Morse to perpetuate the legacy he believed originated with the Mayflower Compact; it led Weir to picture the Pilgrims as the antithesis of poor immigrants then flooding urban areas; and it compelled Matteson to capitalize on the persuasive power of the myth to sell popular prints. The same sense of mission propelled Lyman Beecher westward, armed with Puritan ideals to battle Catholicism; and it provided a convenient stratagem for masking bigoted Know-Nothing propaganda. The crusade to maintain Protestant hegemony over the increasing Catholic population soon merged with a reformist mission. That combination was to dispense a younger New England generation scrambling to reshape the Puritan legacy into a weapon targeted against perceived social and political evils.

Part Three

COMBATING
THE
MYTHS

8

Saints and Sinners

$\mathcal{W}$hen President James Polk declared war on Mexico in 1846, jubilant crowds cheered in front of Richmond's city hall to the accompaniment of bands playing martial music; and when native Virginian general Winfield Scott became a war hero, the Old Dominion was ecstatic. But in Massachusetts, there were few cheers. Many, in fact, considered the annexation of Texas to be a Southern ploy for spreading slavery into the new territories. The abolitionist William Lloyd Garrison called it a "war for slavery," while future senator Charles Sumner cursed the action as "the greatest crime a nation can commit."[1] These differing opinions concerning the Mexican War fueled fiery debates in Congress as legislators argued over whether the huge amount of Western land gained as the spoils of victory should be "slave" or "free."[2] While the fractured nation stood in jeopardy of splitting apart, the origin myth of Massachusetts accelerated its climb to national prominence and the Jamestown legend became the target of increasing scorn and derision. Not only were no dedicated missionaries spreading the Old Dominion's history across the country but in the race to prove which origin legend most influenced the founding of the United States, the story of one Indian girl's bravery could hardly compete with an entire army of self-righteous Pilgrims.

In her role as Virginia's guardian angel, Pocahontas had become a ready target for derision. And every time someone fired at her, a chivalrous Virginian would retaliate, if not by challenging the offender to an actual duel then certainly by goading the perpetrator into a verbal confrontation. The counterattacks were not just aimed at Yankees. In 1847, Waddy Thompson of South Carolina published

a book entitled *Recollections of Mexico,* in which he stated that Doña
Marina, the "Indian interpreter of Cortes," possessed such "great
qualities" that she threw "into the shade our own Pocahontas."[3] A
former resident of Virginia, James Chamberlayne Pickett, was
primed to pounce on Thompson, whom he believed had unjustly advocated a negotiated settlement of the very war that he had supported.[4] To chastise the South Carolinian, Pickett decided to explode
his remark about Virginia's heroine.

"In all history and romance it would be difficult to find a more perfect character than Pocahontas," Pickett wrote angrily, "and taking
her as she has come down to us, it appears to me to be impossible to
say wherein it could have been improved." It is, he contended, "one
of the most incontestable facts in history." Had not Captain Smith, "a
man incapable of falsehood or of exaggeration" described her that
way? And was not his description corroborated by "the sanction and
belief of contemporary thousands, hundreds of them being eye-
witnesses of what he narrated and described?" Included in Pickett's
publication was documentation to demonstrate the superiority of
Pocahontas's character over that of Doña Marina. Pickett insisted
that he was presenting this evidence because of "strong attachments"
to his native state and to the "memory of Pocahontas," "dear to every
son and daughter of the 'Old Dominion.'"[5] In inflating a minor comment to such improbable proportions, Pickett's publication demon-
strates how sensitive Virginians could be about their origin legend
and how willing they were to evoke the Pocahontas myth to symbolize a full array of Southern concerns.

Pickett's obsessive need to defend Virginia's origin legend was fueled by much more than a chance remark by Waddy Thompson. It
was a protective position that many Southerners were adopting as
the lifestyle fueled by slavery was increasingly denounced by outsiders, many of whom traced the evils of that system back to
Jamestown. One of the first of these critics was the French political
analyst Alexis de Tocqueville. In his highly influential *Democracy in
America* of the mid-1830s, de Tocqueville concluded that Jamestown
was founded by "gold seekers" dispatched by the British Crown to
enhance the wealth of the motherland. If that were not bad enough,
these first settlers were "without wealth or standards" and their "rest-
less, turbulent temper endangered the infant colony and made its
progress vacillating." He admitted that "quieter folk with better

morals" did eventually come to the Old Dominion, but these never "rose above the level of the English lower classes," and except for financial profit, "no noble thought or conception" ever made its way to Virginia.

But de Tocqueville had an entirely different opinion of the Plymouth settlers, whom he believed implanted the nucleus of a blossoming democracy: New Englanders "belonged to the well-to-do classes at home" and "from the start" initiated an "unusual phenomenon of a society in which there were no great lords, no common people," and even "no rich or poor." They immigrated as families, had "a fairly advanced education," and "brought with them wonderful elements of order and morality." Furthermore, he elaborated, the "immigrants, or as they so well named themselves, the Pilgrims," came voluntarily, giving up "a desirable social position and assured means of livelihood" to follow "a purely intellectual craving," for "in facing the inevitable sufferings of exile they hoped for the triumph of *an idea*."[6]

Whereas de Tocqueville saw colonial Massachusetts as the seedbed of progressive republicanism and plantation Virginia as the stagnant repository of antiquated autocracy, visitors from the Northeastern United States were challenging portions of the Jamestown legend because it introduced a plantation system fueled by slavery. One of them was the young Frederick Law Olmsted, whose fame rests on his later designs for New York's Central Park and other urban landscapes. In 1853, he spent several weeks observing Old Dominion society, concluding that the degenerate lifestyle of mid-nineteenth-century Virginia had roots in the Jamestown settlement. The Virginia Company's emissaries, Olmsted wrote, had "never done a real day's work in their lives before they left England," and they incorporated those lazy habits into the colony's economic structure, especially after the first boatload of Africans arrived. With the advent of slavery, he continued, "the gentlemen of Virginia" were "relieved from the necessity of personal labor." Their "indolence and imbecility" precipitated the failure of the Jamestown colony, a situation exacerbated by the "large immigration of speculators" who planted tobacco and ultimately divided the colony into "two grand divisions—gentlemen and laborers." In noting that the first Africans came to Virginia shortly before the Pilgrims landed in New England, Olmsted emphasized the differences between the "first cheerful labor" of the "voluntary immigrants" to Plymouth and those who brought their wide-spread inertia to Virginia.[7]

Olmsted's attitude was typical. Many Northerners of the 1840s and 1850s were blaming all the nation's ills on the first boatload of African slaves and then contrasting Southern dependence on slavery with the morally superior and mutually cooperative colony at Plymouth. Boston's Unitarian minister Nathaniel Frothingham proclaimed in 1857 that the "101 souls" who landed in Plymouth were "as sturdy, brave and firm as its own famous rock," a dramatic contrast to the "sadder freight" that came to "the unconscious waters of the Chesapeake Bay." That "dark slave-ship sailed up to Jamestown, with its dusky freight of 20 human souls, stolen from Africa. They came to a colony which had "broken down at home." Its "lazy and shiftless" inhabitants "hailed the coming of their dark-skinned brethren with no brother's welcome; no sympathy for the woes of those broken-hearted men; but work, work, work, in a service harder than that of the children of Israel of old under the taskmasters of Egypt."[8] The views of a French political analyst, a traveling Northerner, and an abolitionist minister all relayed the same message: The ills of nineteenth-century Virginia began in Jamestown, a colony with a shameful history when compared with the exemplary Pilgrim colony at Plymouth.

In response to these accusations, Virginians began to review their colonial history in a frantic attempt to present it in a more favorable light. As early as 1839, writers for Richmond's *Southern Literary Messenger* were begging readers, even scolding them, to study their own beginnings. After presenting a survey of colonial history and a summary of seventeenth and eighteenth-century texts, state historian Charles Campbell lamented that most "old histories" were "out of print, obsolete, seldom seen" and "seldom read." In place of factual information, the press teemed "with myriads of ephemeral fictions, continually emerging on the face of the ocean, bubbles born only to expire." How long, he asked, "shall the old chronicles of Virginia be doomed to slumber in oblivion?"[9]

So many Virginians replied to Campbell's appeal that the *Messenger* was soon inundated with letters and commentaries about the state's colonial history. A series of articles running sequentially during 1843 included reports of tombstone inscriptions, historical sculpture, and an assortment of documents. In 1844, the *Messenger* petitioned the state legislature to allot funds for preserving archival materials and dispatching an emissary to England in search of additional documents. Campbell once more admonished Virginians in January 1845 to keep pace with other states that had already begun collecting historical documents, an activity he thought would "infuse into the breasts of Virginia youth a warmer patriotism and State-pride and a more generous longing to emulate" their predecessors. Meanwhile, the *Messenger* started reprinting colonial documents (including John Smith's *True Relation*) and publishing detailed accounts of Virginia's colonial history.[10]

If they were not discovering "knightly tombs and heirlooms" left by the early planters or searching for Powhatan's settlement of Werowocomoco, Virginians were retelling the story of Smith and Pocahontas.[11] Beginning in February 1847, the *Messenger* ran serialized installments of Campbell's history of Virginia, which was advertised as "a most acceptable offering" to the "residents of Virginia; especially to that large and respectable class who justly pride themselves upon their honorable connection with . . . the deeds of their immediate ancestry." Somewhat defensively, the writer recommended the history to the rest of the nation so that it could learn "what Virginia has been and what she has done," an enlightenment that should "soften" if not "silence" the "aspersions cast upon her."[12] Heavily dependent upon the writings of John Smith, William Stith, and Robert Beverley for documentation, Campbell's history repeated the familiar tales, refreshed with tidbits collected from his archival searches.[13]

When the serialized history was published as a book in 1860, the editors of the *Southern Literary Messenger* praised it lavishly, lauding the author for his treatment of the state's favorite heroine: "Throughout the narrative Pocahontas appears in all her grace and sweetness and purity, a being so beautiful and so pure" that she might have been taken from the pages of Herodotus, or Livy. The writer, however, criticized Campbell for failing to mention that Pocahontas's descendants rank among the "most distinguished" in the state in terms of "graces of eloquence," "personal beauty," and "intrinsic moral worth."[14] In whatever direction Virginia's defense of Jamestown wandered, the compass always seemed to point toward the ancestors who supposedly sired the state's most prominent citizens.

A large part of the campaign to dignify Virginia's colonial history required that all derogatory insinuations about a possible romance between Pocahontas and Smith be firmly squelched and that her marriage to Rolfe be emphasized positively, although the wedding itself, like the baptism, had no verifiable historical documentation. Mary Webster attempted to rectify that deficiency in her epic poem *Pocahontas: A Legend* by providing a lengthy description of her ancestors' wedding.[15] Webster deliberately merged Pocahontas's marriage and baptism, as did the historian Henry Howe, who wrote in his *Historical Collections of Virginia* (1847) that "the nuptial ceremonies at Jamestown" were "solemnized with great pomp, according to the rites of the English church."[16]

A popular print entitled *The Marriage of Pocahontas* also reinforced the linkage of marriage and baptism.[17] Taken from a painting by Henry Brueckner done in 1855, the engraving (Fig. 8.1) depicts the wedding in a crowded church. As was common practice, Brueckner based his composition on a proven format, in this case Chapman's *Baptism of Pocahontas,* which also suggests a merger of the two Christian ceremonies. Brueckner imitated Chapman's placement of figures in the middle ground slightly left of center, with an audience of colonists and Indians grouped around them. Pocahontas wears a sleeveless white tunic, green skirt, red shawl, and sandals; her head is covered by a wreath of flowers topped by a curled feather and short trailing veil. Rolfe, dressed as a Cavalier, clasps his bride's hand and points upward to announce that God had sanctioned the marriage. The minister, Alexander Whitaker, emphasizes that blessing with his gesture of benediction.[18]

In a pamphlet written to accompany the engraved version of Brueckner's *Marriage of Pocahontas,* the popular historian Benson J. Lossing described the wedding as a romantic tale of love and piety. The bride, Lossing explained, "was the daughter of a pagan king who had never heard of Jesus of Nazareth, yet her heart was overflowing with the cardinal virtues of a Christian life." And, he rhapsodized, on that "day in charming April" of 1613, Rolfe and Pocahontas "stood at the marriage altar in the new and pretty chapel at Jamestown, where, not long before the bride had received Christian baptism, and was named the Lady Rebecca."[19] Brueckner's print,

FIGURE 8.1   *John McRae, after Henry Brueckner's* The Marriage of Pocahontas, *lithograph, 1855. Division of Prints and Photographs, Library of Congress, Washington, D.C.*

supported by Lossing's description, thus endowed Virginia's plantation "aristocracy" with visual verification of an event that had no documentation to support it.

Former Virginia governor and local historian Wyndham Robertson, another descendant of Rolfe and Pocahontas, provided additional "proof" that the marriage had taken place. At an 1860 meeting of the Virginia Historical Society, he cited a number of sources to pinpoint the date of the wedding as April 5, 1613, and counteract all claims that Smith and Pocahontas had a love affair.[20] In his *History of the Colony and Ancient Dominion of Virginia,* Charles Campbell not only reiterated that assertion but denounced all hints of a romance between Smith and Pocahontas, insisting that Pocahontas and Rolfe were deeply in love, while she held only a "filial affection" for Smith.[21]

For the Virginia elite, the union of Pocahontas and Rolfe composed the essential link between the Jamestown settlers and Cavalier aristocrats.[22] It marked a merger of cultures anchored in a Christian rite and thereby implied a peaceful move onto Indian lands to build tobacco plantations. This "baptized" blending of two races was in part a subterfuge to divert attention from slavery, the state's most pressing racial problem, barraged at the time by abolitionist condemnation. As another popular print attests, the marriage of Rolfe and Pocahontas continued to carry an important message about Virginia's origins. Designed by the German artist Anton Hohenstein, *The Wedding of Pocahontas* of 1867 (Fig. 8.2) resembled Brueckner's depiction of the same theme and similarly stressed the unique blend of wilderness, chivalry, and Christianity that symbolized Virginia's mythical past, although Hohenstein's wedding scene is situated outdoors.[23]

By 1860, ancestor veneration in the Old Dominion had become almost frantically defensive. Much of this protective attitude was a direct response to a penetrating assault on Virginia history then taking shape in Massachusetts. In 1858, the urbane and well-respected Unitarian minister John Gorham Palfrey published his *History of New England,* in which he included a long footnote accusing John Smith of not being the "sole author of his books" and casting doubts on the captain's veracity.[24] Palfrey's evidence came from Charles Deane, the amateur historian responsible for expediting publication of Bradford's manuscript. When Deane was viewing that document in the Fulham Library, he had also discovered Edward Maria Wingfield's *A Discourse of Virginia,* buried in another London collection. Written by the man who had brought charges against Smith, the *Discourse* characterized the captain as a "rogue without a lycence" and an unscrupulous conspirator. Deane thus concluded—using as documentation Wingfield's memoir and Smith's *True Relation,* which makes no mention of his rescue by Pocahontas—that Smith had fabricated the entire story, a determination he revealed in a speech before the American Antiquarian Society in 1860.[25]

These charges from Massachusetts initiated a volley of historical insults and chauvinistic boasts that passed back and forth across the Mason-Dixon line. Virginians immediately responded to Deane's publication by shoring up their defenses with verbal and visual illustrations of the marriage of Pocahontas and Rolfe and pointing out the gulf that separated their idyllic past from Plymouth's dour history. New documentation repeated justifications of the origin legend, while artwork and poetry underscored those texts with oversimplified interpretations designed to substantiate a marriage that had

FIGURE 8.2   *Anton Hohenstein,* The Wedding of Pocahontas, *lithograph, 1867. Division of Prints and Photographs, Library of Congress, Washington, D.C.*

spawned the state's plantation elite. It was as if Virginians were try-ing to convince themselves—and no doubt, the world—that their way of life was anchored in historical realities that were as serious, family-oriented, and morally uplifting as the Pilgrim foundations of New England. For Northerners, Virginians' reliance on an apocryphal episode from colonial history to justify an economic system depen-dent on slavery rendered their historical arguments ineffective at best and ludicrous at worst.

Although emphasis on a plantation genealogy guaranteed serious ad-miration at home, it inspired those viewing the Old Dominion's gene-sis parable from afar to treat the story lightly. Two foreigners—Irish-born playwright John Brougham and the British novelist William Makepeace Thackeray—smiled at the Jamestown legend. Brougham, in fact, roared with laughter. His musical farce *Po-ca-hon-tas, or The Gentle Savage* opened at Wallack's Theatre on Christmas Eve 1855.

New Yorkers greeted the production with enthusiasm; they snickered at the puns, gags, and comedic pantomimes and hummed along as the cast–led by Brougham as Powhatan and the popular comedian Charles Walcot as John Smith–sang parodies set to popular melodies. Known for his innovative wit and captivating manner, Brougham was a theatrical entrepreneur with a finger on his era's pulse and an eye on audience appeal; therefore, when he decided to satirize the Pocahontas story, he was well aware that the legend was ripe for lampooning.[26] Ever since Barker's *The Indian Princess* had opened almost fifty years earlier, the legend had remained a favorite on the long list of romantic Indian tales that delighted theatergoers during the early nineteenth century. Although Barker had taken liberties with the characterizations, he had treated the tale as if it were an earnest recounting of history. In subsequent decades, Custis, Owen, and Barnes had used Virginia's origin legend as a vehicle through which to express opinions on the Indian question, women's rights, and other current social issues. But Brougham overturned all of his predecessors by borrowing bits and pieces from each to transform their notions of social commentary into a satirical and boisterous farce.

The play begins with a long poem entitled "The Song of Pocahontas," a takeoff on Longfellow's *Hiawatha*, which had been published that same year:

> *Ask you–How about the verses?*
> *Whence this song of Pocahontas,*
> *With its flavor of Tobacco,*
> *And the Stinewerd–the Mundungus,*
> *With its pipe of Old Virginny,*
> *With the echo of the Breakdown,*
> *With its smack of Bourbon whiskey,*
> *With the twangle of the Banjo . . .*

Enter "JOHNSMITH, the valiant soldier, Sailor, Buccaneer, Explorer, Hero, Trader, Colonizer, Gent, Adventurer, Commander, Lawyer, Orator, and Author, Statesman, Pioneer and Bagman." He is traveling with "a crew of Fillibusters, each with matchlocks and revolvers, to take peaceable possession of some transatlantic region." They "incontinently blundered on the shores of Tuscarora near to Werowance, the palace of King Powhatan," a "hospitable monarch" who attempts to fatten them with "rice and pumpkins, Buckwheat-cake and sweet potatoes, Squashes, Hominy, and Doughnuts."

> *Now, the natives knowing nothing*
> *Of the benefits intended*
> *By this foreign congregation*
> *Who had come so far to show them*
> *All how much they'd been mistaken;*
> *In what darkness they were dwelling*
> *And how much obliged they were to*
> *These disinterested people*
> *Who had journeyed to enlighten*
> *Their unfortunate condition,*
> *Through these potent triunited*
> *Anglo-Saxon civilizers,*
> *Rum, Gunpowder, and Religion.*

Because the natives "didn't see the joke precisely in the way it was expected," they decide "the shortest way to settle those gratuitous advisers, would be quietly to knock them on the head." Therefore, JOHNSMITH ends up in the tent of Powhatan, who continues hitting him until Pocahontas "laid her lovely tresses on the pale cheek of the victim" and whispers "you have yet a squeak, old fellow."[27]

After this introduction, the playwright maneuvered the familiar characters through a series of musical outbursts and foolish antics. Smith, a bumbling but lovable fool, finds Pocahontas at Jamestown "some time before it was built"; she is attending a "Finishing Institution" with a group of silly girlfriends. Smith and Pocahontas immediately fall in love, but Powhatan disapproves because he wants his daughter to marry "Mynheer Rolff," a crude and gruff Dutchman. These and other characters deliver ballads, duets, and operatic quartets that parody current events. Although many targets of Brougham's puns and spoofs are now unrecognizable, others are easy to identify. For example, when Smith first meets Pocahontas, she asks if he is "a fugitive come here to seek a railway, underground," and Smith answers that he is:

> *Without a shade of color to excuse*
> *Canadian Agents here to chalk my shoes,*

> *Therefore my passage–money won't be figured,*
> *For on that head Philanthropy is niggard!* [28]

In other scenes, Brougham lampooned women's rights activists, New York city politics, George Bancroft's histories, and congressional lobbying. But most of all, he was mocking the didactic intensity of his predecessors, who feigned historical verisimilitude in plays about Pocahontas that were permeated with personal opinions about current events. By shaking up past and present–and mocking the legend that Virginians took so seriously–Brougham transformed the Jamestown story into a burlesque.

Like Brougham, William Makepeace Thackeray poked fun at Virginia's origin legend, but his more subtle and more gentle appraisal came from the firsthand experience of spending several weeks in the Old Dominion during 1855. His lectures throughout the state were well attended and eagerly received. Unlike New Englanders touring the region during that time, Thackeray found little to criticize. He told the author John Esten Cooke that "he had always looked upon the Virginians as resembling more closely his own people in England than the Americans of other states." He considered Richmond to be "the very prettiest friendliest and pleasantest little town" he had seen "in these here parts" and found Virginians to possess "immense tenderness, romantic personal enthusiasm and a general kindliness and serviceableness and good nature."[29]

When it came to slavery, the English author harbored no sympathy for the abolitionists. In fact, he felt most Virginians were handling their inherited responsibilities in a fairly evenhanded manner, thus his attitude toward blacks differed little from that of his plantation hosts. "They don't seem to me to be the same as white men," he observed, "any more than asses are the same animals as horses; I don't mean this disrespectfully, but simply that there is such a difference of colour, habits, conformation of brains, that we must acknowledge it." Although Thackeray admitted that Harriet Beecher Stowe's "individual instances of cruelty" in *Uncle Tom's Cabin* were "only too true," he believed such occurrences to be infrequent. Generally, he observed that Virginians rarely separated slave families and their slaves seemed happy and well tended. "And for freeing them," he snarled, "Bon Dieu it is an awful measure to contemplate."[30]

Although Thackeray refused to find fault with the slavery system, he was able to mock other foibles of Virginia society, especially its attachment to the Pocahontas legend. He subsequently incorporated his observations into his rambling novel *The Virginians,* issued in serial form in Britain and the United States (1857–1859) and published in two volumes shortly thereafter. Set in eighteenth-century Virginia and England, the novel centers around George and Harry, twin brothers reared on a Virginia plantation. George inherits an English estate, but Harry remains at home; eventually, they end up on opposite sides of the American Revolution. However, before this occurs, George writes a play about Pocahontas and arranges to have it produced in London. "I made acquaintance with brave Captain Smith as a boy in my grandfather's library at home," George recalls, "where I remember how I would sit at the good old man's knees, with my favourite volume on my own spelling out the exploits of our Virginia hero." His play features an "Indian king; a loving princess; a traitor in the English fort; a brave Indian warrior" (who found "himself entertaining an unhappy passion for Pocahontas"), and a "medicine-man," described as a "priest of the Indians." These and other descriptions prepare the reader for Thackeray's gently satirical retelling of Virginia's origin myth in the "'ground-bait' verses" that begin the play:

> *Who will shield the fearless heart?*
> *Who avert the murderous blade?*
> *From the throng, with sudden start,*
> *See, there springs an Indian maid.*
> *Quick she stands before the knight*
> *"Loose the chain, unbind the ring,*
> *I am daughter of the king,*
> *And I claim the Indian right!"*
>
> *Dauntlessly aside she flings*
> *Lifted axe and thirsty knife;*
> *Fondly to his heart she clings,*
> *And her bosom guards his life!*

Through his lighthearted treatment of the Pocahontas legend, Thackeray both demonstrated his keen awareness of the inflated esteem Virginians bestowed upon the story and smiled at the comic quality of current theatrical renditions of the legend. In the novel, George's drama is a dismal failure in London, which leads its author to conclude that he should never have attempted to maintain such an "actual fidelity to history."[31]

In mocking the repertoire of Pocahontas plays, Thackeray followed a less acerbic path than Brougham. Unlike his Irish contemporary, the British novelist's primary purpose was not to belittle the origin legend itself but to tease Virginians about their irrational reverence for the story and use the incident to exemplify cultural misunderstandings. To George, who grew up in Virginia, the story represents historical heroism and bravery, but to the London audience with a different cultural conditioning, it fails to elicit much more than guffaws and catcalls. During his stay in Virginia, Thackeray probably reacted with similar amusement to the planters' regard for their origin myth, thus he was able to use his visitor's perspective to mock the intensity with which Virginians transformed Smith and Pocahontas into regional saints.[32]

While authors and playwrights were laughing at Virginia's beatification of Pocahontas and Smith, Bay Staters were being reminded of flaws in their own origin legend. Foremost among them was the distinction between the terms "Puritan" and "Pilgrim," a matter that had once been merely a question of semantics. Before the mid-1840s, most writers and orators used the words interchangeably, thereby suggesting that they saw little difference between them. But during a time when Congregationalists and Unitarians were split into two competing religions and immigrants were radically changing New England's demographics, the exclusive and highly regulated Puritan society suddenly seemed riddled with defects. At the same time, New England missionaries were "selling" the Pilgrims of Plymouth as national ancestors and everyone in the region wanted to claim them as their own.[33]

Conservatives were insisting that the Pilgrims were the original orthodox Congregationalists and therefore there was no difference between the inhabitants of the Plymouth and Massachusetts Bay colonies. On Forefathers' Day 1852, Charles Porter, a lineal descendant of John Carver, referred to the Plymouth settlers as "Puritan Pil-grims" and implored all heirs of colonial Massachusetts to uphold the "faith and church polity of the Puritans" and "never abandon" it.[34] Other traditionalists were answering condemnations of Puri-tanism by addressing the criticism itself. On that same Forefathers' Day, Reverend William Adams told the New England Association of New York that some had rendered the Puritans "ridiculous by the nakedness of their religion, the sourness of their faces, and the aus-terity of their manners" and had even accused them of "licentious-ness and infidelity." Those faultfinders carping about the "naked-ness" of the religion, Adams entreated, should regard it as "the nakedness of the athlete, entering the arena, stripping himself of every robe which would embarrass his limbs, before wrestling for very life."[35]

At the same time that conservatives were defending the Puritans, Unitarians and other more liberal New Englanders were lambasting them. By midcentury, accusations were even coming from respected Bay Colony descendants like Peter Oliver, a Brahmin lawyer who traced his lineage back to an early settler of the same name. In *The Puritan Commonwealth* (1856), published shortly after his death, Oliver condemned Puritan intolerance and presented a scathing ac-count of John Winthrop and his followers: "Deluded by a fanaticism, which taught that private reasoning was but little removed from in-spiration, breaking away from the easy yoke of the church, to surren-der their whole being to the iron slavery of Puritanism, Christianity, as they endeavored to mould it, was only blackness and darkness and tempest."[36]

Other authors were also attempting to remove the veil from the Calvinist past, chief among them Nathaniel Hawthorne. His love-hate fascination with his Puritan forebears created a lasting image. From "Old News" and "May-pole of Merrymount" of the mid-1830s to *The Scarlet Letter* and *House of the Seven Gables* of the 1850s, Hawthorne painted a picture of a society controlled by dour and re-lentless oppressors who thwarted human development and imposed an iron-fisted jurisdiction on an intimidated population.[37] Less famil-iar, but equally searing, were the writings of the maverick Unitarian minister Sylvester Judd, whose best-known work, *Margaret* (1845), sounded a clarion call for removing unwanted strictures from New England society and religion.[38] The novel is set in the late eighteenth century and concerns the many obstacles facing an innocent girl who refuses to bend to the restraints of the Puritan world around her.[39] Judd, in fact, advocated an ideal religion that mixed formal ritual with the transcendental communion between man and nature, a clear antithesis of orthodox Congregationalism. Despite its seeming offenses to the region's controlling ideology, *Margaret* was immensely popular in Massachusetts, thus providing another indication that the old restraints were fast disappearing.

Liberal New England politicians were also seeking to champion the Pilgrims and downgrade the importance of the Puritans, a theme that pervaded the Plymouth celebration of August 1, 1853. Because the event launched the fund-raising drive for the Pilgrim monument and Plymouth Rock canopy, it was imperative for speakers to elicit a positive image of the Pilgrims and distinguish them from the negative connotations associated with Puritanism. Senator Charles Sumner, for example, insisted that he admired the Pilgrims because they were called "Separatists." That designation meant they "openly disclaimed the National Establishment" to become "a separate sect" and were considered "outcasts, despised in their own day by the proud and great."[40] As part of his plea for New Englanders to take an active role in opposing slavery, Sumner said that the Pilgrims had exhibited courage and dedication through repeated self-sacrifices, whereas the inhabitants of Massachusetts Bay had created a highly structured society predicated on strict regulations and the rewards of worldly success. When the broadminded Separatists merged with the Massachusetts Puritans, Sumner implied, they unwittingly sacrificed their open society of righteous individuals to enter a closed enclave ruled by uncompromising bigots. The assault on Puritanism narrowed the message of the origin myth by negating all unpleasant associations and emphasizing only those qualities then considered desirable.

Ever since Weir's *Embarkation of the Pilgrims* assumed its place in the Capitol rotunda, writers and orators had been describing the forefathers as stalwart martyrs braving turbulent waters to find religious freedom. Midcentury artists soon picked up on that theme, but where Weir had stressed the piety of the immigrants, American

FIGURE 8.3   *Emanuel Leutze,* English Puritans Escaping to America, *engraving, 1847. Author's collection.*

artists working a decade later tended to emphasize the physical perils of the migration. One of the best examples is Emanuel Leutze's *English Puritans Escaping to America,* painted in 1847 (Fig. 8.3). The artist himself had immigrated to America when only a boy. From his birthplace near Munich, he moved with his family to Philadelphia in 1816, and then, in 1840, recrossed the Atlantic to establish a studio in Düsseldorf. There he created some of his most dramatic and arresting historical epics, the most famous being *Washington Crossing the Delaware,* first exhibited in the United States in 1851.

In that oft-reproduced composition, Leutze pictured a diverse group of individuals in a crowded boat; his *English Puritans,* painted four years earlier, also shows heroic people forging through stormy waters to reach a seemingly unattainable destination.[41] Leutze's fleeing Puritans ride precariously high waves, as a dapper man in the bow pulls an oar while his companion in the stern operates the tiller; between them, three shabbily dressed men (one with a bandage wrapped around his head) assist with the rowing, while in the center, a woman leans forward to shelter her baby. A battle in the background between knights in armor and a man standing in a rowboat indicates that the party is escaping from danger to safety, a theme Leutze emphasized by sending his boatload of emigrants from the dark rocky cliffs of the English shore to a larger ship waiting on a lighted horizon.

The concept of escape had additional meaning, as hoards of individuals were seeking refuge in America to flee from the revolutions, famine, and poverty of Europe. In fact, the metaphorical flight from darkness to light and from war to peace had tremendous implications for Leutze, who was painting the escaping Puritans while insurrections were exploding all around him in Germany. The turbulent sea was a favorite theme of romantic literature, and in paintings of the period, the storm-tossed ship was a metaphor for political or social turmoil.[42] Leutze tilted the boat, enlarged the waves, and darkened the sky to imply that impending danger threatened both his own world and that of the fleeing Puritans.[43]

Leutze's dramatic departure was no doubt inspired by more contemporary voyages, because no such imperiled conditions drove away the seventeenth-century Puritans, most of whom left England voluntarily. His *English Puritans* imparted several different messages. For those who had recently left Europe, the Puritans' perilous voyage might remind them of their own threatened escape from turmoil to live in a land of freedom; for New Englanders, the scene hinted at the more recent plight of runaway slaves escaping from Southern plantations and seeking the safe haven of New England.[44] The American print-buying public would perhaps have been touched by these additional meanings and certainly would have admired the theatricality of Leutze's rendition of the embarkation.

Other artistic interpretations of the Pilgrims' departure came from the British Isles at midcentury. Several different incidents were focusing attention on the Puritans, not least of which were the pressures for social change that swept England, the Continent, and the Northeastern United States during the 1840s and 1850s. The reformist zeal had also affected the Church of England, which was already troubled by internal theoretical differences and threats posed by an invigorated British interest in Roman Catholicism on one extreme and Protestant evangelism on the other. All of these currents combined to

FIGURE 8.4   *Charles Lucy,* Departure of the Pilgrim Fathers, *oil on canvas, 1847. Courtesy of the Pilgrim Society, Plymouth, Mass.*

produce revisionary histories of the English Civil War that cast a more favorable light on Cromwell's once-despised Puritans and engendered curiosity about the seventeenth-century dissenters who had dared defy both the Crown and the Anglican establishment.[45]

In 1847, the same year that Leutze painted *English Puritans,* the Englishman Charles Lucy painted *Departure of the Pilgrim Fathers* (Fig. 8.4) and its companion, *The Landing of the Pilgrim Fathers.*[46] The *Departure* (now hanging in Plymouth's Pilgrim Hall) depicts a group of emigrants preparing to leave Delfthaven aboard the *Speedwell,* pictured on their right. It is a more intimate, sorrowful, and placid departure than the one pictured by Leutze. Like Weir, Lucy centered his composition on the praying figure of John Robinson. But the British artist deviated from his American contemporary by forming the figures into a pyramid with Robinson at its apex, his arms outstretched over the mournful crowd. This configuration opens out to the viewer, whereas Weir's closed semicircle faces inward on the

FIGURE 8.5   *Charles Lucy,* The First Landing of the Pilgrims, 1620, *engraving, c. 1850. Division of Prints and Photographs, Library of Congress, Washington, D.C.*

praying minister. By changing this emphasis, Lucy transformed the calm dignity of Weir's *Embarkation* into an operatic melodrama.

Lucy's *First Landing of the Pilgrims, 1620* (Fig. 8.5) takes the immigrants to the other side of the Atlantic and pictures families praying in gratitude for their safe deliverance. Both Lucy's *Landing* and *Departure* were reproduced as prints in the 1850s, the latter engraved by Thomas Agnew and Sons and sold to help the Pilgrim Church in Southwark build a new sanctuary. The Southwark congregation traced its history back to the same Separatist movement that drove John Robinson and his followers from England in the early seventeenth century; its minister, Henry Jacob, also broke with mainstream Puritanism and moved to the Netherlands, but instead of immigrating to America, he led his flock back to England in 1616. The group that survived in the London suburb of Southwark remained bound to the Plymouth settlers for whom they subsequently named their church.[47] In the middle of the nineteenth century, their pastor, John Waddington, persuaded Massachusetts industrialist Abbott Lawrence (then an American minister to Britain) to help raise money for the new church and to agree that he would match any sum raised in England with money collected from Pilgrim descendants in the United States.[48]

To aid the Southwark building campaign–as well as fund-raising efforts for the Pilgrim monument and Plymouth Rock canopy–Congregational clergymen in England delivered a series of public lectures to enhance the sale of Lucy's *Departure of the Pilgrims.* Pointing to the print, the Reverend Hugh Stowell Brown informed his congregation in Liverpool that "these fathers and founders of New England" speak in the language of "busy commerce," of "manly independence," of "wide philanthropy," and "the growth and power of the western confederation of states, which bids fair to make some of the powers of Europe look small, shriveled and contemptible." Similarly, the Reverend William Bevan told a congregation at Wolverhampton in 1854 that Lucy's "memorable picture" commemorates "one of the sublimest and most influential facts that has ever occurred upon the stage of human empire" because the Pilgrims "bequeathed to New England the honor and the good" of the motherland. Around the same time, R. W. Dale advised churchgoers in Birmingham that Lucy's rendition captured the "energy, the freedom, the wealth" of the United States that is "the harvest of that seed-sowing which was done by the hands of the Pilgrim Fathers."[49]

Each of these clergymen stressed the English roots of the Plymouth settlement and the way that influence had shaped the commercial development of the United States. Perhaps it was no coincidence that two of the talks took place in the cities of Liverpool and Birmingham, where merchants were then importing cotton from the southern United States to feed England's thriving textile industries. In addition to supporting the fund-raising campaign, the clergy may well have been trying to prick the consciences of Britain's Congregationalists and engender a feeling of kinship with the antislavery sentiments then preoccupying their coreligionists in Massachusetts. No doubt, that affinity inspired Bevan to end his talk with the following admonition: "There, in New England, has risen the protest against the Southern Slavery which British Virginian Colonists entailed upon" the United States. New England, he stressed, harbors the "bulwarks of protestantism and evangelism" and guards those movements "against the menace of encroachment."[50]

The renewed interest in the Pilgrims sparked other British artists to address the subject. One was Charles W. Cope, who painted the *De-*

FIGURE 8.6   *Charles Cope,* Departure of the Pilgrim Fathers from Delft Haven, 1620, *engraving, c. 1854. Division of Prints and Photographs, Library of Congress, Washington, D.C.*

parture of the Pilgrim Fathers from Delft Haven, 1620 (Fig. 8.6) for the Peers' Corridor of Britain's House of Lords as part of a series of episodes from the English Civil War.[51] It pictures the departing Puritans in a crowded rowboat, while on shore a group of their compatriots pray for the small boat pushing out to sea. Cope eschewed the turbulent seas of Leutze's *English Puritans* and the emotionalism of Lucy's *Departure.* His Puritans seem to be in no immediate danger from pursuing authorities as they prepare to leave the quiet beach in Delfthaven. Equilibrium and worship doubtless seemed more appropriate than flight and pursuit for a composition that would be permanently lodged in the Houses of Parliament.[52] A letter to the editors of the *London Morning Advertiser* from Pilgrim Church pastor John Waddington explained that despite some minor inaccuracies in details, Cope's painting was sure to "command general admiration" because of the "simple, yet grand, sentiment" it imparted. With an eye to his own fund-raising campaign, the reverend pointed out that the

"Pilgrim Fathers were not of the '*Puritan*' party," rather they were '*Independents*.'"[53] To emphasize the difference between the emigrants of 1620 and the Puritans who went to Massachusetts a decade later, Cope printed the word "Mayflower" on the stern of the boat and the phrase "Freedom of Worship" on an unfurled banner held by one of the passengers.

Another Englishman boosting the international significance of New England's origin myth was William H. Bartlett, whose book *The Pilgrim Fathers* came out in 1853. Filled with intricate steel engravings, the combined travelogue and history was a unique production. The artist-author was already recognized for similar publications about Europe and the Middle East and was known in the United States for his illustrations in *American Scenery*, a popular and elaborate volume of landscape vignettes and descriptions.[54] Because Bartlett's views of cities, towns, and the countryside were so widely known, he was readily welcomed when he visited Massachusetts in the early 1850s to sketch locations and investigate material relating to Plymouth's first settlers (Fig. 8.7). In addition to his extensive tour of New England in preparation for his forthcoming publication, Bartlett also traveled to English and Dutch sites associated with the Pilgrims.[55]

In the preface to *The Pilgrim Fathers*, Bartlett played to the revisionists by expressing hopes that the English public would "cast aside the lingering prejudices generated by political and religious animosity" and place the Pilgrims "among the best and worthiest" individuals his "country has ever produced."[56] The author-artist apparently gained access to Bradford's diary before New Englanders discovered it in London, and from it—along with information obtained through English and American assistance—he pieced together the biographies of Brewster, Bradford, Standish, and other leaders of the *Mayflower* contingent. Bartlett's travels allowed him to also include vivid descriptions of their family seats and locations where the Separatists migrated. It was the first popular interpretation of the original Bradford material, and his thorough research opened up new vistas for exploring the Pilgrims' migration. Throughout the book, Bartlett made clear distinctions between the Separatists and Puritans, the former portrayed as courageous and persecuted exiles, the latter as equally pious but more privileged and dictatorial dissenters.[57]

Among the most far-reaching contributions of Bartlett's *Pilgrim Fathers* were two small illustrations described by the author as "a very

FIGURE 8.7 *William Bartlett, "Leyden Street," engraving, 1853, illustration from* The Pilgrim Fathers.

tolerable presentment of the general costume of the Pilgrims, varying slightly according to the station and means of the wearer."[58] Beneath that description, he pictured a man and woman in tall, wide-brimmed hats wearing dark, simple clothing topped by pointed white collars (Fig. 8.8).[59] In those same years Cope, Lucy, and other British artists were imagining the English Puritans in somber outfits, the men's clothes resembling the simple garb worn by Quakers or other renegade Protestant sects and the women's patterned after uniforms of early nineteenth-century matrons, nurses, or governesses.[60] The two drawings in Bartlett's *The Pilgrim Fathers* transmitted those ideas of costume across the ocean, and within the next decade, American artists would begin changing their depictions of the Pilgrims.

Among those influenced by these new interpretations was Peter Frederick Rothermel, who, like Leutze, had grown up in Philadelphia and studied in Düsseldorf.[61] His *Landing of the Pilgrims at Plymouth Rock* of 1854 (Fig. 8.9), in fact, appears to be bringing Leutze's imperiled boat to its final destination; he features a similarly diverse party of individuals in an equally crowded boat enduring the same

FIGURE 8.8 *William Bartlett, "Pilgrim Costumes," engraving, 1853, illustration from* The Pilgrim Fathers.

FIGURE 8.9 *Peter Frederick Rothermel,* Landing of the Pilgrims at Plymouth Rock, *oil on canvas, 1854. Kirby Collection of Historical Paintings, Lafayette College, Easton, Pa.*

blustery weather. But instead of departing from Europe, these passengers are disembarking on the rocky coast of New England. Men on board maneuver the vessel to a huge rock, where a member of the crew attempts to anchor the craft with a towrope. A mother clutches her child; and in the center of the composition, a pale woman, with her fair hair and a veil streaming in the wind, is being helped ashore by a man wearing a jacket and sash.[62] Behind them on the right, other refugees huddle on the rocky shore. Although these men and women have completed their journey, they still seem anxious and their surroundings heighten the feeling of unease. The sky is black, the sea rough, their faces shrouded in sorrow.

Rothermel's *Landing* differed entirely from earlier paintings and prints, which pictured the landing as a secure and stable affair. In the opening decades of the century, Sargent had presented dauntless fighters determined to conquer the land. In the years immediately preceding the Civil War, Rothermel painted elegant gentlemen and well-bred ladies seemingly unprepared to combat the dangers awaiting them beyond the icy shore. These are not the diligent Pilgrims hard at work establishing their community on the edge of a relatively calm sea as seen in the many still-popular "landing" prints. Instead, this rendition blends those earlier forefathers with mid-nineteenth-century reinterpretations of the Pilgrim myth to present the Plymouth settlers as victims of nature and not its conquerors.[63]

As one of the last serious treatments of the debarkation at Plymouth, Rothermel's painting brought the familiar story to its dramatic conclusion. Keenly attuned to the lucrative print market, the artist knew that the Plymouth ancestors had transcended regional boundaries and were now considered to be national ancestors. Therefore, he followed Leutze in designing his *Landing* to encapsulate differing American viewpoints. The frightened immigrants might have been escaping an oppressive European regime; they might be surrogates for fugitive slaves escaping to freedom; or their anxieties might reflect the tense atmosphere in Washington during the 1850s when Southerners were threatening secession and Northerners were sharpening their attacks on slavery. Whatever his reason for creating this emotional scene, Rothermel fully understood that his reproduced image would sell to Americans who considered the Pilgrims as primary forefathers of the nation.

In past years, American artists had varied the clothing to correspond with their intended messages. Sargent had dressed his landing
party in a blend of Elizabethan costume and medieval armor; Weir
had attired his embarking Pilgrims in current fashions with Elizabethan trimmings; Leutze had clothed his fleeing passengers in a variety of outfits, some quite elaborate and seemingly expensive. But
Rothermel's Pilgrims marked a subtle change. Although he followed
Weir by giving the Pilgrims elegant costumes to distinguish them
from poor, recent immigrants, he toned down his palette and simplified his styles in keeping with his English contemporaries, who were
depicting Puritans in the somber clothing of Quakers or the more severe styles of the Victorian period. This revision also corresponded
with conditions in the United States during the 1850s, when Virginians were proudly touting their descent from the more flamboyant
Cavaliers and New Englanders were stressing the pious and sanctimonious Pilgrims. Hence, to draw a sharp visual distinction between
the two societies, Rothermel trimmed down the large feathered hats,
discarded the ruff collars, and gave his women simplified versions of
current fashions.[64]

By the outbreak of the Civil War, the Pilgrims were fully prepared
for sainthood, not only in New England but in old England and
much of the United States as well. Only in Virginia and the other
Southern states did they still symbolize the arrogance of the abolitionists and the misplaced pride of overblown self-righteousness. For
New Englanders, the romantic blend of Cavalier, Indian princess,
and swashbuckling captain so exalted by Virginians made a foolish
comparison when set beside an origin myth that rested on episodes
of piety and sacrifice. When war broke out in 1861, both Virginia
and Massachusetts had amassed a fully developed army of historical
saints and demons to reinforce their barriers of mutual distrust. The
principal issue at stake was slavery, an institution that had no relevance to the original founders of either Jamestown or Plymouth. But
that historical reality did little to deter the combatants from invoking
their ancestors to either justify sectional convictions or denounce
perceived evils.

9

Prelude to Battle

Congressional debates over the status of slavery following the Mexican War reached a crescendo over the omnibus compromise bill of 1850, which included a provision that required federal troops to return all runaway slaves. When the Fugitive Slave Law passed, it so infuriated New England abolitionists that they intensified their drive to spirit blacks across the border into Canada. Many blamed Daniel Webster for the hated bill because he had been a vocal advocate of compromise as the only way to preserve the Union. When he expressed those views in an impassioned speech in the Senate, many of his former Massachusetts supporters were outraged. Charles Sumner called him "Judas Iscariot or Benedict Arnold"; Horace Mann referred to him as "Lucifer descended from Heaven"; and Ralph Waldo Emerson wrote in his diary that the "word liberty in the mouth of a Webster sounds like the word love in the mouth of a courtesan."[1]

Shortly after making that speech, Webster left his senatorial post to become secretary of state in the cabinet of Millard Fillmore; a few months later, in December 1850, the beleaguered statesman presented the Forefathers' Day address at the New England Society of New York. Hurt and infuriated by criticism from so many of his former admirers, Webster was banking on another oration centered upon the Pilgrims to recover a portion of the respect he had once enjoyed. And for that reason, he returned to the landing at Plymouth, a subject that had electrified a similar audience thirty years earlier. The two landmark speeches stand as bookends in Webster's illustrious career. His first was that of an aspiring politician invoking the legend of

the forefathers to prove his allegiance to the principles valued by
New Englanders; the second was that of a resolute warhorse using
the same text to urge support of the Union.[2]

As he began his address in 1850, Webster recalled the Pilgrims'
landing on the "bleak coast of Plymouth" and thanked "Almighty
God" for elevating their descendants to the "height of prosperity and
happiness." Then he proceeded to transform the Pilgrims into champions of moderation and reconciliation. First, he mentioned the forefathers' obligation to uphold the tenets of the Mayflower Compact,
which he insisted obligated their offspring to support the U.S. Constitution. Next, he linked the *Mayflower* with the small, intrepid blossom
of the same name. Then he pretended to summon the spirit of the
Pilgrim elder, William Brewster. If Brewster stood before them, Webster continued, he would ask, "with a voice of exultation, and yet
softened with melancholy," if the present state of the nation was "the
great reward" for which he and his brethren had "endured lives of
toil and hardship?" Webster answered by assuring his audience that
Brewster would have commanded the "worthy descendants of
Carver and Allerton and Bradford" to spread their "children over
the continent; accomplish the whole" of their "great destiny" and be
willing to shed their "heart's blood" to transmit their "love of civil
and religious liberty" to their posterity. A few moments later, he used
the Forefathers' Day platform to urge preservation of the Union, declaring, "There is no longer imminent danger of dissolution in these
United States . . . We shall live as united Americans; and those who
have supposed that they could sever us, that they could rend one
American heart from another, and that speculation and hypothesis,
that secession and metaphysics, could tear us asunder, will find
themselves dreadfully mistaken."[3] Perhaps it is fortunate that the
Massachusetts statesman never lived to witness that bloody severing
of ties.

Webster's call to preserve the Union had widespread support in
1850, when only extremists were urging actual separation.[4] But there
were many New Englanders who were beginning to think the power
of Washington too strong and were outshouting advocates of rapprochement and loudly decrying the Fugitive Slave Law. Those fa-
voring abolition summoned up Pilgrim ghosts and made them into
staunch opponents of slavery. "The spirit of our fathers," intoned the
Reverend Robert B. Hall on Forefathers' Day 1854, "calls upon us to

. . . eradicate from the goodly heritage which they have bestowed on us this festering evil. . . . They call to us from their graves to-day by no word or act of ours to consent to its further prevalence, or unfaithfully to profane the sanctities of the ark of freedom which they deposited here."[5] That ark was sailing straight into the stormy seas of angry discontent.

That turbulence manifested itself in the U.S. Senate on May 22, 1856, when Preston Brooks, a young congressman from South Carolina, angrily pounded his cane on Massachusetts senator Sumner's head until the New Englander lay unconscious and bleeding on the Senate floor. The few onlookers who happened to be in the chamber that day watched dumbfounded, but none attempted to intervene. Brooks later claimed that he was merely seeking to redeem his state's honor, which Sumner had besmirched a few days earlier by accusing another South Carolinian, Senator Andrew Butler, of pandering to his "mistress," the "harlot Slavery."[6] Many Southerners quietly applauded Brooks's attack, for they considered Sumner to be a dangerous firebrand. Outraged Bostonians, however, were demanding an apology.

Although Brooks's tirade was unforgivable, Sumner had incited the ire of Southerners with his fiery opposition to slavery. A Harvard classmate of abolitionist Wendell Phillips and a close friend of Henry Wadsworth Longfellow, Sumner was a composite of scholarly accomplishment and political ambition. Ever since his election to the Senate in 1851, he had been an outspoken antislavery advocate. Having little sympathy for the moderate Whigs of his state, Sumner had joined the Free-Soil Party and became the most vociferous members of its three-man Senate team, in this capacity issuing numerous angry diatribes against slavery.

In August 1853, three years before the encounter with Brooks, Sumner had spoken in Plymouth at the anniversary of the *Mayflower's* embarkation. The speech, entitled "A Finger Point from Plymouth Rock," interjected abolitionist zeal into the commemorative event that kicked off the fund-raising drive for the Plymouth Rock canopy and Pilgrim memorial. The senator began by contrasting the small Plymouth colony with the vast American nation. "From these obscure beginnings of poverty and weakness" to "that marble Capitol, where thirty-one powerful republics" are "bound in indissoluble union," Sumner told the audience, the United States must asso-

ciate the "little band of Pilgrims" with the "lesson" they taught.
"Through them the spirit of modern Freedom made itself potently
felt, in its great warfare with Authority, in Church, in Literature, and
in the State; in other words, for religious, intellectual, and political
emancipation." The Pilgrims "knew by bitter experience all the
sharpness of persecution. Against them the men in power raged like
the heathen. Against them the whole fury of the law was directed.
Some were imprisoned; all were impoverished, while their name became a by-word of reproach." Sumner's intent—to collapse into a single continuum the experiences of the *Mayflower* passengers and those
of the nineteenth-century antislavery activists—designated the abolitionists as the Pilgrims' true spiritual descendants. "Self-sacrifice is
never in vain," he urged. The Pilgrims "foresaw, with the clearness of
prophecy, that out of their trials should come a transcendent future."
He then went on to define the "finger point" of his title:

> Standing on Plymouth Rock, at their great anniversary, we cannot fail
> to be elevated by their example. We see clearly what it has done for the
> world and what it has done for their fame. No pusillanimous soul here
> to-day will declare their self-sacrifice, their deviation from received
> opinions, their unquenchable thirst for liberty, an error or illusion.
> . . . Better be the despised Pilgrim, a fugitive for freedom, than a halting
> politician, forgetful of principle, "with a Senate at his heels."[7]

Sumner's verbal pounding had gained him little popularity in the
U.S. Senate, even among those who shared his views. Hence, his reference to the necessity of "self-sacrifice" was indeed prophetic, although he could not have foreseen the extent to which his own
would soon be required.

Although Southerners labeled him a firebrand, Sumner did not favor direct action; instead, he believed that the best route for achieving emancipation was through relentless pressure to change federal
laws. That placed him somewhere between the moderate clergymen,
who favored solving the dilemma by deporting blacks to Africa, and
the "immediatists" of William Lloyd Garrison's "Boston Clique,"
who endorsed open confrontations with slaveholders.[8] Although the
Massachusetts abolitionists expressed a wide range of opinions, few
advocated total emancipation. In fact, most New Englanders feared
the possibility that hoards of Southern blacks might invade their region and therefore cast a wary eye on Garrison's abolitionist fervor.

Oliver Wendell Holmes, for example, spoke of blacks as a "weaker people" whom whites must "remember and care for." But he insisted, "as in the case of the Indians, or any other inferior natural tribe of men, our sympathies will go with our own color first. . . . The white man must be the master in effect, whatever he is in name; and the only way to make him do right by the Indian, the African, the Chinese, is to make him better by example and loving counsel."[9] Holmes's confident assertion of white superiority epitomized the prevailing New England view, for Puritan consciences notwithstanding, most who boasted of a *Mayflower* heritage were revolted by thoughts of an influx of former slaves disrupting, and perhaps destroying, their region.

Debates over slavery dominated all Northern and Southern discourse between the end of the war with Mexico in 1848 and the outbreak of the Civil War in 1861, as politicians urgently sought a solution to the dilemma posed by division of the continent into slave and free territories. The stopgap Kansas-Nebraska Act of 1854, which replaced the Missouri Compromise, ruled that the two territories must rely upon "popular sovereignty" to decide whether they would enter the nation as slave or free states. Within weeks, Kansas became a battleground for the opposing forces, a situation that drew contenders from both Massachusetts and Virginia. A vocal contingent of Massachusetts clergymen and abolitionists enthusiastically formed the New England Emigrant Aid Company to provide material assistance to those who could be persuaded to relocate in Kansas and join the battle against slavery.[10]

The fighting in Kansas provided a focus for Forefathers' Day oratory in 1855, when two well-known opponents of slavery—New York senator William Seward and Wendell Phillips—delivered the principal addresses at the Pilgrim Society in Plymouth. Like Sumner two years earlier, Seward portrayed the Puritans as nonconformists willing to risk their lives for civil and religious liberty.[11] His speech was long, dense, and repetitious, and when he finally sat down, the tall, gentlemanly Phillips mounted the podium. Wasting little time with preliminaries, he immediately linked the Pilgrims of 1620 with the abolitionists of 1855. "What the Puritans gave the world," he said, "was not thought but ACTION . . . It was ACTION that made them what they were." If "the Carvers and Bradfords of 1620" returned that day, Phillips told the audience, they would not behave as they had in the seventeenth century. "The Pilgrims of 1620 would be, in 1855, not in Plymouth, but in Kansas . . . Do you suppose that if Elder Brewster could come up from his grave to-day, he would be contented with the Congregational Church and the five points of Calvin? No, Sir," Phillips insisted. He would be talking about "the Underground Railroad, and the thousand Sharpe's Rifles, addressed 'Kansas,' and labeled 'Books.'"

Phillips was referring to the extensive shipments of camouflaged weapons sent by Massachusetts abolitionists to antislavery fighters in Kansas. He commanded descendants of the Pilgrims to take direct action, for "to be as good as our fathers, we must be better. Imitation is not discipleship." Fidelity of this sort, he insisted, not only entailed suffering terrible hardships but New Englanders must be ready to choose "death rather than compromise!" Phillips went on to point out that Puritan "institutions were made for man" and for that reason the forefathers wrote "the first constitution ever made . . . Hold on to that idea," he insisted, "with true New England persistence—the sacredness of individual man—and everything else will evolve from it." As he approached the end of his talk, Phillips boasted that he was proud to be considered "a fanatic," because he believed no abolitionist had yet "risen high enough." Encouraged by cheers from his listeners, he proclaimed: "Afar off, I see Carver and Bradford, and I mean to get up to them." On this high note, Phillips sat down to the roar of audience approval.[12]

On that same Forefathers' Day, Holmes was two hundred miles away from Plymouth advising exactly the opposite to the New England Society of New York. In asking for caution when criticizing "this detested social arrangement of our neighbors" in the South, Holmes warned New Englanders to temper their desires to save "every inch of American soil" for "freedom" and reduce their "involuntary participation in slavery to the minimum consistent with our existence as a united people." In short, he asked the audience to apply "the right language" when addressing its "slave holding sister States." The "manly logic in the extreme left of abolition," he charged, could lead to trouble. "Tear the Constitution to tatters, empty the language of its opprobrious epithets on the men of the southern section of what has been foolishly called our common country, and take the consequences."[13] The contrast between Phillips's bellicose challenge and Holmes's cautionary admonition—both uttered on the same Forefathers' Day in 1855–demonstrated that the small and otherwise homogeneous group of antislavery Bostonians were poles apart in their proposed solutions.

The Virginia opposition, though it loudly condemned the abolitionists, never overcame its disadvantage of having to justify slavery. The best it could do was to plead that regardless of rhetoric to the contrary, its plantation owners had higher regard for blacks than those New Englanders doing all the carping.[14] A writer for the Richmond *Whig* dismissed the abolitionists as an organized band spreading "religious and political fanaticism" and conducting a vindictive "crusade against the Southern States."[15] Although they had little trouble labeling current-day abolitionists as fanatics, Virginians had greater problems when trying to use their origin myth to defend their "peculiar institution." Their main drawback was that the Jamestown legend lacked the moral purpose implicit in the story of the Pilgrims. Therefore, to justify an economic system fueled by human bondage, Virginians often bypassed Jamestown and turned to Pocahontas's plantation heirs as a fitting contrast to New England's prim and pious ancestors.

By midcentury, most Virginians were exonerating slavery and conjuring up images of a fabled Camelot, where a benighted plantation elite treated docile and compliant "darkies" with paternalistic kindness. Residents of the Old Dominion, however, had not always presented this ludicrous image of their "peculiar institution." In fact, at one time Virginians had been divided on the issue, and several leaders of the Revolutionary generation had even made provisions for emancipating their slaves. In 1796, St. George Tucker–the William and Mary law professor whose son, Nathaniel Beverley Tucker, became a staunch defender of slavery–petitioned the Virginia House of Delegates with a plan for gradual emancipation.[16] The legislature, however, rejected Tucker's proposal, and the idea of manumission simmered on the back burner until Nat Turner's 1832 slave insurrection in Southampton County shocked Virginians into calling a special session of the House of Delegates. Although many prominent citizens–including Thomas Jefferson Randolph, the grandson of Thomas Jefferson–argued in favor of freeing the slaves, the measure failed to win enough votes and was once again tabled.[17]

Nat Turner's raid and the House of Delegates' decision to reject emancipation propelled Virginians in two directions. On the one hand, the legislature gradually fortified the "peculiar institution" by passing strong laws forbidding literacy among slaves. On the other hand, several prominent Virginians began transferring their attention from freeing the slaves to colonizing them. Many joined the American Colonization Society and even established a local offshoot known as the Virginia Colonization Society, which procured a $100,000 commitment from the House of Delegates to help repatriate hundreds of blacks in the new nation of Liberia. One of the chief supporters of this project was future U.S. president John Tyler, elected to preside over the Virginia society in 1838. When accepting that office, Tyler admitted his initial reservations about resettling the slaves, but his "doubts vanished after learning of the successful landing of the first emigrants." He rejoiced that "thousands of civilized beings have made it their home, and the wilderness may be considered as reclaimed." With enthusiasm, Tyler announced, Monrovia "will be to Africa what Jamestown and Plymouth have been to America."[18] By reversing the Atlantic crossing and transforming the steamy jungle into a "reclaimed" wilderness, Tyler and his cohorts were cleansing their own consciences through a reenactment of America's fabled origins.

Despite these measures aimed at skirting the real issue, protection of slavery as an institution slowly became the dominant theme of Old Dominion politics as adamant proslavery Virginians began reshaping the state's ideological arguments to refute the challenges of Northern abolitionists.[19] One *Southern Literary Messenger* columnist reminded New Englanders that many of their forebears made fortunes in the slave trade: "Pecuniary profit is a great salvo to tender consciences," especially when the guilty are "pious descendants of the Pilgrims," adding that if "they are really so horrified as they pretend," they should donate "a portion of that wealth to purchase the freedom of those whose fathers were sold into bondage by their fathers to obtain it."[20]

A few years later, an anonymous writer in the *Messenger* charged Boston's outspoken abolitionist, Theodore Parker, of planning "to fight from State to State and from line to line, until he reaches Massachusetts," where "he will fight from town to town until he reaches Plymouth Rock and from that embark either for Greenland or

Africa." The writer went on to anticipate that the vessel for that voyage should be named "the *Happy Riddance*" which will "rank with the Mayflower in historical value and importance, and that Plymouth Rock will be doubly blessed in our annals for what it gave and what it sent away!"[21] But the heirs of Pocahontas were so greatly challenged by verbal attack from the expanding ranks of *Mayflower* descendants that their acid retorts were only pebbles tossed against a barrage of abolitionist ammunition.

With all varieties of New Englanders slandering the Old Dominion for separating slave families and torturing blacks, Virginians answered such charges by canonizing an Indian. Although Powhatan's daughter might seem an unlikely representation for a state with few visible Native Americans in its population, the link between slavery and the origin myth did have its own peculiar rationale. If a nonwhite woman sat at the apex of the state's social pyramid and her blood supposedly flowed in most aristocratic veins, then weren't Virginians more tolerant than their Northern detractors?

Meanwhile, Harriet Beecher Stowe was stirring her region's conscience. In May 1852, Henry Wadsworth Longfellow noted in his diary that he was reading her "pathetic and droll book on Slavery" to his family. "Every evening we read ourselves into despair in that tragic book," he wrote. "It is too melancholy, and makes one's blood boil too hotly."[22] Around the nation, Americans of all persuasions were passionate about *Uncle Tom's Cabin*—some exhilarated, others enraged. Her passionate attack on slavery emanated from the Puritan conscience instilled by her father, Lyman Beecher, and nurtured during her childhood in Litchfield, Connecticut. While she and her many siblings—especially her sister Catharine and brother Henry—eschewed the bigoted intensity of their opinionated father, they channeled much of his zealousness into reforming the society around them.

When Lyman Beecher moved to Cincinnati in 1832, Harriet went with him and after several years married Calvin Stowe, one of her father's ministerial colleagues at the Lane Seminary. In addition to raising their large family, she spent much of her time writing fiction and publishing a variety of articles in national magazines. One of her earliest books, a collection of short stories about her childhood, was entitled *The Mayflower; or, Sketches of Scenes and Characters, Among the Descendants of the Pilgrims* (1844). Although the book had nothing to do with the first Plymouth settlers, its title reveals that Stowe and her readers were so deeply rooted in the Pilgrim myth that she could use it to identify a publication about life in early nineteenth-century New England.[23] Stowe's Calvinist upbringing perhaps surfaced most vividly in *Uncle Tom's Cabin*, the book that Longfellow and other descendants of the Pilgrims took as a call to arms. Its strong antislavery message, in fact, galvanized many heirs of New England Puritanism to spearhead the abolitionists' crusade.

Antislavery rhetoric reverberated throughout Massachusetts during the 1850s, a decade in which political fervor was matched by intellectual ferment. The Bay State could boast not only of such literary notables as Nathaniel Hawthorne, Herman Melville, and Henry David Thoreau but also of Ralph Waldo Emerson, then dominating the lecture circuit and composing essays in his Concord home, and James Russell Lowell, then editing the newly founded *Atlantic Monthly,* in which portions of Oliver Wendell Holmes's *Autocrat of the Breakfast Table* first appeared.[24] All of these works signaled a shift in emphasis for heirs of the Puritan tradition. Their parents had spent their energies on religious controversies, but the next generation of New England intellectuals transfigured those passions into spearheading moral crusades. Abolition was not the only cause to engage them; with equal vigor, they embraced temperance, worker's benefits, women's rights, prison reform, and a variety of other social causes.

John Greenleaf Whittier, a precursor of New England's reformist movement, wrote a series of antislavery poems in the 1830s. Outraged when Boston authorities tried to censure an abolitionist meeting in 1835, the Quaker pacifist inveighed: "Shall Honor bleed?— shall Truth succumb? / Shall pen, and press, and soul be dumb?" He answered that query by proclaiming:

> *No; by each spot of haunted ground,*
> *Where Freedom weeps her children's fall;*
> *By Plymouth's rock, and Bunker's mound;*
> *By Griswold's stained and shattered wall;*
> *By Warren's ghost, by Langdon's shade;*
> *By all the memories of our dead!*

> *By their enlarging souls, which burst*
> *The bands and fetters round them set;*
> *By the free Pilgrim spirit nursed*
> *Within our inmost bosoms, yet,*
> *By all above, around, below,*
> *Be ours the indignant answer,—No!*

A year later, he again invoked the ancestors in his response to John C. Calhoun's bill forbidding the Senate from accepting petitions against slavery:

> *Is the old Pilgrim spirit quenched within us,*
> *Stoops the strong manhood of our souls so low,*
> *That Mammon's lure or Party's wile can win us*
> *To silence now?*

Although Whittier was a devout Quaker and not doctrinally linked with the Puritan tradition, he was first and foremost a loyal son of Massachusetts who perceived "the Pilgrim spirit" to be part of his legacy. Well aware that a contrast of the region's ancestors with "Mammon's lure or Party's wile" would arouse the consciousness of New Englanders, the poet applied such references liberally in hopes of prodding his readers into voicing their opposition to slavery.[25]

Whittier's impassioned plea was antithetical to the urbane intellectualism of James Russell Lowell, but he, too, made use of the Pilgrim legend to prick the conscience of his region. His "Conversation with Miles Standish" of 1848 employs a barbed wit to chastise New Englanders for falling short of the high-minded courage displayed by their ancestors. One of Lowell's targets was the hallowed Forefathers' Day rite, which comes to the forefront in an imagined conversation between the poet and the ghost of Miles Standish. The spectral Standish begins by explaining the purpose of his surprise visit:

> *I come from Plymouth, deadly bored*
> *With toasts, and songs, and speeches,*
> *As long and flat as my old sword*
> *As threadbare as my breeches;*
> They *understand us Pilgrims! they,*
> *Smooth men with rosy faces,*

> *Strength's knots and gnarls all pared away,*
> *And varnish in their places! . . .*

The old soldier then takes specific aim at those New England politicians who failed to stand up against the war with Mexico.

> *These loud ancestral boasts of yours,*
> *How can they else than vex us?*
> *Where were your dinner orators*
> *When slavery grasped at Texas?*
> *Dumb on his knees was every one*
> *That now is bold as Caesar,*
> *Mere pegs to hang an office on*
> *Such stalwart men as these are.*

Remarking that his visitor seemed "much stirred when talking about the "sacred compromises," the poet-narrator prompts Standish to explode: "Now God confound the dastard word!" He then follows this invective with a specific charge against the region's failure to confront the evils of slavery head on:

> *My gall thereat arises*
> *Northward it hath this sense alone,*
> *That you, your conscience blinding,*
> *Shall bow your fool's nose to the stone,*
> *When slavery feels like grinding.*
>
> *"T'is shame to see such painted sticks*
> *In Vane's and Winthrop's places,*

But Lowell's ghostly conscience stops short of urging armed conflict:

> *To see your spirit of Seventy-six*
> *Drag humbly in the traces,*
> *With slavery's lash upon her back*
> *And herds of office holders*
> *To shout applause, as, with a crack,*
> *It peels her patient shoulders.*

> *"We forefathers to such a rout!—*
> *No, by my faith in God's word!"*
> *Half rose the ghost, and half drew out*
> *The ghost of his old broadsword,*
> *Then thrust it slowly back again*
> *And said with reverent gesture,*
> *"No, Freedom, no! blood should not stain*
> *The hem of thy white vesture. . .* [26]

Although Lowell's poem ridiculed Forefathers' Day oratory, those annual speeches had frequently contained abolitionist sentiments, one of the first being Webster's opposition to the slave trade in 1820. William Sullivan and George Blagden both addressed the issue during the 1830s. and Mark Hopkins ended his 1846 Forefathers' Day talk by insisting that the nation expunge all that "is incompatible" with "the spirit and forms" of New England's institutions. "It is this which has swept slavery from the soil of the Puritans, and which we ought to labor with every energy to infuse, till it shall sweep every vestige of that dreadful curse from this land."[27]

Other New Englanders were resorting to the Virginia myth as a vehicle for condemning the plantation system. One of them, Emily Clemens Pearson, published *Cousin Franck's Household* a year after Stowe's *Uncle Tom's Cabin* startled the nation by exposing the horrors of slavery. Through her narrator and pseudonymous author "Pocahontas," Pearson mocked the Old Dominion's origin myth and the plantation elite that boasted of its descent from the Indian "princess."[28] Pearson's "Pocahontas," who comes from New England to visit her cousin Franck Cameron in Port Royal, Virginia, proffers her antislavery criticism through a series of letters.[29] Franck is married to Regina Hartley, mistress of a wealthy plantation, who has two daughters by a previous marriage. Regina is depicted as a shallow and arrogant Southerner, her daughters as stereotypical opposites. One taunts and belittles blacks; the other not only ministers to the slaves but arranges to hustle them across the Mason-Dixon line. These one-dimensional white women—complemented by the cruel overseer, the foolish senator, the conniving doctor, and the ignorant and drunk poor whites—are far less believable than the parade of downtrodden blacks. Like Stowe, Pearson sermonized about the savagery of slavery, including the breakup of black families, the humiliation of forced

servitude, and the callousness of planters. By adopting the name "Pocahontas" for the compassionate New England observer, the author
transformed the Old Dominion's favorite ancestor into a critic of the
Cavalier lifestyle that her marriage to Rolfe allegedly propagated.

Although "Pocahontas" says that in general Virginians are "the
most agreeable and delightful people in the world," she is appalled
by the "pestiferous atmosphere" of the slave system. In the course of
her stay with the Camerons, "Pocahontas" discovers that the family
nursemaid, Selma, is Regina's half-sister, the result of a union between Regina's father and a slave woman who also produced two
sons and another daughter. Selma's siblings had long ago been sold
to another plantation, and a series of implausible coincidences brings
Selma together with her sister and surviving brother, both of whom
have been passing for white. As the story progresses, Selma herself
becomes whiter and whiter. Soon visitors begin mistaking her for the
plantation mistress, much to the consternation of Regina, who rages:
"'Such impertinence in her to resemble me so strongly' and 'to ape
my manners, and carry herself like a lady! As if it was not mortifica-
tion enough for her to be of my family, she must be a living proclamation of it, having written in face, figure, mind and manner.'"[30]

In introducing the theme of miscegenation, Pearson insistently
spotlighted the byproduct of the slave system that Southerners most
wanted to forget. To make this point, she identified her narrator as
the very person whose mixed-race marriage was at the heart of the
planter class's aristocratic pretensions. The name "Pocahontas" reinforced the notion that miscegenation had sired Virginia's vaunted
origin myth. Pearson underscored this offense to the Old Dominion's
pride by suggesting that the system of slavery was collapsing because
race mixing was so widespread that even the color of one's skin was
no longer a plausible rationale for bondage.

The miscegenation theme coupled with the narrator's name added
a provocative dimension to what would otherwise simply have been
another sanctimonious antislavery tract. In the end, Regina breaks
down because her kinship to blacks entirely destroys her. "Pocahontas" then convinces Cousin Franck to liberate his slaves and bring
them with his family to New England where they could all be freed
from the "loathsome burden" of slavery. In the end, as the Cameron
family joyously moves north, the fictitious "Pocahontas" becomes a
savior, redeeming the sinning Virginians through their rebirth as

New Englanders, a clever reversal of the Smith-Pocahontas rescue. Pearson's tale of redemption through emancipation and acceptance of a rival culture presaged a series of attempts by Northerners to twist Virginia's origin legend into a mockery of itself.

No appropriation of either origin legend could match Henry Wadsworth Longfellow's *Courtship of Miles Standish*, which was to redefine the verbal and visual images of the Pilgrims for many years to come. On the eve of its release in October 1858, the poet felt optimistic enough about its success to boast to his friend Charles Sumner that the poem would "do very well; and is rather a triumph in its way, considering the hard times."[31] Within two months after it first appeared, the Boston publisher Ticknor and Fields had not only distributed 25,000 copies but had given the poet an advance for the English edition, a handsome volume with illustrations by John Gilbert. In the United States, artists were clamoring to illustrate the poem, and before year's end, the American artist John Whetten Ehninger had completed eight paintings taken from the epic, and Felix O.C. Darley and Joseph Alexander Ames had contacted the author to inform him that they had already illustrated specific scenes. Thus, Longfellow could gloat in a letter to Sumner that "'Miles Standish' has had a most extraordinary 'march.'"[32]

Both Gilbert and Ehninger turned Longfellow's *Courtship of Miles Standish* into a series of lasting images (Figs. 9.1, 9.2, 9.3, 9.4).[33] Both men depicted Standish as a short, pudgy buffoon; both drew Priscilla at her spinning wheel with Alden at her side; both showed the young couple courting in a woodland setting; and both pictured the wedding procession with Priscilla riding a large white bull. Significantly, Gilbert and Ehninger both dressed the Pilgrim men in dark suits with white collars and gave them tall top hats, an indication that by 1858, artists in the United States as well as in England were avoiding all vestiges of flamboyance. The entrepreneurial Ehninger, who had studied with Leutze in Düsseldorf before returning to his New York home, combined the eight drawings into a holiday gift book, with each drawing accompanied by quotations from the poem.[34] As these illustrations were frequently imitated during the next few decades, they had a tremendous impact on future Pilgrim imagery.

FIGURE 9.1 *John W. Ehninger, "Priscilla and John Alden," illustration for* Courtship of Miles Standish, *1859.*

FIGURE 9.2 *John W. Ehninger, "The Council," illustration for* Courtship of Miles Standish, *1859.*

FIGURE 9.3 *John Gilbert, "Priscilla at the Wheel," illustration for* Courtship of Miles Standish, *1859.*

FIGURE 9.4 *John Gilbert, "The Wedding Procession," illustration for* Courtship of Miles Standish, *1859.*

When he published *The Courtship of Miles Standish* in 1858, Longfellow was reveling in success. Comfortably ensconced at the historic "Craigie House" in Cambridge with his wife, the former Fanny Appleton, and their five children, he had recently retired as Smith Professor of Modern Languages at Harvard and had already amassed a large following due to the popularity of his historical epics taken from American folklore, especially *Evangeline* (1847) and *The Song of Hiawatha* (1855). Although he wrote *Miles Standish* at the high point in his career, three years later he would experience a series of multiple shocks. First came the firing on Fort Sumter and the war he had long dreaded; then shortly afterward, his wife burned to death in an accidental fire in which he was also injured. Following this tragedy, the once handsome, ebullient poet lost much of the innocent optimism that characterized his facile writing. He lived on until 1882, receiving a stream of admirers, translating Dante, writing serious prose, and turning out those gentle rhymes that so delighted nineteenth-century readers.[35]

In the years since his death in 1882, Longfellow's exalted reputation has slowly declined. No longer do schoolchildren memorize "The Village Blacksmith" or "Paul Revere's Ride." Few anthologies of American poetry even carry his verses, and professors of literature dismiss him as trivial and passé. Thomas Wortham of the University of California is typical in objecting that Longfellow's poetry is "banal in its poetic craftsmanship, at times nonsensical in its linguistic and metaphoric incoherence."[36] In other words, the once-fashionable poet has been deposed from the canon, defeated in part by the facility of his rhymes and the magnitude of his popularity while he was alive.

There is, however, a great deal more in *The Courtship of Miles Standish* than modern scholars acknowledge. Longfellow was well attuned to his times, and those times were turbulent.[37] He often condemned slavery and faulted Congress for pandering to Southern interests, a complaint he addressed in a volume entitled *Poems on Slavery*, published in 1842. Although his protests were mild compared to those of many New Englanders, he consistently denounced the system that subjected human beings to a life of servitude.[38] On many occasions, Longfellow praised Sumner for speaking out boldly against slavery, and when the senator paid for that bravado with the blow from Brooks, Longfellow's support increased. As Sumner recovered from his wounds in late 1857 and early 1858, Longfellow wrote: "I groan with you over the iniquity of the times. It is deplorable; it is heart-breaking." A few weeks later he advised his friend to "keep aloof" from the "great political barracoon of Congress."[39]

Conditions in Washington greatly troubled Longfellow. When James Buchanan became president, the poet called it "a poor piece of business" which would surely bring about "a sad state of things." Four years later, after Abraham Lincoln was elected, he wrote: "This is a great victory; one can hardly overrate its importance. It is the redemption of the country. Freedom is triumphant." But as the threat of war increased, Longfellow's optimism waned, and he filled his diary entries with apprehensions. "Six States have left the Union, led by South Carolina," he wrote on January 28, 1861, five weeks before Lincoln's inauguration. "President Buchanan is an antediluvian, an *après-moi-le-déluge* President, who does not care what happens, if he gets safely through his term. We owe the present state of things mainly to him. He has sympathized with the disunionists. It is now too late to put the fire out. We must let it *burn* out."[40]

In the shadow of such political worries, Longfellow began to compose *The Courtship of Miles Standish.* Although he recorded no trips to Plymouth until 1870, he researched the Old Colony thoroughly by visiting Boston's New England Historical Society and reading everything from Deane's edition of Bradford's journal to Peter Oliver's abrasive account of the Puritan Commonwealth.[41] The poem recapitulated an old legend about the triangular romance between the elder Miles Standish, John Alden, and Priscilla Mullens. Longfellow told Sumner that it was "the well-known adventure" of his maternal ancestor John Alden.[42]

The narrative begins with an examination of Standish's character as he struts around his quarters instructing Alden to be his emissary in proposing marriage. The young man faithfully follows orders, even though he loves Priscilla himself. During their visit, Priscilla tells her suitor she is homesick for England, refuses Standish's proposal, and delivers her oft-quoted response ("Speak for yourself, John"). Alden subsequently prepares to return to England on the *Mayflower* but changes his mind when he sees Priscilla; meanwhile, Standish leads an army into an Indian camp, ignores the inhabitants' peaceful overtures, and blusters into a battle. Back in Plymouth,

Priscilla sits at her spinning wheel entertaining the entreaties of Alden, when a messenger reports that Standish has been killed in battle. Hearing this, the couple hastens to marry, but just as the ceremony finishes, the captain reappears. In the end, he forgives them, and the poem concludes with Alden transporting his bride homeward "like a queen" atop a "snow-white bull."

The popularity of the *Courtship of Miles Standish* persuaded most twentieth-century critics that the poem was merely an appealing glimpse into an imagined Pilgrim world. But the romance, with its juxtaposition of love and war, was not merely a sentimental view of New England's past but also a critique of American politics in the years preceding the Civil War. Longfellow's apprehensions about warmongering in the Buchanan White House surfaced in the personality of the title character. He had a literary precedent; a decade earlier, Lowell had used Standish to chastise New Englanders for not acting more forcefully in the fight against slavery. Ten years later, Longfellow turned Lowell's intrepid hero into a blustering bully. In the first canto of the *Courtship*, Standish compares himself to Julius Caesar and boasts that he could wipe out every "sagamore, sachem, or powow" in the vicinity (15–24).[43] This characterization of the military leader—issuing orders and making tough threats but fearing to propose marriage—matches Longfellow's negative appraisal of the "antediluvian" Buchanan rattling swords but never taking a firm stance. By emphasizing Standish's false bravado, Longfellow was also suggesting his mistrust of Southerners' threatening war if the government failed to meet their demands.

If Standish was a buffoon, the poet's ancestor John Alden emerged as a man of honor. Not only had he carried out the captain's errand and refused to marry Priscilla until he believed Standish to be dead but he often demonstrated his incorruptible character with such aphorisms as, "Better be dead and forgotten, than living in shame and dishonor" (69). In Alden's character there are traces of Longfellow himself, afraid and uncertain about taking a decisive position, and traces of Sumner, holding firm to his beliefs and willing to face the necessary consequences.

Unlike the flood of literature then picturing the Pilgrims as superhuman paragons of virtue, Longfellow treated the Plymouth inhabitants as ordinary folk going about their everyday lives. His romance turned the first colony into a democratically governed and idealized

New England village, with its industrious workers "intent on their labors," gardeners, fishermen, hunters, farmers, and a town council making all decisions (129). This egalitarian Eden offered a comforting antidote to uncertainties of the present. As Alden and his bride ride into the wilderness, the closing verse envisions that lost Camelot:

> *Like a picture it seemed of the primitive, pastoral ages,*
> *Fresh with the youth of the world, and recalling Rebecca*
> * and Isaac,*
> *Old and yet ever new, and simple and beautiful always,*
> *Love immortal and young in the endless succession of lovers*
> *So through the Plymouth woods passed onward the bridal*
> * procession. (152)*

In that "primitive, pastoral" time, beauty and courage (Rebecca and Isaac) rode off on a white bull to sire a nation despite the fatuous Standish. In other words, there was still a glimmer of hope that beyond the current troubles, the paradise of Plymouth might be recaptured.

A review that appeared in the *Southern Literary Messenger* in 1859 derides *The Courtship of Miles Standish* for its decided bias. The author began by accusing his "New England brethren" of having "a headstrong looseness in morals" and "a passion for making an *auto da fe* of all institutions and opinions different from their own." Although the reviewer acknowledged that Longfellow had written "a pleasant book," he complained about the price of seventy-five cents and jibed: "Let us not be understood as assailing the Bostonians for devouring twenty thousand copies of hexametrical classicity." He then criticized the poet for being "especially endeared to the descendants of the Pilgrims" even though he was unable to capture the "spirit of the time" in "any very palpable way."[44] If New Englanders were smitten with Longfellow's poem, this reviewer asserted, discriminating Southerners would never follow suit. His snide appraisal indicates that the old rivalry between the origin legends of Virginia and Massachusetts had become a key factor in determining the value of literary works. And the author's bitterness also signals recognition that the Pilgrim legend had grown beyond its initial task of pinpointing New England's beginnings and now reigned as the origin myth for the entire United States.

❧

But not all Virginians were sulking about New England's successful campaign to implant its ancestors as the nation's founders. Rather, most were bragging about their own glorious colonial past, a dominant theme when leaders of the Old Dominion gathered on the "sacred soil" of Jamestown to celebrate the 250th anniversary of John Smith's landing, a year before publication of Longfellow's *Courtship of Miles Standish.* Pilgrimages to the island had been happening with regularity prior to the 1857 Jamestown Jubilee, and by the time May 13 rolled around, the journey down the James River had become almost obligatory for loyal Virginians. But revelry, not worship, was the predominant theme of the anniversary celebration. The missionary intensity that fueled New England's crusade to end slavery was foreign in Virginia, where a Tidewater pedigree in and of itself was sufficient to engender state pride. Although the upper crust of society cared deeply about its mixed Cavalier-Pocahontas lineage—and the growing middle class was eager to share that heritage—most Virginians were able to revere their forebears while at the same time treating the past with a nonchalance that eluded the most fervent, mission-driven New Englanders.

The scope and message of the 250th Jamestown anniversary differed from the bicentenary celebration held there fifty years earlier. In 1807, William and Mary College had orchestrated the ceremonies in which students delivered speeches to residents from nearby towns; in 1857, the Jamestown Committee (centered in the nation's capital) organized events and invited regional notables to address an audience that came from all over the area. Whereas the orators of 1807 had talked of nation building and republican values, the rostrums of 1857 resounded with pointed sectional chauvinism.

Only the moss-draped island seemed the same, with its old church tower, decaying gravestones, a powder magazine, a few old wells, and the remnants of ancient walls. The island's nineteenth-century proprietor, William Allen, who lived in the old Ambler house part of the year, grew corn and grain amid the sacred relics. But the depressed condition of the Jamestown peninsula was not indicative of the state at large.[45] In fact, the 1857 jubilee took place during a time when Virginia was experiencing an economic upswing, and that undoubtedly contributed to the buoyant mood that brought visitors to the Jamestown Jubilee.

After disembarking from steamers bearing multicolored banners, people lingered by the tower to recall the historic events that had transpired in the demolished church. A columnist for the *Richmond Daily Dispatch* captured the day's reverential mood when he mused that a "stretch of fancy might bring to the mind of the observer a vision of Pocahontas, the queenly daughter of a noble kind, and of the sturdy Captain John Smith, kneeling at the chancel and pledging their faith to the service of the Most High God."[46] If this writer's "stretch of fancy" lacked historical verisimilitude, it exemplified the desire of Virginians to invoke colonial beginnings in hopes of rousing regional passions.

At noon, members of the Jamestown Society took their places on a platform situated near the church tower. Seated with them was former President John Tyler, Governor Henry Wise, and George Washington Parke Custis, whose play *Pocahontas* was still a favorite in the Old Dominion. Philip R. Fendall, president of the Jamestown Society, began the ceremony with a short speech that sounded as if it had been lifted from Plymouth. "We are here," he said, "on the site of what once was Jamestown—pilgrims to the graves of our forefathers." And it was on this spot, he gestured, that they "planted the seeds of a mighty republic, now reaching from ocean to ocean, dispensing to millions the blessings of civil and religious liberty, and animating by its example the cause of human rights throughout the world."[47] Fendall clearly envisioned the Jamestown Jubilee as a chance for Virginians to combat the verbal attacks from Massachusetts with proof that their colonial roots reached equally as deep and their humanitarian mission extended equally as far.

A similar, though more subtle, adaptation of the Plymouth rhetoric filtered into the main address by former President Tyler. He devoted the better part of his speech to a detailed recital of Virginia's colonial past, at one point gesturing toward the old church tower to remind the audience that the chapel once standing beside it had held the altar at which "Pocahontas had knelt when she received the rite of baptism and at which she also plighted her faith in marriage." The ex-president then carried his historical lesson through a laudatory account of Virginia's revolutionary heroes and ended by uniting that history with a rebuttal of the abolitionists: "Political demagogues may revile and abuse but they cannot detract from the high and lofty fame which belongs to this time-honored Commonwealth, or disturb" that "conservative and national" policy "which she has through all times pursued." Then he called upon the audience to support its homeland by renewing its "pledges to those principles of self-government" embedded in the ancestral legacy.[48]

Tyler's phraseology was loaded. By suggesting a renewal of pledges to the "principles of self-government," he was asserting that Virginia would make its own decisions about the status of slavery within its borders. In the White House, he had attempted to maintain an equilibrium among his Whig brethren while also fighting to uphold his state's interests. In the twelve years since leaving office, he had become a leading spokesman in matters concerning the Old Dominion, and that meant defending slavery and the social system it fostered. His measured, well-researched perusal of Virginia history in the Jamestown Jubilee speech challenged his listeners to stand on the precedents of their forebears and aggressively combat unwanted interference from the North.

The summons to pose historical examples as a defense of Virginia's rights echoed through in a long poem written and read by native son James Barron Hope. After taking a lugubrious excursion through Virginia history—with all the expected tributes to that "peerless maid, the pearl of all her tribe" and the "great captain"—the poet concluded with an allusion to the state's "splendor" inherited from the sun. He then carried that reference one step further by linking it to a willingness to fight to retain that "splendor":

> *As I aspire, in any song of mine,*
> *To make that name in greater lustre shine.*
> *Its fittest place is on Virginia's brow,*
> *As, kneeling down, to God she sends her vow—*
> *That, as her great son left her, she will be;*
> *And live on proudly—free among the free;*
> *Or, finding that she may not thus remain,*
> *Like SAMSON, grasp the pillars of the fane,*
> *And leave all wreck, where erst in pride it rose,*
> *Tomb for herself in common with her foes.*

In short, Virginians should vow to either live "free amid the free" or wreck the Union with the strength of Samson. It was all but a call to arms. Governor Wise sounded an even stronger note in his short, unprepared address. "Virginians!" he charged, "the Fountain-head of this mighty river of Life and Liberty is ours—ours to keep, ours to guard." Therefore, "we will but wait, and watch, and be worthy, and be bold to be free, *we have the bridle of magic reins and golden bit in our own hands*, and we may mount the Pegasus to slay every Hydra and Gorgon dire, which threaten our peace or our fate."[49]

As the visitors boarded their steamers with the words of Tyler, Hope, and Wise ringing in their ears, many must have been inspired to defend their state and its history at all costs. Although most of the dignitaries departed when the formal ceremony ended, a group of diehards remained to participate in a banquet at which a round of toasts amplified the blend of history and sectional belligerence heard in that afternoon's speeches. F. McNerhany saluted Governor Wise as "a noble champion of Constitutional liberty; a watchful guardian of Southern rights; and a sleepless sentinel on the ramparts of the Union." But Colonel W. F. Phillips best captured the mixture of history and defiance when he cheered both the U.S. Constitution and the Old Dominion and then reminded his listeners that in the famous rescue legend "the death-club of Fanaticism" threatened the "safety" of Smith until "the arms" of Pocahontas were "uplifted to ward off the impending blow."[50] Such were the jumbled communications that fired up regional consciousness at the 1857 Jamestown Jubilee.

There still remained some scattered indications that North and South might end their ancient enmity peaceably. One surfaced at the 1857 Jamestown celebration when a "daughter of Massachusetts" submitted a toast for one of the men to read at the banquet. The reader hailed the guest as a resident of "the time honored and patriotic State which annually assembles her children around the ice-bound base of Plymouth Rock, and there teaches them to worship at a country's shrine." The Bay Stater, he continued, wished to "tender in the presence of this honored company her gratitude for the privilege of assembling with them around the altar where Freedom and a Nation *first* sprang to light."[51] It was a small tribute but nevertheless a sign that not all citizens of Massachusetts were denigrating Virginians.

Another example of guarded cooperation between the Bay State and Old Dominion involved a campaign to preserve George Washington's home. During the 1850s, members of Washington's family let it be known that they could no longer afford to maintain Mount Vernon and were thus planning to sell it. While the state of Virginia and the federal government argued about which of them should bear the responsibility of appropriating funds to purchase the grave site and home, private citizens on both sides of the Mason-Dixon line were endeavoring to preserve the property and make it available for public visitation. Spearheading the campaign was the Mount Vernon Ladies Association, an organization composed primarily of Virginia women. Cooperating closely with them was Sarah Josepha Hale, who published requests for money to save Mount Vernon in *Godey's Lady's Book* alongside pleas for making New England's Thanksgiving into a national holiday; both appeals were considered to be patriotic.

Because worship of George Washington transcended sectional lines, his Virginia home was considered a national shrine and—in the tense atmosphere of the late 1850s—saving it became tantamount to preserving the Union. Former Massachusetts senator and governor Edward Everett embarked on a cross-country speaking tour in which he closely allied the nation's first president with the unified nation. Washington's Farewell Address, Everett insisted, was not about "the love of liberty" or "the preservation of State rights" but "Union, Union, Union," was "the first, the last, the constant strain of this immortal address."[52] Everett's marathon efforts ultimately succeeded in raising more than $69,000. In 1859, the Mount Vernon Ladies Association announced that it had enough money to buy the estate, and subsequently George Washington's home and grave site came under its jurisdiction.[53] While still in Virginia during April 1859, Everett joined a pilgrimage to Jamestown; its purpose was to plant ivy roots around the base of the church tower. After that symbolic gesture, the Massachusetts orator paid homage to "the chivalrous Smith, the friendly Powhatan," and "the gentle and compassionate Pocahontas." Then he expressed hopes that until the end of all time, "the great Republic of which it is our privilege to be the citizens, will stand unshaken upon the foundations of Jamestown and Plymouth!"[54] Although other moderate New Englanders might endorse the sentiments, those speeches and ceremonies were quiet voices in an ever louder cacophony of hatreds.

Another vain attempt to maintain cooperation between North and South pervaded the first meeting of the Old Dominion Society, held in New York City in May 1860. Aping its predecessor and rival, the New England Society—which had been celebrating Forefathers' Day in the metropolis for over half a century—the new organization gathered at the Great Hall of the Cooper Institute to commemorate the landing of John Smith's fleet. Guests included members of the St. Patrick's Society, the St. Nicholas Society, the St. George's Society, and the New England Society, all of whom shared the platform with current and former residents of Virginia. On the surface, therefore, an atmosphere of sectional harmony prevailed.

Former Virginia congressman George W. Summers tried to follow the theme of sectional equanimity, but he seemed to have trouble masking all regional chauvinism. "The founders of Virginia," he proclaimed, "were not driven to America by religious persecution and intolerance as were the Puritan fathers of New-England" and subsequently in Virginia there was "no account of any general persecution for religious opinion." In fact, the Jamestown settlement invited the Pilgrims to "remove to the Delaware within the limits of Virginia, and thus escape the rigors of their more northern latitude." This in itself, Summers emphasized, was proof enough of religious tolerance. While he defended the South's position on the return of fugitive slaves and the right of new territories to vote on the status of slavery within their boundaries, he tempered those opinions with solicitations that the Union not "be dissolved on account of any abstract opinion." He stressed that both sides were responsible for the current turmoil and pled for harmony, amplified by the hope that "the stars and stripes still float over a free and united people . . . proudly cherishing the memory of their origin in the colonies of Jamestown and Plymouth."[55]

A similar call for a moratorium on sectional bitterness and a return to an amiable, regional rivalry pervaded the Old Dominion Society's banquet held the following evening. The first toast was an anonymous poem read by the presiding official, Colonel William M. Peyton. Its opening verse set the tone for the commemoration:

> *Virginia! In our flowing bowls*
> *Thy name we would remember*
> *Dear as is Plymouth to the souls*
> *Of Pilgrims in December,—*
> They *hold their banquet as the gloom*

> *Of Winter round them closes;*
> Our *festive board is all abloom*
> With *Spring's returning roses.*

The verses that followed lauded the present day over the "age of Smith and Standish" and heaped praise on Virginia, the "ancient Mother of the States." The poem ended with a good-humored solicitation for moderation of sectional tensions:

> *Here North and South and East and West*
> *Are met in sweet communion—*
> *Now drain the cup—this toast is best,*
> *VIRGINIA AND THE UNION!*[56]

Perhaps because the Old Dominion Society was meeting in New York, the mood could remain conciliatory. Actually, most Virginians, unlike many of their Southern neighbors, were reticent to abandon the Union, and it was these moderates who encouraged the congenial bantering heard at the 1860 banquet. But deeper south and further north, pleas for respectful but cautious coexistence had fewer and fewer adherents as angry sectionalism swiftly began to dominate all interchanges. Before long, Massachusetts and Virginia would be embroiled in an armed struggle to settle their long-held grudges. That war, with all of its needless carnage, brought to a bloody climax two hundred years of cultural, political, and economic misunderstanding.

10

The Pilgrims Versus Pocahontas

John Brown and his ragtag band took over the federal arsenal at Harpers Ferry, Virginia, on October 16, 1859, with intentions of inciting a slave rebellion, a motive that instantly made the raw-boned and eccentric Brown (often called the "Old Puritan") into a hero in Massachusetts and villain in the Old Dominion. Brown's incursion onto Virginia soil received the backing of a group of prominent Bostonians, thus the confrontation that followed inflamed the long-standing rivalry. Primed for decades to employ the origin myths to argue for contemporary points of view, the residents of Virginia and Massachusetts perceived the raid at Harpers Ferry as the first battle of an inevitable clash.

Long before Harpers Ferry, Brown was known to be mentally unstable and financially irresponsible.[1] In 1854, he took several of his sons to "Bloody Kansas" with the sole purpose of conducting a guerrilla war to fight the slaveholders threatening to invade the territory. He there engaged in a series of raids that became known as the Potawatomi Massacre, a rampage in which five proslavery men were murdered and dismembered in front of their horrified families. Shortly after this bloody assault, Brown visited Boston in search of cash and ammunition for further action in Kansas, identifying himself as a descendant of Peter Brown (or Browne), a *Mayflower* passenger. Perhaps for this reason, the Boston intelligentsia welcomed him with open arms. Recalling their first meeting many years later,

Franklin Sanborn—a Concord educator who became one of Brown's principal sponsors—said that the antislavery fighter had impressed him as "a historic character; that is, he had, like Cromwell a certain predestined relation to the political crisis of his time," and like "Cromwell and all the great Calvinists, he was an unquestioning believer in God's fore-ordination and the divine guidance of human affairs."[2]

Sanborn presented Brown to the social activist Samuel Gridley Howe, the Unitarian ministers Thomas Wentworth Higginson and Theodore Parker, and the prosperous entrepreneur George L. Stearns. All four of these New Englanders had worked with Sanborn in financing the Free Kansas movement, and when Brown revealed his plans for leading an incursion into Virginia, they agreed to join with Gerrit Smith (a wealthy landowner from upstate New York) to provide funds for the expedition. This group, later dubbed the Secret Six, supplied most of the cash for Brown's raid on Harpers Ferry. Sanborn also arranged for the antislavery fighter to meet Ralph Waldo Emerson, Henry David Thoreau, William Lloyd Garrison, and Wendell Phillips, all of whom lent moral support, though little cash, to the abolitionist campaign.[3] All of these men and their spouses were eager to translate their antislavery zeal into action, and who could be a better recipient of their support than a *Mayflower* heir who seemed to be a reincarnated Roundhead ready to sacrifice his life for a noble cause?

New Englanders who met Brown—with his gaunt frame, fiery eyes, and frequent biblical quotation—saw him as a reminder of their forebears. Julia Ward Howe called him "a Puritan of the Puritans, forceful, concentrated, and self-contained"; and the millionaire Amos Lawrence labeled him the "Miles Standish of Kansas." While Brown was soliciting money in Boston, Sanborn composed a poem that began with these lines:

> *In thee still sternly lives our fathers' heart,*
> *Brave Puritan. Stout Standish had praised God*
> *For such as thou,—of Mayflower blood thou art.*
> *And worthier feet on Plymouth Rock ne'er trod.* [4]

Such mergers of the terms "Puritan" and "Pilgrim" indicate that many of the New Englanders who had been so careful to disparage the one and emphasize their spiritual descent from the other would forget that distinction when appraising a man whom they perceived as a personification of their inbred Calvinist conscience. Little of that moral rectitude impressed Brown, however. Disappointed by his inability to collect enough money among the "'Heaven exalted' people" of Boston, he left for Kansas in April 1857, but not before penning a bitter memo entitled "Old Browns Farewell to The Plymouth Rocks, Bunker Hill Monuments, Charter Oaks, and Uncle Thoms Cabbins," in which he complained about the "extreme cruel treatment" he had received in New England.[5]

During the next two years, Brown conducted erratic forays to wipe out slaveholders, all the while plotting his attack on Harpers Ferry and collecting surreptitious contributions from his Massachusetts backers for that purpose.[6] Within the next year, he gathered an "army" of volunteers, including three of his own sons, a son-in-law, Will Thompson, and five former slaves. With the goal of capturing a federal arsenal and fomenting a slave rebellion, Brown rented a farm in Maryland near the western Virginia border, and on October 16, 1859, he led eighteen of his followers into Harpers Ferry.

The raid was ill-fated from the start. Brown had expected the non-slaveholding western Virginians to join his campaign, but none did. He was even unable to rouse slaves to join him, and worst of all, one of the first people Brown's men killed was Hayward Shepard, a free black working at the railroad station. After the raiders captured the arsenal, took several hostages, and fortified themselves in the armory, they realized that they were facing hostile townspeople, an armed local militia, and eventually a U.S. cavalry unit led by Colonel Robert E. Lee and his deputy, Lieutenant J.E.B. (Jeb) Stuart. Sporadic exchanges of gunfire killed several Virginians and ten of Brown's band, including two of his sons and his son-in-law. When the smoke cleared, the authorities had captured the Old Puritan along with four of his deputies, hauling them off to the Charlestown jail; two escaped raiders were subsequently seized and also imprisoned. All six were eventually executed.

Almost immediately after Brown's arrest, rumors of a widespread slave rebellion incited so much hysteria in Virginia that Governor Henry A. Wise, whose eccentricity and intensity paralleled that of his prisoner, charged into action. Infuriated that federal troops had been required to end the insurrection and fearful that the recalcitrant western Virginians would rise up against the state, Wise stationed thousands of militia units around Harpers Ferry. Brown's maneuver had been reduced to a standoff between defenders of a brave, if misdirected, Puritan and an army of Cavalier guards.[7] The Secret Six provided little support to their hero after the venture failed, an indication that their ardor had been programmed by the belief that they were conducting a Puritan crusade. After that fiasco threatened to land them in jail, most of the six retreated in terror.[8]

Other New Englanders, however, filled the void in the weeks between Brown's arrest and trial. The most aggressive was the abolitionist Lydia Maria Child, who petitioned Governor Wise to spare the man whom she described to a friend as "a real psalm-singing, praying Puritan, of the old stamp."[9] In her letter to Wise, Child asked permission to visit Brown in prison because he needed "a mother or sister to dress his wounds, and speak soothingly to him." She also asked the governor to deliver a letter to the prisoner, in which she expressed her longing to administer "sisterly words of sympathy and consolation" to him. Wise, then harboring presidential ambitions, attempted to follow a middle course by publicly expressing admiration for Brown's courage and even calling the former Kansas fighter "the gamest man he ever saw." Privately, however, he vowed to see Brown hanged.[10]

As loyal champions of two opposing regional mythologies, Wise and Child proceeded to act out their prescribed roles with dramatic precision. First, the governor answered Child's offer with courtly, if caustic, condescension by assuring her that "Virginia and Massachusetts are involved in no civil war" and indeed that Virginians would treat her "in a chivalrous" and "Christian spirit" if she visited. Although perhaps a "few unenlightened and inconsiderate persons, fanatical in their modes of thought and action" might wrongly "molest" her, because the people of Virginia were "much excited by the crimes" that she seemed to condone. Nevertheless, the state would be "weak indeed" if it failed to adhere to the "letter of morality as well as of law" and remiss in its "chivalry" if it could not "courteously receive a lady's visit to a prisoner." Then the Governor dug in. He would never insult a woman, he oozed, even though "her walk of charity" came from "one who whetted knives of butchery for our mothers, sisters, daughters and babes." For that reason, neither he nor his fellow Virginians could share her "sentiments of sympathy with Brown." With his eye still focused on presidential politics, Wise submitted the correspondence to the Richmond press, a misguided move that left the governor with few friends and enabled Child to mount a more determined abolitionist assault.[11]

In the meantime, Brown received Child's letter. Apparently puzzled by her request, he cordially thanked the New Englander for her "great sympathy" to a stranger and requested that instead of making the trip to Virginia he would be pleased if she would aid his wife and remaining children.[12] Brown's letter—combined with her own misgivings about the safety of such a journey—convinced Child to stay home, although she did contact Brown's wife and worked to raise money for the family. After the Virginia court pronounced its guilty verdict and condemned Brown to a swift execution, Child sent Wise a lengthy discourse reiterating her reasons for opposing slavery and repeating her admiration for Brown. "I believe," she said, "that old hero to be no criminal, but a martyr to righteous principles which he sought to advance by methods sanctioned by his own religious views, though not by mine." The "free, enlightened yeomanry of New England," she warned, "would rejoice to have the Slave States fulfill their oft-repeated threat of withdrawal from the Union."

When Margaretta Mason, the wife of Virginia senator James Mason, saw the correspondence between Wise and Child in the Richmond papers, she jumped into the fray. "Do you read your Bible, Mrs. Child?" she taunted. "If you do, read there, 'Woe unto you hypocrites,' and take to yourself with two-fold damnation that terrible sentence." Mason further charged that Child should be ashamed for wanting to "soothe with sisterly and motherly care" a "hoary-headed murderer." How dare she interfere in Virginia law when she knew nothing of the situation! "Do *you* soften the pangs of maternity in those around you by all the care and comfort you can give? Do *you* grieve with those near you, even though their sorrows resulted from their own misconduct?" Then Mason twisted her dagger: "We do these and more for our servants, and why? Because we *endeavor to do our duty in that state of life it has pleased God to place us*."[13]

Child answered her accuser with a list of biblical texts that not only proved her knowledge of the holy book but also substantiated her dedication to abolitionism. "Men, however great they be," she wrote, "are of small consequence in comparison with principles; and the principle for which John Brown died is the question at issue between us." She followed this reproach with a lengthy condemnation of slavery and then emulated Wise by sending the entire correspondence to Horace Greeley's *New York Tribune.* Subsequently, the American Anti-Slavery Society agreed to combine all eight letters into a book that became a runaway bestseller in the Northern states. The bitter exchange between two women bred to execute opposing missions—Mason's protestations about Virginia's code of honor and Child's formulaic denunciation of slavery—revealed that extremists in both camps had won the ideological battle, and all rational dialogue between Massachusetts and Virginia was henceforth impossible.

After he was pronounced guilty, the stalwart Old Puritan became a symbol of the Pilgrims' sacrifice. Brown himself set the stage in a letter written to his cousin two weeks before his execution. He speculated that he was the first in the family "since the landing of Peter Brown from the Mayflower that has *either been sentenced to imprisonment*; or to the Gallows." But even though "a man dies under the hand of an executioner," he explained, it "has but little to do with his true character," for he was following the path God had chosen for him.[14]

Ralph Waldo Emerson elaborated on this theme when addressing a meeting at Boston's Tremont Temple two weeks before the scheduled hanging. In his short speech, Emerson pictured Brown as a symbol of Pilgrim suffering and Wise as the devil incarnate. He told the audience about Peter Brown, "who came to Plymouth in the Mayflower, in 1620," explaining then that John Brown "joins that perfect Puritan faith, which brought his fifth ancestor to Plymouth Rock, with his grandfather's ardor in the Revolution." Emerson scolded Wise for allowing such a one-sided trial and asked: "Is there a man in Massachusetts so simple as to believe that when a United States Court in Virginia, now, in its present reign of terror, sends to Connecticut, or New York, or Massachusetts, for a witness, it wants him for a witness? No; it wants him for a party; it wants him for meat to slaughter and eat."[15] Around the same time, Henry David Thoreau pled for release of Brown by interjecting a historical corollary: "He was one of that class of whom we hear a great deal, but, for the most part, see nothing at all—the Puritans. It would be in vain to kill him. He died lately in the time of Cromwell, but he reappeared here."[16] For Thoreau, Brown was a reincarnated Cromwell, a man of his own stamp who remained unafraid of authorities. Brown's foray into Virginia to foment a slave rebellion was a reenactment of the battle between Puritans and Cavaliers.

Proclamations of Brown's martyrdom became the dominant note throughout New England on December 2, 1859, the day of his execution. On both sides of the Atlantic, Brown's deeds were justified as a manifestation of his Puritan conscience. In a widely publicized letter written to the editor of the *London News*, the French novelist Victor Hugo remarked: "Brown wished to begin the good work by the deliverance of the slaves in Virginia. Being a Puritan, a religious and austere man, and full of the Gospel, he cried aloud to these men—his brothers—the cry of emancipation."[17] On the day of the hanging, Emerson, Thoreau, Bronson Alcott, and other sympathizers attended a memorial service in Concord, where they sang a hymn that Franklin Sanborn had written to the tune of "Auld Lang Syne":

> *Today beside Potomac's wave*
> *Beneath Virginia's sky,*
> *They slay the man who loved the slave,*
> *And dared for him to die.*
>
> *The Pilgrim Fathers' earnest creed,*
> *Virginia's ancient faith,*
> *Inspired this hero's noblest deed,*
> *And his reward is—Death!*[18]

After the execution, attention turned from Brown's Puritanism to the sins of Virginia.[19] Wendell Phillips made a pointed historical reference to the regional rivalry in a speech delivered at the Boston Music Hall ten days after Brown's burial. The Puritans under Cromwell, he said, "tore off the mask" of "enlightened tyranny" in England, and "John Brown has done the same for us today." Then Phillips proceeded to elevate his hero to Pilgrim sainthood:

Lo this event! Brewster, and Carver, and Bradford, and Winthrop faced a New England winter and defied law for themselves . . . John Brown goes a stride beyond them. . . . Braver than Carver or Winthrop, more disinterested than Bradford, broader than Hancock or Washington, pure as the brightest name on our catalogue . . . He sits in that heaven of which he showed us the open door, with the great men of Saxon blood ministering below his feet. And yet they have a right to say, "We created him."[20]

Phillips also invoked the Old Dominion's own origin myth to demonstrate how ineffective the legend had been in justifying the action of Virginians. He recalled the story of a young Harpers Ferry woman, Miss C.C. Fouke, who threw her body between Brown's son-in-law, Will Thompson, and his Virginia attacker. This episode, he said, resembled the action of an "Indian girl" who "flung herself before her father's tomahawk on the bosom of the English gentleman." He then asked: "What has dragged her [Virginia] down from Pocahontas in 1608 to John Brown in 1859, when humanity is disgraceful, and despotism treads it out under its iron heel?"[21] The Reverend Stephen H. Taft in Martinsburgh, New York, also told the tale of Miss Fouke on that same December 12. "Many years ago," he began, "when Indian chiefs ruled in Virginia, instead of Governor Wise, a gallant captain by the name of John Smith—instead of John Brown—was tried before a council of chiefs, and sentenced to death." Taft repeated the story of Pocahontas's intervention and added: "Such was Virginia chivalry and magnanimity two hundred and fifty years ago under Indian rule." The main difference between the two scenes, he said, was that Thompson was "wholly in the power of his captors" and thus ultimately received a bullet in his head. "Where is now the *chivalry*," Taft asked, "*where the mercy* which dwelt in the bosom of savages in the days of Powhatan? *Gone, quite gone!*" Eaten out by the barbarism of slavery."[22]

For Taft and Phillips, Virginia's origin myth had failed because its moral message was rendered meaningless when used to defend the slave power that its heroine purportedly sired. And for most Northerners, Brown's execution was a clear case of virtue versus villainy, with the latter the victor. Indeed, it had become such a pervasive theme in December 1859 that the justification for fighting seemed rooted in the old Puritan-Cavalier rivalry. Virginia, they said, murdered Brown because his Puritan conscience led him to sacrifice his life in fulfillment of a preordained calling. The belief that Brown's mission began when the *Mayflower* landed helped convince the Secret Six that they were historically bound to finance the Harpers Ferry raid. At the same time, that historical rationale frightened Virginians into realizing that their old nemesis was quite serious about invading the Old Dominion to pay off an ancestral obligation.

The English Civil War was part of the rhetorical feud between Virginia and Massachusetts and provided a rationale for increasing animosity between North and South.[23] The connection between the seventeenth-century war and antebellum America was not as far-fetched as it might seem, because the English confrontation between Puritans and Cavaliers occurred just as the Anglican Church was gaining a foothold in colonial Virginia and the English Puritans were settling the Massachusetts Bay Colony. "We . . . of the south, and especially we of Virginia," proclaimed a *Southern Literary Messenger* columnist in 1837, "are the descendants, for the most part, of the old Cavaliers—the enemies and persecutors of those old puritans—and entertain, perhaps, unwittingly, something of an hereditary and historical antipathy against the children, for their father's sakes."[24] Similar statements came from Massachusetts: "Oliver Cromwell was New England working on British soil," proclaimed the Reverend William Adams. "Puritanism has had two homes and histories, trans-Atlantic and cis-Atlantic."[25] Bay Staters, in other words, believed themselves to be heirs of Oliver Cromwell's Puritan Roundheads, whereas Virginians claimed kinship to the Cavaliers' defending themselves against Puritan aggression and fighting to restore the Stuart Crown.

The best conveyors of such reasoning were nineteenth-century histories of colonial Virginia and Massachusetts. Accounts written by residents of Massachusetts celebrated Cromwell's victory as a triumph, whereas those written by Virginians decried the Puritan "revolution" as a black period in English history. George Bancroft, the loyal son of Massachusetts, described replacement of the Stuart monarchy with the Puritans' Long Parliament as the first step toward founding a democratic nation. In volume 1 of his *History of the United States*, Bancroft employed the present tense to create a sense of excitement. "There is now no time to oppress New England," he rhapsodized, "the throne itself totters;—there is no need to forbid emigration; England is at once become the theatre of wonderful events, and many fiery spirits, who had fled for a refuge to the colonies, rush back to share in the open struggle for liberty." In Bancroft's view, the

Long Parliament removed export and import taxes, expanding commerce between New England and the mother country and benefiting both the mercantile trade and the shipbuilding industry. Thus, during the brief period that the Puritans controlled the British government, New England and the mother country coexisted as equals; Massachusetts enlarged its territory, Rhode Island became a separate colony, and all New England residents came together in a Puritan union. "With the increase of English freedom, the dangers which had menaced Massachusetts" under the Stuarts disappeared, and the colony developed "a more lenient policy" toward its inhabitants.[26] As a dedicated Democrat, Bancroft viewed the English Civil War as a seminal event in the ever-expanding spiral toward universal equality that culminated with Andrew Jackson's presidency.

A Southern historian, writing during those same years, interpreted the English war in reverse. In his history of Virginia (1847), Henry Howe explained that during the "usurpation of Cromwell" the Virginia colony "refused to acknowledge his authority, and declared itself independent." According to Howe, the colonists discovered "that Cromwell threatened to send a fleet and an army to reduce Virginia to subjection," and thus they dispatched "a messenger to Charles II, then an exile in Breda, Flanders." The monarch apparently accepted their "invitation to come over, and be king of Virginia," Howe wrote, and he "was on the eve of embarking when he was recalled to the throne of England." After the Restoration, the king "in gratitude for the loyalty of Virginia . . . caused her coat of arms to be quartered with those of England, Scotland, and Ireland, as an independent member of the empire," granting the colony the title of "Old Dominion."[27] But Bancroft gave this same story a different twist. He wrote that although Virginians resisted entreaties from the Long Parliament and refused to approve the Puritan commonwealth, they profited from the cessation of taxation and absence of royal authority. Bancroft concluded that despite these benefits acquired from "the democratic revolution in England," the wave of religious intolerance that followed the Restoration led Virginia to banish all Puritan ministers.[28]

Romantic poetry of the antebellum years provides an excellent indicator of the opposing interpretations of seventeenth-century English history. In a paean to the Old Dominion that appeared in the *Southern Literary Messenger* in 1841, Spencer Wallace Cone explained how Virginians perceived their chivalric heritage.

Gentle, and eloquent, and bold,
Fit champions of the free,
The "Lion Heart"—had loved of old
Virginia's chivalry.
The OLD DOMINION! 'Tis a name
Should ring the world around,
'Til every babbling tongue of fame made music to the sound;
That kings might learn to know their peers
In her untitled Cavaliers! . . .

It is a weary time since first
We left Potomac's side,
Where noble hearts are nobly nursed
By old Virginia's pride:—
Where the blood of Charles' Cavaliers,
The jovial, true and bold,
Runs purely down the stream of years
As from the font it rolled;—
And men are of as princely sort
As ever ruled in regal court.[29]

Similarly, New Englanders glorified their colonial beginnings, but in their case, it was pious sufferers, not "jovial" men of the "princely sort," of whom they sang. Look, for example, at these lyrics composed by Grenville Mellen in 1832 for the New England Society of New York:

We sing of heroes who outdid
The boast of chivalry:
Whose valor braved the shock amid
A stormy sea and sky;
Whose deeds were deeds of mercy, done
To persecuted man—
Whose wreaths were wreaths of triumph, won
In VIRTUE'S fearless van!

NEW ENGLAND'S FATHERS!—men who dar'd
The agony of years—
Whom pale OPPRESSION never spar'd

> *But could not bow to tears!*
> *Who mid the howl of winter fled,*
> *And your banner here unfurl'd,*
> *And CONSCIENCE in her pride outled*
> *Unfetter'd to the world!*[30]

As the United States became embroiled in its own internal conflict, the verbal battle between Puritan and Cavalier intensified. The American Civil War was to many a reenactment of seventeenth-century enmity. Massachusetts believed it was reviving a Puritan democratic conscience to justify fighting fellow countrymen; Virginia conjured up fabled Cavalier stability to incite a feeling of camaraderie among Southerners. As these two historical arguments fused with the larger issues of slavery and opposing economic systems, they filtered into the familiar rhetoric that drove the United States across the brink of compromise and into the irreversible chasm of destruction.[31]

Shortly before the presidential election of 1860, which pitted Republican Abraham Lincoln against Democrat Stephen Douglas, James P. Holcombe, a law professor at the University of Virginia, published a pamphlet urging people to vote against the "Black Republican." His argument was passionate and emphatic: "If the Union cannot be preserved without an eternal strife between the North and the South, it cannot be abandoned too soon." He then barraged his audience with loaded questions. "If you are prepared to submit to the election of a Black Republican President, when, may I ask, ought resistance to begin?" Holcombe's answer was resoundingly clear. "We would be false to the traditions and memories of patriotism, false to the principles of liberty, false to that glorious sentiment which our fathers first baptized in their blood. . . . So long as Northern sentiment upon African slavery remains unaltered, the Constitution, as it stands, furnishes us no permanent security against Northern injustice."[32]

As the election drew near, a contributor to the *Southern Literary Messenger* stated that the period in history most like the North's "present moral and political status" was to be found in "Round-head scenes of the Cromwellian period." At the present time, the writer complained, "an asceticism under the pretenses of religion" is "more proscriptive and more brutal" than any "since the middle ages." But he assured his readers that such pressures would not impede Southerners when defending their convictions. "The power and the charm of slavery is over the land," he declared, "and the men and the women of Plymouth Rock may rave and scream as they will, they yet live under its law, and prosper by its fruits."[33]

After Lincoln's victory, the avalanche toward secession began in earnest. South Carolina took the first step in December 1860, and gradually, other Southern states followed. The majority of Virginians, however, were reluctant to abandon the Union, although several vociferous spokesmen were pleading for secession. One of them, John Esten Cooke—who would soon join the Confederate army—published a poem entitled "A Dream of the Cavaliers" in *Harper's New Monthly Magazine*. In it, Cooke turned Smith and Pocahontas into a knight and his lady, both dressed in battle gear. His "dream" of the title is a "great procession" of "gallant Cavaliers" led by

> *John Smith, the fearless captain*
> *Of the mighty days of old,*
> *With the beard and swarthy forehead,*
> *And the bearing free and bold!*

He is accompanied by "a fawn of the forest," who carries the "blood of a line of chieftains" and wears "a crown of nodding feathers."

> *Our own dear Pocahontas!*
> *The Virgin Queen of the West—*
> *With the heart of a Christian hero*
> *In a timid maiden's breast!*
>
> *You have heard the moving story*
> *Of the days of long ago,*
> *How the tender girlish bosom*
> *Shrunk not from the deadly blow;*
>
> *How the valiant son of England,*
> *In the woodland drear and wild,*
> *Was saved from the savage war-club*
> *By the courage of a child.*

> *And now in the light of glory*
> *The noble figures stand—*
> *The founder of Virginia,*
> *And the pride of the Southern land!*[34]

Behind them in the parade were Sir William Berkeley, Nathaniel Bacon, William Byrd, many "gay young Cavaliers," and "the men of Revolution, who live on the storied page— / The great old race of giants of the great heroic age!" Now primed for war, the fabled "Cavalier" world that Cooke imagined brought the mélange of Virginia myths together to embody a "dream" of plantation chivalry that Southerners believed they were defending.

As state leaders debated between loyalty to the Union and defense of state pride, another poet, Joseph Brenan, also issued an argument for joining the Confederacy. But instead of following Cooke and posing secession in the romantic guise of Old Dominion history, Brenan's verses—published in the *Messenger* two months before Virginia voted to secede—belligerently attacked Massachusetts:

> *Men of the South! Our foes are up*
> *In fierce and grim array;*
> *Their sable banner laps the air—*
> *An insult to the day!*
> *The Saints of Cromwell rise again*
> *In sanctimonious hordes,*
> *Hiding behind the garb of peace*
> *A million ruthless swords. . . .*
>
> *Hark to the howling demagogues—*
> *A fierce and ravenous pack—*
> *With nostrils prone, and bark and bay,*
> *Which run upon our track!*
> *The waddling bull-pup Hale—the cur*
> *Of Massachusetts breed—*
> *The moping mongrel, sparsely crossed*
> *With Puritanic seed—*
> *The Boston bards who join the chase*
> *With genuine beagle chime,*
> *And Sumner, snarling poodle-pet*

Of virgins past their prime;
And even the sluts of Women's Rights—
Tray, Blanche and Sweet-heart, all—
Are yelping shrill against us still,
And hunger for our fall! . . .
Men of the South! ye have no kin
With fanatics or fools;
You are not bound by breed or birth
To Massachusetts rules. . . . [35]

Brenan's belligerence mirrored the mounting anger that propelled the undecided Old Dominion to vote for secession on April 17, 1861, four days after the Confederates captured Fort Sumter. When Northern troops began moving into their state, Virginians became increasingly convinced that they were engaged in an ancient ideological confrontation with New Englanders. By believing they were righting a historic wrong, soldiers from the Old Dominion could justify taking up arms against fellow Americans because they represented the fanaticism and insanity of Cromwell's army. And by the same token, New Englanders could kill sons of the satanic Cavaliers who had instituted a tyranny of bondage that profiteers initiated and ignorant barbarians were perpetuating. Perhaps the only axiom upon which both sides agreed was that North and South had been united under false pretenses for eighty years.

In search of a common spirit of Confederate nationalism, Southerners especially needed a historical footing. A few months after the Old Dominion joined the Confederacy, the Virginian William Archer Cocke contributed an article to *De Bow's Review* entitled "The Puritan and the Cavalier; or, The Elements of American Colonial Society." The author therein denounced Puritanism and its New England heirs as "intolerant, tyrannical and anti-republican." All of these flaws, he explained, were planted when New England's earliest settlers renounced their motherland. The Puritans, who had emigrated "to establish a religious government, in opposition to that of England," attempted to "subvert the charter that Charles had granted to Massachusetts." But, Cocke insisted, "Virginia, true to her Cavalier sentiment," remained loyal to the Crown. Consequently, the "fundamental differences between the colonies of. Massachusetts and Virginia were that the latter, proud of the constitution of their mother country, sought not to overthrow the government."

In other words, Virginia's settlers brought Britain's legal system to Jamestown, whereas the New England Puritans disobeyed the very laws that they boasted about perpetuating. Furthermore, Cocke continued, "it has been the habit of every New England writer and orator to mislead the public mind by dwelling on a few prominent traits of Puritan character" while ignoring all negative appraisals of the past. The author then attempted to set the story straight. The principal culprit was the "reformation of Luther and Calvin," which unleashed such a "storm" that the Puritans became "eager to overthrow even consecrated principles" if they stood "in the way of their own selfishness." He contrasted the Cavaliers, who imported to Virginia the "moral social and political" influences of England, with the Puritans in Massachusetts, who established "a government to pander to their own religious dogmas" and discriminate against every other religious sect. All of Cocke's arguments pointed toward two distinctly separate societies: one in Massachusetts formed by the "agitators" of the English revolution, the other founded by the "high-toned, honor-loving brave class" of Cavaliers.[36]

New Englanders took a different tack when seeking a historical basis for the war. Following Charles Deane's publication of Edward Maria Wingfield's manuscript in 1860, they chose contempt and condescension as their principal verbal weapon. An article in the *Atlantic Monthly* combined historical documentation with satire to denounce Virginia's origin legend as a fictitious romance. The anonymous author of this article suggested a strong attachment between Pocahontas and Smith, for whom she felt "tender palpitations." She married Rolfe, the author jibed, to insure a "link of friendship between the Reds and the Whites," and that made him harbor "very ill-natured" feelings toward "Rolfe and Company for the cruel deception" that separated Pocahontas from her true love. This critic wrote that after Smith departed from Jamestown,

> the soul seems to have left the Colony . . . the beautiful lands became a prey to the worn-out English gentry, who spent their time cheating the simple-hearted red men. These called themselves gentlemen, because they could do nothing. . . . To this day there seems to be a large number in that vicinity who have no other occupation than that of being gentlemen, and it is evidently in many cases just as much as they can do.[37]

The *Atlantic Monthly* article also touched upon the issue that provided Massachusetts with its strongest historical rationale for fighting Virginia. "The most fatal ship that ever cast anchor in American waters," the author wrote, "was that which brought the first twenty negroes to the settlers of Jamestown," for slavery promoted widespread ignorance and an underclass of "poor white trash."[38] In a report about his journey to the Virginia front in 1862, Nathaniel Hawthorne also commented on the Dutch ship that brought the first slaves to Jamestown a year before the *Mayflower* arrived:

> There is an historical circumstance, known to few, that connects the children of the Puritans with these Africans of Virginia in a very singular way. They are our brethren, as being lineal descendants from the Mayflower, the fated womb of which, in her first voyage, sent forth a brood of Pilgrims upon Plymouth Rock, and, in a subsequent one, spawned slaves upon the Southern soil,—a monstrous birth, but with which we have an instinctive sense of kindred, and so are stirred by an irresistible impulse to attempt their rescue, even at the cost of blood and ruin.[39]

The connection between the first slave ship to Jamestown and the *Mayflower* activated so many symbolic triggers that Hawthorne had only to suggest an antithetical affinity between the two voyages—one black, the other white, one rescuer, the other victim—to imply that New Englanders were more firmly attached to black slaves than to white Southerners.

Shortly after Virginia joined the Confederacy and the capital was transferred from Montgomery to Richmond, officials moved to fortify Jamestown because of its strategic location. The only inhabitable structure on the island was the large Ambler house. Its proprietor, William Allen, had enlisted as a captain in the Virginia militia and his first job in that capacity was mobilizing his slaves to build an earthworks fort on the riverbank. While Allen's involuntary brigade was still at work, a battery of Confederate soldiers under the command of Catesby Jones moved to Jamestown and recruited additional slaves from nearby plantations to complete the fort. By the end of May 1861, 1,000 men lived at the garrison and eight guns stood atop the earthworks mound, which its builders christened Fort Pocahontas. Upriver nearer Richmond at another critical spot on the James stood its companion, Fort Powhatan. Meanwhile, the Union was mobilizing its fleet of steamships, sloops, and frigates, many of which had been named *Pocahontas* and *Powhatan* before the war started. Ironically, both sides were going into battle under the nominative aegis of the Indians, who were an integral part of Virginia's origin myth.[40]

Not far from Jamestown at Fort Monroe near Hampton Roads camped Company B of the Third Regiment of Militia from Plymouth, Massachusetts, better known as the Standish Guards, one of the first units of Union troops to be mustered. Most were volunteers who had signed up for three months of service. They left home in April 1861, wearing uniforms and carrying swords donated by the citizens of the town, merging with similar units in Boston before traveling southward to join Major General Benjamin F. Butler's Sixth Massachusetts Volunteer Infantry Regiment at Fort Monroe. Heirs of the original settlers were now facing each other on the very turf that scions of Jamestown had been verbally defending and descendants of the Pilgrim had been slandering.[41] The historic dimensions of this encounter did not escape Bay Staters. After completing their three months of service, the Standish Guards returned to Plymouth. As they stepped off the train, they were greeted by an enthusiastic crowd of flag-waving residents and a band playing "Home Sweet Home." In his speech of welcome, Charles C. Davis thanked God for delivering the men safely and prayed that "if Plymouth Rock and Jamestown" were to "meet in conflict," God would "defend the Right," which meant that "the Puritan flag of Emancipation" would "wipe away THE CURSE of the Cavalier."[42]

Meanwhile, Virginians were deciding whether or not to celebrate the traditional Fourth of July holiday in 1861. Many Confederate soldiers refused to commemorate the birth of a nation from which they were seceding; but other Southerners saw the holiday as confirming their own cause, because they were resisting a tyranny similar to the English threat that had prompted the rebellion of 1776. On that Independence Day of 1861, John Tyler decided to visit the Confederate troops at Jamestown and express his support for those fighting to defend his state. Six months later, the former president would be dead, thus spared from witnessing Virginia's four years of Union occupation.[43]

Both sides were poised for a decisive battle in March 1862, when the *Monitor* and the *Merrimac* (captured by the Confederates and rechristened the *Virginia*) had their historic encounter at Hampton Roads near Jamestown. This battle of the two "ironclads" ended in a draw after six hours of hand-to-hand combat and marked a turning point in the fortunes of the peninsula adjacent to Jamestown.[44] The potential threat of Confederate naval strength convinced General George B. McClellan that he must attempt to reach Richmond and that the peninsula between Jamestown at Yorktown offered the best route. A clash between McClellan's army and Confederate forces under the command of General John B. Magruder took place in April 1862, when Union troops invaded the mainland. Within a few weeks, they moved to capture Williamsburg in a battle that incurred heavy casualties on both sides. Ultimately, McClellan's forces occupied the old colonial capital and forced the Confederates to abandon their outpost on Jamestown Island, although their final objective of capturing Richmond eluded them for the time being.[45]

After the South's retreat from Jamestown, the island became a favorite hiding place for runaway slaves hoping to be rescued by Union ships. Before departing, one of these groups set fire to the old Ambler residence. Rumor had it that the perpetrators were the very slaves whom the mansion's owner had coerced into building the Confederate fort.[46] If true, that blaze must have seemed a sweet revenge. In July 1862, the Union army occupied Jamestown and set up a communications outpost from which telegraph wires were stretched to the mainland. A few months later, General McClellan visited the island and—like so many before and after him—he wandered through the graveyard, moved by the history that seemed to haunt the ruins.[47]

Virginians, however, could not tolerate Yankee occupation of the hallowed grounds of their colonial past. Some mounted guerrilla attacks, others cut telegraph wires, and in September 1862, a battalion commanded by former Virginia governor Henry A. Wise (now a brigadier general in the Confederate army) attempted to recapture Williamsburg. Although the maneuver succeeded in seizing a few soldiers and temporarily advancing through the city, it failed to dislodge the Northern troops. Ten months later, Wise tried again and once again was defeated. Jamestown and Williamsburg, therefore, remained under Union control until the war ended.[48]

As the Union army swept through the Old Dominion in 1862, a Virginian named J. H. Martin published a long epic poem about Pocahontas and John Smith. Written as a panegyric to the Old Dominion and its contributions to the Confederacy, the poem at once distorts and magnifies the origin myth that had become a motivating credo for Virginians during the war years. Beginning with Powhatan's "beauteous daughter" preventing "the death-club" from smashing the head of John Smith, Martin proceeds to a mythical recounting of Smith's career that propels the legendary captain on globe-trotting excursions from Europe to the Middle East, from Turkey to South America, finally coming to rest in the antebellum United States. At one point, the poet catapults the legendary captain to Mexico, where he beholds the Virginian Winfield Scott leading "a brave, determined, gallant band" into battle. Martin first uses that war to praise the valor of Virginians and then to excoriate Scott for deserting the Old Dominion and remaining in the Union army:

> *. . . Scott, and Harney, Quitman, Lee,*
> *Our columns led to victory*
> *But now the first a traitor turns,*
> *His native State deserts and spurns,*
> *And with the sword his mother gave*
> *Virginia—parent of the brave,—*
> *Her precious life-blood seeks to draw,*
> *Preferring gold to honor's law.*
> *A matricide shall be his name,*
> *The synonyme of guilt and shame . . .*

Scott's perfidy is more than redeemed by Robert E. Lee and other Confederate leaders, whom Martin exalts:

> *But higher yet in Glory's skies*
> *The star of gallant Lee shall rise.*
> *The brow of Johnston shall be seen*
> *Entwined with laurels ever-green. . . .*
> *O! blessing be upon them all,*
> *Who, when they heard Virginia's call,*

> *Surrendered wealth, and place, and power,*
> *To stand by her in danger's hour.*[49]

Martin's fusion of the origin legend with the battles of the war then destroying his state indicates just how fully Pocahontas had been designated Virginia's patron saint.

The exigencies of war inspired another southerner, W. S. Bogart of Savannah, Georgia, to glorify Pocahontas in a tribute published in the *Southern Literary Messenger.* "Her story is still fresh in our minds," Bogart insisted, "and her character of gentle mercy and guileless purity still appeals to the sympathies of every generation." In addition to praising Pocahontas's virtue, bravery, and Christian valor, Bogart explained why she was so important to Southerners: "Pocahontas united her destiny with the white race, and thenceforth shared its blessings." Or to put it more bluntly, he validated the claim of "white superiority," which Pocahontas ostensibly acknowledged when she vowed to become as English as possible. By so doing, she earned the right to enjoy the "blessings" of a higher "civilization," even if it required the enslavement of nonwhites to achieve its ultimate objective. Bogart ended with an outline of the Rolfe-Pocahontas genealogy and a plea for Virginians to "erect, in enduring stone or bronze," an "effigy of the savior of the Colony." Bogart concluded that if such a tribute were placed at the Richmond capitol, Virginia "would at least attest" its "grateful appreciation of her lovely daughter, born in her forest wilds."[50]

Although that statue never materialized, Bogart's musings pose several insights into the meaning of Virginia's origin legend during the Civil War. The Savannah poet not only labeled Smith the "Father of the Colony" but—as the word "savior" indicates—made Pocahontas into a Southern Joan of Arc, a native leader whose Indian blood empowered the cause with an inner ferocity. In a recent study, Robert Tilton notes that the Pocahontas image was "crucial to the South's growing sense of otherness"; its Indian foundations not only made Southerners believe they were strong and invincible but separated them racially from their Northern enemies.[51] This merger of Indian courage and the Southern cause indicates why the name and image of Pocahontas and Powhatan appeared on everything from the fort at Jamestown to the flag of a Virginia cavalry unit known as the Powhatan Guards.[52]

Throughout the war, the Confederate capital was threatened with invasion, even though Generals Robert E. Lee and Thomas J. (Stonewall) Jackson had been able to turn back McClellan's forces during the peninsula campaign of 1862. Fighting continued to rage all around them, however, and by 1864, Richmond's residents were enduring a state of siege as the encircling enemy moved inexorably nearer. On Sunday April 2, 1865, most inhabitants of the city were in church when news arrived that Grant's forces had reached Richmond's outskirts. In the ensuing flight, mobs of retreating Southerners performed a final act of defiance by setting the downtown aflame.[53] Two days after Richmond fell, President Lincoln visited the conquered capital, and five days later, Lee surrendered at Appomattox. The war was over, but the humiliations of defeat were only beginning. Before the triumphant Union army quitted the area, its leaders decreed that Jamestown—the symbolic heart of the state's origin legend—would be the site where former Confederate administrators and officers would be required to take an oath of allegiance to the government of the United States.[54] It was a bittersweet end to a conflict of cultures and ideologies. With much of Virginia bearing severe battle scars, the origin legend that had been a proud emblem of Confederate ideology was now ripped to shreds.

Part Four

TRANSFORMING THE MYTHS

11

The Pilgrims
Triumphant

Victory's vengeance took its toll, not only on the decimated South but on the legend that helped shape Virginia's self-perception before and during the war. Merged with the Cavalier myth, the tale of the Christianized Indian who saved "white" civilization from destruction by "savages" became a Confederate scapegoat. In the heat of battle, Virginians had made wildly exaggerated claims about the heroic deeds of Pocahontas and Smith, thus setting up the pair as idols for the conquerors to smash. Smith had already fallen prey to New England iconoclasts when Palfrey published his *History of New England* in 1858, and Deane released Wingfield's *Discourse* two years later. After the North's victory, Deane stepped up his attack on the Virginia legend by releasing an annotated edition of Smith's *True Relation* in 1866. Before long, Deane's young protégé Henry Adams—an aspiring historian and scion of Massachusetts's most distinguished political family—would greatly outshine his master in Smith-bashing.

Adams became absorbed in the Jamestown story while living in London and serving as private secretary to his father, Charles Francis Adams, American minister to the Court of St. James during the Civil War. His interest in the Virginia colony had been piqued earlier in Boston when Palfrey mentioned his own "historic doubts as to Capt. John Smith and Pocahontas." Remembering that remark several months later, Adams wandered into the library of the British Museum in search of a diversion from menial chores at the embassy.

245

His initial findings, however, seemed to confirm the existence of Pocahontas and substantiate Smith's stories. But after Palfrey sent him Wingfield's criticism of Smith, Adams changed his mind. On the basis of that evidence, he told Palfrey he had "ruled out" the captain's "authority" and decided that Smith was "as powerful a liar as he was a seaman."[1] Five years elapsed while the young writer waited for an opportunity to present his "elaborate argument" to condemn "the old pirate." It came in summer 1866, when Palfrey asked Charles Eliot Norton, editor of the *North American Review,* to assign Adams a critique of Deane's recently published editions of Wingfield's *Discourse* and Smith's *True Relation.*[2]

Writing from an overseas perspective while the war at home was growing increasingly bloody, Adams could not fully separate the Smith-Pocahontas legend from his own mistrust of Virginians.[3] In the early phase of his research, he readily admitted to planning

> a rear attack on the Virginia aristocracy, who will be utterly gravelled by it if it is successful. I can imagine to myself the shade of John Randolf turned green at that quaint picture which [William] Strachey gives of Pocahontas "clothed in virgin purity" and "wanton" at that, turning somersets [somersaults] with all the little ragamuffins and "decayed serving-men's" sons of Jamestowne.[4]

Two months before the January 1867 issue of the *North American Review* appeared, Adams wrote Deane: "It is not likely that our case can be established without a long battle, especially if there are any hot-headed literary Southerners left, to put on the war-paint and feathers and scalp us for our treatment of their hero. Therefore I prefer in a cowardly manner to hide myself under your name."[5]

As Adams recalled fifty years later, Palfrey had advised him that his critique would "break as much glass, as any other stone that could be thrown by a beginner." The article of 1867 not only "broke glass" but launched Adams's literary career.[6] The review begins by praising Deane for presenting "an argument which aims at nothing less than the entire erasure of one of the most attractive portions of American history." He followed this with a summary of the once-sacrosanct Smith legend and a parallel examination of passages from the *True Relation* and *Generall Historie.* From this comparison, Adams concluded that the *Generall Historie* was "remarkable for a curious air of exaggeration" and that the rescue story survived because historians perpetuated it; even Bancroft had relayed it as fact in the first version of his epic history, although the historian had corrected the "blunder" in later editions.[7]

Perhaps Adams's greatest contribution was discerning the potential for polemic in the ongoing debate over the rescue. "The quiet investigations of Mr. Deane," he wrote, "now make it absolutely necessary" for every historian to take a side, though "unfortunately, there is no possibility of compromise in the dispute." Adams left no doubt about which side of the "serious question" he preferred. In the course of the article, he underscored complaints by Smith's contemporaries; he attacked Pocahontas's morality by quoting Strachey's description of her as "a well featured but wanton yong girle" who romped naked with the boys of Jamestown; he dismissed Van de Passe's portrait of Lady Rebecca as "a somewhat hard-featured figure" that did not resemble an Indian; and he accused Smith of inventing the rescue in order to link himself with Pocahontas after she had impressed the English upper crust during her London visit. He ended with a censure of the *Generall Historie*:

> Pocahontas was made to appear ... as a kind of stage deity on every possible occasion, and his [Smith's] own share in the affairs of the colony is magnified at the expense of all his companions. None of those whose reputations he treated with so much harshness appeared to vindicate their own characters, far less to assert the facts in regard to Pocahontas ... but in the absence of criticism, due perhaps to the political excitement of the times, his book survived to become the standard authority on Virginian history. The readiness with which it was received is scarcely so remarkable as the credulity which has left it unquestioned almost to the present day.[8]

With this closing statement, Adams succeeded in delivering a death blow to the Virginia myth by falsifying its very core. And by insisting that historians must be forced to take sides, he fired the initial shot in a debate that would rage for two decades. One of the first to take up the cudgels for the Yankees was Edward Duffield Neill. Born in Philadelphia, Neill was educated in New England and ordained there as a Presbyterian minister; he then served as an army chaplain during the Civil War, later becoming assistant secretary to Presidents Abraham Lincoln and Andrew Johnson. After the war, he briefly acted as consul in Dublin but gave up public service to settle in Minnesota and become the first president of Macalester College.[9] Like Palfrey, Neill conducted historical research with a missionary zeal that produced several publications, among them the *History of the Virginia Company* (1869) and *Virginia Vetusta* (1885).

Both books pose an alternative history for the Jamestown colony that comes close to ignoring Smith and Pocahontas altogether. But in that small portion of the text devoted to the Virginia heroes, Neill charged with a vengeance. Although he could produce little verifiable documentation to back up his argument, he confidently proclaimed that Rolfe had arrived in Virginia with a white wife and child, both of whom subsequently died, and shortly thereafter, he "formed a connection with the Indian woman Pocahontas." To substantiate his case, Neill insisted not only that there was no evidence to prove that the pair ever married but that Pocahontas was buried in England "as the wife of Thomas Wroth," not John Rolfe. According to Neill, a few years after Pocahontas died, Rolfe returned to Virginia and married a woman named Jane Pierce with whom he had a son, Thomas, and a daughter, Jane. It was *those* children who sired the plantation aristocracy from which so many Virginians claimed descent. As proof of this allegation, Neill disclosed that Rolfe's will bestowed his entire estate to the offspring of this last marriage and no child by Pocahontas was even mentioned. This left little doubt, Neill concluded, that the bluebloods of Virginia should trace their lineage to John Rolfe and Jane Pierce, not to Pocahontas.[10]

Neill's largely undocumented text was more than Virginians could stomach. William Wirt Henry—grandson of the legendary Patrick Henry and namesake of the lawyer William Wirt—published a rebuttal in 1875 and enlarged it in an address delivered to the Virginia Historical Society in 1882.[11] His defense of Pocahontas, Rolfe, and Smith was calculated to rescue the state's origin legend from its thorough lambasting by Northerners. If the "feeble colony" of Jamestown had perished, Henry observed, Spaniards "who were already planted in Florida and Mexico, would alike present the wretched appearance of a mongrel population, in the admixture of three races—Spanish, Indian and African. In a word, North America would have been Mexicanized."[12] The well-respected lawyer certainly chose a peculiar argument to introduce his defense of an interracial union that ostensibly produced Virginia's first families.

Nevertheless, in the detailed history of Jamestown that followed, Henry presented a well-crafted answer to the accusations leveled by all who "sneer at the veracity of Smith, the virtue of Pocahontas, and the honesty of Rolfe." He dismantled publications that the critics of Smith had cited as evidence; he avowed that because Wingfield and Smith were "bitter enemies," the former's credibility should be doubted; and he indicated that William Strachey's oft-quoted passage about the young Pocahontas romping with the Jamestown boys was merely an elaboration of Smith's descriptions and not a contradiction. Many other measured and legalistic responses to specific points compose the body of the text, in which Henry pointed an angry finger at the recent critics and condemned their research as being not only highly biased but also riddled with obvious omissions and unjust insinuations.[13]

Toward Neill, Henry leveled his angriest reproof, chiefly because the clergyman implied that Rolfe and Pocahontas were never lawfully married. In answer to these accusations, he ended his long defense with a standard justification of Virginia's origin myth. Rolfe, he insisted, "will ever be remembered in history" as the

> husband of Pocahontas, who, born the daughter of a savage King, was endowed with all the graces of character which become a Christian princess; who was the first of her people to embrace Christianity, and to unite in marriage with the English race; who, like a guardian angel, watched over and preserved the infant colony which has developed into a great people, among whom her own descendants have ever been conspicuous for true nobility; and whose name will be honored while this great people occupy the land upon which she so signally aided in establishing them.[14]

Repetition of the tired and overblown rhetoric only seemed to undercut Henry's valid criticism of New England's partisan accusations, thus rendering his account of Virginia's genesis legend convincing only to survivors of the plantation South.[15]

John Esten Cooke's novel *My Lady Pokahontas*, which came out in 1885, the same year that Neill published *Virginia Vetusta*, was a fictitious corollary to William Wirt Henry's legalistic defense of John Smith. Cooke treated his state's genesis legend as if it were an actual seventeenth-century document related by the "brave and trusty soldier" Anas Todkill. The book's subtitle proclaims that Todkill—who had actually been an aide to John Smith—was a "Puritan and Pilgrim," a clear declaration that Cooke was trying to counteract the New England critics by making the Virginia tale appear to be a Puritan testimony. The book's introduction summarizes the author's intentions:

> When that blessed damozel, my dear Lady Pokahontas, died untimely, I fell into a great wonder at the mysterious ways of Providence that put out that bright light of our time so sudden. Virginia had much need of her to bring her people to the knowledge of our Saviour. But she went away to heaven even at the moment when she was returning to her country, and her hope to have builded up a New Jerusalem in that Heathennesse had no fruit, but was buried in her grave. She had surely done her work to God's honour and immortal glory natheless, ne'er was it begun.[16]

In the course of the narrative, Todkill condemns the captain's enemies (Wingfield, "a fat merchant"; Ratcliffe, "a counterfeit impostor") while portraying Pocahontas as a playful child with the maturity of a woman. She often visited the town, he recalls, "decently clad in her robe of birds' feathers" and during those visits formed a close but chaste friendship with Smith, who taught her the English language and the customs of his homeland. Cooke enlivened the story by hinting that Pocahontas loved Smith more deeply than Rolfe, although the author always described their relationship as the infatuation of a pure young maiden for an older and wiser father figure. Because of her many kind deeds, Todkill calls Pocahontas his "guardian angel" and implies that she is a Puritan "saint." Subsequently, the narrator, who remains at Jamestown after Smith's departure, witnesses the courtship of Pocahontas and Rolfe ("a grave, staid man, much given to religious exercises") and attends both her baptism and marriage. He accompanies the Rolfes to London, visiting the Globe Theatre with them, where they view *The Tempest* and talk to Shakespeare. Later, Todkill witnesses the tearful reunion of Pocahontas and Smith, shortly after which the heroine meets her "melancholy" death.[17]

Cooke's fictitious romance and Wirt's legalistic defense signify the Old Dominion's frantic attempt to resuscitate the Jamestown legend and redeem the colony's rightful place as the first English settlement in America. But the Virginians were working against overwhelming odds. In the postbellum United States, the Pilgrims reigned as primary founders of a reunited nation. Lincoln's proclamation of 1863 making Thanksgiving a national holiday helped accelerate the process that was already well underway due to the many New England missionaries who had spread their origin myth from coast to coast. After Appomattox, the Pilgrims were even credited with influencing the Union victory, a message that pervaded the 250th anniversary commemoration of the Pilgrims' landing in 1870.

Robert Winthrop, a veteran of Forefathers' Day orations, delivered the principal address for the celebration at Plymouth. Now an old man who had served his state in the United States Senate and House, he once more reiterated the familiar story and in the course of his address hinted about New England's leading role in establishing the ideology that had held together the Union and conquered Southern "tyranny . . . in the great struggle which has so recently terminated."[18] Other speakers at the banquet were far more belligerent. The master of ceremonies asked Major General Oliver Otis Howard (later a primary founder of Howard University) to respond to the toast: "Plymouth and Jamestown—the Pilgrims and the Cavaliers—Freedom and Slavery. They met on the field of Gettysburg, and Freedom conquered." As one of the heroes of that battle, Howard attributed the triumph of "Freedom" over "Slavery" to "that little compact which was made before the Pilgrims landed." Former senator Henry Wilson declared: "The example of the Pilgrims . . . inspired William Lloyd Garrison when he proclaimed immediate emancipation" and "inspired Abraham Lincoln in his immortal Proclamation of Emancipation, which smote the fetters from the limbs of three and a half million men."[19] Garrison himself attributed the success of his abolition campaign to lessons learned from the Pilgrims. In a letter to the Pilgrim Society in which he expressed regrets that he would be unable to attend the celebration, the aging abolitionist wrote:

> It was in support of civil and religious liberty that the Pilgrims of the Mayflower encountered the most formidable dangers, and made the most heroic sacrifices . . . no commemoration of their worth is deserving of record which is not inspired by a noble purpose to draw from their example incentives to higher aspirations and a broader recognition of human rights than has yet been attained even in our own land.[20]

Most prominent New Englanders of 1870 were firmly convinced that the conquest of the South and termination of slavery were linked directly to the ideals of "civil and religious liberty" that the Pilgrims brought to America. That seventeenth-century Massachusetts had virtually no civil or religious liberty as then understood made little difference; the correlation between Pilgrim ideals and the Union victory had been so often repeated that most Northerners accepted it without question. But at the same time, Massachusetts was beginning to smile about absurdities inherent in its overblown past, even when celebrating the 250th anniversary of the Pilgrims' landing. For example, the old hair-splitting dispute over distinctions between Puritans and Pilgrims had so lost its controversial edge by 1870 that Edward Everett could joke about it in a poem written especially for the Forefathers' Day banquet:

> *We know the fun you love so well at Puritans to poke,*
> *Your witches and your Quakers and every threadbare joke.*
> *Go read your history, school-boys; learn on one glorious page,*
> *The Pilgrim towers untainted above that iron age.*
> *From stains of mightiest heroes the Pilgrims' hands are clean,*
> *In Plymouth's free and peaceful streets no bigot's stake was seen;*
> *The sons of other saints may wince and pale beneath your mock,*
> *Harmless the fool-born jesting flows back from Plymouth Rock.*[21]

Everett's humorous dismissal of a subject that had provoked thoughtful historical investigations and even heated squabbles only two decades earlier marked a sea change in attitudes. When it spread from its regional base to become a national genesis legend, the Plymouth story lost its grip on New England. No longer relevant as a blanket ancestral legacy for a now-diversified region, the Pilgrim tale joined such staples as George Washington's cherry tree and Abraham Lincoln's log cabin to become an emblem of American patriotism.

One need look no further than the U.S. Centennial Exposition of 1876 to find proof that the founders of Plymouth had entered the realm of popular Americana. At the Philadelphia fair, paintings, decorative arts, home furnishings, and architecture all focused on Pilgrim themes; and in the next fifty years—during the so-called Colonial Revival—American material culture became saturated with "authentic" Pilgrim styles and practices.[22] The 1876 centennial also announced to the world that the United States wanted to forget the war and diminish sectional animosities, a pacifistic attitude that signaled new ways to evaluate the Virginia and Massachusetts origin myths.[23] As wartime tempers cooled and the nation began assessing its unprecedented losses, an intense conflict between genesis legends seemed foolish, if not perilous. Although many Virginians still clung tenaciously to the veracity of the Jamestown romance and numerous Bay Staters still boasted about their *Mayflower* ancestry, only the diehards felt it was worth fighting about. But the North's victory assured the Massachusetts legend of its prominent place in history books, whereas its Virginia counterpart was relegated to the realm of fiction.

Two paintings exemplify these perceptions of the Plymouth and Jamestown origin myths during the 1870s. Both are oversized canvases, both reproduced as popular prints. One is George Henry Boughton's *Pilgrims Going to Church* (Fig. 11.1); the other is Victor Nehlig's *Pocahontas Saving the Life of John Smith* (Fig. 11.2). The English-born Boughton was living in London when he painted *Pilgrims Going to Church,* but he had spent his childhood in Albany, New York; Nehlig created *Pocahontas* in New York City, but he had grown up in France. Both artists, therefore, were able to approach their subjects from the perspective of knowledgeable outsiders with a full understanding of how the origin legends were interpreted in the United States.

Boughton's *Pilgrims Going to Church*—first exhibited at London's Royal Academy in 1867 and featured nine years later at the Philadelphia centennial—pictures a group of somberly dressed Pilgrims trudging through a snowy wilderness. An elderly, bearded clergyman clutching his bible accompanies them, and all appear earnest and peaceful, even though several men carry muskets to protect the churchgoers from possible dangers that lurk in the frozen woodlands. The composition is conceived in terms of straight lines and right angles, with few diagonals to break the horizontal procession as it moves silently along the white surface. No one is animated, no one speaks; even the children seem subdued as they accompany their parents in this ritual family outing. Nor is there much color in Boughton's palette: Only the dull green or blue of shadows, the deep red of a child's coat, and the pale pink of faces break the gray monotony.

254

FIGURE 11.1   *George Henry Boughton,* Pilgrims Going to Church, *oil on canvas,*
1867. Collection of the New York Historical Society, New York, N.Y.

FIGURE 11.2
Victor Nehlig, Pocahontas
Saving the Life of John
Smith, *oil on canvas,*
1870. Courtesy of Museum
of Art, Brigham Young
University, Provo, Utah.
All Rights Reserved.

The mood and the subjects of Boughton's composition seemed appropriately sober and pious. Following the artistic trends of the time, he aligned his subjects in the horizontal procession familiar from English and European salon paintings of a few years earlier; and as in those works, he included children and old people within the group.[24] These were familiar neighbors with prayer book in hand walking through the snow on a wintry Sunday. They look "right" because the costume that had been slowly aggrandizing since the 1850s was fully accepted by the 1870s. The men wear knee breeches, their dark, belted military-style jackets and tall black top hats reminiscent of contemporary fashions of the previous generation; the girls and women have on plain gray or black dresses with wide white collars, some wearing aprons and hooded capes, others white or black caps, and one has a felt top hat similar to the illustration in Bartlett's book. By the 1880s, that "uniform" had become codified into a standard Pilgrim costume and was permanently attached to all future representations of the Plymouth settlers (Figs. 11.3 and 11.4).

The prominence of Boughton's *Pilgrims Going to Church* at the 1876 centennial was but one of many indications that the artist had captured a proper notion of America's colonial past that matched late nineteenth-century popular perceptions of the Pilgrims.[25] Nehlig elicited a very different mood in *Pocahontas Saving the Life of John Smith* (see Fig. 11.2), which he painted on a seven-foot vertical canvas in 1870 and copied as a slightly altered horizontal lithograph four years later.[26] In both media, Nehlig turned the rescue of Smith into a study in turbulence. Unlike Boughton's calm, angular procession, Nehlig designed a dramatic swirl of overlapping lines and jutting diagonals.

A rather youthful Powhatan, dominating the upper portion of the painting, stands on a rocky ledge with arms extended and is the only stationary figure above a mélange of tangled forms. Directly below him is an adolescent Pocahontas, described in a pamphlet printed to accompany the lithograph as "a lovely Indian maiden just budding into womanhood."[27] Bare to the waist, this nubile young woman stands poised between Smith (awkwardly resting on one knee with his head tipped backward) and a muscular brave with his axe hoisted for the strike. On the right, two other male Indians tug on the rope that tethers Smith to his rock. Smoke from a fire billows behind Smith's head; other Indians (including a medicine man in a horned

FIGURE 11.3
George Henry Boughton, Priscilla
and John Alden, *engraving,
1889. Division of Prints and
Photograps , Library of Congress,
Washington, D.C.*

FIGURE 11.4   *Howard Chandler
Christy,* Priscilla Mullen and John
Alden, *1903, Illustration for Henry
Wadsworth Longfellow,* Courtship of
Miles Standish.

headdress at the top left) form a circle around the periphery. Like Boughton and other artists of the period, Nehlig avoided bright colors, but instead of the cool grays used by his English contemporary, he chose warm browns and coppery crimson to emphasize the "redman's" skin tones. Therefore, both the color scheme and the smoking fire create a heated intensity that invokes an opposite sensory response to the icy landscape of Boughton's work. Nehlig's *Pocahontas,* in fact, not only revives the half-nude, sexy portrayal of Pocahontas but depicts the stereotypical violent, uncontrollable Indians then associated with the Wild West. Both characterizations were designed to enhance print sales.

Writing about the Nehlig's painting during its first exhibition, a New York critic remarked:

> The love of the Indian princess for the daring white adventurer, Captain Smith, has always been a favorite theme with Americans. It was one of the few striking romantic incidents which relieved the correct, but somewhat dull, foundation of the infant republic. In spite of the cant about "our ancestors" who came over on that eternal Mayflower, there is a well founded, though not oft expressed, suspicion that the Pilgrim Fathers were rather a heavy set of people after all, very much given to psalm singing, but with a rather sharp eye to business. They were not good subjects for pictures, being too angular and demure, and not even making GOOD RELIGIOUS SUBJECTS, for their severity was rather that of soldiers than of apostles. From this type of muscular christians the artist turns away in despair and seeks in foreign lands kindlier subjects for his pencil.
>
> The story of Pocahontas and her romantic affection for the buccaneering captain stands boldly relieved in the melancholy records of the colonization, and, as it is surrounded by something of the mystery and uncertainty of the fable, possesses an interest that no other incident in our early history can calm [claim].[28]

This observation, reproduced in the advertising pamphlet for the lithograph, opens a window onto popular perceptions of the origin legends in the postwar years. In a narrow sense, the author treated the two stories as polarities, thereby offering Americans a choice between the "eternal Mayflower" and Pocahontas's "romantic affection." For this writer—and indeed for the nation—the Pilgrims connoted a moral parable about goodness and piety, whereas the

Pocahontas story was a fanciful romance, therefore considered salacious and exciting. The individual who bought a print of the Pilgrims
to hang over the mantle might be a patriot wanting to touch the colonial past or perhaps a religious person wanting to be reminded of
early American devotion. The buyer choosing Pocahontas, however,
wanted adventure, fun, and perhaps even a bit of naughtiness. In the
broader sense, the New York reviewer not only made an observation
about why people purchased works of art but, more significantly,
also observed the manner in which both origin legends had entered
the realm of popular culture by 1870.

The commentary also indicates that both genesis legends were being treated lightly. Although Pocahontas had been the brunt of
Northern jokes for several decades, it was not until well after the
Civil War that the nation could laugh at the overinflated Pilgrims. No
one did it better than Mark Twain. In an after-dinner speech delivered to the first annual meeting of the New England Society of
Philadelphia in 1881, he questioned why on earth they were celebrating the Pilgrims' landing. "It was as cold as death off Cape Code
there," he jibed. "Why shouldn't they come ashore? If they *hadn't*
landed there would be some reason for celebrating the fact."

Then he joked that he was "a border ruffian" from the state of Missouri and his first American ancestor was an Indian. "Your ancestors," he said, "skinned him alive"; his other ancestors were Quakers
and "your tribe chased them out of the country for their religion's
sake. . . . Your ancestors—yes, they were a hard lot but nevertheless
they gave us religious liberty to worship as they required us to worship, and political liberty to vote as the church required." Following
this line, Twain claimed numerous ancestors—from Salem witches to
slaves—and admitted that he was "a mixed breed, an infinitely
shaded and exquisite Mongrel." For this reason, he suggested that
they "disband these New England societies," which were "nurseries
of a system of steady augmenting laudation and hosannaing" and
hold an auction to sell Plymouth Rock. "The Pilgrims were a simple
and ignorant race," he teased. "They never had seen any good rocks
before, or at least any that were not watched, and so they were ex-
cusable for hopping ashore in frantic delight and clapping an iron
fence around this one."[29]

The members of the Forefathers' Day audience who laughed at
this typical Mark Twain put-down had moved beyond their parents.

They had grown weary of writers quibbling about the ideological differences between Virginia and Massachusetts and realized it was time to redress the meanings of the origin myth.[30] In the battle to sanctify their forebears and demean their opponents, the antebellum mythmakers had so expanded and exaggerated their regional genesis legends that the message had lost its persuasiveness. Twain's jesting sent a clear signal that a scarred and maturing nation was learning from the devastations of war that excessive regional chauvinism could have deadly consequences.

12

The Myths Triumphant

By the 1870s, the diehards—who included chauvinistic Massachusetts superpatriots and Virginians lamenting their "lost cause"—became even more determined to reinvigorate the legends as a means of reviving regional consciousness. In their zeal to accomplish this, the New England and Virginia loyalists set off on a fifty-year campaign to memorialize their ancestors with a panoply of monuments and memorials. The town of Plymouth was the logical starting point, forced as it was to take the Pilgrims seriously. Indeed thousands of tourists streamed in each year, keeping local businesses alive. With an eye toward enhancing its tourist attractions, the Pilgrim Society had planned to build a canopy over Plymouth Rock and a large Pilgrim monument well before the Civil War began. In the 1850s, the society had hired Boston artist Hammatt Billings—a descendant of the Mayflower passenger John Howland—to draw up plans for both structures. Best known as an illustrator of children's books and romantic fiction, Billings carried his love of fantasy into his designs.[1] He conceived the Plymouth Rock canopy as a two-tiered granite edifice bolstered on the corners by pairs of Doric piers, with each of the four facades opened by massive arches (Fig. 12.1).[2] Stone scallop shells—symbols of pilgrimages to the tomb of St. James on the coast of Spain—crowned all four vaults of the roof, thus giving the canopy a paradoxical link to one of Europe's most sacred Catholic shrines. In fact, its Baroque design resembled the ornate baldachinos (altars)

FIGURE 12.1   *Hammatt Billings, Plymouth Rock canopy, photograph, c. 1866. Courtesy of the Pilgrim Society, Plymouth, Mass.*

found in many Italian cathedrals, thus posing another unlikely association with the Roman Church.

The Plymouth sponsors apparently ignored these contradictions, and plans for expediting the canopy progressed rapidly. By 1859, the cornerstone and base were in place, but construction halted during the Civil War. Finally, in 1867, engineers hoisted the bottom section of the rock from under the wharf, moved it to the waterfront, and placed it under the new canopy. Meanwhile, the top half of the relic rested in its cage outside Pilgrim Hall while members of the society sought funds and technical advice to expedite coupling the two segments. The reunification of Plymouth Rock occurred in 1880, when Pilgrim Society member J. Henry Stickney underwrote transportation of the upper portion to the waterfront. Before the crew placed it under Billings's canopy, a stonecutter carved "1620" into the cracked facade, after which the two halves of Plymouth Rock were rejoined after more than a century of separation.[3]

At the same time, a short distance from the center of Plymouth, the Forefathers Monument (Fig. 12.2) was slowly rising.[4] For many years, Billings had been designing imaginary colossal statues, and when the Pilgrim Society granted the commission in 1853, he eagerly began making sketches. He had originally hoped to erect the "grandest work of its kind in the world," one dwarfed only by the colossi of Egypt. Had the National Monument to the Forefathers been constructed in accordance with the designer's grandiose vision, it would have been equal in size to the Statue of Liberty. With

Billings's mammoth design in mind, the Pilgrim Society designated a hill adjacent to Allerton Street as the site for the monument, and by 1859, the cornerstone—filled with historical papers, books, maps, diplomas, and a small piece of Plymouth Rock—was in place.[5] After the interruption of the Civil War, the Pilgrim Society decided to delay work on the monument until the Plymouth Rock project was completed. As time passed, however, the enthusiasm that had once made Bay Staters eager to fund the ambitious monument waned, and as the coffers diminished, so did the size of the statue. In 1874, Billings

FIGURE 12.2   *Hammatt Billings, National Monument to the Forefathers, Plymouth, Mass., photograph, n.d. Pilgrim Hall, Plymouth, Mass.*

reluctantly agreed to reduce the dimensions by half.[6] A few months after making that concession, the designer died, and construction halted once more.

Two years later, it resumed under the supervision of the designer's brother, Joseph Billings, but in 1880, he too expired, and when his successor, Reverend Willard M. Harding, also died a few months after assuming his duties, it appeared that the ancestors were expressing doubts about the projected colossus and its overseers. Despite its ill-fated start, the monument slowly began to rise under the general direction of the Pilgrim Society. In 1886, with construction in Plymouth still underway, the city of New York unveiled Frederic-Auguste Bartholdi's much larger Statue of Liberty; three years went by before Plymouth was at last ready to dedicate its own long-awaited monument.[7]

The eighty-one-foot colossus that now towers over the town is compelling—not so much as a tribute to the Pilgrim past but rather as a manifestation of the then popular Beaux Arts style. During the latter part of the nineteenth century, female statues were typically seen as personifications of abstract principles, a mindset that enabled Bartholdi to consider his sculpture to be a symbol of American "liberty" and Billings to designate the statue atop the Forefathers Monument as a stone embodiment of "faith." In formal design, therefore, the two statues are similar; both are gigantic women draped in Greco-Roman robes, and both stand erect with the right arm raised. Faith clutches the bible with her left hand; Liberty holds a tablet inscribed with the date of American independence. Faith's title, her index finger pointing to heaven, and her opened bible all suggest the Pilgrims' religious foundation; the four allegorical figures—two male and two female—grouped around the octagonal pedestal are meant to represent "Morality," "Education," "Law," and "Liberty," those pillars of society and government that the Pilgrim fathers supposedly brought to America.[8]

Following the then current trend toward French-inspired classicism, Billings believed it perfectly logical to memorialize a simple and pious band of early seventeenth-century English men and women with a huge classical "goddess." But today the Forefathers Monument seems little more than an awkward imitation of a fashionable artistic convention. In some ways, the more sensitively executed and highly symbolic Statue of Liberty is different, because Bartholdi designed it as a tribute to republicanism and therefore included the classical torch and drapery to symbolize the Greco-Roman roots of the American republic.[9] Billing's Faith, by contrast, was meant to commemorate a band of religious separatists, and therefore the ersatz Grecian references echo the Beaux Arts style but reveal little about the Pilgrims. Not only was classicism an inappropriate means for conveying the elementary Puritanism of the separatists but the very size and complexity of the monument seems to contradict the notion that the Pilgrims came to escape the excessive materialism of Europe. Perhaps the initial concept somehow became lost in the shuffle of supervisors after Hammatt Billings's death, but as it stands, the Pilgrim Monument seems rife with contradictions. Its gigantic proportions and self-conscious monumentality best illustrate the boastful confidence of the victors in the wake of Lee's surrender, and the monument therefore reigns as a supreme example of the Pilgrim heritage's bloated prominence during the late nineteenth century.

The inconsistencies of the Pilgrim Monument apparently seemed less offensive to Plymouth residents than Billings's Baroque baldachino covering their sacred rock. Beyond the fact that the papal-altar style appeared jarring and old-fashioned, many devoted descendants were dissatisfied that the canopy stood amidst warehouses a good distance from the shoreline. As the tercentenary of the Pilgrims' landing approached in 1920, members of the Pilgrim Society decided it was time to properly venerate New England's most treasured relic by relocating it near the water's edge. Assured that modern technology would prevent further destruction, the society proceeded with plans for redesigning the harbor, with Plymouth Rock as its centerpiece. The National Society of Colonial Dames agreed to sponsor construction of the park and engaged the architectural firm McKim, Mead, and White to devise a new neoclassical canopy to shelter the rock. Several years and $51,800 later, Plymouth Rock rested under a flat roof surrounded by sixteen Doric columns topped by a simple frieze (Fig. 12.3). As the town had to contend with a classical goddess to memorialize the hallowed forefathers, few seemed to mind that an updated replica of the temples built to consecrate Greek deities was covering the iconic representation of a breakaway Protestant sect.[10]

On November 29, 1921, the day set aside for the dedication, torrential rains and heavy winds inspired Pilgrim Society president Arthur Lord to greet the crowd packed inside the First Parish Church with the opening lines of William Cullen Bryant's poem: "Wild was the day; the wintry sea / Moaned sadly on New England's strand." The rock, Lord said, now "rests in its original position by the waterside, and the waves of the Bay which the keel of the Mayflower once plowed, again and forever break upon it as in the Pilgrim days."[11] Nobody questioned the fact that the "original position" of the hallowed rock had been altered, as was the appearance of "the encircling shore." With a new sea wall, paved sidewalks, and neoclassical portico, Plymouth harbor had changed markedly in three hundred years. Indeed, the original Mayflower passengers would surely have been shocked, if not repelled, by the array of monuments and quaint restored homes that had transformed their simple village into a historic shrine.

FIGURE 12.3   *McKim, Mead, and White, Plymouth Rock canopy, photograph, c. 1925. Courtesy of the Pilgrim Society, Plymouth, Mass.*

In 1920, Lyon G. Tyler (son of John Tyler, then serving as president of William and Mary College) lamented Virginia's historical ostracism. "The world is now perfectly convinced that the birthplace of the nation was really on the shores of Cape Cod," he wrote, "and this belief is due entirely to the vociferous propaganda that has been going on ever since the fall of the Confederacy. . . . We were conquered, and one of the penalties was the stealing of our history."[12] The war-torn Old Dominion had indeed lacked the wherewithal—but not the desire—to build elaborate monuments in the late nineteenth century. With their fabled Cavalier myth in shambles, heirs of the once-proud plantation elite became suddenly desperate to preserve and refurbish their colonial heritage.

For that purpose, the Association for the Preservation of Virginia Antiquities was born in 1889; and within only a few years after receiving its charter, the APVA had become one of the most active and influential of all Southern memorial organizations. Spearheaded by a formidable array of socially prominent Richmond women, the APVA's primary mission was safeguarding the state's historical landmarks. At the top of the list was Jamestown. Even in its desolate state, the island's historical significance convinced a series of entrepreneurs that the site might be turned into a profitable venture. The property exchanged hands several times, but each investor watched his money become mired in the intemperate climate and murky bogs.[13] The last of these speculators, Ohio industrialist Edward E. Barney, purchased Jamestown in 1892 for $15,000. Scarcely was the ink dry on the contract before APVA members petitioned him to relinquish a 22.5-acre stretch along the waterfront. A mere four months later, these guardians of Virginia tradition had convinced Barney to reluctantly deed the desired acreage to the preservation society.

The APVA wasted no time in establishing machinery to protect its historic district. Until 1895, visitors had been free to dock excursion boats on the riverfront, picnic along the shore, and roam all around the island, but the APVA restricted free access to the ruins and limited admission to its twenty-two-acre site.[14]

On the APVA's property stood the graveyard, the remains of the Confederate fort, and the old church tower. Residents of the Old Dominion had the opportunity to place that icon in its proper perspective when the Colonial Dames—that predominantly Yankee lifeline for memorials—offered to finance a new church adjacent to the tower, to be ready for dedication during the 1907 tercentenary. Although Virginia traditionalists and preservation purists opposed building any permanent structure on the island, the opportunity to reconstruct the old church was too tempting to refuse.[15] Much to the chagrin of loyal Virginians, the Colonial Dames selected a Boston architect, Edward M. Wheelwright, to design the reconstructed edifice. His model for the project was St. Luke's Church in Isle of Wight County, Virginia, built in 1632 and believed to be the oldest remaining Protestant house of worship in North America.

Because the old brick tower was so revered, the architect decided to alter it little and merely attach it as an entrance to the new building (Fig. 12.4). Preservation of the tower, however, was the only conservation measure taken. Before and during the reconstruction, APVA members and other prestigious onlookers were allowed to rummage through the ancient rubble, their excavations resulting in

FIGURE 12.4 *Jamestown Church,*
Jamestown, Va., 1994. Photograph by author.

the displacement, if not the removal, of priceless artifacts. Even more unsettling was the search for facing materials. In an attempt to provide an "authentic" facade, two seventeenth-century homes met the wrecker's ball so that their salt-glazed brick could be used to cover the new church's exterior.[16] The Jamestown Memorial Church was therefore a conglomerate of demolished authenticity and ersatz verisimilitude.

A week before the scheduled dedication of the new church, the Colonial Dames formally presented the building to the APVA, whose members may have blanched at being dependent on Yankee largesse but received the gift with professed gratitude.

A spirit of brotherhood between former enemies governed the dedication on May 13, 1907, the 300th anniversary of the British landing at Jamestown. In an address prepared for the occasion, author Thomas Nelson Page advised the South to accept its diminished role graciously. "Virginian, as I am in every fiber of my being," Page proclaimed, "I declare my belief before the high God that this spot belongs by indefeasible title to all the people of this country."[17] The island had been saved from further deterioration, the church had risen phoenix-like out of the ruins, and memories of the state's original ancestors had been preserved for posterity.

The Jamestown tercentenary also seemed an ideal time to commemorate Pocahontas by placing a statue of the Indian heroine on the island. In April 1906, Mrs. Thomas Bagby of West Point, Virginia, announced formation of a new society in Washington, D.C., its mission to erect a testimonial to "the fidelity and devotion of this Indian maiden." The Pocahontas Association, which was composed primarily of women who traced their heritage back to the union between Powhatan's daughter and John Rolfe, then commissioned William Ordway Partridge to design the sculpture.[18] After conducting research at the Anthropological Bureau of the Smithsonian Institution and making sketches of Algonquian models, the sculptor determined to depict Pocahontas "at the moment when she comes from the tent of Powhattan, her father, to beg colonists to flee from death."[19] Although a model of the statue stood on the grounds of the 1907 Jamestown Tercentenary Exposition, the sponsoring organization did not have sufficient funds to allow casting of the piece in bronze. In 1911, Partridge told Cuyler Reynolds that the model for "poor little Pocahontas" still lived in his studio, awaiting its larger reincarnation. Five years later, the Pocahontas Association did manage to underwrite the casting of an eighteen-inch bronze replica to present as a gift to Edith Bolling Galt when she married President Woodrow Wilson. It was well after the conclusion of World War I, however, before Partridge's completed statue (Fig. 12.5) occupied "her permanent abiding place" at Jamestown.[20]

The dedication of Pocahontas in June 1922 typified the strange mixture of genealogical pride and inherent condescension that overshadowed the Virginia legend. Gathered at Jamestown that June day were some of the state's most prominent citizens, along with a "full blooded Indian of the Rappahannock tribe in native dress" accompanied by some of his kinsmen. All claimed to be descendants of Powhatan. At that time, the Rappahannocks were seeking to change the Virginia law that prohibited them from voting in local elections. Although the APVA and the Pocahontas Association, joint sponsors of the ceremony, offered verbal support for the Rappahannocks' campaign, their speeches at the dedication rang with echoes of ingrained bigotry. When Richmond socialite Cynthia Tucker Coleman, daughter of Nathaniel Beverley Tucker, summarized the familiar story of the "gentle" Pocahontas's marriage and conversion, she remarked: "The time had come when this fair western world was to be redeemed from the dominion of the savage to yield its wealth of soil and climate to that race which should dominate the world."[21] These were hardly conciliatory words for the Rappahannocks in the audience.

Mrs. Coleman's rhetoric does characterize Partridge's bronze Pocahontas, who seems to burst from the wilderness to "save" the white

Figure 12.5 *William Ordway Partridge,* Pocahontas, *bronze,* 1907–1922, *Jamestown, Va., Photograph courtesy of the Association for the Preservation of Virginia Antiquities.*

community from slaughter by her relatives. Not only does she look far older than a girl whose entire life spanned only twenty-two years, but her long hair topped by a feather and her hawk-beaked features epitomize early twentieth-century stereotypical notions about the Indians. Despite this, Partridge's statue is dramatically different from earlier representations of Pocahontas. No longer the half-dressed, vulnerable object of male voyeurism, she is in command of her surroundings.[22] And she also transcends the one-dimensional "Lady Rebecca" of the Cavalier past. This mature Pocahontas personifies the proud and defiant women of the APVA, who staked their claim on Jamestown Island, and the determined women of the Pocahontas Association, who persisted in procuring and installing the statue. In short, she was an emblem of reconstructed Virginia–forceful, determined, and proud.

By 1922, when that dedication on Jamestown took place, the historical legend that the statue commemorated no longer had the same meaning as a century earlier. Standing near the entrance to the APVA's protected area, Partridge's sculpture symbolizes a postbellum version of the old tale, renovated to conform with the reconstructed Jamestown Memorial Church that Pocahontas seems to be guarding. Both statue and edifice were intended to evoke the ethos of a mythic past, but neither succeeds. The exaggerated chauvinism that drove the Old Dominion origin myth to the forefront of sectional propaganda a half-century earlier had vanished, taking with it the central motivation for Virginians to defend a legend about the courageous young Indian, purported ancestor of the leading Tidewater planters.

Two vignettes seem to sum up the legacies of Pocahontas and the Pilgrims in the antebellum years. The first comes from Oklahoma, where in June 1899, "a group of fun loving girls" in the Oowala Community of the old Cherokee nation organized a society named after "this country's first Indian heroine." Soon, the Pocahontas Club had spread to other Oklahoma towns. "The pride of our Ancient Race we nourish and support," declared a spokesperson for the Claremore chapter, in order that "its traditions, lore and legends may not perish from the earth."[23] Just as the New England Societies of Charleston and New York became a nucleus for perpetuating a transplanted culture, the Cherokees in Oklahoma similarly safeguarded the heritage of their people.

Ironically, the society's early activities, though centered upon tribal traditions, evoked many symbols that today seem derisive. At their "Evening with Hiawatha" of 1901, for example, Will Rogers (a supporter of the organization) appeared decked out in Indian regalia, replete with "war paint, a tomahawk and other paraphernalia." Later that year, the Oklahoma club sponsored a float in the local parade which "depicted a party of warriors in full dress preparing to execute Captain John Smith with Pocahontas intervening."[24] If Pocahontas's rescue of Smith did allow the English to remain in America, as Virginians claimed, then reenactment of that scene in a Cherokee parade indicates that the romanticism of the legend overshadowed any logical analysis of its meaning.

The ladies of Virginia shared more with their counterparts in Oklahoma than might first appear. Both groups chose Pocahontas to represent their ancestral link to a distant world that had been subsumed by the complexities of industrial America. Whether their identities were European or Native American, these two Pocahontas societies mimicked each other by attempting to recreate a mythic past that was rapidly degenerating into a kind of souvenir-shop kitsch.

The second vignette concerns an attempt by Pilgrim descendants to preserve their forebears' remains. While workmen were completing the new Plymouth Rock canopy in December 1920, the General Society of Mayflower Descendants decided to entomb a collection of ancestral bones on Coles Hill, the supposed burial ground of the *Mayflower* passengers. The bodies in those graves just above Plymouth Rock had never been allowed to rest in peace. First a storm in 1735 destroyed the cemetery and carried many skeletons out to sea. Then, more than a century later, workers for the Plymouth Water Department dislodged another cache of bones while laying pipes in 1855.

Taking no chance of further loss, the *Mayflower* descendants gathered all the remains, had them certified as those of seventeenth-century Europeans (not Native Americans, as many had suspected), and lodged them in a vault on Coles Hill. But it was not by any means to be their final entombment. In 1867, the bones were again displaced, this time into what was hoped to prove an even safer repository—a box secured within Hammatt Billings's Plymouth Rock canopy. Then, when laborers were demolishing the canopy over Plymouth Rock in December 1920 to make way for the McKim, Mead, and White structure, they discovered that the presumably airtight reliquary had not been lined in a harmless metal or wood as everyone had assumed. Rather, it was coated with a type of lead that had caused the skeletons to almost totally disintegrate. As funds had already been set aside for refurbishing the Coles Hill burial ground, a cement receptacle was simply added to the growing list of expenditures.

By this time the fragments of ancestral bones had become tantamount to holy relics, and the reburial procedure resembled a religious ritual. First, authorities held a small ceremony to transfer the remains from the ill-fated lead receptacle to a plain pine box. After that, a carriage conveyed the wooden casket in a solemn procession to Coles Hill, where the *Mayflower* descendants gathered to witness placement of the remains in what they hoped would be their final resting place. Several months later, those same descendants gathered to dedicate a sarcophagus erected to cover the concrete tomb. Inscribed on its side are the names of the *Mayflower* passengers believed to have died during the first winter.[25] Barring further intervention by the powers that be, these relics—and the spirits they embody—will remain imprisoned in their weather-tight vault into eternity. The entombment of these "sacred" bones—like the reenactment of the rescue of John Smith in a Cherokee parade—provides strong evidence to indicate that myth had become a substitute for documented fact.

The triumph of the myths reached full fruition with Jamestown's tercentenary of 1907 and Plymouth's similar commemoration of 1920–1921. Virginia celebrated its anniversary in two ways, thus producing an updated version of the split imagery that had characterized its origin myth for three centuries. One celebration was a loud and commercial world's fair that ran from April through November at Hampton Roads near Norfolk; the other was a quiet and private reaffirmation of the state's origin legend held on Jamestown Island, where members (and would-be members) of the old elite gathered on May 13 to dedicate the newly rebuilt Jamestown Church. By the end of the tercentenary year, memorials dotted the once-vacant island, among them a bronze gate at the entrance to the APVA territory (donated by the Colonial Dames), a house funded by the Daughters of the American Revolution for the APVA's on-site superintendent, and a museum built by the APVA to hold recently excavated artifacts and relics dating back to the original settlement.

The most outstanding memorial of all was the giant obelisk—with huge stone eagles surrounding its base—constructed with a $50,000 congressional grant (Fig. 12.6). Ever since 1807, Virginians had been dreaming of such a tribute to the founders of Jamestown. But concepts of memorials changed during that century, and by 1907, the classical stone shaft patterned after the Washington Monument seemed anachronistic.[26] As the largest and most visible structure on the island, it looms as a testimony to the nation that financed it but carries neither symbol nor suggestion of the colony it commemorates. Instead, the stark obelisk with its guardian eagles abuts the APVA's land as if to remind the heirs of Virginia's Cavalier past that

FIGURE 12.6   *U.S. government obelisk,*
Jamestown, Va., 1994. Photograph by author.

they could not escape the shadow of the omnipotent Union that conquered it.

The contrast between the solemn memorializing on Jamestown Island and the Tercentenary Exposition at Hampton Roads was one of both mood and message. In the short boat ride between the two sites, visitors were propelled from the somber ruins of the seventeenth century to the commercial glitter of the twentieth. The highlight of the exposition's opening day was a speech by President Theodore Roosevelt, who arrived on the presidential yacht *Mayflower*.[27] Although some Virginians may have considered the name of the president's vessel to be yet one more reminder of the Yankee conquest, the crowd that day was willing to overlook such minor details because Roosevelt was a popular president.

The purpose of his speech was to stress America's leadership role in world commerce, a theme that fit into the aspirations of the fair's organizers. But he camouflaged this message behind laudatory remarks about that "little band of daring men who had planted themselves alone on the edge of a frowning continent" in 1607. They "took root in the land," he said, "and were already prospering when the Pilgrims landed at Plymouth." Although Roosevelt acknowledged that the Dutch, Spanish, German, French, Scottish, and Irish had also contributed to the development of the nation, he stressed the "early English colonial stock" that impressed "its strong twin individualities, the mark of the Cavalier and of the Puritan," on the United States. He called upon the two former colonial (and nineteenth-century) enemies to join together to spread American entrepreneurship across the world.[28]

It was an appropriate beginning for a commercial spectacular designed to focus attention on the region and thereby bolster the state's advantages in the growing world market. For this reason, the Hampton Roads organizers hoped to outdo the glitz and bravado of the Chicago World's Columbian Exposition of 1893 and the more recent St. Louis Exposition of 1904. Several of Richmond's leading citizens who abhorred the fair's commercial orientation had been endeavoring for years to wrest control away from the coastal entrepreneurs.[29] Their criticism was justified as it turned out, because the grandiose ambitions of the planners overshot their mark. In fact, the fair would have gone under before the opening had not it been for a bailout by the federal government, a contribution that financed construction of the waterfront docks, a Soldiers and Sailors Rendezvous, a huge United States Building, and a Negro Building.[30] Constant setbacks prevented completion of these and other projects for the April opening, and some of the buildings were still unfinished as late as September. Worse yet, too few visitors passed through the turnstiles to compensate for the extravagant budget, and when the fair closed in November, sponsors were socked with a $2-million deficit.[31]

The Jamestown Tercentenary Exposition displayed an arts and crafts village, a variety of international exhibitions, impressive displays of leading American manufacturers, a number of restaurants, and an amusement arcade.[32] Tradition-bound Virginians, infuriated enough by the blatant commercialism, were even more incensed to discover that a project inspired by the founding of Jamestown paid scant attention to the colony itself. On the exposition grounds only the *names* of the legendary Indians–from the Pocahontas Hospital and Pocahontas Avenue to Powhatan Street and the Powhatan Guards–survived as reminders of the original settlement. Visitors, however, could tour "Old Jamestown," a profit-making venture that sold relics from Virginia's first colony and tickets to view reconstructed historical vignettes.[33] Despite its garish exterior and financial difficulties, the Jamestown Exposition did leave one enduring legacy. During World War I, the U.S. government purchased the fairgrounds and transformed it into the Norfolk Naval Station. And as part of the project, the thirty state pavilions (all replicas of famous mansions) that lined tree-shaded walkways became "Admiral's Row" where naval officers could continue to enjoy the remains of an ill-fated, tercentennial folly.[34]

Part of the failure of the Jamestown tercentenary was the myth's in-adequacy to inspire patriotism during an era of intense nationalism. The Pilgrims had already preempted that territory, and despite Vir-ginians' arguments to the contrary, there was little national import implicit in Pocahontas's rescue of English civilization in the persona of John Smith. In contrast, the Pilgrims had become *the* colonial an-cestors for the entire United States. Each November, Americans commemorated them on Thanksgiving; and fashions in architecture, furniture, and the decorative arts carried perceived Pilgrim motifs. The settlers of Plymouth had, in fact, become so popular by the time the 1920 tercentenary began that the entire nation was inundated with a variety of Pilgrim novels and histories, an early Thomas Edi-son film depicting the Pilgrim story, and an array of Pilgrim paint-ings, illustrations, and statues.[35]

This popularity ensured the success of the Plymouth tercente-nary.[36] Like the *Mayflower* passengers they were commemorating, planners of the two-year celebration were also able to benefit from Virginia's mistakes. Not only did they vow to avoid the hype and commercialism of their Southern predecessor, but a state commis-sion apportioned huge amounts to underwrite activities, corporations donated large sums of money, and Congress authorized Massachu-setts senator Henry Cabot Lodge to form an unprecedented board to administer federal spending. Secure with financial backing and a popular history, the Plymouth tercentenary needed no midway or sideshows to capture world attention.[37]

The prolonged observance began in the spring of 1920 with tableaux and memorial dedications on the coast of the English Chan-nel, followed during the summer with a trek around East Anglia trac-ing Pilgrim footsteps, a journey to the Netherlands for more pageants and tributes, and a ceremony to dispatch a *Mayflower* replica across the Atlantic. In late September, academics from Europe and the United States assembled in Plymouth, England, for a weeklong con-ference focused on the colonization of Massachusetts, thus launching the Pilgrim tercentenary with a fitting mixture of scholarly dignity and international finesse.[38] Meanwhile, residents of Massachusetts were preparing for a surfeit of ancestor veneration on their side of the ocean. In November 1920, they marked the 300th anniversary of the signing of the Mayflower Compact, and on Forefathers' Day in late December, they celebrated the Pilgrims' landing. As in Virginia, preparations for the tercentenary ran behind schedule. But with assured financing, the Massachusetts committee had no reason to rush, and the anniversary celebration continued throughout 1921.[39]

The highlight of the Plymouth tercentenary was an extravagant pageant, *The Pilgrim Spirit,* written and directed by Harvard professor George Pierce Baker.[40] Periodic evening performances took place throughout the summer of 1921 on a specially constructed stage at the edge of Plymouth Bay. Elaborate lighting and audio equipment made the pageant technically spectacular. It began with a voice from the darkness booming: "I, the rock of Plymouth, speak to you, Americans . . . Of me a rock in the ooze, they have made a corner-stone of the Republic." Then the spotlights focused on a Norse galley heading toward the harbor, but before it could land, Indian canoes drove it away; that scene recurred several times as other explorers met similar fates. The next act portrayed a century of Puritan suffering in England and Holland, highlighted by the appearance of King James I shouting above a cacophony of bagpipes: "A Puritan is a Protestant scared out of his wits! . . . I shall make them conform or I will harry them out of this land—or else do worse."

Eventually, actors portraying William Brewster, John Carver, John Robinson, and William Bradford stepped forward to escort their band from England to Holland and finally across the Atlantic. In the last act, the cast formed a series of familiar tableaux vivants taken from well-known paintings that depicted episodes of the embarkation and colonization. A party of pious Pilgrims knelt in prayer as they departed from Delfthaven; another group signed the Mayflower Compact. Others recreated the landing on Plymouth Rock; then additional players struggled through the first winter and feasted at the first Thanksgiving. One scene enacted the banishment of two "strangers," John Oldham and John Lyford, who had refused to conform to the dictates of the Plymouth elders. "Let this be for a warning," the pageant's Governor Bradford cautioned the renegades: "[W]hat we established here for personal liberty and self-government . . . [we will] hold as a heritage for our children and our children's children." This message pervaded the entire performance. The perpetuation of "liberty and self-government" moved in an unbroken line from the Plymouth settlement to the twentieth-century United States.

The pageant climaxed with players dressed as Washington and Lincoln reading the "Return of the Pilgrims" by Robert Frost, another New England literary giant who invoked the origin legend. As their young voices resounded into the night, the emotion intensified:

> *First Speaker*
> This was the port of entry for our freedom.
> Men brought it in a box of alabaster,
> And broke the box, and spilled it to the west
> Here on the granite wharf prepared for them.
>
> *Second Speaker*
> And so we have it.
>
> *First Speaker*
> Have it to achieve;
> We have it as they had it in their day,
> A little in the grasp—more to achieve.
> I wonder what the Pilgrims if they came
> Would say to us as freemen? Is our freedom
> Their freedom as they left it in our keeping—
> Or would they know their own modern guise?[41]

Frost's inquiry about the Pilgrims' modern reincarnation came late in the evening's lengthy performance, when the audience had been so saturated with ancestor veneration that the poet's reflection attracted little notice. All cheered, however, when for the grand finale the large cast marched back and forth across the stage, waving flags of the World War allies and shouting, "The path of the *Mayflower* must forever be kept free."[42]

Far grander than most other pageants popular during that era, Baker's historical panorama drew large crowds throughout the summer of 1921. Most admired the repeated assurance that the Pilgrims and their offspring formed the bedrock of the leaders and guiding ideology of the nation.[43] Among those admirers was President Warren G. Harding, who attended a performance on August 1 and spoke briefly before the lights dimmed. As did Theodore Roosevelt fourteen years earlier, Harding arrived aboard the presidential yacht *Mayflower*—but at least in Plymouth, the name fit the occasion. In fact, the ship's replica rested at anchor a few feet away from the speakers' platform. Harding's address—sprinkled with a jumble of mixed metaphors and skewed historical analogies—was less polished but otherwise akin to the oration that Roosevelt had delivered at Hampton Roads. With the settlers of Plymouth, Harding said, came "the fruits of the revolution, the strengthened parliamentary institutions, and the restrictions on the royal prerogative. No one ever will dispute the large part New England played in the rearing of new standards of freedom."[44] As the words "freedom," "democracy," and "liberty" echoed across the harbor, the realities of seventeenth-century Massachusetts became totally subsumed by myth.

The Jamestown and Plymouth tercentenaries ironically turned out to be confirmations of the regional myths as they had evolved through three centuries. Whereas the commercialism of the 1907 celebration eclipsed all serious gestures of remembrance, the 1920–1921 commemoration never seemed to waver from its focus on the ancestors. The serious and dedicated Plymouth commemoration took advantage of the patriotic and moral messages inherent in the myth. Jamestown, by contrast, sent out the usual opposing signals, which in 1907 were the division between excessive sentimentality and unbridled commercialism. In many ways, this disparity between the two tercentenaries reflected the strength of the Pilgrim myth to command nationwide attention and the inability of its Virginia counterpart to elicit comparable notice.

The tercentenaries of 1907 and 1920–1921 also marked the end of an era. No longer did a heated rivalry between Massachusetts and Virginia fuel the mythmakers' passions. When that regional chauvinism played itself out during the Civil War and Reconstruction, both myths transmogrified to meet modern needs. In the turn-of-the-century Colonial Revival, the Pilgrims remained in the forefront as patriotic representatives of early America. Undermined by the assault of Massachusetts historians, Pocahontas hung in the shadows as the key player in a semihistorical romance. After World War II, however, a new generation of scholars began to return her to the spotlight with long overdue investigations of early Virginia history, a search now greatly enhanced by archeological excavations that are uncovering artifacts that will help to create a valid history of the Jamestown settlement (Fig. 12.7). Now bifurcated between archeologists searching for "truths" and the Disney Studio exploring new realms of fantasy, the Virginia legacy will probably never have the single focus of the Pilgrim heritage. But even that once-solid representative of wholesome Americana is under scrutiny. Recent scholars have begun to scrape away the layers of mythologizing in Massachusetts in an attempt to separate fact from fantasy.

FIGURE 12.7   *Excavations at Jamestown, 1997. Photograph by author.*

As the twentieth century draws to a close, there is a renewed interest in the early colonies, perhaps because the quatercentenaries of
the landings at Jamestown and Plymouth lie just over the horizon.
Tourism has overrun both locations, and both have been declared
national landmarks. In 1934, the U.S. government and the Commonwealth of Virginia purchased Jamestown from the widow of Edward Barney, and except for the twenty-two acres controlled by the
APVA, the site is now under the purview of the National Park Service. Although still a thriving town, Plymouth, too, is covered with
historical markers and designated shrines, especially Burial Hill and
the park that surrounds Plymouth Rock. In both Plymouth and
Jamestown, sections of land have been set aside for recreated villages. Thatch-roofed houses line dirt roads; roleplayers in period costumes speak seventeenth-century dialect and pretend they are the
original settlers. They saw wood, weave cloth, make shoes, forge
iron, and perform other duties that presumably absorbed the lives of
the seventeenth-century inhabitants (Figs. 12.8 and 12.9).

FIGURE 12.8   *James Fort, Jamestown Settlement, Va., c. 1997. Photograph by author.*

FIGURE 12.9
*Interior scene, Plimoth
Plantation c. 1997.
Photograph by author.*

With every strike of the gavel at a memorial meeting, with each groundbreaking for a new monument, with every parade float adorned by costumed colonials, the American genesis legends mutated and expanded. Most actual events dissolved into symbolic totems designed to match current fashions. Thus, a bronze Pocahontas could rush toward a recreated church in Jamestown, a neoclassical canopy could guard Plymouth Rock, a stone tomb on Coles Hill could enshrine the now sacrosanct remains of the Pilgrim forefathers; the ladies of Richmond and the Oowala Community could pursue good works in commemoration of a mutual legend, and the Pilgrim Society could construct a colossal Victorian goddess to memorialize a pious seventeenth-century Christian community. And all the while, few of the participants would dare comment on the incongruities inherent in such observances. For most, the legends themselves had developed lives of their own and were realities in and of their own right.

For the twenty-first century, there will be new myths and heroes, and as the founders of colonial America sink further and further into the distant past, the myths will once more mutate to accommodate a changing culture. Soon the Pilgrims and Pocahontas will merely be minor players in a global culture that has unanticipated ideological battles to wager and unforeseen invented traditions to bolster.

Notes

Preface

1. Mircea Eliade, *Myth and Reality* (New York, 1963), 34.

2. For comments on the feminine nature of the Pocahontas myth, see Anne Norton, *Alternative Americas: A Reading of Antebellum Political Culture* (Chicago, 1986), 86–87, 182–183; Mary V. Dearborn, *Pocahontas's Daughters: Gender and Ethnicity in American Culture* (New York and Oxford, 1986), 12–30; and Philip Young, "The Mother of Us All: Pocahontas Reconsidered," *Kenyon Review* 24 (Summer 1962):391–415.

3. See Peter Hulme, *Colonial Encounters: Europe and the Native Caribbean, 1492–1792* (New York, 1986), 137–173.

4. Studies dealing with the roles of myths in shaping concepts of history include John Bodnar's *Remaking America: Public Memory, Commemoration, and Patriotism in the Twentieth Century* (Princeton, 1992); Paul K. Longmore's *The Invention of George Washington* (Berkeley, 1988); Barry Schwartz's *George Washington: The Making of an American Symbol* (New York, 1987); Garry Wills's *Cincinnatus: George Washington and the Enlightenment* (New York, 1984); William H. Truettner, ed., *The West as America: Reinterpreting Images of the Frontier, 1820–1920* (Washington, 1991); and Michael Kammen's many publications, including *Mystic Chords of Memory: The Transformation of Tradition in American Culture* (New York, 1991), *Spheres of Liberty: Changing Perceptions of Liberty in American Culture* (Madison, Wis., 1986), *A Machine That Would Go By Itself: The Constitution in American Culture* (New York, 1986), and *A Season of Youth: The American Revolution and the Historical Imagination* (New York, 1978). Other books of recent years take the idea of myths beyond national borders. See Simon Schama's *Landscape and Memory* (New York, 1995), and David Lowenthal's *The Past Is a Foreign Country* (Cambridge, Eng., and New York, 1985).

5. The classic twentieth-century cultural studies of New England–Vernon L. Parrington's *Main Currents of American Thought: The Colonial Mind* (New York, 1927), and Perry Miller's *Errand into the Wilderness* (Cambridge, Mass., 1956)–have been up-

dated by Sacvan Bercovitch's *The Puritan Origins of the American Self* (New York, 1975) and *The American Jeremiad* (Madison, Wis., 1978). More recently, Andrew Delbanco, *The Puritan Ordeal* (Cambridge, Mass., and London, 1989), and John Canup, *Out of the Wilderness: The Emergence of an American Identity in Colonial New England* (Middletown, Conn., 1990), have explored other areas of early New England thought.

6. Earlier scholars of American culture emphasized a common American mindset and minimized regional differences. See such seminal works as Rush Welter's *The Mind of America, 1820–1860* (New York and London, 1975), and R.W.B. Lewis's *The American Adam: Innocence, Tragedy, and Tradition in the Nineteenth Century* (Chicago, 1955). More recent emphasis on regional differences, such as E. Digby Baltzell's *Puritan Boston and Quaker Philadelphia: Two Protestant Ethics and the Spirit of Class Authority and Leadership* (New York, 1979), do compare localized differences, although the broad brush used to do so often overlooks nuances of difference within each society.

7. An excellent introduction to these diverse sources is Jack P. Greene, *Interpreting Early America: Historiographical Essays* (Charlottesville, Va., and London, 1996). Among the more comprehensive studies are Jack P. Greene, *The Intellectual Construction of America: Exceptionalism and Identity from 1492 to 1800* (Chapel Hill, N.C., 1993), and *Pursuits of Happiness: The Social Development of Early Modern British Colonies and the Formation of American Culture* (Chapel Hill, N.C., 1988); Bernard Bailyn and Philip D. Morgan, eds., *Strangers Within the Realm: Cultural Margins of the First British Empire* (Chapel Hill, N.C., 1991); Bernard Bailyn, *The Peopling of British North America: An Introduction* (New York, 1986); David Hackett Fischer, *Albion's Seed: Four British Folkways in America* (New York and Oxford, 1989); D. W. Meinig, *The Shaping of America*, 2 vols. (New Haven, 1986 and 1993); Jack P. Green and J. R. Pole, eds., *Colonial British America: Essays in the New History of the Early Modern Era* (Baltimore, 1984); and Arthur Quinn, *A New World: An Epic of Colonial America from the Founding of Jamestown to the Fall of Quebec* (New York, 1994). For specific studies of the two colonies, see John Demos, *A Little Commonwealth: Family Life in Plymouth Colony* (London, New York, and Oxford, 1970); James Horn, *Adapting to a New World: English Society in the Seventeenth-Century Chesapeake* (Williamsburg, Va., and Chapel Hill, N.C., 1994); Carl Bridenbaugh, *Jamestown 1544–1699* (New York and Oxford, 1980); Ivor Noël Hume, *The Virginia Adventure: Roanoke to James Towne: An Archeological and Historical Odyssey* (New York, 1994); and Stephen Foster, *The Long Argument: English Puritanism and the Shaping of New England Culture, 1570–1700* (Williamsburg, Va., and Chapel Hill, N.C., 1991). For views on Native Americans and African Americans, see Winthrop D. Jordan, *White over Black: American Attitudes Toward the Negro, 1550–1812* (New York, 1968); Edmund S. Morgan, *American Slavery, American Freedom: The Ordeal of Colonial Virginia* (New York and London, 1975); Helen C. Rountree, *The Powhatan Indians of Virginia: Their Traditional Culture* (Norman, Okla., 1989); William S. Simmons, *Spirit of the New England Tribes: Indian History and Folklore, 1620–1984* (Hanover, N.H., 1986); and Betty Wood, *The Origins of American Slavery: Freedom and Bondage in the English Colonies* (New York, 1997).

8. Of the many analyses of antebellum history and culture, I found among the most interesting Robert W. Wiebe, *The Opening of American Society from the Adoption of the Constitution to the Eve of Disunion* (New York, 1984); Lewis Perry, *Boats Against the Current: American Culture Between Revolution and Modernity, 1820–1860* (New York and Oxford, 1993); Fred Sompkin, *Unquiet Eagle Memory and Desire in the Idea of American Freedom, 1815–1860* (Ithaca and New York, 1967); and Edward Pessen, *Jacksonian America: Society, Personality, and Politics,* rev. ed. (Urbana, Ill., and Chicago, 1985).

9. Among the best new cultural studies from specific points of view are Nathan O. Hatch, *The Democratization of American Christianity* (New Haven, 1989); Daniel Walker Howe, *The Political Culture of the American Whigs* (Chicago, 1979); Roger G. Kennedy, *Architecture, Men, Women, and Money in America, 1600–1860* (New York, 1985); James M. Lindgren, *Preserving Historic New England: Preservation, Progressivism, and the Remaking of Memory* (New York and Oxford, 1995); Jean Fagan Yellin's *Women and Sisters: The Antislavery Feminists in American Culture* (New Haven and London, 1989); Robert F. Berkhofer Jr., *The White Man's Indian: Images of the American Indian from Columbus to the Present* (New York, 1978); and Ann Douglas, *The Feminization of American Culture* (New York, 1977).

10. The classic study of regional myths in nineteenth-century literature of antebellum Virginia and Massachusetts is William R. Taylor, *Cavalier and Yankee: The Old South and American National Character* (Cambridge, Mass., 1957). For a recent look at the Pocahontas myth, see Robert S. Tilton, *Pocahontas: The Evolution of an American Narrative* (Cambridge, Eng., and New York, 1994); and William S. Rasmussen and Robert S. Tilton, *Pocahontas: Her Life and Legend* (Richmond, Va., 1994), the catalog of a recent exhibition at the Virginia Historical Society. For a thorough and perceptive analysis of the Pilgrim myth, see John Seelye's recent publication, *Memory's Nation: The Place of Plymouth Rock* (Chapel Hill, N.C., 1998).

Chapter 1

1. Drew Gilpin Faust, *The Creation of Confederate Nationalism: Ideology and Identity in the Civil War South* (Baton Rouge, La., 1988), 6.

2. Eric Hobsbawm, "Introduction: Inventing Traditions," in Eric Hobsbawm and Terence Ranger, eds., *The Invention of Tradition* (Cambridge, London, and New York, 1983), 1.

3. See Albert Matthews, "The Term 'Pilgrim Fathers' and Early Celebrations of Forefathers' Day," *Proceedings of the Colonial Society of Massachusetts* 19 (1914):297, 312, 351.

4. See Sacvan Bercovitch, *Puritan Origins of the American Self* (New Haven, 1975), 35–71.

5. Robert C. Winthrop, *An Address Before the New England Society in the City of New York, December 23, 1839* (Boston, 1840), 51–54.

6. *An Account of the Pilgrim Celebration at Plymouth,* August 1, 1853 (Boston, 1853), 61.

7. Although this may be an apocryphal account, Thomas Faunce is said to have identified the rock when he heard a new wharf was to be built above it and asked friends to carry him to the water's edge so he might "take a last farewell of the cherished object." Upon reaching the shoreline, the church elder tearfully informed the assembled crowd that his father once "assured him" the rock "had received the footsteps of our fathers on their first arrival." See James Thacher, *History of the Town of Plymouth from Its First Settlement in 1629 to the Year 1832* (Boston, 1832), 30, 201–202. On Plymouth Rock, see Rose T. Briggs, *Plymouth Rock: History and Significance* (Plymouth, Mass., 1968), 6–7; William S. Russell, *Guide to Plymouth and Recollections of the Pilgrims* (Boston, 1846), 176–183; Robert D. Arner, "Plymouth Rock Revisited: The Landing of the Pilgrim Fathers," *Journal of American Culture* 6 (Winter 1983):25–35; and John McPhee, "Travels of the Rock," *New Yorker* 66 (February 26, 1990):108–117.

8. William H. Bartlett, *The Pilgrim Fathers; or, The Founders of New England in the Reign of James the First* (London, 1853), 164, 171.

9. Randolph Harrison McKim, "Historical Address," in *The Pilgrimage to Jamestown, Va., of the Bishops and Deputies of the General Convention of the Protestant Episcopal Church in the United States of America* (New York, 1898), 9.

10. Quoted in Marshall Fishwick, *The Virginia Tradition* (Washington, 1956), 36.

11. James Barron Hope, "Poem," in *Celebration of the Two-Hundred and Fiftieth Anniversary of the English Settlement at Jamestown, May 13, 1857* (Washington, 1857), 25.

12. Raymond Firth, *Symbols: Public and Private* (Ithaca, 1973), 166.

13. That kind of commemoration, writes Barry Schwartz, "lifts from an ordinary historical sequence those extraordinary events which embody our deepest and most fundamental values." By seeking to recreate the nation's origins, Americans sought "unique cultural traditions to stand beside its newfound political unity." See Barry Schwartz, "The Social Context of Commemoration: A Study in Collective Memory," *Social Forces* 61 (December 1982):377, 389.

14. William Bradford had recorded the date as December 11, according to the "old-style" (or Julian) calendar, but it was changed in 1752, when England accepted the Gregorian calendar, which added ten or eleven days to shift the landing date to December 21 or 22.

15. See Stephen Nissenbaum, *The Battle for Christmas: A Cultural History of America's Most Cherished Holiday* (New York, 1996), 3–48. Henry Wadsworth Longfellow commented about this prohibition in his diary entry of Christmas Day, 1856: "We are in a transition state about Christmas here in New England," he mused. "The old Puritan feeling prevents it from being a cheerful, hearty holiday; though every year makes it more so." Samuel Longfellow, *Life of Henry Wadsworth Longfellow, with Extracts from His Journals and Correspondence* (Boston, 1886), 2:290. During the Civil War, Plymouth began to celebrate Christmas, replete with dancing, decorated trees, and Santa Claus. See "Christmas and Forefathers," *Old Colony Memorial,* December 27, 1862.

16. The first Forefathers' Day feast consisted of "succatach," clams, oysters, codfish, venison, Indian whortleberry pudding, apple pie, cranberry tarts, and other

delicacies of the region. Writing many years later about the first commemoration of the Pilgrims' landing, James Thacher noted that the banquet was "dressed in the plainest manner" because "all appearance of luxury and extravagance" would have been inappropriate at an event honoring "our ancestors, whose memory we shall ever respect." Thacher, *History of Plymouth*, 180–181.

17. There is also a tangential link to the British autumnal celebration known as "Harvest Home," an Anglican and Catholic tradition that the Puritans of New England were loath to accept. Concerning the first harvest celebration with the Indians, see William Bradford, *History of Plymouth Plantation* (Boston, 1912), vol. 1, 230–231; and Edward Winslow, *Mourt's Relation*, ed. D. B. Heath (Cambridge, Mass., 1986), 82. Both are quoted in *The Thanksgiving Primer* (Plymouth, Mass., 1987), 7.

18. In 1777, Washington asked the Continental Congress to issue a Thanksgiving proclamation to celebrate victories against the British. For more information, see Diana Karter Appelbaum, *Thanksgiving: An American Holiday, an American History* (New York, 1984), 109–127; *Columbian Centinel*, October 14, 1789.

19. Sylvester Judd, *Margaret: A Tale of the Real and the Ideal, Blight and Bloom; Including Sketches of a Place not Before Described, Called Mons Christi* (Boston, 1851), vol. 2, 80.

20. *Old Colony Memorial*, December 14, 1850.

21. See Patricia Okker, *Our Sister Editors: Sarah J. Hale and the Tradition of Nineteenth-Century American Women Editors* (Athens, Ga., 1995); Ruth E. Finley, *The Lady of Godey's: Sarah Josepha Hale* (Philadelphia and London, 1931), 195–204; and Sherbrooke Rogers, *Sarah Josepha Hale: A New England Pioneer, 1788–1879* (Grantham, N.H., 1985).

22. See Appelbaum, *Thanksgiving*, 140–161, 234–242; Matthews, "The Term 'Pilgrim Fathers,'" 309–317; Wesley Frank Craven, *The Legend of the Founding Fathers* (New York, 1956), 30–32, 82–83; and George F. Willison, *Saints and Strangers* (New York, 1945), 408–415; and Stephen Eddy Snow, *Performing the Pilgrims: A Study of Ethnohistorical Role-Playing at Plimoth Plantation* (Jackson, Miss., 1993), 12–20.

23. An author signing his name "A Farmer of the Ancient Dominion" admitted as much. In the introductory essay of a booklet printed for the bicentenary, he told how New Englanders frequently added "fresh oil to the lamp of their patriotism" by organizing "annual festivals" to commemorate the "debarkation at Plymouth." But "in the ancient dominion of Virginia, which may be called the principal fountain of American population, not the slightest notice is taken of an event in which the whole world is interested." *Report of the Proceedings of the Late Jubilee at Jamestown in Commemoration of the 13th May, the Second Centesimal Anniversary of the Settlement of Virginia* (Petersburg, 1807), 6.

24. Ibid., 42–47.

25. See Edith Bolling Wilson, *My Memoir* (New York and Indianapolis, 1938) 228; and Isabel Ross, *Power with Grace: The Life Story of Mrs. Woodrow Wilson* (New York, 1975), 13–14, 175.

26. From the union of Jane Rolfe and Robert Bolling came one son, John Bolling, and five daughters. The latter married Colonel Richard Randolph, Colonel John

Fleming, Dr. William Gay, Thomas Eldridge, and James Murray. For a listing of the many offspring, see Stuart E. Brown Jr. et al., eds., *Pocahontas' Descendants* (Richmond, 1985), and Wyndham Robertson, *Pocahontas, Alias Matoaka, and Her Descendants* (1887; reprint, Baltimore, 1968).

27. James Thacher, *History of the Town of Plymouth from Its First Settlement in 1629 to the Year 1832* (Boston, 1831), 179–180.

28. Oliver Wendell Holmes, *Oration Before the New England Society in the City of New York at their Semi-Centennial Anniversary, December 22, 1855* (New York, n.d.), 9–10, 19–20.

29. "Liberal historians," writes Peter Gomes, "were forced to resort to a useful distinction which would provide them a set of respectable ancestors to whom they could attribute their own values while maintaining a healthy separation from less agreeable ancestors whose ideas they disapproved and whose church and state institutions they fully possessed." Thus, "the myth of the mild religious hospitality of the Pilgrims vs. the perception of the corrupting and intolerant power of the Puritan oligarchy" developed. Peter Gomes, "Pilgrims and Puritans: 'Heroes' and 'Villains' in the Creation of the American Past," *Proceedings of the Massachusetts Historical Society* 95 (1983), 12.

30. See *Sixtieth Anniversary Celebration of the New England Society in the City of New York* (New York, 1866); William Way, *History of the New England Society of Charleston, South Carolina, 1819–1919* (Charleston, S.C., 1920); and *Rules of the New-England Society of Charleston, S.C.* (Charleston, S.C., 1850).

31. The Jamestown Committee was formed in the 1850s; the Old Dominion Society held its first meeting in 1860.

32. See William H. Newell, "Good and Bad Ancestors," in William H. Newell, ed., *Ancestors* (The Hague and Paris, 1976), 17–29.

Chapter 2

1. See Charles Campbell, "An Introduction to the History of the Colony and Ancient Dominion of Virginia," *Southern Literary Messenger* (hereafter *SLM*) 13 (February 1847):73–80 and (March 1847):129–140; *History of the Colony and Ancient Dominion of Virginia* (Philadelphia, 1860), 30–84; and "A Monument at Jamestown to Captain John Smith," *SLM* 22 (August 1858):112–114.

2. William Henry Foote, *Sketches of Virginia: Historical and Biographical* (1850; reprint, Richmond, 1966), 14.

3. For historiographical and literary sources of the Pocahontas legend, see Robert S. Tilton, *Pocahontas: The Evolution of an American Narrative* (Cambridge, Eng., and New York, 1994); Frances Mossiker, *Pocahontas: The Life and the Legend* (New York, 1976), 321–337; Wayne Franklin, *Discoverers, Explorers, Settlers: The Diligent Writers of Early America* (Chicago, 1979), 187–190; and Jay B. Hubbell, "The Smith-Pocahontas Story in Literature," *Virginia Magazine of History and Biography,* 65 (July 1957):275–312.

4. The full title of the 1608 publication was *A True Relation of such occurences and accidents of noate as hath hapned in Virginia since the first planting of that Collony.* All three of these are reprinted in Philip L. Barbour, ed., *The Complete Works of Captain John Smith (1580–1631)* (Chapel Hill, N.C., 1986).

5. The most respected of these geographical surveys were written by the Richard Hakluyts, senior and junior. See E.G.R. Taylor, ed., *The Original Writings and Correspondence of the Two Richard Hakluyts* (London, 1935). See also Thomas Hariot's *Briefe and True Report of the New Found Land of Virginia*, first published in 1588.

6. Philip Barbour, *The Three Worlds of Captain John Smith* (Boston, 1964), 350–369.

7. Ibid., 355. An important firsthand account of life in Jamestown was the diary of a young man named George Percy, which had been published by the Reverend Samuel Purchas in *Hakluytus Posthumus.* See *Purchas His Pilgrimes: In Five Bookes* (London, 1625–1626). For Percy's actual diary, see George Percy, "A Trewe Relacyon of the Precedings and occurrentes of Momente . . . 1609 . . . 1612," *Tyler's Quarterly Magazine* 3 (1922):259–282. Other contemporary recorders were William Strachey, who served briefly as secretary of the colony in 1610–1611, during which he sent a letter to the Virginia Company that was published as *The History of Travell into Virginia Britania*, eds. Louis B. Wright and Virginia Freund (1612), and *For the Colony in Virginia . . .* , ed. David H. Flaherty (1610–1611; reprint, Charlottesville, 1969); and Ralph Hamor, *A True Discourse of the Present State of Virginia* (1615; reprint, Richmond, 1957). For discussion of the Smith, Percy, and Strachey histories, see Barbour, *Three Worlds*, 98, 111, 298–300, and 354.

8. Barbour, *Three Worlds*, vol. 2, 151–262; also see Edward Arber, ed., *Travels and Works of Captain John Smith* (Edinburgh, 1910), 38, 400–401, 410, 436, 455, 511–512. For other interpretations, see Philip L. Barbour, *Pocahontas and Her World* (Boston, 1970); Mossiker, *Pocahontas.*

9. Barbour, *Complete Works*, vol. 2, 260–262.

10. See Lawrence W. Towner, "*Ars Poetica et Sculptura:* Pocahontas on the Boston Common," *Journal of Southern History* 28 (November 1962):482–485.

11. See Henry Adams, "Captain John Smith," *North American Review* 104 (January 1867):1–30; and Edward D. Neill, *Virginia Vetusta, During the Reign of James the First: Containing Letters and Documents Never Before Printed* (Albany, N.Y., 1885). For a summary of the historians' views, see Philip L. Barbour, introduction to *Complete Works*, vol. 2, 26–32, and J. A. Leo Lemay, *Did Pocahontas Save Captain John Smith?* (Athens, Ga., 1992), 7–18, 102–105. For more recent criticism of Smith, see Arthur Quinn, *A New World: An Epic of Colonial America from the Founding of Jamestown to the Fall of Quebec* (Boston, 1994), 1–43, and Bert J. Loewenberg, *American History in American Thought: Christopher Columbus to Henry Adams* (New York, 1972), 110–115.

12. Until the mid-1960s, most scholars treated the Pocahontas story as fiction, some suggesting that Smith crafted the rescue anecdote and other Pocahontas episodes from tales told by previous explorers or that he took these incidents from archetypal universal myths. Elemire Zolla, for example, poses the theory that Smith

created the Pocahontas episode to give the Stuart court a persuasive myth for encouraging colonization, pointing to "the element of chivalry, the missionary, the savage, not to mention given the protagonist's rank of princess, [and] the continuity of royal rule" as fundamental ingredients of a classic myth. See Elemire Zolla, *The Writer and the Shaman: A Morphology of the American Indian*, trans. Raymond Rosenthal (New York, 1969), 20–24. Philip Young suggests that Smith borrowed the rescue story from a similar tale about Juan Ortiz, a member of de Soto's exploration party, published in Richard Hakluyt's writing of 1609. See Philip Young, "The Mother of Us All: Pocahontas Reconsidered," *Kenyon Review* 24 (Summer 1962):397. Also see Lewis Leary, "The Adventures of Captain John Smith as Heroic Legend," in J. A. Leo Lemay, ed., *Essays in Early Virginia Literature Honoring Richard Beale Davis* (New York, 1977), 13–33.

13. For the classic nineteenth-century defense of Smith, see William Wirt Henry, "The Address," *Proceedings of the Virginia Historical Society* (Richmond, 1882), 10–63. For discussion of recent reevaluations of Smith, see Laura Polanyi Striker and Bradford Smith, "The Rehabilitation of Captain John Smith," *Journal of Southern History* 28 (November 1962):474–481; Kevin J. Hayes, "Defining the Ideal Colonist: Captain John Smith's Revisions from *A True Relation* to the *Proceedings* to the *Third Book of the Generall Historie*," *Virginia Magazine of History and Biography* 99 (April 1991):123–144; and Frederic W. Gleach, *Powhatan's World and Colonial Virginia: A Conflict of Cultures* (Lincoln, Nebr., and London, 1997), 106–122.

14. Gleach, *Powhatan's World*, 115–122; and Philip L. Barbour, introduction to *Complete Works*, vol. 1, lxiii–lxiv. Samuel Purchas commented upon Pocahontas's appearance at the Stuart Court in *Purchas His Pilgrimes*; and Ralph Hamor mentioned her in *A True Discourse*.

15. In fact, Smith set a precedent for shaping the history of colonial Virginia by using descriptive narrative to air personal concerns, especially during the eighteenth century. See, e.g., Robert Beverley, *The History and Present State of Virginia*, ed. Louis B. Wright (1705; reprint, Chapel Hill, N.C., 1947); William Byrd, *Histories of the Dividing Line Betwixt Virginia and North Carolina*, introduction and notes by William K. Boyd and Percy G. Adams (New York, 1967); William Stith, *The History of the First Discovery and Settlement of Virginia* (1747; reprint, Spartanburg, S.C., 1965); and Thomas Jefferson, *Notes on the State of Virginia* (Chapel Hill, N.C., 1982); For summary analysis of these histories, see Michael Kraus, *The Writing of American History* (Norman, Okla., 1953), 39–43, 51–52; and David Van Tassel, *Recording America's Past: An Interpretation of the Development of Historical Studies in America, 1607–1884* (Chicago, 1960), 25–27.

16. Smith's contemporaries described him as short in stature, tough, fearless, and ill-tempered. For a full account of his exploits, see Barbour, *Three Worlds*; Ivor Noël Hume, *The Virginia Adventure, Roanoke to James Towne: An Archeological and Historical Odyssey* (New York, 1994), 121–254; J. A. Leo Lemay, *The American Dream of Captain John Smith* (Charlottesville, Va., and London, 1991).

17. They were Christopher Newport, Bartholomew Gosnold, John Ratcliffe, John Martin, Edward Maria Wingfield, and George Kendall.

18. Hume, *Virginia Adventure,* 20–129; Warren M. Billings, ed., *The Old Dominion in the Seventeenth Century: A Documentary History of Virginia, 1606–1689* (Chapel Hill, N.C., 1975), 17–22.

19. "George Percy's Account of the Voyage to Virginia and the Colony's First Days," in Billings, *Old Dominion,* 25.

20. See James Horn, *Adapting to a New World: English Society in the Seventeenth-Century Chesapeake* (Williamsburg, Va., and Chapel Hill, N.C., 1994), 131–133; Hume, *Virginia Adventure,* 120–166; and Carl Bridenbaugh, *Jamestown 1544–1699* (New York and Oxford, 1980).

21. See Helen C. Rountree, *The Powhatan Indians of Virginia: Their Traditional Culture* (Norman, Okla., and London, 1989), 17–31, and "The Powhatans and the English: A Case of Multiple Conflicting Agendas," in Rountree, ed., *Powhatan Foreign Relations* (Charlottesville, Va., and London, 1993), 173–205; Helen Rountree and Rudolph Turner III, "On the Fringe of the Southeast: The Powhatan Paramount Chiefdom in Virginia," in Charles Hudson and Carmen Chaves Tesser, eds., *The Forgotton Centuries: Indians and Europeans in the American South, 1521–1704* (Athens, Ga., 1994), 365–372; J. Frederick Fausz, "An 'Abundance of Blood Shed on Both Sides': England's First Indian War, 1609–1614," *Virginia Magazine of History and Biography* 98 (January 1990):3–56; Hume, *Virginia Adventure,* 127–136; and Gleach, *Powhatan's World, 23–87.*

22. Scientists studying trees made this discovery. See *New York Times,* April 24, 1998.

23. One of the first ships to return to Jamestown brought two women, Mrs. Thomas Forrest and her maid, Anne Burras. Historians have recorded the latter's marriage to John Laydon as the first English wedding held in North America. See Martha W. McCartney, *James City County: Keystone of the Commonwealth* (James City County, Va., 1997), 28–39; and Horn, *New World,* 24–31.

24. The letter is reprinted in *The Old Dominion in the Seventeenth Century,* 216–219. Ralph Hamor indicated that Dale had hoped to further improve relations with the Indians by arranging an English marriage for another of Powhatan's daughters, but the *weroance* refused to sacrifice a second child. See Gleach, *Powhatan's World,* 134–135.

25. Tobacco itself was not new to the Englishmen because small quantities had been grown in the British Isles since 1570; only the type of tobacco and scale of operation was unique to Virginia. See Horn, *New World,* 131.

26. See David R. Ransome, "Pocahontas and the Mission to the Indians," *Virginia Magazine of History and Biography* 99 (January 1991):81–94.

27. Gleach indicates that the title "brother" for Opechancanough might have suggested dual tribal leadership and not that they were siblings. See Gleach, *Powhatan's World,* 140–145; also see J. Frederick Fausz, "An 'Abundance of Blood Shed on Both Sides,'" 44–50.

28. See Edmund S. Morgan, *American Slavery, American Freedom: The Ordeal of Colonial Virginia* (New York and London, 1975), 71–91; T. H. Breen, *Tobacco Culture: The*

Mentality of the Great Tidewater Planters on the Eve of Revolution (Princeton, 1985); Billings, *Old Dominion*, 175–204; and Horn, *New World*, 123–136.

29. Horn, *New World*, 58–64; and James Horn, "Cavalier Culture? The Social Development of Colonial Virginia," *William and Mary Quarterly* 48 (1991):238–245.

30. Edmund Morgan, however, argues that the Africans may have already been slaves in the Bahamas. Morgan, *American Slavery*, 297.

31. See ibid., 295–337; Betty Wood, *The Origins of American Slavery: Freedom and Bondage in the English Colonies* (New York, 1997), 68–93; Robert S. Cope, *Carry Me Back: Slavery and Servitude in Seventeenth Century Virginia* (Pikeville, Ky., 1973); Billings, *Old Dominion*, 127–174; Wesley Frank Craven, *White, Red, and Black: The Seventeenth Century Virginian* (Charlottesville, Va., 1971); and Winthrop D. Jordan, *White over Black: American Attitudes Toward the Negro, 1550–1812* (New York, 1968), 44–56, 71–82.

32. Horn, *New World*, 372–380; John B. Frantz, ed., *Bacon's Rebellion: Prologue to Revolution?* (Lexington, Mass., 1969); Wilcomb E. Washburn, *The Governor and the Rebel: A History of Bacon's Rebellion in Virginia* (Chapel Hill, N.C., 1957); Billings, *Old Dominion*, 267–282; and Jane D. Carson, *Bacon's Rebellion in Virginia, 1676–1976* (Jamestown, Va., 1976). For the historiography of early Virginia, see Jack P. Greene, *Interpreting Early America: Historiographical Essays* (Charlottesville, Va., and London, 1996), 200–213.

33. For biographical information, see Bradford Smith, *Bradford of Plymouth* (Philadelphia and New York, 1951).

34. The first to use the manuscript was Bradford's nephew Nathaniel Morton, who copied large portions in his *New England Memorial* (1669); subsequently, Cotton Mather used it for his *Magnalia Christi Americana, or The Ecclesiastical History of New England* (1702); and Thomas Prince included portions of it in his *Chronological History of New England* (1736).

35. See further "Editorial Preface by Charles Deane," reprinted in Verna M. Hall and Rosalie J. Slater, *The Hand of God in the Return of the Bradford Manuscript* (San Francisco, 1971), 17–33; Harvey Wish, "William Bradford and *Of Plymouth Plantation*," introduction to *Of Plymouth Plantation* (New York, 1962), 21–22; "Recovery of the Bradford Manuscript," *Proceedings of the Massachusetts Historical Society* 3 (1855–1858):19–23; and George F. Willison, *Saints and Strangers* (New York, 1945), 427–432.

36. For an interesting discussion of Puritan historiography, see Lawrence Buell, *New England Literary Culture: From Revolution Through Renaissance* (Cambridge, London, and New York, 1986), 214–238.

37. See Stephen Foster, *The Long Argument: English Puritanism and the Shaping of New England Culture, 1570–1700* (Williamsburg, Va., and Chapel Hill, N.C., 1991), 4, 13–14, 63, 156–158.

38. William Bradford, *History of Plymouth Plantation* (Boston, 1912), vol. 1, 9, 11.

39. In his 1669 history, Nathaniel Morton stated they feared "their Posterity would in a few generations become Dutch and so lose their interest in the English

Nation." Quoted in John Canup, *Out of the Wilderness: The Emergence of an American Identity in Colonial New England* (Middletown, Conn., 1990), 58. A nineteenth-century British clergyman gave a more colorful twist to this interpretation: "The Pilgrims, with their true English hearts began to fear that in a generation or two their descendants would become Dutchmen. Intolerable! And, what was still worse, they feared that their darling Independency might disappear under the influence of Dutch Presbyterianism. And so they resolved to colonize." R. W. Dale, *The Pilgrim Fathers: A Lecture* (London, 1854), 21. Also see Andrew Delbanco, *The Puritan Ordeal* (Cambridge, Mass., and London, 1989), 70.

40. For details of the voyage and events preceding it, see George D. Langdon Jr., *Pilgrim Colony: A History of New Plymouth, 1620–1691* (New Haven, 1966); and H. Roger King, *Cape Cod and Plymouth Colony in the Seventeenth Century* (Latham, Md., 1994).

41. See Emmanuel Altham to Sir Edward Altham, September 1623, in Sydney V. James Jr., ed., *Three Visitors to Early Plymouth: Letters About the Pilgrim Settlement in New England During Its First Seven Years* (1963; reprint, Bedford, Mass., 1997), 24.

42. See Mark Sargent, "The Conservative Covenant: The Rise of the *Mayflower* Compact in American Myth," *New England Quarterly* 61 (June 1988):239–246.

43. John Demos, *A Little Commonwealth: Family Life in Plymouth Colony* (Oxford and New York, 1970), 6–7.

44. Samoset learned English from fishermen off the Maine coast; Squanto had been kidnapped by an exploring party and sold as a slave in Spain before escaping to London, but eventually returned to the American coast on an English ship. Bradford, *Plymouth Plantation*, vol. 1, 198–202; Canup, *Out of the Wilderness*, 94–95. For insights into Native American life in New England, see William S. Simmons, *Spirit of the New England Tribes: Indian History and Folklore, 1620–1984* (Hanover, N.H., and London, 1986); and Delores Bird Carpenter, *Early Encounters–Native Americans and Europeans in New England: From the Papers of W. Sears Nickerson* (East Lansing, Mich., 1994), 9–14, 102–105, 145–246; and Emmanuel Altham to Sir Edward Altham, September 1623, in James, *Three Visitors*, 29–31. Also see "Tisquantum" in *Dictionary of Canadian Biography* (Toronto, 1966), vol. 1, 649–650; L. N. Kinnicutt, "Plymouth Settlement and Tisquantum," in *Massachusetts Historical Society Proceedings* 48 (1914–1915):103–108; and Arthur Lord, "Massasoit," and Stanley E. Goodman, "Squanto," in L. D. Geller, ed., *They Knew They Were Pilgrims, Essays in Plymouth History* (New York, 1971), 9–31.

45. Canup, *Out of the Wilderness*, 62–73.

46. Bradford, *Plymouth Plantation*, vol. 1, 382.

47. Ibid., 383–407.

48. Ibid., vol. 2, 47–48.

49. Ibid., vol. 2, 48–58. Also see Canup, *Out of the Wilderness*, 105–125.

50. Bradford, *Plymouth Plantation*, vol. 2, 369.

51. On demographics of the Massachusetts Bay immigrants, see T. H. Breen and Stephen Foster, "Moving to the New World: The Character of Early Massachusetts

Immigration," *William and Mary Quarterly* 30 (1973):189–222; also see T. H. Breen, *Puritans and Adventurers: Change and Persistence in Early America* (New York and Oxford, 1980), 46–67; Foster, *The Long Argument,* 108–174; and Greene, *Interpreting Early America,* 240–243.

52. Perry Miller, "Errand into the Wilderness" in *Errand into the Wilderness* (Cambridge, Mass., 1956).

53. For discussion of Miller's theory, see Delbanco, *The Puritan Ordeal,* 216–217, and "The Puritan Errand Re-Viewed," *Journal of American Studies* 18 (December 1984):343–360; Greene, *Interpreting Early America,* 76–77, 222–226; Russell J. Reising, *The Unusable Past: Theory and the Study of American Literature* (New York and London, 1986), 49–91; Theodore Dwight Bozeman, "The Puritan's 'Errand into the Wilderness' Reconsidered," *New England Quarterly* 59 (June 1986):231–251; Bruce Tucker, "The Reinvention of New England, 1691–1770," *New England Quarterly* 59 (September 1986):315–340. For the most prolific and controversial of these critics, see Sacvan Bercovitch, *The American Jeremiad* (Madison, Wis., 1978), 3–30, and "New England's Errand Reappraised," in John Higham and Paul K. Conklin, eds., *New Directions in American Intellectual History* (Baltimore, 1979), 85–104, and "Rhetoric and History in Early New England: The Puritan Errand Reassessed" in L. J. Budd et al., eds., *Toward a New Literary History* (Durham, N.C., 1980), 54–68.

54. David Hackett Fischer, *Albion's Seed: Four British Folkways in America* (New York and Oxford, 1989), 117–125, 131–134, 189–199; Virginia DeJohn Anderson, "The Origins of New England Culture," *William and Mary Quarterly* 48 (April 1991):231–237; D. W. Meinig, *The Shaping of America: A Geographical Perspective on Five Hundred Years of History,* vol. 1, *Atlantic America, 1492–1800* (New Haven, 1986), 91–109. For an interpretation of these sources, see Greene, *Interpreting Early America,* 244–248, 281–307.

55. Perry Miller pointed this out in his 1952 essay, explaining that the migration to Plymouth "was not so much an errand as a shrewd forecast, a plan to get out while the getting was good." According to Miller, Winthrop's settlement of Boston left England armed with a fully developed "errand" to create a Puritan utopia, but the Separatists did not believe they were "propagating the gospel in remote parts of the world" until well after they arrived at Plymouth. Miller, "Errand into the Wilderness," 4–5. Whereas Miller and his followers have pointed out differences between the Plymouth and Massachusetts Bay colonies, others have argued that the two colonies were essentially the same. See Samuel Eliot Morison, "The Pilgrim Fathers: Their Significance in History," *Publications of the Colonial Society of Massachusetts* 38 (September 13, 1951):364–379; and Peter J. Gomes, "Pilgrims and Puritans: 'Heroes' and 'Villains' in the Creation of the American Past," *Proceedings of the Massachusetts Historical Society* 95 (1983):1–16.

56. Notwithstanding their doctrinal disagreements, the Puritans in England before the civil war of the 1640s considered both colonies to be rebels and often referred to both groups as "Separatists." See Foster, *The Long Argument,* 166–167, 198–199.

There is also some indication that the aborted Lyford-Oldham "coup" may have been an attempt to strengthen Plymouth's ties with the dominant English Puritan movement. See John A. Goodwin, *The Puritan Conspiracy Against the Pilgrim Fathers and the Congregational Church, 1624* (Boston, 1883), 5–6. For further discussion of the differences between the two colonies, see Delbanco, *The Puritan Ordeal,* 41–80; Demos, *A Little Commonwealth,* 8–10; and Perry Miller, "The Marrow of Puritan Divinity," in *Errand into the Wilderness,* 48–98.

57. See Jill Lepore, *The Name of War: King Philip's War and the Origins of American Identity* (New York, 1998), 71–170.

58. Canup, *Out of the Wilderness,* 12–13.

59. See Samuel Eliot Morison, "The Plymouth Colony and Virginia," *Virginia Magazine of History and Biography* 62 (April 1954):147–165; and Fischer, *Albion's Seed,* 57–62, 139–146, 256–264, 354–360.

60. John Pory to the Earl of Southampton, January 13, 1622/1623, in James, *Three Visitors,* 11.

61. Quoted in Canup, *Out of the Wilderness,* 96–97.

62. See "Reflections on the Census of 1840," *SLM* 9 (June 1843):349.

63. See Anne Norton, *Alternative Americas: A Reading of Antebellum Political Culture* (Chicago, 1986), 148; and Richard Beale Davis, *Intellectual Life in the Colonial South, 1585–1763* (Knoxville, Tenn., 1978), vol. 1, 204–208.

64. See Meinig, *Shaping of America,* vol. 1, 91–109; 144–160; Ransome, "Pocahontas and the Mission," 91–94; Horn, *New World,* 54. For seventeenth-century documentation, see Billings, *Old Dominion,* 205–235.

65. See Davis, *Intellectual Life,* vol. 1, 262–269, 276–282, 330–349, and vol. 2, 633–650; Fischer, *Albion's Seed,* 117–125, 207–240, 332–340; and Horn, *New World,* 55–56, 164, 381.

66. T. H. Breen believes this "scramble for riches" began when the first Jamestown settlers came in search of economic enhancement and found its logical outlet with the advent of tobacco farming. Breen, *Puritans and Adventurers,* 106–126. Also see Fischer, *Albion's Seed,* 130–134, 151–180, 365–382.

Chapter 3

1. Trumbull's paintings are *The Declaration of Independence, Resignation of General Washington, Surrender of Lord Cornwallis at Yorktown,* and *Surrender of General Burgoyne at Saratoga.*

2. *Annals of Congress, Register of Debates,* 12, pt. 4, Appendix, 24th Cong., sess. 1 (June 23, 1836), Res. 8, 23. On the congressional commission, see Ann Uhry Abrams, "National Paintings and American Character: Historical Murals in the Capitol Rotunda," *Picturing History* (New York, 1993), 65–79; Vivien Green Fryd, *Art and Empire: The Politics of Ethnicity in the United States Capitol, 1815–1860* (New Haven, 1992), 42–47; Lillian B. Miller, *Patrons and Patriotism: The Encouragement of the*

Fine Arts in the United States, 1790–1860 (Chicago, 1966), 3–84; Sally Webster, "Writing History/Painting History: Early Chronicles of the United States and Pictures for the Capitol Rotunda," in Harriet F. Seine and Sally Webster, eds., *Critical Issues in Public Art: Context, Content, and Controversy* (New York, 1992), 33–43; George R. Nielsen, "Paintings and Politics in Jacksonian America, *Capitol Studies* 1 (Spring 1972):87–92; and Kent Ahrens, "Nineteenth Century History Painting and the United States Capitol," *Records of the Columbia Historical Society of Washington, D.C.* 15 (1980):191–120.

3. See Chapter 8.

4. *New-York Mirror* 15 (September 2, 1837).

5. Ibid.

6. For more details on the sculpture, see Fryd, *Art and Empire,* 16–34.

7. See Peter C. Marzio, *The Democratic Art: Pictures for a Nineteenth Century America: Chromolithography, 1840–1900* (Boston and Fort Worth, Tex., 1979).

8. As reprinted in William S. Russell, *Guide to Plymouth and Recollections of the Pilgrims* (Boston, 1846), appendix, 50.

9. Blair Bolling, "Commonplace Book," (Mss 5:5B 6383:1 o.s.), Virginia Historical Society, Richmond.

10. Unlike its predecessor, the Old Colony Club, the Pilgrim Society never restricted membership to descendants of the original settlers. In keeping with the New England tradition of scholarship, the founders structured their society along the lines of the Massachusetts Historical Society in Boston (founded in 1791) and the American Antiquarian Society in Worcester, Massachusetts (founded in 1812). See James Thacher, *History of the Town of Plymouth, from Its First Settlement in 1620 to the Year 1832* (Boston, 1832), 247.

11. Minutes transcribed by Samuel Davis at a meeting of the Pilgrim Society, September 22, 1822, Pilgrim Hall, Plymouth, Mass.

12. Although Parris's plans called for a "monumental" portico adorning the front entrance, it took a few years for the Pilgrim Society to raise enough money to engage the Providence architect Russell Warren to design a more imposing exterior. In place of Parris's severe neoclassicism, Warren turned to the newer Greek Revival style. Consequently, the Pilgrim Hall facade, completed in 1833, displayed a wooden portico with fluted Doric columns and a double staircase leading to a doorway on the building's upper floor. See Peter J. Gomes, ed., *The Pilgrim Society, 1820–1970: An Informal Commemorative Essay* (Plymouth, Mass., 1971); L. D. Geller, "Plymouth and Pilgrim Hall Museum After Three Hundred and Fifty Years," in *They Knew They Were Pilgrims: Essays in Plymouth History* (New York, 1971), 211–213; Thacher, *History of Plymouth,* 262–268; Russell, *Guide to Plymouth,* 230–234; and Edward Francis Zimmer, *The Architectural Career of Alexander Parris (1780–1852),* Ph.D. diss., Boston University, 1984, vol. 1, 498–501.

13. The author was mistaken—the wharf was made of stone, not wood. "The Celebration at Plymouth," reprinted in *An Account of the Pilgrim Celebration at Plymouth,*

August 1, 1853 (Boston, 1853), 175. For further discussion of the new monuments, see Chapter 12.

14. John Henry Strobia, "Journal of an Excursion to the North and East in the Summer of 1817," and Henry Beaumont, "A Short Journal of a Voyage to North America," Virginia Historical Society, Richmond.

Chapter 4

1. The source of the original painting has never been firmly established. Some attribute it to Van de Passe; others think that unlikely because Van de Passe and his family were primarily printmakers, not painters. The National Portrait Gallery in Washington owns the so-called Booton Hall portrait, which many believe to be the original. I agree with Philip Barbour and Ivor Noël Hume that it was probably copied from the engraving instead of being the original source for that print. See Philip L. Barbour, *Pocahontas and Her World* (Boston, 1970), 233–345, and Ivor Noël Hume, "No Fayre Lady: The Several Faces of Pocahontas," *Colonial Williamsburg* (Autumn 1994):62–65. Also see F. H., "The Pocahontas Portrait," *Virginia Magazine of History and Biography* 35 (October 1927):431–436; handwritten notes in the Charles Henry Hart Papers, Archives of American Art, Smithsonian Institution, Washington, D.C. (hereafter AAA); Catalogue of American Portraits, National Portrait Gallery, Smithsonian Institution, Washington, D.C.; and Robert S. Tilton, *Pocahontas: The Evolution of an American Narrative* (Cambridge, Eng., and New York, 1994), 105–109. I am grateful for the help provided by Dr. Ellen Miles, Wendy Wick Reaves, and other members of the National Portrait Gallery staff.

2. Henry Holand, ed., *Baziliologia: A Booke of Kings* (London, 1618), National Portrait Gallery, Smithsonian Institution, Washington, D.C., is a compendium of engraved portraits of British royalty.

3. That oval format was, in fact, standard for depicting members of the British court at the time. See Wayne Craven, *Colonial American Portraiture: The Economic, Religious, Social, Cultural, Philosophical, Scientific, and Aesthetic Foundations* (Cambridge, Eng., and New York, 1986), 22–24. The inscription of the National Portrait Gallery painting, *MATOAKA ALS REBECCA FILIA POTENTISS PRINC: POWHATANI IMP: VIRGINIAE,* differs from that in the engraving.

4. For additional information about her sitting for the portrait, see David R. Ransome, "Pocahontas and the Mission to the Indians," *Virginia Magazine of History and Biography* 99 (January 1991):87.

5. Theodore de Bry engraved the drawings that were published in Thomas Hariot's *Briefe and True Report of the New Found Land of Virginia* of 1590. See Paul Hulton, *America 1585: The Complete Drawings of John White* (Chapel Hill, N.C., 1984), plate 36; and Wayne Franklin, *Discoverers, Explorers, Settlers: The Diligent Writers of Early America* (Chicago, 1979), description accompanying plate 30; Ivor Noël Hume, *The Virginia Adventure, Roanoke to James Towne: An Archeological and Historical Odyssey* (New

York, 1994), 29, 31–32, 56–72; and William S. Rasmussen and Robert S. Tilton, *Pocahontas: Her Life and Legend* (Richmond, Va., 1994), 8.

6. The rest of the inscription is: "[H]is thankfulness and how he subiected 39 of their kings. reade and history." See Philip Barbour, ed., *The Complete Works of Captain John Smith* (Chapel Hill, N.C., 1986), vol. 2, 97; and Hugh Honour, *The European Vision of America* (Cleveland, 1975), description accompanying plate 69.

7. The engraving of 1793 was published by W. Richardson, Castle Street, Leicester Square, London.

8. Barbour, *Complete Works*, vol. 2, 150–151. For details about the rescue story, see J. A. Leo Lemay, *Did Pocahontas Save Captain John Smith?* (Athens, Ga., 1992), 34–45.

9. Barbour, *Complete Works*, vol. 2, 182–183.

10. Ibid., 261.

11. Stith repeated Smith's story almost verbatim, and Beverley related the encounter between Englishman and Indian as a mere cultural misunderstanding. See William Stith, *History of the First Discovery and Settlement of Virginia* (1747; reprint, Spartanberg, S.C., 1965), 143; Robert Beverley, *The History and Present State of Virginia*, ed. Louis B. Wright (Chapel Hill, N.C., 1947), 43. Also see Peter Hulme, *Colonial Encounters: Europe and the Native Caribbean, 1492–1792* (New York, 1986), 146–147; and Frederic W. Gleach, *Powhatan's World and Colonial Virginia: A Conflict of Cultures* (Lincoln, Nebr., and London, 1997), 120–121.

12. The earliest utilization of the legend, *The Female American*, was released in London in 1767 and in the United States around 1790 and thus predated republication of Smith's *Generall Historie*. Its anonymous author narrates in the first person under the pseudonym of the book's main character, Unca Eliza Winkfield. The novel begins with a thinly disguised version of the Pocahontas story in which the author's Indian mother, Unca, rescues and subsequently marries an Englishman named Winkfield. The male protagonist is actually a parody of Virginia's first governor, Edward Maria Wingfield (often spelled "Wynckfield"), whom the captain lambasted in his *Generall Historie* as one of the corrupt officials appointed by the Virginia Company. See Anonymous, *The Female American: or, The Adventures of Unca Eliza Winkfield Compiled by Herself* (1767; reprint, New York and London, 1974). On Wingfield, see Hume, *Virginia Adventure*, 109, 128.

13. "Anecdotes of Pocahunta," *Columbian Magazine*, July 1787, 548–51. See "The Marquis and the Chevalier," *Jamestown Magazine* 2 (August 1907):43; and Tilton, *Pocahontas*, 9–11. Chastellux spelled the family name "Bowling."

14. The Marquis de Chastellux, *Travels in North America in the Years 1780–81–82* (American publication of the 1787 French edition: reprint, New York, 1968), 270. Stith and Beverley also wrote about Pocahontas's *head*, not her *body*. Beverley, *Present State*, 39; Stith, *First Discovery*, 55.

15. Chastellux, *Travels*, 270–272.

16. John Davis, *Travels of Four Years and a Half in the United States of America During 1798, 1799, 1800, 1801, and 1802* (New York, 1909), 296–320.

17. For further discussion of Davis's prurient descriptions, see Philip Young, "The Mother of Us All: Pocahontas Reconsidered," *Kenyon Review* 24 (Summer 1962):391–415. Also see William Warren Jenkins, "The Princess Pocahontas and Three Englishmen Named John," in J. Lasley Dameron and James W. Mathews, eds., *No Fairer Land: Studies in Southern Literature before 1900* (Troy, N.Y., 1986), 8–20.

18. John Davis to Henry Carey, March 10, 1805, Historical Society of Pennsylvania, Philadelphia.

19. See John Davis, *The First Settlers of Virginia* (New York, 1806), v–viii, and *Captain Smith and Princess Pocahontas* (Philadelphia, 1805), 25; and Young, "Mother of Us All," 400–401.

20. Ibid., 19–26; George C.D. Odell, *Annals of the New York Stage* (New York, 1927), vol. 2, 318–319; William Dunlap, *History of the American Theatre* (New York, 1832), 378–379; Walter J. Meserve, *An Emerging Entertainment: The Drama of the American People to 1828* (Bloomington, Ind., 1977), 180–181; and Arthur Hobson Quinn, *A History of the American Drama, from the Beginning to the Civil War* (New York, 1943), 138–139.

21. Perhaps the Indian theme reflects the democratic political leanings of Barker and his father, then the outspoken mayor of Philadelphia, a position the playwright himself would assume one day. For further discussion of Barker's political activities, see Paul H. Musser, *James Nelson Barker, 1784–1858* (Philadelphia, 1929), 6–12, 80–82.

22. Although Barker announced that the "principal materials" came from Smith's *Generall Historie*, it is clear that his source of inspiration was Davis, an attribution corroborated by the appearance of the playwright's name on the subscription list appended to Davis's *Travels*.

23. J. N. Barker, "The Indian Princess or La Belle Sauvage," in Montrose J. Moses, *Representative American Plays by American Dramatists, 1765–1819* (New York, 1918), 595.

24. Ibid., 611–612.

25. A Philadelphia *Ordeal* critic commended this scene as being "superior" to that in most European plays. See Meserve, *Emerging Entertainment,* 175.

26. William Gilmore Simms, "Pocahontas: Subject for the Historical Painter," in C. Hugh Holman, ed., *Views and Reviews in American Literature, History and Fiction* (London, 1962), 114–115.

27. See Rasmussen and Tilton, *Pocahontas,* 14–15.

28. See Jill Lapore, *The Name of War: King Philip's War and the Origins of American Identity* (New York, 1998), 80.

29. The handprint on the rear shank of the horse was probably copied from Catlin's *Keokuck (the Watchful Fox), Chief of the Tribe Sauk and Fox* (National Museum of American Art, Smithsonian Institution, Washington, D.C.). The Corbould version of the rescue had several reincarnations, most notably a color lithograph of 1870 by Christian Inger and a folk painting now belonging to Colonial Williamsburg. I wish

to thank Douglas E. Bradley, curator of ethnographic arts, Snite Museum of Art, University of Notre Dame, for helping me identify the Plains symbolism. For details on Catlin, see William Treuttner, *The Natural Man Observed: A Study of Catlin's Indian Gallery* (Washington, D.C., 1979), 41–43, 141–142, 147–148. Information on Corbould is in Edward Henry to R. Griffin, April 28, 1860, and the obituary of January 21, 1905, Additional Manuscripts, Department of Manuscripts, The British Library, London.

30. "The press of the country . . . that powerful engine of American action, is in New-England hands. The professions, generally, are theirs. The manufactures, and the artisans, and the commerce, are theirs, as a general remark, which all, as agents of action, powerfully predominate over the public mind." "Fourth of July Thoughts," *Knickerbocker* 14 (July 1839):68.

31. See Beverley, *Present State*, 37–44.

32. Stith, *First Discovery*, 137, 144. For his full account of the Pocahontas story, see ibid., 54–56, 61, 89–90, 127–129, 136–147.

33. Chastellux, *Travels*, 272.

34. Beverley, *Present State*, 38–39. For the rationale that seemed to persist through the nineteenth century, see David D. Smits, "'Squaw Men,' 'Half-Breeds,' and 'Amalgamators': Late Nineteenth-Century Anglo-American Attitudes Toward Indian-White Race Mixing," *American Indian Culture and Research Journal* 15 (1991): 29–61.

35. The best biography of Wirt is still John P. Kennedy, *Memoirs of the Life of William Wirt*, 2 vols. (Philadelphia, 1850; reprint, Buffalo, N.Y., 1973). Also see Michael L. Oberg, "William Wirt and the Trials of Republicanism," *Virginia Magazine of History and Biography*, 99 (July 1991):305–326; and Charles Frederick Stansbury, "Literary Landmarks of the Jamestown Exposition: William Wirt," *Jamestown Magazine* 2 (July 1907):1–7.

36. William Wirt, *The Letters of the British Spy* (1803; reprint, Chapel Hill, N.C., 1970), 168–170.

37. For discussion of Virginians and miscegenation, see Tilton, *Pocahontas*, 9–33.

38. Some authors have claimed that the 1793 republication of the Van de Passe *Lady Rebecca* engraving made Pocahontas appear more European than she had in the 1618 version. After closely examining the two prints, I believe that slight differences between the two engravings should be attributed to the poorer quality of the late eighteenth-century print and not to a deliberate attempt of the printmaker to make her appear "whiter." I wish to thank Wendy Wick Reaves for advising me on this matter. For the opposite opinion, see Tilton, *Pocahontas*, 9–10, 106–109.

39. See T. H. Breen, *Tobacco Culture: The Mentality of the Great Tidewater Planters on the Eve of Revolution* (Princeton, 1985).

40. Portions of the history were published in the late nineteenth century. See Arthur H. Shaffer, Introduction to *Edmund Randolph, History of Virginia* (Charlottesville, Va., 1970), xi–xliv.

41. Ibid., 24–25, 31, 62, 74, 77.

42. John Daly Burk, *History of Virginia from its First Settlement to the Present Day,* 4 vols. (Petersburg, Va., 1804–1816), vol. 1, 113, 186–187.

43. Ibid., 188–190.

44. A family anecdote alleged that Ryland Randolph, a prominent descendant, had obtained the portrait along with one of John Rolfe from a member of the British branch of the Rolfe (Rolf) family. The paintings remained at Randolph's James River plantation, Turkey Island, until 1784, when a distant relative, Thomas Bolling, purchased the pair and transported them to his estate near Petersburg. The Virginian Hugh Grigsby reported that the originals were "fixed permanently in a panel of the wooden wainscot over the mantle" of Randolph's home and were badly damaged when pried from the wall. Hugh Grigsby to Charles Deane, March 6, March 25, and April 17, 1875, Massachusetts Historical Society, Boston. Also see Thomas L. McKenney and James Hall, *The Indian Tribes of North America . . .* (Totowa, N.J., 1972), vol. 3, ix–x; and *Collections of the State Historical Society of Wisconsin* (Madison, 1903):63–69.

45. Linnaeus Bolling to William Bolling, September 14, 1830, and William Bolling, "History of Two Portraits Said to be Those of John Rolfe and Pocahontas," Bolling Papers, Virginia Historical Society, Richmond. The same sentiments were expressed by Archibald Robertson in a letter of September 20, 1830, and in an accompanying memorandum. See McKenney and Hall, *Indian Tribes,* x–xii, and *Historical Collections of the Wisconsin Historical Society* 2 (1855):43–47.

46. Grigsby claimed that it was Thomas Sully who copied the original Turkey Island portrait, but no other evidence substantiates this. See Hugh Gribsby to Charles Deane, March 6, 1875, Massachusetts Historical Society, Boston.

47. William Bolling was, in fact, convinced that the companion portrait of Rolfe might have been genuine but that the one alleged to be Pocahontas was a picture of somebody else. Thomas Sully apparently copied both the Indian Gallery print and his nephew's portrait. William Bolling, "Two Portraits." Also see Rasmussen and Tilton, *Pocahontas,* 35–37; Virginius C. Hall, *Portraits in the Collection of the Virginia Historical Society* (Richmond, 1981), 196–197; and citation in the *Catalogue of American Portraits,* National Portrait Gallery, Smithsonian Institution, Washington, D.C.

48. Quoted in Louise Phelps Kellogg, "Pocahontas and Jamestown," *Wisconsin Magazine of History* 25 (September 1941):41–42. Sully had apparently been anticipating a portrait of Pocahontas before 1830, because a sketch attributed to the artist and dated c. 1828 at the Valentine Museum in Richmond pictures a young and lithe maiden who strongly resembles the later Pocahontas portrait.

49. Quoted in Anthony Faiola, "Little Dove vs. 'Pocahontas,'" *Washington Post,* May 25, 1995.

50. Ibid.

Chapter 5

1. Felicia Hemans, "The Landing of the Pilgrim Fathers," in William S. Russell, *Guide to Plymouth and Recollections of the Pilgrims* (Boston, 1846), appendix, 50–52.

2. The speech that inspired Hemans was probably Edward Everett's Forefathers' Day address of 1824. She told Bancroft that she had read the hymn by J. Pierpont written that same year. Felicia Hemans to George Bancroft, July 24, 1826, Massachusetts Historical Society, Boston. Also see "Mrs. Hemans and the Pilgrim Fathers: Speech of Rev. Charles Brooks at the Cape Cod Association," *Littell's Living Age* 31 (December 1851):553; and *Old Colony Memorial,* December 6, 1851.

3. Preface, *The Poetical Works of Mrs. Felicia Hemans, Complete in One Volume* (Philadelphia, 1836), xii.

4. See Felicia Hemans to William Jack, May 1, 1823, Department of Manuscripts, British Library, London; and Peter W. Trinder, *Mrs. Hemans* (Cardiff, Wales, 1984), 33–34.

5. Long ignored in literary circles, Hemans has received recent attention, especially from feminists who cite her failed marriage, unyielding dedication to work, and poems about hearth and home as evidence of the difficulties suffered by women authors during the nineteenth century. See John Seelye, *Memory's Nation: The Place of Plymouth Rock* (Chapel Hill, N.C., 1998), 91–96; Norma Clarke, *Ambitious Heights, Writing, Friendship, Love: The Jewsbury Sisters, Felicia Hemans, and Jane Welsh Carlyle* (London and New York, 1990), 44–51ff.; and Virginia Blair et al., *The Feminist Companion to Literature in English: Women Writers from the Middle Ages to the Present* (New Haven, 1990), 510. For older sources, see Harriet Hughes, *The Poetical Works of Mrs. Hemans, with a Memoir of Her Life, by Her Sister* (Edinburgh, 1839); John Correll, *Felicia Hemans: Her Life and Poems . . .* (Dublin, 1865); and Lucy B. Walford, *Twelve English Authoresses* (1893; reprint, Freeport, N.Y., 1972), 85–100.

6. Henry Tuckerman explained her appeal: "The bleak arrival of the New-England pilgrims, and the evening devotion of the Italian peasant-girl are equally consecrated by her muse. . . . Her best verses glow with emotion. When once truly interested in a subject, she cast over it such an air of feeling that our sympathies are won at once." Henry T. Tuckerman, "Essay," in Rufus Griswold, ed., *Poems of Felicia Hemans with an Essay on Her Genius* (Philadelphia, 1849), x–xii. Also see "The Poetical Works of Felicia D. Hemans," *SLM* 11 (December 1845):716–719.

7. Felicia Hemans and Harriet Browne to George Bancroft, February 20, 1824, December 15, 1824, July 24, 1826, and April 24, 1827, Massachusetts Historical Society, Boston. She also corresponded with such British literary figures as Samuel Butler, Sir Walter Scott, and Joanna Baillie. See the Butler-Hemans Correspondence, Department of Manuscripts, British Library, London; and Henry F. Chorley, *Memorials of Mrs. Hemans with Illustrations of Her Literary Character from Her Private Correspondence* (London, 1836), vol. 1, 107–109, 244–247.

8. See "Landing of the Pilgrim Fathers by Mrs. Hemans and Her Sister" (London, 183); and for a later musical version, see Otto Singer, "The Landing of the Pilgrim Fathers: A Cantata" (Cincinnati, 1876).

9. Bradford, *History of Plymouth Plantation* (Boston, 1912), vol. 1, 155–156.

10. Appended to Jedidiah Morse and Elijah Parish, *Compendious History of New England* (Charlestown, Mass., 1804), 377.

11. The last verse of Berkeley's "On the Prospect of Planting Arts and Learning in America" (1728?) begins with this line: "Westward the course of empire takes its way."

12. John Adams to Benjamin Rush, May 23, 1807, in John A. Schutz and Douglass Adair, eds., *The Spur of Fame: Dialogues of John Adams and Benjamin Rush, 1805–1813* (San Marino, Calif., 1966), 89.

13. *Old Colony Memorial,* January 15 and January 29, 1853.

14. For mid-nineteenth-century deliberations over the date, see "The 22nd of December," *Old Colony Memorial,* December 21, 1850. For other information about the date, see George F. Willison, *Saints and Strangers* (New York, 1945), 425; Nathaniel Morton, *New England Memoriall,* ed. Howard J. Hall (New York, 1937), 22; Cotton Mather, *Magnalia Christi Americana,* ed. Kenneth B. Murdock (Cambridge, Mass., 1977), 132; and William Hubbard, "General History of New England," *Collections of the Massachusetts Historical Society* 5 (1815):53.

15. See Wendy Greenhouse, "The Landing of the Fathers: Representing the National Past in American History Painting, 1770–1865," in *Picturing History: American Painting, 1770–1930* (New York, 1993), 45–63; Ann Uhry Abrams, "Visions of Columbus: The 'Discovery' Legend in Antebellum American Paintings and Prints," *American Art Journal* 25 (1–2) (1993):74–101.

16. See Anne Cannon Palumbo, "Averting 'Present Commotions': History as Politics in *Penn's Treaty,*" *American Art* 9 (Fall 1995):29–55.

17. G.N.G. Clarke, "Taking Possession: The Cartouche as Cultural Text in Eighteenth-Century American Maps," *Word and Image* 4 (April–June 1988):459. I wish to thank Jeremy Bangs and James Baker for calling my attention to this cartouche and Anne Palumbo for her helpful comments. Also see Peter Benes, *New England Prospect: A Loan Exhibition of Maps at the Currier Gallery of Art in Manchester, New Hampshire* (Boston, 1980), 13.

18. See Harold W. Sniffen, "Views of Port Cities as Depicted by Vernet and Other Eighteenth-Century Artists," in Joan D. Dolmetch, ed., *Eighteenth-Century Prints in Colonial America: To Educate and Decorate* (Williamsburg, Va., 1979), 32–50; and Sinclair Hitchings, "London's Images of Colonial America," in Dolmetch, *Eighteenth-Century Prints in Colonial America,* 11–31.

19. See Carl L. Crossman and Charles R. Strickland, "Early Depictings of the Landing of the Pilgrims," *Magazine Antiques* 98 (November 1970):777–780.

20. Three known versions of the painting are in Pilgrim Hall, Plymouth, Mass.; the State Department, Washington, D.C.; and the Vose Gallery, Boston.

21. Another (and more likely) version of the legend states that Corné came as an apprentice to Captain Elias Derby, a Salem merchant. Known primarily for his ma-

rine paintings and house decorations, the Italian artist did only a few historical compositions. Among these are *The Landing of Columbus* and *Columbus and the Egg.* See Nina Fletcher Little, "Michele Felice Corné, 1752–1845," *Magazine Antiques* 102 (August 1972):262–269; Robert E. Peabody, "A War Refugee of 1800," *Publications of the Colonial Society of Massachusetts* 34 (1941):404–411; and Philip Chadwick Foster Smith and Nina Fletcher Little, *Michele Felice Corné, 1752–1845* (Salem, Mass., 1972).

22. Two of the earliest such illustrations appeared in James Seward's *History of the Discovery of America and the Landing of Our Forefathers at Plymouth,* published in 1809.

23. See S. Elizabeth Bird, "Introduction: Constructing the Indian, 1830s–1990s," in *Dressing in Feathers: The Construction of the Indian in American Popular Culture* (Boulder, 1996), 1–12; Frederick Drimmer, ed., *Captured by the Indians, 15 Firsthand Accounts, 1750–1870* (New York, 1961); and Robert F. Berkhofer Jr., *The White Man's Indian: Images of the American Indian from Columbus to the Present* (New York, 1978), 72–111.

24. The best source for this history is still Jacob C. Meyer, *Church and State in Massachusetts from 1740–1833* (Cleveland, 1930), 32–68, 90–132.

25. See "Plymouth Church Records," *Publications of the Colonial Society of Massachusetts* 22 (1920):xxxiv–xlvii; Peter Gomes, "George Whitefield in the Old Colony: 1740," in L. D. Geller, ed., *They Knew They Were Pilgrims: Essays in Plymouth History* (Plymouth, Mass., and New York, 1971), 91–99; and Harold Field Worthley, "Doctrinal Divisions in the Church of Christ at Plymouth, 1744–1801," in Geller, *They Knew,* 101–112.

26. The terms "liberal" and "conservative" were then applied to the two sides of the Congregational schism, although the meanings differed from more recent applications.

27. John Allyn, *A Sermon Delivered at Plimouth, December 22, 1801* (Boston, 1802), 33–34.

28. Abiel Holmes, *A Discourse Delivered at Plymouth, 22 December, 1806, at the Anniversary Commemoration of the First Landing of the Fathers, A.D. 1620* (Cambridge, Mass., 1620), 17–20.

29. To emphasize the conservative Calvinists' link to the past, the prominent minister Lyman Beecher named his anti-Unitarian periodical *The Spirit of the Pilgrims.* See Martin Moore, *The Old Ways of the Pilgrim Fathers* (Hingham, Mass., 1835), 4, 6, 16; and Samuel Joseph May, *Letters to Rev. Joel Hawes, D.D. in Review of His Tribute to the Memory of the Pilgrims* (Hartford, Conn., 1831). Also see Joseph Conforti, "Edwards, Unitarians, and the Memory of the Great Awakening, 1800–1840," in Conrad Edick Wright, ed., *American Unitarianism, 1805–1865* (Boston, 1989), 42; Nathan O. Hatch, *The Democratization of American Christianity* (New Haven and London, 1989), 170–179; and Meyer, *Church and State in Massachusetts,* 133–159.

30. See James M. Banner Jr., *To the Hartford Convention: The Federalists and the Origins of Party Politics in Massachusetts, 1789–1815* (New York, 1970), 152–167.

31. The Boston Forefathers' Day celebration was orchestrated by such leading Federalists as Stephen Higginson, Benjamin Lincoln, George Cabot, Christopher

Gore, and William Tudor Jr. See "The 'Feast of the Shells,'" *Independent Chronicle,* December 31, 1798, reproduced in Albert Matthews, "The Term 'Pilgrim Fathers' and Early Celebrations of Forefather's Day," *Publications of the Colonial Society of Massachusetts* 19 (1914):328. On the political rivalry, see Linda K. Kerber, *Federalists in Dissent: Imagery and Ideology in Jeffersonian America* (Ithaca, 1970); Steven Watts, *The Republic Reborn: War and the Making of Liberal America, 1790–1820* (Baltimore and London, 1987); and Robert W. Wiebe, *The Opening of American Society from the Adoption of the Constitution to the Eve of Disunion* (New York, 1984).

32. Quoted in Matthews, "'Pilgrim Fathers,'" 324.

33. At the celebrations of 1797, for example, the participants toasted the Federalist presidents George Washington and John Adams, then moved on to speeches praising Timothy Pickering, John Jay, Alexander Hamilton, Governor Increase Sumner, and other prominent Federalists. *Massachusetts Mercury*, December 28, 1797, reproduced in Matthews, "'Pilgrim Fathers,'" 324–325. *Columbian Centinel*, December 24, 1800, quoted in Matthews, "'Pilgrim Fathers,'" 333. The political nature of such toasts did not go unnoticed by the opposition. A series of articles in the Jeffersonian *Independent Chronicle* between 1799 and 1805 ridiculed the banquets for their strident Federalist content. See ibid., 328–329, 344–349.

34. Born in 1761 into a close-knit and pious Woodstock, Connecticut, household, Jedidiah Morse graduated from Yale in 1783 and was ordained as a Congregational minister in 1786. His father held a number of minor local offices and served for many years as one of two deacons in the local church. For biographical information, see Richard J. Moss, *The Life of Jedidiah Morse: A Station of Peculiar Exposure* (Knoxville, Tenn., 1995); and Joseph W. Phillips, *Jedidiah Morse and New England Congregationalism* (New Brunswick, N.J., 1983).

35. Richard J. Moss, "Republicanism, Liberalism, and Identity: the Case of Jedidiah Morse," *Essex Institute Historical Collections* 126 (October 1990):215, 230.

36. A "Citizen of Williamsburg" [St. George Tucker], *A Letter to the Rev. Jedediah Morse, A.M. Author of the "American Universal Geography,"* ed. and intro. L. H. Butterfield (1795; reprint, Richmond, Va., 1953), 8–9. Judge John Tyler congratulated Tucker on his bold response to Morse and added: "Jedediah's universality is like his mental Faculties confined within a very narrow circle indeed." John Tyler to St. George Tucker, July 10, 1795, in Lyon Tyler, *Letters and Times of the Tylers* (1896; reprint, New York, 1970), 12.

37. Although he often preached against the evil influence of capitalism, Morse was reaping its benefits by accumulating a comfortable nest egg through publication of his geographical and historical texts. See Moss, "Republicanism," 221–223, 230–231, and Moss, *Jedidiah Morse*, 81–115.

38. He subsequently established a periodical entitled the *Panoplist* as a vehicle for excoriating Unitarianism, a movement he angrily dubbed "the *democracy* of Christianity." See Moss, *Jedidiah Morse*, 87.

39. When it became clear that Unitarians would hold sway at Harvard, Morse led the drive to establish several conservative institutions, including the First Sabbath-School Society in 1806, the Andover Theological Seminary in 1808, and the American Board of Foreign Missions in 1810. See Jedidiah Morse, *A Sermon, Preached at Charlestown, November 29, 1798, on the Anniversary of Thanksgiving . . .* , quoted in Vernon Stauffer, *New England and the Bavarian Illuminati* (1918; reprint, New York, 1967), 268; Gary B. Nash, "The American Clergy and the French Revolution," *William and Mary Quarterly* 22 (July 1965):392–412; and Phillips, *Jedidiah Morse*, 73–101. For J. Morse's theological orientation, see Sidney E. Morse, *Memorabilia in the Life of Jedidiah Morse, DD* (Boston, 1867), 15; Moss, *Jedidiah Morse*, 54–58.

40. See Paul J. Staiti, *Samuel F.B. Morse* (New York and Cambridge, Eng., 1989), 1–6, 13–15; and Moss, "Republicanism," 217–221.

41. Morse had returned to Charlestown and found himself under the unrelenting scrutiny of his parents while painting this first large history painting. In February 1811, he wrote to his brothers Edward and Richard, then students at Yale, that he was working on a large rendition of "the landing of our forefathers at Plymouth," which he hoped to finish before spring. Samuel F.B. Morse to Edward and Richard Morse, October 24 and December 8, 1810, January 11 and Feb. ?, 1811, Manuscript Division, Library of Congress, Washington, D.C. Also see Moss, *Jedidiah Morse*, 127–130.

42. Staiti, *Samuel F.B. Morse*, 14.

43. See Jedidiah Morse and Elijah Parish, *Compendious History of New England* (Charlestown, Mass., 1804), 39–43; and Davis oration in ibid., 375.

44. Shortly after completing *The Landing of the Forefathers,* Samuel Morse left America for London, where he spent four years studying painting with the American expatriate Benjamin West, during which time he fine-tuned his painting techniques and completed several classical history paintings, the best-known being *The Dying Hercules.* After returning home, he tried for a while to placate his father by becoming involved in religious affairs, but he soon left Massachusetts to pursue his career as an artist in New York. See S.E. Morse, *Memorabilia*, 5, 16; S.F.B. Morse to Henry Thacher, July 10, 1817, Massachusetts Historical Society, Boston; Paul Staiti and Gary A. Reynolds, *Samuel F.B. Morse* (New York, 1982), 16–17; Carleton Mabee, *The American Leonardo: A Life of Samuel F.B. Morse* (New York, 1943), 24–25; and Edward Lind Morse, *Samuel F.B. Morse: His Letters and Journals* (Boston and New York, 1914), 30.

45. *Dictionary of American Biography*, under "Paine, Robert Treat, Sr."; and David Hackett Fischer, *The Revolution of American Conservatism: The Federalist Party in the Era of Jeffersonian Democracy* (New York, 1965), xi.

46. R. T. Paine, "Rule New-England," in *The Works in Verse and Prose of the Late Robert Treat Paine, Jr.* (Boston, 1812), 252–253.

47. Charles Prentiss, introduction to *Works of Paine,* vi–xl; *Dictionary of American Biography*, under "Paine, Robert Treat, Jr."; E. M. and S. B. Puknat, "An American Critic and a German Vogue, the Theatrical Pioneering of Robert Treat Paine," *Publi-*

cations of the Colonial Society of Massachusetts 43 (February 1957):203–289; and Joseph Peirce to General Henry Knox, September 15, 1895, Massachusetts Historical Society, Boston.

48. New Englanders lost their respect for the English rebel Thomas Paine during the 1790s, when he sided with the Jacobins in France. See Nash, "The American Clergy and the French Revolution," 400–402.

49. The first verse, perhaps for reasons of expedience, denounced the Jacobin violence Paine had once defended: "While France her huge limbs bathes recumbent in blood, / And Society's base threats with wide dissolution; / May Peace like the dove, who returned from the flood, / Find an ark of abode in our mild constitution." See Robert Treat Paine Jr., "Adams and Liberty," in *Works of Paine*, 245–247.

50. Prentiss, introduction to *Works of Paine*, xlvi–xlvii.

51. "Song of Jefferson and Liberty" (1874), 1, 3–7, Miscellaneous Bound Manuscripts, Boston Public Library.

52. See, for example, "Festival of the Sons of the Pilgrims," song sheet, n.d., Pilgrim Hall, Plymouth, Mass.

53. Robert Treat Paine Jr., "Ode," in *Works of Paine*, 265–266; and Matthews, "'Pilgrim Fathers,'" 326–327.

54. The senior Paine complained that a "person for whom Nature, Education . . . connections & family beneficent assistance have done so much to qualify for introduction to an honorable & profitable situation in life" should reject it all. Robert Treat Paine to Robert Treat Paine Jr., February 24, 1810, Massachusetts Historical Society, Boston.

55. Charles Prentiss summarized his friend's problems: "A supercilious pride had, at least, partially excluded him from higher society, and compelled him to intercourses, not always the most reputable or useful." Prentiss, introduction to *Works of Paine*, xliv.

56. Joseph Croswell to Albert Gallatin, November 18, 1801, Gallatin Papers, New York Historical Society, New York.

57. Joseph Croswell, *A New World Planted; or, The Adventures of the Forefathers of New England Who Landed in Plymouth, December 1620* (Boston, 1802). Walter Meserve wrote that Croswell's *New World* "reads better" than some plays that did reach the stage. See Walter J. Meserve, *An Emerging Entertainment: The Drama of the American People to 1828* (Bloomington, Ind., 1977), 189.

58. He wrote Gallatin that his father had been in Boston for forty years as a "settled minister" known to Samuel Adams and others of his generation. His father may have been the Reverend Andrew Croswell, whose preaching led to the schism that divided the First Plymouth Church in 1743, or the itinerant evangelist Joseph Croswell, who conducted a long trek of missionary wanderings around New England during the Great Awakening. Andrew Croswell died in Boston in 1785, and Joseph Croswell died in Bridgewater, Mass., in 1799. In the available genealogical information, neither man is recorded as having a son named Joseph. See Simon G. Croswell, *A Memoir of the Lives of Some of the Croswell Family* (privately printed, 1916).

Also see *Sketches and Extracts from the Journals and Other Writings of the Late Joseph Croswell, 1712–1799* (Boston, 1809); James Thacher, *History of the Town of Plymouth from Its First Settlement in 1629 to the Year 1832* (Boston, 1831), 308–309; "Plymouth Church Records," *Publications of the Colonial Society of Massachusetts* 22 (1920):xxxiv–xxxv, 295; and Mark L. Sargent, "Plymouth Rock and the Great Awakening," *Journal of American Studies* 22 (August 1988):251–523.

59. Croswell to Gallatin, November 18, 1801; Joseph Croswell, "Ode to Liberty," appended to Chandler Robbins, *Address Delivered at Plymouth on the 24th Day of January, 1793 . . . to Celebrate the Victories of the French Republic* (Boston, 1793); and "A True Acct of All the . . . Estate of Jo. Croswell," Pilgrim Society, Plymouth, Mass.

60. As a defense during their trial, Oldham told the court: "We form'd a plan to put you all in fear, / That our terrific noise might stimulate, / To adequate concessions on your part / For the indignity confer'd on us." See Croswell, *New World*, 33; and Margaret G. Mayorga, *A Short History of American Drama: Commentaries on Plays Prior to 1920* (New York, 1940), 343.

61. Croswell, *New World*, 45. Also see Matthews, "'Pilgrim Fathers,'" 342.

62. For a different interpretation, see Seelye, *Memory's Nation*, 47–49; Robert S. Tilton, *Pocahontas: the Evolution of an American Narrative* (Cambridge, Eng., and New York, 1994), 48–49; and Mark L. Sargent, "Rekindled Fires: Jamestown and Plymouth in American Literature, 1765–1863" (Ph.D. diss., Claremont Graduate School, 1985), 70–89.

63. Although the first known exhibition of Sargent's *Landing of the Fathers* was the Boston exhibition of 1815, he may have exhibited it as early as 1802. Shortly after the 1815 exhibition, sap leaking from the pole around which it was wrapped damaged the canvas, and the artist created a duplicate that he exhibited several times before he presented it to the Pilgrim Society in 1835. See Dunlap, *History* 2:61–62; and Mabel Munson Swan, *The Athenaeum Gallery, 1827–1873: The Boston Athenaeum as an Early Patron of Art* (Boston, 1940), 39–40; Matthews, "'Pilgrim Fathers,'" 335–336; and curator's files, Pilgrim Hall, Plymouth, Mass.

64. The helmeted figure of John Carver with his wife beside him dominates the center of the composition; William Bradford is positioned behind Carver; the Indian, Samoset, loosely clad in a toga-style animal skin, stands in the foreground, bowing submissively to the European strangers; Edward Winslow is on the far right; the elderly William Brewster in the middle, and a debonair Miles Standish (in a jaunty white hat) stands just behind Samoset. Sargent may well have patterned Standish's hat after a white felt hat said to have belonged to one of the original Plymouth settlers in the collection of Pilgrim Hall, Plymouth.

65. The Massachusetts Historical Society, in fact, possesses an invitation to the Forefathers' Day celebration of 1798 addressed to the artist's father, Daniel Sargent (spelled "Sargeant"), and bearing the Samuel Hill illustration at the top. See Fig. 5.2.

66. In 1651, when Winslow returned to England on colony business, he sat for the portrait. After his death it passed down through the Winslow family of Marshfield and Boston and finally ended up in Pilgrim Hall, Plymouth, Mass. Examples of the

commentaries that praise the individual character of the landing party are in *Old Colony Memorial,* January 1, 1825, and October 31, 1835. For more on the Winslow portrait, see Wayne Craven, *Colonial American Portraiture* (New York and Cambridge, Eng., 1986), 51–52; and Alexander Young, *Chronicles of the Pilgrim Fathers of the Colony of Plymouth, 1602–1625* (Boston, 1841), xi.

67. John Singleton Copley had painted portraits of his grandfather, Epes Sargent, his mother, Mary Turner Sargent, and numerous other relatives. John Singer Sargent was a descendant of the same Massachusetts family. See Jules Prown, *John Singleton Copley* (Cambridge, Mass., 1966), vol. 1, 33, 38, 190–191, 227–228; and E. P. Richardson, *American Art: An Exhibition from the Collection of Mr. and Mrs. John D. Rockefeller 3rd* (San Francisco, 1976), 38.

68. Letters to and from Sargent to his family (1793–1797) and letters from H. C. Pratt, January 20 and February 28, 1845, Massachusetts Historical Society, Boston. Also see Dorinda Evans, *Benjamin West and His American Students* (Washington, D.C., 1980), 113–115; Ann Uhry Abrams, *The Valiant Hero: Benjamin West and Grand Style History Painting* (Washington, D.C., 1985), and *Dictionary of American Biography,* under "Sargent, Henry."

69. Henry Sargent to William Dunlap, May 5, 1833, Pennsylvania Academy of Fine Arts Papers, AAA. Also see William Dunlap, *History of the Rise and Progress of the Arts of Design in the United States* (1834; reprint, New York, 1969), vol. 2, 58–63; and William Dunlap, *Diary of William Dunlap* (New York, 1931), vol. 3, 682. Late in life, Sargent became an honorary member of the American Academy of Fine Arts, received an honorary Master of Arts degree from Harvard, and was elected president of the Artist's Association; he died, however, before assuming the post. See Julia De-Wolf Addison, "Henry Sargent: A Boston Painter," *Art in America* 17 (1929–1930):279–284.

70. His large *Christ Entering Jerusalem* (unlocated) was well received when exhibited in 1817. In addition, Sargent painted numerous portraits, including those of John Randolph, De Witt Clinton, Jeremy Belknap, and Commodore Oliver Hazard Perry. See Henry T. Tuckerman, *Book of the Artists* (1867; reprint, New York, 1966), 56–58; and *Columbian Centinel,* February 15, 1817.

71. "The Landing of the Fathers," *Palladium,* March 14 and 17, 1815, reproduced in *Collections of the Massachusetts Historical Society* 13 (1915):225, 230; and *Old Colony Memorial,* October 31, 1835.

72. Russell, *Guide to Plymouth,* appendix, 28.

73. The problems began when Jefferson imposed an embargo in 1807 that affected New England's export and import trade. See Banner, *Hartford Convention,* 41–44.

74. A group of aging Federalists, who called themselves the "Essex Junto," made it clear that they favored secession rather than fight with England. The group was led by George Cabot, Stephen Higginson, Theophilus Parsons, Jonathan Jackson, and John Lowell. See David Hackett Fischer, "The Myth of the Essex Junto,"

William and Mary Quarterly 21 (April 1964):191–235; and Fischer, *American Conservatism,* 153–154, 250, 262.

75. See Banner, *Hartford Convention,* 327–350.

76. Dunlap, *History,* vol. 2, 62.

77. *Old Colony Memorial,* October 31, 1835.

78. Another columnist wrote: "An historical painting is a species of drama presented to the eye, where . . . colouring forms the dialogue and all that remains belongs to invention, plot and character." "Peregrinus," "The Landing of the Fathers," 232.

79. See Thacher, *History of Plymouth,* 246–254; Peter J. Gomes, ed., *The Pilgrim Society, 1820–1970, an Informal Commemorative Essay* (Plymouth, Mass., 1971), 6–8; Robert V. Remini, *Daniel Webster: The Man and His Time* (New York, 1997), 178–187; and Walker Lewis, ed., *Speak for Yourself, Daniel: A Life of Webster in His Own Words* (New York, 1969), 79–81.

80. *The Writings and Speeches of Daniel Webster* (Boston, 1903), vol. 1, 183–84.

81. Ibid., 181–226.

82. The compromise, which established a dividing line at 36° by 30' between the slave and free states, established a precedent that governed admission of territories for the next two decades. See Don E. Fehrenbacher, *The South and Three Sectional Crises* (Baton Rouge, La., 1980), 9–23; and William W. Freehling, *The Road to Disunion, Secessionists at Bay, 1776–1854* (New York and Oxford, Eng., 1990), 144–161.

83. Paul D. Erickson argues that Webster's 1820 speech spawned the "myth of the Pilgrims." The New England politician, Erickson claims, "rewrote the past into a set of factually simple and splendid tales resembling myth more than documentary history," fashioning such expropriations of the past into self-serving aids of his own political ambitions. See Paul D. Erickson, "Daniel Webster's Myth of the Pilgrims," *New England Quarterly* 57 (March 1984):44–64; and Seelye, *Memory's Nation,* 73–85.

84. Edward Everett, *Oration December 22, 1824* (Boston, 1825), 21–23, 38; and "First Settlement of New England," *Orations and Speeches on Various Occasions by Edward Everett* (Boston, 1850), vol. 1, 46, 48–49, 52–53, 69. For information on Everett, see Paul A. Varg, *Edward Everett, the Intellectual in the Turmoil of Politics* (London and Toronto, 1992).

85. The 1824 presidential race was between Adams (whose support came from the Northeastern states), Andrew Jackson (whose backers lived along the frontier), the Georgian William Crawford (who represented the Deep South), and Kentucky's Henry Clay (who was endorsed by moderates from the Midwest and North). Jackson garnered the most votes, but none of the candidates received the needed majority; the election had to be settled by the House of Representatives, which voted in Adams's favor.

86. Minutes of Pilgrim Society, September 22, 1821, Samuel Davis account book, Pilgrim Hall, Plymouth, Mass.

87. Thacher, *History of Plymouth,* 268–269. A Massachusetts guidebook of 1849 describes Sargent's *Landing* as "a most valuable and interesting acquisition" of the Pil-

grim Society, "valued at three thousand dollars." *Gazetteer of Massachusetts* (Boston, 1849), 239. Also see Thacher, *History of Plymouth,* 268–69; James Thacher to Henry Sargent, October 14, 1835, Massachusetts Historical Society, Boston; John Trumbull to James Thacher, May 1, 1835, and James Thacher to Charles Warren, March 8, 1840, Pilgrim Society, Plymouth, Mass.

88. *Old Colony Memorial,* January 1, 1825. A resident of Philadelphia visiting Pilgrim Hall was deeply moved by Sargent's "faithful representation of the incident . . . Its excellence entitles it to a high rank among the finished productions of the art," equal to works by two current favorites, the Boston history painter Washington Allston and the Spanish religious painter Bartolomé Murillo. *Old Colony Memorial,* November 25, 1826.

89. For the various poems and hymns, see Russell, *Guide to Plymouth,* appendix, 49–74.

90. George Bancroft, *History of the United States from the Discovery of the American Continent,* vol. 1, *History of the Colonization of the United States* (1834; reprint, Boston, 1848), 313. Bancroft's use of the "old-style" date may well explain why so many of the *Landing* prints have it inscribed below the picture.

91. On Bancroft's youth, see Lillian Handlin, *George Bancroft: The Intellectual as Democrat* (New York, 1984), 3–50.

Chapter 6

1. James Bouldin, a Virginia congressman, best summed up the net impact of Custis's play when he said that *Pocahontas* was "the most supremely ridiculous play" he had ever seen. Quoted in Benjamin Brown French, *Witness to the Young Republic: A Yankee's Journal, 1828–1870,* eds. Donald B. Cole and John J. McDonough (Hanover, N.H., and London, 1989), 69.

2. Although Custis's own lineage stretched back to Dutch, Belgian, and British aristocracy, he always seemed at odds with Virginia society and politics. Yet as the self-professed heir to the Washington legacy, he could command a measure of distinction despite his reputation as an eccentric. On Custis's life, see Roger G. Kennedy, *Architecture, Men, Women, and Money in America, 1600–1860* (New York, 1985), 202–214; and George Washington Parke Custis, *Recollections and Private Memoirs of Washington* (New York, 1860). Also see data in an obituary in the scrapbook of Mary Curtis Lee, Virginia Historical Society, Richmond; *Dictionary of American Biography,* under "Custis, George Washington Parke"; Milton Rubicam, "The Royal Ancestry of George Washington Parke Custis," *Virginia Magazine of History and Biography* 65 (April 1957):222–228; and Arthur Hobson Quinn, *A History of the American Drama from the Beginning to the Civil War* (New York, 1943), 270, 272–273.

3. At that time, enclaves of Creeks, Choctaws, Chickasaws, and Cherokees lived in undeveloped areas of the Deep South. For Jackson's policies, see Edward Pessen, *Jacksonian America: Society, Personality, and Politics,* rev. ed. (Urbana and Chicago, 1985), 296–301. On the Cherokees, see William G. McLoughlin, *Cherokee Renascence*

in the New Republic (Princeton, 1986); Thomas E. Mails, *The Cherokee People: The Story of the Cherokees from Earliest Origins to Contemporary Times* (Tulsa, Okla., 1992); and William L. Anderson, *Cherokee Removal: Before and After* (Athens, Ga., 1991).

4. Quoted in Robert F. Berkhofer Jr., *The White Man's Indian: Images of the American Indian from Columbus to the Present* (New York, 1978), 161.

5. Wirt had made a name for himself in legal circles by appearing before the Supreme Court in such landmark cases as *McCulloch v. Maryland* and the Dartmouth College case. A poor orphan boy from Maryland, he soon evolved into the quintessential Virginia legal scholar and man of letters, seeming to imitate Jefferson, who had helped launch his career. The Richmond-based lawyer served as attorney general from 1817 to 1825 under Presidents James Monroe and John Quincy Adams, but his political orientation turned him vehemently against Jackson in 1828, and by 1831, he had cast his lot with the Whigs. When the Anti-Masons asked him to become their presidential candidate in 1832, he accepted mainly as a way to oppose Jackson. See John P. Kennedy, *Memoirs of the Life of William Wirt*, 2 vols. (Philadelphia, 1850; reprint, Buffalo, N.Y., 1973). Also see Michael L. Oberg, "William Wirt and the Trials of Republicanism," *Virginia Magazine of History and Biography* 99 (July 1991):305–326; and Charles Frederick Stansbury, "Literary Landmarks of the Jamestown Exposition: William Wirt," *Jamestown Magazine* 2 (July 1907):1–7.

6. Wirt's Speech before the Court is in Kennedy, *Memoirs*, vol. 2, 295.

7. Quoted in Pessen, *Jacksonian America*, 300.

8. See John Ehle, *Trail of Tears: The Rise and Fall of the Cherokee Nation* (New York, 1988).

9. G.W.P. Custis, "Pocahontas, or the Settlers of Virginia," in Arthur Hobson Quinn, ed., *Representative American Plays from 1767 to the Present Day* (New York, 1953), 187–192.

10. Ibid., 175, 182, 192.

11. Ibid., 191.

12. Ibid., 192.

13. See Jill Lepore, *The Name of War: King Philip's War and the Origins of American Identity* (New York, 1998), 191–226.

14. Custis, "Pocahontas," 192.

15. See Berkhofer, *White Man's Indian*, 23–31, and S. Elizabeth Bird, "Introduction: Constructing the Image, 1830s–1990s," in Bird, ed., *Dressing in Feathers: The Construction of the Indian in American Popular Culture* (Boulder, 1996), 1–12.

16. Much of the biographical information on Chapman comes from the files and unfinished manuscript of the late William Pardee Campbell (hereafter either Campbell Papers or Campbell mss.), AAA. Also see William P. Campbell, *John Gadsby Chapman* (Washington, 1962); "John Gadsby Chapman and Son: American Etchers in Italy, 1850–1884," *Tamarind Papers* 12 (1989):28–37; William J. Dickman, "John Gadsby Chapman: Alexandria's Foremost 19th Century Painter," *Northern Virginia*

Heritage 2 (February 1980):15–18; and Edward F. Heite, "Painter of the Old Dominion," *Virginia Cavalcade* 11 (Winter 1968):11–29.

17. Chapman received art instruction from the artists George Cooke, Charles Bird King, and Thomas Sully. He was apparently enrolled in Judge Henry Tucker's school in Winchester. Campbell mss., AAA. For an interesting insight into their friendship, see J. G. Chapman to H. A. Wise, December 26, 1857, printed in "Editor's Table," *SLM* 26 (February 1851):148–154.

18. These included portraits of old family friend Jane C. Washington (proprietor of Mount Vernon), former president James Madison, and Tennessee congressman Davy Crockett. See Georgia S. Chamberlain, "Madison and Montpelier by John Gadsby Chapman," *Antiques Journal* (March 1959):36–37; Curtis Carroll Davis, "A Legend at Full-Length, Mr. Chapman Paints Colonel Crockett–and Tells About It," *Proceedings of the American Antiquarian Society* 69–70 (October 1959):155–174; and Jane C. Washington to J. G. Chapman, March 30, 1835, Campbell Papers, AAA.

19. Chapman wrote to Representative Joshua S. Johnston of Louisiana: "I looked to the land of my home and every feeling with flattering promises." He sent a similar plea to John Trumbull shortly after the latter installed his last painting in the rotunda; in response, Trumbull wrote a letter of recommendation for Chapman. J. G. Chapman to J. S. Johnson, March 10, 1832, Historical Society of Pennsylvania, Philadelphia; Thomas Sully Journal, New York Public Library; and Campbell Papers, AAA.

20. J. G. Chapman to H. A. Wise, June 29, 1836, and H. A. Wise to J. G. Chapman, January 17, 1836, Historical Society of Pennsylvania, Philadelphia, copy in Campbell Papers, AAA.

21. J. G. Chapman to J. S. Johnson, March 10, 1832; and J. G. Chapman to H. A. Wise, June 29, 1836, Historical Society of Pennsylvania, Philadelphia, copies in Campbell Papers, AAA; J. K. Paulding to Richard Henry Wilde, February 13, 1835, *Letters of James Kirke Paulding*, ed. Ralph M. Aderman (Madison, Wis., 1962), 164; *Old Print Shop Portfolio* 18 (October 1958):27–33; and *New-York Mirror* 12 (March 21, 1835):301–302, (May 16, 1835):366.

22. Campbell mss., AAA. In preparation for Paulding's book, Chapman created nine oil paintings–*View of Washington's Mother's Residence in Fredericksburg, View of the Birthplace of Washington, View from the Old Mansion House of the Washington Family near Fredericksburg, Distant View of Mount Vernon, The Bed Chamber of Washington, The Tomb of Washington,* three different *Views of Yorktown*–and a series of supplemental sketches. See Georgia S. Chamberlain, *John Gadsby Chapman, 1808–1889* (privately printed, 1963), 8; and James K. Paulding to Jared Sparks, October 28, 1835, *Letters of James Kirke Paulding,* 169.

23. *Coronation of Powhatan* and *Warning of Pocahontas* were done as preparatory works for engravings; *Good Times at Jamestown* also appeared as an engraving in the *New-York Mirror,* and *Pocahontas Saving the Life of Captain John Smith* was subsequently

distributed as a lithograph. See *New-York Mirror* 12 (March 21, 1835):302, and 18 (May 8, 1841):144; and *Knickerbocker* 8 (July 1836):114.

24. See Philip L. Barbour, ed., *The Complete Works of Captain John Smith (1580–1631)* (Chapel Hill, N.C., 1986), vol. 2, 258. For an interpretation of the ceremony in a different light, see Frederic W. Gleach, *Powhatan's World and Colonial Virginia: A Conflict of Cultures* (Lincoln, Nebr., and London, 1997), 126–127.

25. Because Smith wrote that the native leader had refused to don the "scarlet Cloke" sent by James I, Chapman pictured it lying on the ground behind him.

26. An analogous message pervades Chapman's *First Ship* of 1837, picturing an Indian man standing on a rocky cliff presumably witnessing the landing of John Smith and his party. Chapman exhibited a painting of it at the National Academy of Design in 1837, but that work is unlocated, known only from an engraving that appeared in *The Token* gift book of 1842.

27. Although the scene was not intended to portray the first landing at Jamestown, it follows the "landing" formula in that a ship is at anchor on the horizon and people await the passengers on the shore. Chapman's engraving of the *Landing of Columbus* appeared in the *New-York Mirror* 14 (January 7, 1837):217. See Ann Uhry Abrams, "Visions of Columbus: The 'Discovery' Legend in Antebellum American Paintings and Prints," *American Art Journal* 25 (1, 2) (1993):83–85.

28. Paulding wrote that as the ship neared the harbor "shouts were now heard in the village mingled with exclamations of 'They're come–they're come!' . . . A boat was now seen to put off from the ships and make for the shore. There were no strangers here. They had met in a new world, and all felt like brothers." See "The Engraving: An American Author," *New-York Mirror* 17 (October 19, 1839):129.

29. For example, in his speech to the New England Society of New York in 1839, Robert Winthrop insinuated that cargoes of women were "sold to the planters for wives" in exchange for tobacco. Robert C. Winthrop, *Address to the New England Society of New York City*, December 23, 1839 (Boston and New York, 1840), 44–56.

30. Chapman combined his first paycheck from Congress with donations from friends and patrons to finance the English trip. See J. G. Chapman to William Bolling, January 27, 1838, Virginia Historical Society, Richmond; J. G. Chapman to William Kemble, June 6, 1837, and J. G. Chapman to James Herring, June 15, 1837, Campbell Papers, AAA; and Chapman's account book, property of Robert Mayo, Richmond, Virginia. I wish to thank Mr. Mayo for sharing this material with me.

31. J. G. Chapman to William Bolling, January 27, 1838, November 28, 1837, and March 13, 1837; William Bolling Diary, March 22, 1838; and William Bolling, "History of Two Portraits," Bolling Papers, Virginia Historical Society, Richmond.

32. Some of those sketches now belong to the Jamestown-Yorktown Foundation. I wish to thank Mark Cattanach for showing them to me. Also see *The Picture of the Baptism of Pocahontas. Painted by the Order of Congress for the Rotundo of the Capitol, by J.G. Chapman, of Washington* (Washington 1840), 5–6; Heite, "Painter," 15; and Chamberlain, "Chapman," 6.

33. J. G. Chapman to William Kemble, October 17, 1838, November 18, 1838, February 15, 1839, October 1, 1839, January 29, 1840, June 6, 1840, Campbell Papers, AAA.

34. J. G. Chapman to William Kemble, November 20, 1840, Campbell Papers, AAA. As the first of the four artists to complete his rotunda painting, Chapman was troubled by the physical problems of mounting the canvas, a task made increasingly difficult by indifference of the Capitol staff. To solve such dilemmas and seek the best methods for preserving the painting against "the effects of dampness," he consulted the elderly John Trumbull, the only other person who had placed paintings in the rotunda. See J. G. Chapman to John Trumbull, December 22, 1839, Campbell Papers, AAA.

35. Quoted in Chamberlain, "The Baptism of Pocahontas," *Iron Worker* 23 (Summer 1959): 21. Benjamin French, the House of Representatives clerk, noted in his journal that although he saw the painting still on the floor and obstructed by "a large trestle," he could detect "several great defects" along with "some admirable points" and predicted that the picture would "be harshly criticised" and thus "do the painter little credit." The writer for the *National Intelligencer* also remarked that the painting "certainly left on our mind a vivid impression of its beauty as a work of art," yet there was a "want of grace in attitude and expression in the countenance" of Pocahontas and "a want of picturesqueness on the whole." French, *Witness to the Young Republic,* 105–106; *New York Herald,* December 3, 1840; and *National Intelligencer* December 1, 1840.

36. *Picture of the Baptism,* 4–5.

37. J. G. Chapman to William Kemble, November 20, 1840, Campbell Papers, AAA.

38. *Picture of the Baptism,* 3.

39. Dale does not appear in the preliminary sketch and was no doubt added to wear the suit of armor that Horatio Greenough sent Chapman from Italy. Maria Heath Cooke, Chapman's cousin and wife of his friend George Cooke, is supposed to have posed for Pocahontas. The interior of the church came from a chapel similar to the one believed to have been in Jamestown; the chair in the left corner–said to be from the time of James I–came from sketches made in England. J. G. Chapman to William Kemble, October 1, 1839, Campbell Papers, AAA. Also see William S. Rasmussen and Robert S. Tilton, *Pocahontas: Her Life and Legend* (Richmond, 1994), 23–29.

40. Smith mentioned Nantequas, Opechancanough, and Opachisco in the *Generall Historie.* Powhatan is absent from the ceremony because the apocrypha attached to the tale alleges that he refused to watch his daughter convert to the white man's religion. See Chamberlain, "Baptism," 18–19.

41. Georgia Chamberlain has rightly suggested that the heads of Nantequas, Opechancanough, and Opachisco strongly resemble the chiefs in Charles Bird King's *Young Omahaw, War Eagle, Little Missouri, and Pawnees,* whereas the face of

Pocahontas was probably taken from King's *Eagle's Delight.* See Chamberlain, "Baptism," 19.

42. *Picture of the Baptism,* 3.

43. Chapman also used the native mother and baby to link his painting with Benjamin West's *Penn's Treaty with the Indians,* which had a similar configuration in the foreground and also depicts a meeting between English settlers and Native Americans. The merger of the marriage and baptism is suggested by Diana McClintock, "Chapman's Baptism of Pocahontas: Princess or Squaw?" paper delivered at the Southern College Art Conference, October 23, 1993. I thank the author for sharing the paper with me.

44. William Gilmore Simms, "Pocahontas: A Subject for the Historical Painter," in C. Hugh Holman, ed., *Views and Reviews in American Literature and Fiction* (Cambridge, Mass., 1962), 116–117.

45. Mrs. M. M. [Mary] Webster, *Pocahontas: A Legend* (Philadelphia, 1840), vi–vii, 134, 136.

46. For the classic twentieth-century definition of that term, see Barbara Welter, "The Cult of True Womanhood," *American Quarterly* 18 (Summer 1966):151–174; also in her *Dimity Convictions: The American Woman in the Nineteenth Century* (Athens, Ohio, 1976), 21–41.

47. *New-York Mirror* 18 (July 11, 1840):17.

48. William Watson Waldron, *Pocahontas, Princess of Virginia and Other Poems* (New York, 1841), 9.

49. "Pocahontas, the Indian Princess," *SLM* 4 (April 4, 1838):227–228.

50. For views on Indian theatrical depictions during the 1830s, see Sally L. Jones, "The First but Not the Last of the 'Vanishing Indians': Edwin Forrest and Mythic Recreations of the Native Population," in Bird, *Dressing in Feathers,* 13–27.

51. William Gilmore Simms, "The Forest Maiden," in *The Book of My Lady: A Melange by a Bachelor Knight* (Boston, 1833), 52. For more information on Simms, see Charles S. Watson, *From Nationalism to Secessionism: The Changing Fiction of William Gilmore Simms* (Westport, Conn., 1993); Mary Ann Wimsatt, *The Major Fiction of William Gilmore Simms: Cultural Traditions and Literary Form* (Baton Rouge, La., 1989); and William R. Taylor, *Cavalier and Yankee: The Old South and American National Character* (1957; Cambridge, Mass., and London, 1977), 267–270.

52. Simms, "Forest Maiden," 52–59.

53. From the mid-1830s through the mid-1840s, Simms struggled to resolve the true meaning behind the rescue of Smith through two essays, "Pocahontas: A Legend of Virginia" (1846) and "Pocahontas: A Subject for the Historical Painter" (1845), and a biography, *The Life of Captain John Smith* (1846).

54. During his tenure in Congress, Owen helped establish the Smithsonian Institution and fought to remove Great Britain from partial ownership of the Oregon Territory; in his later years, he served as minister to Italy and was an avid abolitionist. A prolific writer, he composed a number of political tracts, a novel, a memoir,

and several books on spiritualism. See Richard W. Leopold, *Robert Dale Owen: A Biography* (Cambridge, Mass, 1940); Robert Dale Owen, *Threading My Way* (New York, 1874); and *Dictionary of American Biography,* under "Owen, Robert Dale."

55. "A Citizen of the West" [Robert Dale Owen], *Pocahontas: A Historical Drama* (New York, 1837), 21. For critical notices of the book, see Leopold, *Robert Dale Owen,* 137.

56. Owen does comment on the sad plight of the vanquished natives, whose fate he compares at one point to that of a panther felled by arrows. [Owen], *Pocahontas,* 68. For Owen's views on Indians, see Robert Dale Owen, introduction to *Report of the Organization Committee of the Smithsonian Institution* (Washington, 1837), 8.

57. [Owen], *Pocahontas,* 81–82.

58. What will the "bestial heathens" think of "their white neighbors?" Smith asks his adversary. "How will they venerate Christian morality, and English honor, gallantry, good faith" when they learn that the settlers conspire to murder Pocahontas and her tribesmen? Ibid., 190–191.

59. Ibid., 149, 184–187, 189.

60. Some of Owen's concern about the position of women came from his friendship with Frances Wright; the remainder grew out of his own obsession with aiding victims of the capitalist system. When he married Mary Jane Robinson in 1832, he renounced his claim on her property as a gesture of his respect for a wife's independence. For commentaries on Owen's views of women, see Elinor and Anne E. Pancoast, *The Incorrigible Idealist, Robert Dale Owen in America* (Bloomington, Ind., 1940), 21; Frances Mossiker, *Pocahontas: The Life and the Legend* (New York, 1976), 326–327; and Robert S. Tilton, *Pocahontas: The Evolution of an American Narrative* (Cambridge, Eng., and New York, 1994), 74.

61. The reviewer for *Graham's Magazine,* for example, called it an "absurdly flat affair" that must have been written by his wife, an accomplished author in her own right. See "Powhatan: A Metrical Romance, in Seven Cantos," *Graham's Lady's and Gentleman's Magazine* 19 (July 1841):46–47; and "Powhatan: A Poem by Mr. Seba Smith," *Knickerbocker* 17 (April 1841):350. For more information on the Smiths, see Milton and Patricia Rickels, *Seba Smith* (Boston, 1977), 81–86; and Mary Alice Wyman, *Two American Pioneers: Seba Smith and Elizabeth Oakes Smith* (New York, 1972), 151–154;

62. [Seba Smith], *John Smith's Letters with 'Picters' to Match* (New York, 1839), 27–28.

63. Mrs. Seba Smith, "The Worthies of Virginia," *SLM* 6 (January 1840):50.

64. Seba Smith, *Powhatan: A Metrical Romance in Seven Cantos* (New York, 1841), 98–99, 117–118.

65. Ibid., 152, 154–155.

66. Seba Smith's juxtaposition of masculine pride and feminine strength may well have been a gentle ribbing of his wife, Elizabeth Oakes Prince Smith, who acted out her views on women's rights. A perfect example was her pen name "Elizabeth Oak-

smith," a conflation of her middle and married names. She also had her children's names officially changed to Oaksmith. See Rickels, *Seba Smith*, 22–23, 81–85.

67. "Powhatan: A Metrical Romance, in Seven Cantos," *SLM* 7 (July 1841): 588–589.

68. Lydia H. Sigourney, "Pocahontas," in *Pocahontas and Other Poems* (London, 1841), 13.

69. Haight, *Mrs. Sigourney*, 75–107.

70. Ibid., 6, 10.

71. Ibid., 22.

72. Charlotte M.S. Barnes, "The Forest Princess, or Two Centuries Ago: An Historical Play in Three Parts," in *Plays, Prose, and Poetry* (Philadelphia, 1848), 148, 176. Also see *Dictionary of American Biography*, under "Charlotte Mary Sanford Barnes"; and Quinn, *History of American Drama*, 273.

73. Tailored to suit the English audiences that viewed the melodrama four years before it arrived in the United States, the play showed the leading English settlers treating the Native Americans honorably and chastising those who acted otherwise.

74. Barnes, "Forest Princess," 209, 223.

75. Ibid., 262–264, 267–268.

76. The painting is in a private collection and is unavailable for reproduction. For information, see American Art Union Catalog, 1848, Roll P38, AAA; and Rasmussen and Tilton, *Pocahontas: Her Life and Legend*, 31.

Chapter 7

1. For a description of this event, see Edward Lind Morse, *Samuel F.B. Morse: His Letters and Journals* (Boston and New York, 1914), vol. 2, 221–222.

2. Samuel F.B. Morse, "The Germ of the Republic," unpublished letter to the *New-York Mirror*, 1841–1842, Morse Papers (hereafter MP), Library of Congress.

3. Morse began his campaign to place a painting in the Capitol in 1826 when he contacted New York congressman Gulian Verplanck with an intricate plan about how the competition should be organized. Shortly thereafter, he began soliciting support among his wide circle of friends, which included such artistic and literary luminaries as James Fenimore Cooper, William Cullen Bryant, Asher B. Durand, and William Dunlap; and he also contacted then president John Quincy Adams, Congressmen Edward Everett and Henry Clay, as well as Senators Daniel Webster, John C. Calhoun, and Robert Hayne. "Note to Several Members of Congress when the subject of national pictures was before Congress in 1834," and S.F.B. Morse to Washington Allston, March 21, 1837, MP. Also see Paul Staiti, *Samuel F.B. Morse* (New York and London, 1989), 149–154, 175–176, 208; Lillian B. Miller, *Patrons and Patriotism: The Encouragement of the Fine Arts in the United States, 1790–1860* (Chicago, 1966), 51–52, 247, n. 14; and Carleton Mabee, *The American Leonardo: A Life of Samuel F.B. Morse* (New York, 1943), 184–185.

4. Morse, "Germ of the Republic"; and *New-York Mirror* 15 (September 2, 1837):80.

5. "Brutus" [Samuel F.B. Morse], *Foreign Conspiracy Against the Liberties of the United States* (1835; reprint, New York, 1977).

6. See Ray Allen Billington, *The Protestant Crusade, 1800–1860: A Study of the Origins of American Nativism* (New York, 1938), 121–125; Tyler Anbinder, *Nativism and Slavery: The Northern Know-Nothings and the Politics of the 1850s* (New York and Oxford, Eng., 1992), 9; and Louis Dow Sisco, *Political Nativism in New York State* (New York, 1901), 21–22.

7. See Billington, *Origins of Nativism*, 49–110; Ira M. Leonard and Robert D. Parmet, *American Nativism, 1830–1860* (New York, 1971); and "Review of William Godwin, 'An Inquiry Concerning the Power of Increase in the Numbers of Mankind,' *North American Review* 15 (1822):293–298.

8. See Handlin, *Boston's Immigrants*, 42–47, 242; David Fitzpatrick, *Irish Emigration, 1801–1921* (Dublin, 1985); and Dudley Baines, *Emigration from Europe, 1815–1930* (London, 1991).

9. Morse, *Foreign Conspiracy*, 140. In *Imminent Dangers to the Free Institutions of the United States,* published a year after *Foreign Conspiracy,* Morse intensified his attack.

10. The Whig candidate, Seth Geer, also championed the Nativist cause and thus split the vote to allow the Democratic candidate to win by a landslide. See Leo Hershkowitz, "The Native-American Democratic Association in New York City, 1835–36," *New York Historical Society Quarterly* 46 (January 1962):56–59.

11. Morse said he was told that Inman was planning to refuse the commission and name him as a replacement. When this gossip proved to be ill founded, the paranoid artist began lashing out at suspected "enemies" in Congress, especially John Quincy Adams, whom he believed had adopted a "decided and openly hostile attitude" toward him. S.F.B. Morse to Washington Allston, March 21, 1837, MP.

12. R. W. Weir to Verplanck, March 15, 1837, Verplanck Papers (hereafter VP), New York Historical Society.

13. Ibid.

14. S.F.B. Morse to Mary ?, April 28, 1837, and "Germ of the Republic," MP.

15. Thomas Cole to S.F.B. Morse, March 14, 1837; J. G. Chapman to S.F.B. Morse, May 2, 1839, and December 3, 1841, MP.

16. "Mr. Morse's '*Cabin of the Mayflower,*'" *New-York Mirror* 19 (October 16, 1841):335.

17. See James Franklin Beard, ed., *The Letters and Journals of James Fenimore Cooper* (Cambridge, Mass., 1960+), vol. 3, 259; E. L. Morse, *Samuel Morse, 30–34*; Thomas S. Cummings, *Historic Annals of the National Academy of Design* (Philadelphia, 1865; reprint, New York, 1969), 144–146; Carleton Mabee, *The American Leonard: A Life of Samuel F.B. Morse* (New York, 1943), 184–188, 193; Staiti, *Samuel Morse*, 208–212; and Harry B. Wehle, *Samuel F.B. Morse, American Painter* (New York, 1932), 25–26.

18. When commemorating the bicentenary of 1820, for example, William Crafts told South Carolina's New England Society that if Protestants had not settled in Plymouth, North America would have become "another Rome," with the pope scheming to wrest control of the continent. William Crafts, *Address Delivered Before the New England Society of South Carolina on 22 December, 1820* (Charleston, S.C., 1820), 9–10.

19. Among the recent studies of Beecher are James W. Fraser, *Pedagogue for God's Kingdom: Lyman Beecher and the Second Great Awakening* (Lanham, Md., 1985); and Stephen H. Snyder, *Lyman Beecher and His Children: The Transformation of a Religious Tradition* (Brooklyn, 1991).

20. Lyman Beecher, *Plea for the West* (Cincinnati, 1835), 61.

21. Thomas H. O'Connor, *The Boston Irish: A Political History* (Boston, 1995), 14–29.

22. Billington, *Protestant Crusade*, 18, 70–75; O'Connor, *Boston Irish*, 30–58; Oscar Handlin, *Boston's Immigrants, 1790–1880: A Study in Acculturation* (1969; rev. ed., Cambridge, Mass., 1991), 150; and Theodore M. Hammett, "Two Mobs of Jacksonian Boston: Ideology and Interest," *Journal of American History* 62 (March 1976):845–868.

23. Beecher, *Plea for the West*, 95.

24. Ibid., 125–126.

25. [Jacob Abbott], *New England and Her Institutions by One of Her Sons,* The American Popular Library (Boston, 1835), 245–246.

26. See "Immigration," *North American Review* 40 (April 1835):457–476.

27. James Sabine, *Fathers of New England . . . A Sermon at Plymouth* (Boston, 1821), 4, 14, 27.

28. P. M. Whelpley, *A Discourse Delivered Before the New England Society of the City and State of New York . . .* (New York, 1823), 11, 18–19. A similar pronouncement came from William Sullivan, eminent lawyer and author of historical schoolbooks, when he spoke at Plymouth on Forefathers' Day in 1829: "The class of Christians to whom we owe our origin were alike distinguished from the adherents to papal authority, and from those who adhered to the English church. They abhorred the doctrines and ritual of Rome; but they abhorred no less, the forms and ceremonies imitated therefrom . . . They preserved through all sufferings . . . [a religion] *purified* from human errors, and follies." William Sullivan, *Discourse Delivered Before the Pilgrim Society on the 22nd Day of December, 1829* (Boston, 1830), 12.

29. Pelig Sprague, *Address . . . Pilgrim Society, Plymouth, December 22, 1835* (Boston, 1836), 7–8, 11, 30. For similar sentiments, see "The New England Character," *North American Review* 44 (January 1837):237–238.

30. Robert C. Winthrop, *An Address Before the New England Society in the City of New York, December 23, 1839* (Boston, 1840), 35, 40.

31. For information on the New York coterie, see James T. Callow, *Kindred Spirits: Knickerbocker Writers and American Artists, 1807–1855* (Chapel Hill, N.C., 1967).

32. In the 1820s, Weir had toured Italy, a sojourn that constituted the better part of his artistic education, save a brief period of study with John Wesley Jarvis in New

York. Upon returning home, Weir established himself as an illustrator and soon was creating drawings for the *Talisman* and the *New-York Mirror*. His history paintings include *Columbus Before the Council at Salamanca* and *The Landing of Henry Hudson*; among his religious works is a mural for the chapel at West Point. See *Robert Weir: Artist and Teacher of West Point* (West Point, N.Y., 1976); J. E. Kent Ahrens, "Robert Walter Weir (1803–1889)," Ph.D. diss., University of Delaware, 1972; Irene Weir, *Robert W. Weir, Artist* (New York, 1947); Michael E. Moss, ed., *Robert W. Weir of West Point: Illustrator, Teacher, and Poet* (West Point, N.Y., 1976); and Susan P. Casteras, "Robert W. Weir's *Taking the Veil* and The Value of Art as a Handmaid of Religion," *Yale University Art Gallery Bulletin* 39 (Winter 1986):12–23.

33. He had the backing of then congressman Gulian Verplanck and Secretary of War Lewis Cass. See Lewis Cass to G. C. Verplanck, March 22, 1834, roll 531, AAA.

34. That was the way it was described in *The Picture of the Embarkation of the Pilgrims . . .* (New York, 1843), 6; and shortly after being commissioned, Weir indicated that he was expected to illustrate the Pilgrims. See T.(?) Benton to R. W. Weir, July 4, 1836, roll, 531, nos. 795–796, AAA.

35. When Gulian Verplanck wrote Washington Allston in 1830 urging him to enter the Capitol rotunda competition, he suggested the "Landing of the Pilgrims" as a possible topic. Allston replied that he would not consider painting that subject because Henry Sargent, "a high-minded, honorable man," considered it "his ground." Weir also briefly considered painting the "Storming of Stony Point" during the Revolution. See Weir to Verplanck, March 15, 1837, VP; and Washington Allston to Gulian Verplanck, March 1830, in Nathalia Wright, ed., *The Correspondence of Washington Allston* (Lexington, Ky., 1993), 286. Also see J. E. Kent Ahrens, "Robert Weir's 'Embarkation of the Pilgrims,'" *Capitol Studies* 1 (Fall, 1972):60.

36. The board would consist of Gulian Verplanck, William Cullen Bryant, and Dr. James DeKay, each of whom had just donated money to allow the would-be inventor to paint his "Germ of the Republick." Verplanck to Morse, April 20, 1837, VP; Joseph Sills Diary, roll P29, AAA; and Weir to Verplanck, April 19, 1837, in I. Weir, *Robert Weir*, 76.

37. Eliza Robbins to R. W. Weir, April 10, 1837, roll 531, AAA.

38. R. W. Weir to William C. Preston, in I. Weir, *Robert Weir*, 76–77; and Ahrens, "R. Weir," 60.

39. A number of sketches indicate that Weir attempted to situate the departing party "by the *Sea-side*" instead of on the ship's deck to conform with the passage in Mather's text, but in the end, he combined Mather's account with a narration in Mount's *Memorial* that placed them aboard ship for their "sad and mournful parting." See Cotton Mather, *Magnalia Christi Americana, Books I and II*, ed. Kenneth B. Murdock, (Cambridge, Mass, 1977), 127; *Picture of the Embarcation*, 9–13; C. Leslie to R. W. Weir, October 12, 1838, in I. Weir, *Robert Weir*, 77–78; Ahrens, "Weir's 'Embarkation,'" 63–66; and *Robert Weir: Artist and Teacher*, 34–36, 67–68.

40. Weir's penchant for detail and the diversity of costume displeased some of his artistic colleagues. Thomas Cole complained in a letter to Jonathan Mason that the

eye was "distracted" by the "discordant colour and chiaroscuro," which left the spectator doubting that they were "men who were about to abandon all enjoyments and blessings of civilized life to seek a home in the howling wilderness—for conscience sake." Horatio Greenough, too, complained about Weir's distribution of light and shadow, which obscured faces and rendered details of clothing and accessories "so real" that it "mocks my desire to see men." See Ahrens, "Weir's 'Embarkation,'" 70; Henry T. Tuckerman, *Book of the Artists* (1867; reprint, New York, 1966), 210.

41. Weir dressed the men in the knee breeches, doublets, and hose of the seventeenth century. William Bradford and John White have starched ruffs; Miles Standish displays his military orientation through his metal corslet; Mrs. Winslow and Mrs. White wear the ample taffeta skirts, puffed sleeves, and feathered hats of the artist's own day and have only sketchy suggestions of the jerkins, ruffs, and fitted bodices of the Pilgrims' era. Russell's *Guide* explains that Mrs. Winslow was a bride "and of the wealthier class" and therefore Weir dressed her fashionably. William S. Russell, *Guide to Plymouth* (Boston, 1846), appendix A, ii.

42. All are quoted in I. Weir, *Robert Weir*, 80–89.

43. In New York, the canvas hung briefly at the National Academy of Design, where Morse still presided. The academy president never recorded his opinions of Weir's successful exhibit, but one can easily imagine his reaction. Before the painting went to the academy, it was lodged above New York's City Library, and actors from the nearby Olympic Theater presented a "tableau vivant" of the composition. Ibid., 90–91.

44. Rufus Choate, "The Age of the Pilgrims: The Heroic Period of Our History," in Samuel Gilman Brown, ed., *The Works of Rufus Choate, with a Memoir of His Life* (Boston, 1862), 374, 383.

45. T. D. Rogers, "Embarkation of the Pilgrims" (1844), clipping at Pilgrim Hall, Plymouth, Mass.

46. "Nell" and "An Artist's Studio," *Knickerbocker* 37 (January 1851):41–42.

47. S. G. Bulfinch, *A Discourse Suggested by Weir's Picture of the Embarkation of the Pilgrims* (Washington, D.C., 1844).

48. Beecher, *Plea for the West*, 45–51, 102–103, 113.

49. James F. Clarke, *The Pilgrim Fathers: A Poem Recited in the Church of the Disciples, Boston, on the Festival of the Pilgrims, December 22d, 1842* (Boston, 1843), 10–11.

50. Samuel W. Worcester, *A Discourse Delivered at Plymouth, Massachusetts, December 22, 1848* (Salem, Mass., 1849), 49.

51. *Old Colony Memorial*, December 22, 1849.

52. Lydia Sigourney, "The Pilgrims," in William S. Russell, ed., *Guide to Plymouth* (Boston, 1846), appendix, 61–63.

53. Daniel Webster, *Address Before the New England Society of New York* (New York, 1850), 9–10.

54. *Old Colony Memorial*, March 20, 1852.

55. ["Nobody Knows Who"], *To Those Born on the Soil Who Know Nothing but the Advancement of their Country's Good* (Brooklyn, N.Y., 1854), 6.

56. See John R. Mulkern, *The Know-Nothing Party in Massachusetts: The Rise and Fall of a People's Movement* (Boston, 1990); Dale Baum, "Know-Nothingism and the Republican Majority in Massachusetts: The Political Realignment of the 1850s," *Journal of American History* 64 (March 1978):959–86; Billington, *The Protestant Crusade*, 380–436; Anbinder, *Nativism and Slavery*, 105–134; and David Harry Bennett, *The Party of Fear: From Nativist Movements to the New Right in American History* (Chapel Hill, N.C., 1988), 113–134.

57. "The Native American," *Old Colony Memorial*, December 2, 1854.

58. See Mrs. N. S. Monroe, "Landing of the Pilgrims," in William H. Ryder, ed., *Our Country; or, The American Parlor Keepsake* (Boston, c. 1854); and ["One of 'Em," ed.], *The Wide-Awake Gift: A Know-Nothing for 1855* (New York, 1855).

59. T. Whittemore, "My Native Land," in Ryder, *Our Country*, 13–26.

60. See Billington, *Protestant Crusade*, 295; and ["Nobody Knows Who"], *To Those Born on the Soil*, 3.

61. "Archbishop Hughes on the Pilgrims, &c," *Boston Evening Transcript*, March 11, 1852, clipping in the Newberry Library, Chicago.

62. William Bradford, *History of Plymouth Plantation* (Boston, 1912), vol. 1, 191.

63. Ibid., 189–190. Also see Arthur Lord, "The *Mayflower* Compact," *American Antiquarian Society Proceedings* 30 (October 1920):278–294; and Morison, "Pilgrim Fathers," 368–370.

64. Some of the Separatists were apparently worried that their sponsors would believe that by not colonizing in the proscribed location, they were trying to renege on their loan. I wish to thank Leo Lemay for this suggestion.

65. See Mark Sargent, "The Conservative Covenant: The Rise of the *Mayflower* Compact in American Myth," *New England Quarterly* 61 (June 1988):239–246.

66. *The Writings and Speeches of Daniel Webster* (Boston, 1903), vol. 1, 198.

67. Webster, *Address*, 7.

68. Choate, "Age of the Pilgrims," 385.

69. George Bancroft, *History of the United States*, 14th ed. (1848), vol. 1, 310.

70. S.F.B. Morse to Washington Allston, March 21, 1837, and Morse, "Germ of the Republic," MP.

71. Although Matteson spent most of his life in upstate New York, his ancestors came from New England, and family legends coupled with ancestral pride might have inspired the artist to gravitate toward the Pilgrim subjects he painted throughout his career. *The Mayflower Compact* was printed and distributed by the art dealer William Schaus. See *Thompkins H. Matteson, 1813–1884* (Sherburne, N.Y., 1949); Tuckerman, *Book of the Artists*, 432–434; and Georgia S. Chamberlain, *Studies on American Painters and Sculptors of the Nineteenth Century* (Annendale, Va., 1965), 19–23. I wish to thank Wendy Greenhouse for providing information on Matteson's paintings.

72. *Literary World* 6 (May 29, 1847):397. Matteson's *First Sabbath* was exhibited at the National Academy of Design in 1847 and was also purchased by Schaus to be distributed as a print. T. P. Rossiter contributed *The Puritans of New England Reading the Bible* to that same exhibition.

Chapter 8

1. Robert W. Johannsen, *To the Halls of Montezumas: The Mexican War in the American Imagination* (New York and Oxford, Eng., 1985), 8, 195, 215–217, 270–301; and Charles Sumner to Nathan Appleton, August 22, 1846, *The Selected Letters of Charles Sumner*, ed., Beverly Wilson Palmer (Boston, 1990), vol. 1, 175.

2. Debates on the subject had raged while the war was still in progress and exploded into a major conflagration when Congressman David Wilmot of Pennsylvania proposed an amendment to the war appropriations bill that would forbid slavery in all territories acquired from Mexico. That so-called Wilmot Proviso dropped a firebomb in Washington that divided the nation into two opposing camps. After months of wrangling, Congress finally eked out a temporary agreement, known as the Compromise of 1850. This patchwork legislation placated Northerners by admitting California as a free state and abolishing the slave trade in the District of Columbia. Southerners were granted the admission of Utah and New Mexico with no restrictions on slavery and a strong bill for returning fugitive slaves to their owners. For discussion of the Compromise of 1850, see David M. Potter, *The Impending Crisis, 1848–1861*, completed and edited by Don E. Fehrenbacher (New York, 1976), 90–120; and Don E. Fehrenbacher, *The South and Three Sectional Crises* (Baton Rouge, La., 1980), 25–44.

3. Waddy Thompson, *Recollections of Mexico* (New York, 1847), 29.

4. Thompson, who began his career as a Whig representative in Congress between 1835 and 1841, conducted a diplomatic mission to Mexico in 1842, during which he developed a pleasant working relationship with the Mexican leader, Santa Anna, and became an outspoken advocate of a peaceful settlement of the Texas situation. See Henry T. Thompson, *General Waddy Thompson* (Columbia, S.C. [?], 1919).

5. James Chamberlayne Pickett, *The Memory of Pocahontas Vindicated Against the Erroneous Judgment of the Honorable Waddy Thompson, Late Envoy Extraordinary and Minister Plenipotentiary to Mexico* (Washington, D.C., 1847), 4–6.

6. Alexis de Tocqueville, *Democracy in America*, ed. J. P. Mayer (New York, 1969), 34–36. For further comments on de Tocqueville, see Lewis Perry, *Boats Against the Current: American Culture Between Revolution and Modernity, 1820–1860* (New York and Oxford, 1993), 66–68, 89–103.

7. Frederick Law Olmsted, *A Journey in the Seaboard Slave States, with Remarks on their Economy* (1856; reprint, New York, 1968), 146–148, 216–223.

8. Nathaniel L. Frothingham, *The Significance of the Struggle Between Liberty and Slavery in America: A Discourse at Portland, Maine, on Fast Day, April 16, 1857* (New York, 1857), 12.

9. C. C., "The History of Virginia," *SLM* 5 (December 1839):788–792. In June 1839, the magazine had published "John Rolf's Relation to the State of Virginia" of 1617, which had been copied from the original manuscript in the British Museum. "Interesting Account of Virginia, in 1617," *SLM* 5 (June 1839):401–407.

10. "Colonial History of Virginia," *SLM* 10 (October 1844):634–635 and (November 1844):691–699.

11. "Colonial History of Virginia," *SLM* 11 (January 1845):3–5, 48–51; "True Relation," *SLM* 11 (February 1845):65–82; "Antiquities of Virginia," *SLM* 9 (September 1843):560–562, (October 1843):591–592, (November 1843):693–696, (December 1843):728–729, (June 1845):351–353, and (October 1845):631–633; and "Contributions to the History of Virginia," *SLM* 12 (August 1846):477–479, (September 1846):533–539, and (October 1846):605–614; John R. Thompson, "Colonial Life of Virginia," *SLM* 10 (October 1844):634–635, and 23 (June 1854):330–342. Other histories of Virginia appeared during the late 1840s and early 1850s, most notably Henry Howe's *Historical Collections of Virginia* (Charleston, S.C., 1847), and William Henry Foote's *Sketches of Virginia Historical and Biographical* (1850; reprint, Richmond, Va., 1966).

12. Charles Campbell, "History of the Colony and Ancient Dominion of Virginia," *SLM* 13 (February 1847):66. See also *SLM* (March 1847):129–144, and (April 1847):193–208; and Benjamin Blake Minor, *The Southern Literary Messenger, 1834–1864* (New York and Washington, D.C., 1905), 157–158.

13. *SLM* 14 (April 1847):200–201.

14. "Campbell's History of Virginia," *SLM* 30 (March 1860):210.

15. She told how the "gallant Soldier and the dark-browed Queen" pledged "a twofold vow . . . of Faith and Love / United here on earth, and bending oft above." Mrs. M. M. [Mary] Webster, *Pocahontas: A Legend* (Philadelphia, 1840), 140–141.

16. Howe, *Historical Collections,* 38.

17. An oil painting entitled *The Marriage of Pocahontas* and dated 1842 was supposedly done by an artist with the unlikely name of J. Rolfe. See Denver Art Museum, *The American Panorama: An Exhibition* (Denver, 1968), 4–5.

18. Virginians must have relished the image, for the print was widely distributed throughout the state. William S. Rasmussen and Robert S. Tilton, *Pocahontas: Her Life and Legend* (Richmond, Va., 1994), 27–29, and 54, n. 71.

19. Because Lossing based his narrative on Brueckner's composition, there were obvious conflicts with the facts as then understood. One was the presence of white women and children at the ceremony. These, the author explained, came from England with Sir Thomas Dale and returned "soon after this memorable event" because the "ninety young women, pure and uncorrupted . . . did not arrive until seven years later." By conflating the apocryphal account of Pocahontas's baptism with a wedding ceremony, Lossing told the story exactly as Virginians wanted to hear it. The pamphlet ends with a brief description of Rolfe's journey to England and Pocahontas's reception at the court of James I, where "she was received with the courtesy due to her rank as a princess." See Benson J. Lossing, *The Marriage of Pocahontas* (New York, 1855), 4–6.

20. His sources were letters from Sir Thomas Dale and Alexander Whitaker, along with historical accounts by Ralph Hamor and William Strachey. See Wyndham Robertson, "The Marriage of Pocahontas," *SLM* 31 (August 1860):81–91. Robinson also chronicled the Pocahontas-Rolfe lineage. See Wyndham Robertson, *Pocahontas, alias Matoaka, and Her Descendants* (1887; reprint, Baltimore, 1968).

21. Charles Campbell, *History of the Colony and Ancient Dominion of Virginia* (1860; reprint, Spartanburg, S.C., 1965), 123. Campbell included a similar description in the "History of Virginia," *SLM* 13 (April 1847):201.

22. In a poem published in 1862, a Virginian named J. H. Martin wrote: "[T]he flower of savage life became the youthful Briton's wife," and in the same chapel she received "baptismal rites" and became "the holy first fruits of her race / Redeemed to God by sovereign grace." J. H. Martin, *Smith and Pocahontas: A Poem* (Richmond, Va., 1862), 135. Mary Jane Windle also made similar assertions in *Life at White Sulfur Springs* (Philadelphia, 1857), 257–275.

23. Prints of Brueckner's *Marriage* were also republished during Reconstruction. I wish to thank Donna Sadler for pointing out that a framed Brueckner print hangs in a recreated Georgia pioneer village. A framed copy of "The Wedding of Pocahontas with John Rolff," lithograph by George Spohme after Hohenstein, published by Joseph Hoover in 1867, belongs to the Virginia Historical Society.

24. John Gorham Palfrey, *History of New England* (Boston, 1858), vol. 1, 89–92.

25. *Transactions of the American Antiquarian Society* 4 (1860):67–103; Justin Winsor, "Memoir of Charles Deane, LL.D.," *Proceedings of the Massachusetts Historical Society*, 2d ser. 7 (November 1891):60–61; and Tilton, *Pocahontas*, 164–165.

26. "John Brougham," *Dictionary of American Biography*; John Brougham, *Life, Stories, and Poems of John Brougham*, ed. William Winter (Boston: 1881), 75–76, 126; and John Stewart Hawes, "John Brougham as American Playwright and Man of the Theatre," Ph.D. diss., Stanford University, 1954, 423–434. Brougham wrote a similar parody of *Metamora* that opened in Boston in 1847. See Jill Lapore, *The Name of War: King Philip's War and The Origins of American Identity* (New York, 1998), 220–223.

27. John Brougham, *Po-ca-hon-tas, or the Gentle Savage* (New York, 1856), 3–4.

28. Ibid., 21. Brougham again made a crack about slavery during the scene in which Powhatan insists that his daughter marry Rolfe. To this demand Pocahontas responds: "The king who would enslave his daughter so, / Deserves a hint from Mrs. Beecher Stowe!" Ibid., 17.

29. John Esten Cooke, "An Hour with Thackeray," *Appleton's Journal* 7 (1879):252; W. M. Thackeray to Anne Thackeray, March 3, 1853, and W. M. Thackeray to Albany Fonblanque, March 4, 1853, in *Letters and Private Papers of William Makepeace Thackeray*, ed. Gordon N. Ray (Cambridge, Mass., 1946), vol. 3, 223, 227.

30. For Thackeray's views on slavery, see W. M. Thackeray to Mrs. Carmichael-Smyth, February 13, 1853; W. M. Thackeray to Anne Thackeray, March 3, 1853; and W. M. Thackeray to Albany Fonblanque, March 4, 1853, in *Letters and Papers*, vol. 3, 199, 223–229. Also see Deborah A. Thomas, *Thackeray and Slavery* (Athens, Ohio, 1993).

31. William Makepeace Thackeray, *The Virginians: A Tale of the Last Century* (1858–1859; London, 1911), 713–716.

32. Perhaps in response to this element of derision, some Virginians were unhappy. John Thompson elaborated on Thackeray's inaccuracies in his portrayals of

Smith and the Washington family. See "Editor's Table," *SLM* 26 (February 1851):152–153.

33. See Samuel Eliot Morison, "The Pilgrim Fathers: Their Significance in History," *Publications of the Colonial Society of Massachusetts* 38 (September 13, 1951):364–379; Peter J. Gomes, "Pilgrims and Puritans: 'Heroes' and 'Villains' in the Creation of the American Past," *Proceedings of the Massachusetts Historical Society* 95 (1983):1–16; and Anne Norton, *Alternative Americas: A Reading of Antebellum Political Culture* (Chicago, 1986), 64–96.

34. Charles S. Porter, *The Paramount Claims of the Gospel: A Semi-Centennial Discourse, Delivered October 1, 1851, Commemorative of the Organization of the Third Church, Plymouth, Mass.* (Boston, 1851), 16–19, 35, 42.

35. William Adams, *An Address Delivered Before the New England Society in the City of New York, December 22, 1852* (New York, 1853), 32–33, 36.

36. Peter Oliver, *The Puritan Commonwealth . . .* (Boston, 1856), 88. A columnist in the *North American Review* launched into Oliver's *Puritan Commonwealth,* saying that the "spirit of the book," was "almost as bad as can possess a man who is writing of the motives and deeds" of people who suffered "for a cause which they esteemed the holiest." See "Oliver's *The Puritan Commonwealth,*" *North American Review* 84 (April 1857):431–433.

37. David S. Reynolds, *Beneath the American Renaissance: The Subversive Imagination in the Age of Emerson and Melville* (Cambridge, Mass., and London, 1988), 249–274.

38. Judd's quest for spiritual fulfillment ultimately led him to break from his orthodox upbringing in Westhampton, Massachusetts, and embrace a spiritualistic form of Unitarianism. From his pulpit in Augusta, Maine, he became an energetic spokesman for reform. See Richard D. Hathaway, *Sylvester Judd's New England* (University Park, Pa., 1981); Francis B. Dedmond, *Sylvester Judd* (Boston, 1980); and Reynolds, *American Renaissance,* 37–43.

39. The clash between nature and custom was a leitmotif for the entire text, which ended with Margaret embracing her own version of Christianity practiced beside her favorite pond that she called "Mons Christi." There in the wilderness, she and her minister husband invited music and sculpture, festivals and flowers into their religious services. See Sylvester Judd, *Margaret: A Tale of the Real and the Ideal, Blight and Bloom; Including Sketches of a Place Not Before Described, Called Mons Christi* (Boston, 1851).

40. *An Account of the Pilgrim Celebration at Plymouth,* August 1, 1853 (Boston, 1853), 37–38, 40, 82–84; and Charles Sumner, *A Finger-Point from Plymouth Rock, Remarks at the Plymouth Festival on the First of August, 1853, in Commemoration of the Embarkation of the Pilgrims* (Boston, 1853), 7, 9–10.

41. The *Escape of the Puritans* may have been a prototype for *Washington Crossing the Delaware,* upon which Leutze was then working. See Barbara S. Groseclose, *Emanuel Leutze, 1816–1868: Freedom Is the Only King* (Washington, D.C., 1975), 27–37, 78. Leutze painted *Escape of the Puritans* as part of a series on the English Puritans.

42. The sea also suggests the opening lines of Hemans's "Landing of the Fathers" ("The breaking waves dash'd high") and Lydia Sigourney's "The Pilgrims" ("How slow yon tiny vessel ploughs the main! Amid the heavy billows"). Sigourney, "The Pilgrims," in William S. Russell, *Guide to Plymouth and Recollections of the Pilgrims* (Boston, 1846), appendix, 61–63. For the precedents in art, see Lorenz Eitner, "The Open Window and the Storm-Tossed Boat: An Essay in the Iconography of Romanticism," *Art Bulletin* 37 (December, 1957):279–290; and Roger B. Stein, *Seascape and the American Imagination* (New York, 1975).

43. While he was working on *Escape of the Puritans* in Düsseldorf, the people of several German states were fomenting revolutions aimed toward overthrowing autocratic rule and establishing constitutional governments; most such revolts prompted authorities in the individual states to respond with arrests and persecution. See Barbara Groseclose, "*Washington Crossing the Delaware*: The Political Context," *American Art Journal* 7 (November 1975):70–78. In a memoir published in the *Bulletin of the American Art-Union* in 1851, Leutze explained that he often used historical episodes to symbolize the American republic's struggle for "freedom" and "liberty." *Bulletin of the American Art-Union* (September, 1851), 95.

44. Leutze's *Escape of the Puritans* was exhibited in New York in 1848. William Appleton, of the well-known Boston mercantile family, purchased the painting for his collection, and engravings of the composition circulated during the next two decades. Martin, Johnson and Co. published a print of it, engraved by G. R. Hall in 1856; and it was an illustration in Jesse Ames Spencer's *History of the United States*, published in 1874.

45. British authors were already exploring aspects of the English Civil War; Scott had produced his novel *Woodstock* in 1826, and Thomas Carlyle published his biography of Oliver Cromwell in 1843. See J. B. Priestley, *Victoria's Heyday* (New York and London, 1972), 30, 69, 120–129; and Walter E. Houghton, *The Victorian Frame of Mind, 1830–1870* (New Haven and London, 1957), 124–126, 218–222.

46. Known primarily for portraits of English leaders, Lucy had studied at the Royal Academy in London and the Ecole des Beaux Arts in Paris before becoming a drawing instructor in Camden Town, a post he held for many years. Although his *Landing of the Pilgrim Fathers* is now missing, it survives in two prints, one reproduced by Martin and Johnson around 1848, the other published by Currier and Ives in 1876. See "Obituary," *Art-Journal* 35 (1873):208; Samuel Redgrave, *A Dictionary of Artists of the English School* (London, 1878), 278; *Cyclopedia of Paintings and Painters* (New York, 1887), vol. 7, 111; and Ethelwyn Manning to Henry Royal, May 4, 1944, Pilgrim Society, Plymouth, Mass. I wish to thank Wendy Greenhouse for providing me with this information, which came from a catalog issued by the Buffalo Fine Arts Academy.

47. See Stephen Foster, *The Long Argument: English Puritanism and the Shaping of New England Culture, 1570–1700* (Williamsburg, Va., and Chapel Hill, N.C., 1991), 63.

48. See John Waddington, *Church of the Pilgrim Fathers, Southwark* (London, 1851), 17–20.

49. Hugh Stowell Brown, *Pilgrim Fathers: A Lecture . . . Illustrative of the Government Prize Picture by Charles Lucy, The Departure of the Pilgrim Fathers* (Manchester, 1853), 45; William Bevan, *The Pilgrim Fathers: The Defenders of Congregational Order, the True Successors of the Apostles and the First Anglican Reformers: A Lecture Illustrated by Lucy's Prize Picture . . . December 4, 1854* (London, 1854), 1, 5; and R. W. Dale, *The Pilgrim Fathers: A Lecture* (London, 1854), 5.

50. Bevan, *The Pilgrim Fathers*, 28.

51. Cope painted his *Embarkation* as both a fresco and on canvas. See Charles Henry Cope, *Reminiscences of Charles West Cope, R.A.* (London, 1891), 146–158, 207; T.S.R. Boase, "The Decoration of the New Palace of Westminster, 1841–1863," *Journal of the Warburg and Courtauld Institute* 17 (1954):319–358; Thomas Archer, *Pictures and Royal Portraits* (London, 1880) vol. 1, 139–143; Richard and Samuel Redgrave, *A Century of British Painters* (1947; reprint, Ithaca, 1981), 459–468; and John Steegman, *Victorian Taste: A Study of the Arts and Architecture from 1830–1870* (1950; reprint, London, 1970), 129–153.

52. As it turned out, Cope's frescoes were anything but permanent; only a few years after their installation, they began to disintegrate, due to the combined effects of sunlight and pollution. But before his *Embarkation* disappeared entirely, Cope duplicated the composition in oils and arranged for its reproduction as an engraving. So popular was the subject that the oil painting soon entered an American collection and the Philadelphia Academy of Fine Arts invited the artist to become an honorary member. See Cope, *Reminiscences*, 157–158, 206–207.

53. Reprinted in *Historical Magazine and Notes and Queries* 1 (May 1857):149–150.

54. See Nathaniel P. Willis, *American Scenery*, with illustrations by W. H. Bartlett (London, 1840), and Eugene C. Worman Jr., "A Geographical Catalog of Bartlett Prints in *American Scenery*," *Imprint* 19 (Autumn 1994):2–16.

55. Unfortunately, Bartlett did not live long enough to enjoy the laurels granted him by the successful publication of *The Pilgrim Fathers*. A year after the book appeared, Bartlett died suddenly at age forty-five while returning from a research trip to the Middle East. See Alexander M. Ross, *William Henry Bartlett: Artist, Author, and Traveller* (Toronto, 1973).

56. William H. Bartlett, *The Pilgrim Fathers; or, The Founders of New England in the Reign of James the First* (London, 1853), xi–xii; and Ross, *Bartlett*, 70–72.

57. Bartlett attributed discovery of the Bradford diary and information about the birthplaces of the Pilgrims to "a distinguished antiquary," the Rev. Joseph Hunter, who had helped Deane transcribe the manuscript. See Bartlett, *Pilgrim Fathers*, xi, 26, 45, 13–107.

58. Ibid., 211.

59. Bartlett actually copied the woman's outfit from a print of *The Merchant's Wife* by the seventeenth-century Dutch artist, Wenceslas Hollar; and he adapted the

man's long jacket and knee-length breeches from earlier nineteenth-century fashions and his pointed collar from the portrait of Edward Winslow that he saw in Pilgrim Hall. He included the Winslow portrait in *Pilgrim Fathers* as a full-page engraving. The few surviving contemporaneous portrayals of the English Puritans show the men wearing tall top hats (but with feathers), capes, and ruff collars. See Maurice Ashley, *Oliver Cromwell and His World* (London, 1972), 17; Valerie Cumming, *A Visual History of Costume: The Seventeenth Century* (London, 1984).

60. William Firth's *The Pilgrim's Daughter*, for example, (an illustration of Scott's *Woodstock*, done in 1853) features a Puritan woman wearing a pointed white collar and a man in a long frock coat and tall black hat. For discussion of how such costumes were adapted, see Beverly Gordon, "Fossilized Fashion: 'Old Fashioned' Dress as a Symbol of Work-Oriented Identity," *Dress* 13 (1987):49–60.

61. For more information on Rothermel, see Mark Thistlethwaite, *Painting in the Grand Manner: The Art of Peter Frederick Rothermel (1812–1895)* (Chadds Ford, Pa., 1995), and "Peter F. Rothermel: A Forgotten History Painter," *Magazine Antiques* 124 (November 1983):1016–1022.

62. The woman is probably meant to represent either Mary Chilton, whom legend credits with having been the first person to land at Plymouth, or Rose Standish, who was designated in a key that accompanied the engraving; and the man is likely John Alden, whose descendants claim it was he who took that first step onto the rock. Other speculations are that the two men in the stern represent John Allerton, William Bradford, and Edward Winslow and that the couple is Rose and Miles Standish. See Lafayette College, *The Kirby Collection of Historical Paintings, Lafayette College, Easton, Pennsylvania* (Easton, Pa., 1963).

63. Around the time he painted *The Pilgrims' First Sabbath at Clark's Island* (often called *First New England Sabbath*), Rothermel did a curious painting that pictures a group of men gathered on the shore beneath snow-covered rocks. A leader–perhaps meant to represent Bradford–lifts his arms heavenward while some of his cohorts kneel in prayer and others assume poses of utter despair. Rothermel also painted other works related to Puritan history, notably *Cromwell Breaking Up the Service in an English Church* (1850) and *The Banishment of Roger Williams* (1851–1852). Joseph Sill confirmed the notion of patriotism when he recorded in his diary that Rothermel had received the commission for *Landing of the Pilgrims* from a Mr. Baldwin. The subject, Sill noted, provided the artist with "an opportunity to shew his skill in a great National Subject." Diary of Joseph Sill, November 20, 1852, and February 17, 1854, reel P30, AAA. I wish to thank Wendy Greenhouse for calling this notation to my attention.

64. Numerous mid-nineteenth-century publications helped perpetuate the Pilgrim legend. See, for example, James G. Miall, *Footsteps of Our Forefathers: What They Suffered and What They Sought . . .* (Boston, 1852); John Winthrop, *The History of New England from 1630 to 1649*, ed. James Savage, 2 vols. (Boston, 1853); and Nathaniel B. Shurtleff, ed., *Records of the Governor and Company of the Massachusetts Bay in New*

England (Boston, 1853). For reviews of these books, see *North American Review* 77 (October 1853):331–373, and 79 (July 1854):53–66.

Chapter 9

1. See Charles Sumner to George Sumner, March 18, 1850, *Selected Letters of Charles Sumner*, 288; Edward J. Renehan Jr., *The Secret Six: The True Tale of the Men Who Conspired with John Brown* (New York, 1995), 48.

2. When Webster criticized the slave trade in his 1820 Forefathers' Day speech, heirs of the old Puritan hierarchy still controlled Massachusetts politics, and the unpopular slave trade was aiding a small coterie of nouveau riche merchants then profiting from importing Africans. In 1850, Webster indicated how much had changed in a letter to the citizens of Newburyport, Massachusetts, written shortly after his speech in the Senate supporting the compromise. The "subject of slavery," he wrote, had been transformed from "a political question" into "a question of religion and humanity," and to support his position on the Fugitive Slave Bill, he pointed out that the New England colonies had passed an ordinance in 1643 ensuring the return of runaway servants. See Paul D. Erickson, "Daniel Webster's Myth of the Pilgrims," *New England Quarterly* 57 (March 1984):45–53; Merrill D. Peterson, "Webster and Slavery," in Conrad Edick Wright, ed., *Massachusetts and the New Nation* (Boston, 1992), 229–230; Daniel Walker Howe, *The Political Culture of the American Whigs* (Chicago, 1979), 205, 216; and Daniel Webster to Edward Sprague Rand et al., May 15, 1850, *The Writings and Speeches of Daniel Webster* (Boston, 1903), vol. 7, 86–87.

3. Daniel Webster, *Address Before the New England Society of New York* (New York, 1850), 4–12, and "Pilgrim Festival at New York in 1850," in *Writings and Speeches of Webster,* vol. 4, 217–226.

4. When touring the South in 1857, James Stirling wrote: "The more I study American character and American opinion, the less I believe in the probability of disunion. No doubt the violence of politicians, and the impulsiveness of the people, may precipitate the country into disunion policy, contrary to their sober judgment and desire, but, barring such political accidents, the sense of the American people in both sections will preserve the Union." James Stirling, *Letters from the Slave States* (London, 1857), 347.

5. Robert H. Hall, "Oration Delivered on the Occasion of the 234th Anniversary of the Landing of the Pilgrims," *Old Colony Messenger*, December 30, 1854.

6. Quoted in Edward L. Pierce, *Memoir and Letters of Charles Sumner* (Boston, 1893), vol. 3, 446. For recent studies of Sumner, see Frederick J. Blue, *Charles Sumner and the Conscience of the North* (Arlington Heights, Ill., 1994); and David Donald, *Charles Sumner and the Coming of the Civil War* (New York, 1960).

7. Charles Sumner, *A Finger Point from Plymouth Rock: Remarks at the Plymouth Festival on the First of August, 1853, in Commemoration of the Embarkation of the Pilgrims* (Boston, 1853), 4–5, 10–11; and *An Account of the Pilgrim Celebration at Plymouth,* Au-

gust 1, 1853 (Boston, 1853), 80–83, 85. Also see John Seelye, _Memory's Nation: The Place of Plymouth Rock_ (Chapel Hill, N.C., 1998), 259–261ff.

8. The "Boston Clique"—its nucleus being William Lloyd Garrison, Maria Chapman, Ellis Gray Loring, Samuel Joseph May, Oliver Johnson, Francis Jackson, Edmund Quincy, Parker Pillsbury, Henry Clark Wright, and Caroline and Deborah Weston—represented the radical extreme. Although most came from prominent New England families, their radical views rendered them pariahs in many Brahmin social circles, so they clustered around Garrison, who served as both mentor and father figure. Garrison had established his newspaper _The Liberator_ in 1831 to criticize the American Antislavery Society, the American Peace Society, the American Missionary Association, and all other organizations that advocated working through the political process to free the slaves gradually. See Lawrence J. Friedman, _Gregarious Saints: Self and Community in American Abolitionism, 1830–1870_ (Cambridge, London, and New York, 1982); Herbert Aptheker, _Abolitionism: A Revolutionary Movement_ (Boston, 1982); and Larry Gara, "Who Was an Abolitionist?" in Martin Duberman, ed., _The Anti-Slavery Vanguard: New Essays on the Abolitionists_ (Princeton, 1965), 32–51.

9. Oliver Wendell Holmes, _Oration Before the New England Society in the City of New York at Their Semi-Centennial Anniversary, December 22, 1855_ (New York, 1855), 42–43.

10. See, for example, the lead editorial in _Old Colony Messenger_, August 11, 1855.

11. The Pilgrims "persisted and prevailed," Seward said, "because they had adopted one true, singular, and sublime principle of civil conduct, namely: that the subject in every State has a natural right to religious liberty of conscience." Instead of deriving "the right of toleration from the common law, or the statutes of the realm," the forefathers "resorted directly to a law broader, older, and more stable . . . a law universal in its application and in its obligation, established by the Creator and Judge of all men, and therefore paramount to all human constitutions." See William H. Seward, _Oration at Plymouth, December 21, 1855_ (Washington, D.C., 1856), 4, 7, and Seelye, _Memory's Nation_, 268–273.

12. Wendell Phillips, "The Pilgrims," in Phillips, _Speeches, Lectures, and Letters_ (Boston, 1864), 228–236. Audience reaction is printed in the text.

13. Holmes, _Oration Before the New England Society_, 38.

14. Defenders of slavery had long claimed that Southerners harbored fewer racial prejudices than Northerners. "The truly Southern man acknowledges the principle of humanity in his servant," wrote John Thompson in 1854. Unlike the "Northern man," the Southerner "feels no degradation in the touch of the negro's hand" and "in sickness watches by his bed, and often with tearful eye and sorrowing heart, attends the remains of some faithful follower to the grave." "A Few Thoughts on Slavery," _SLM_ 20 (April 1854):198. Also see "Gov. Wise's Oration," _SLM_ 23 (July 1856):10–13.

15. Quoted in Mitchell Snay, _Gospel of Disunion: Religion and Separatism in the Antebellum South_ (Cambridge, Eng., and New York, 1993), 32.

16. Included in his proposal were release of black females and their descendants, altering the status of domestic help from slaves to indentured servants, a program of controlled emancipation of other slaves, and state funds to compensate planters for their lost "property." See St. George Tucker, "A Dissertation on Slavery: With a Proposal for the Gradual Abolition of It, in the State of Virginia," reprinted in Cynthia Tucker Coleman, *Virginia Silhouettes* (Richmond, 1934), appendix.

17. Strongest opposition came from a block of Tidewater and Eastern Virginia planters, who still held the reins of state government, even though Western farmers, along with a growing middle class of merchants and lawyers, were slowly eroding their majority. The debate on slavery in the House of Delegates came a year after those same Tidewater planters blocked a change in the new constitution that would have broadened the franchise and brought other democratic measures into Virginia. See Alison Goodyear Freehling, *Drift Toward Dissolution: The Virginia Slavery Debate of 1831–1832* (Baton Rouge, 1982); and William G. Shade, *Democratizing the Old Dominion: Virginia and the Second Party System, 1824–1861* (Charlottesville, Va., and London, 1996), 50–77; 191–211.

18. See Lyon Tyler, *Letters and Times of the Tylers* (1884; reprint, New York, 1970), vol. 1, 568.

19. A *Southern Literary Messenger* columnist stated in 1843, "[W]e lament and deplore it as the greatest evil that could have been inflicted on our country." But he swiftly added: "[W]e lament it not for the sake of the black race, but of the white," asserting that the former "are not only far happier in a state of slavery than of freedom, but we believe the happiest class on this continent." He further explained that if "the slaves of the Southern States had been treated like those of the British West, Indies," they "would have been extinct long ago. Or, if they had been placed in the situation of the free blacks of the North, particularly of New England," they would also have disappeared. But, he boasted, "they have increased in an enormous ratio, alike injurious to the prosperity, and dangerous to the safety of the white race when stimulated to dissatisfaction by the traitorous intrigues of Northern fanatics." See "Reflections on the Census of 1840," *SLM* 9 (June 1843):350. For discussion of the abolitionist argument and the South's response, see Lewis P. Simpson, *Mind and the American Civil War: A Meditation on Lost Causes* (Baton Rouge, La., 1989); Drew Gilpin Faust, *Creation of Confederate Nationalism* (Baton Rouge, La., 1988); John McCardell, *The Idea of a Southern Nation: Southern Nationalists and Southern Nationalism, 1830–1860* (New York and London, 1979); and Fred Hobson, "The Savage South: An Inquiry into the Origins, Endurance, and Presumed Demise of an Image," *Virginia Quarterly Review* 61 (Summer 1985):377–395.

20. "Publicola," "The Present Aspect of Abolitionism," *SLM* 13 (July 1847): 431–432.

21. "A Few Thoughts on Slavery," *SLM* 20 (April 1854):194.

22. Samuel Longfellow, *Life of Henry Wadsworth Longfellow, with Extracts from His Journals and Correspondence* (Boston, 1886), vol. 2, 222–223.

23. Harriet Beecher Stowe, *The Mayflower; or, Sketches of Scenes and Characters, Among the Descendants of the Pilgrims* (Boston, 1844). Similarly, her more polished novel *Oldtown Folks* (Boston, 1869) presented homespun portraits of New England situations and Yankee types. On these works, see Joan D. Hedrick, *Harriet Beecher Stowe: A Life* (New York and Oxford, 1994), 141–142, 330–352.

24. Hawthorne's *Scarlet Letter* came out in 1850, *The House of the Seven Gables* and *Twice-Told Tales* in 1851, *The Blithedale Romance* and *Mosses from an Old Manse* in 1854. Melville published *Moby Dick* in 1851, and Thoreau's *Walden* came out in 1854. For a thorough study of this period, see Van Wyck Brooks, *The Flowering of New England, 1815–1865* (New York, 1936); F. O. Matthiessen, *The American Renaissance: Art and Expression in the Age of Emerson and Whitman* (London, Oxford, and New York, 1941); and David S. Reynolds, *Beneath the American Renaissance: The Subversive Imagination in the Age of Emerson and Melville* (Cambridge, Mass., and London, 1988).

25. John Greenleaf Whittier, "Stanzas for the Times" (1835) and "A Summons" (1836) in *Anti-Slavery Poems: Songs of Labor and Reform* (1888; reprint, New York, 1969), 36 and 41. Also see Robert Penn Warren, *John Greenleaf Whittier's Poetry: An Appraisal and a Selection* (Minneapolis, 1971); and Lewis Leary, *John Greenleaf Whittier* (New York, 1971).

26. James Russell Lowell, "An Interview with Miles Standish," in *The Poetical Works of James Russell Lowell,* ed. Marjorie R. Kaufman (Boston, 1978), 80–81.

27. Mark Hopkins, *Sermon Delivered at Plymouth on the 22nd of December, 1846* (Boston, 1846), 31. Also see William Sullivan, *Discourse Delivered Before the Pilgrim Society on the 22nd Day of December, 1829* (Boston, 1830), 33–35; George W. Blagden, *Address . . . Before the Pilgrim Society, December 22, 1834* (Boston, 1835), 28.

28. "Pocahontas" [Emily Clemens Pearson], *Cousin Franck's Household, or Scenes in the Old Dominion* (Boston, 1853).

29. Very little is known about Pearson, who has been completely overlooked in literary histories, although she wrote a number of books, most with strong moral messages. Her *Jamie Parker: The Fugitive* (Hartford, 1851) gives an account of Virginia plantation life similar to that in her later novels; *Uncle Franck's Household* was reissued under the title *Ruth's Sacrifice, or Life on the Rappahannock* (Boston, 1864). After the Civil War, she published *Prince Paul: The Freedman Soldier* (Boston, 1867), about runaway slaves in Virginia who fight with the Union army. She noted in the preface that she had taken "some pains" during a "residence in Virginia" to record the "nondescript vernacular of the cabin and the hut" and to study the condition of "poor whites," whose miserable existence is "not an accident of the slave system" but its "necessary result." This statement–along with her acknowledgment that portions of *Uncle Franck's Household* had already appeared in religious magazines–prepared the reader for the moralizing that followed. *Uncle Franck's Household,* v–vii. For a discussion of *Jamie Parker* and *Uncle Franck's Household,* see Robert S. Tilton, *Pocahontas: the Evolution of an American Narrative* (Cambridge, Mass., and New York, 1994), 153–158. Also see Sterling Brown, *The Negro in American Fiction* (Washington, D.C., 1937),

33–34; and Lorenzo Dow Turner, *Anti-Slavery Sentiment in Literature Prior to 1865* (1929; reprint, Port Washington, N.Y., 1966), 79.

30. Pearson, *Cousin Franck's Household,* 233–234.

31. H. W. Longfellow to C. Sumner, October 17, 1858, *The Letters of Henry Wadsworth Longfellow,* ed. Andrew Hilen (Cambridge, Mass., 1972), vol. 4, 99.

32. H. W. Longfellow to C. Sumner, August 12, 1858, and November 21, 1958, and H. W. Longfellow to James Thomas Fields, December 5, 1858, in *Letters of Longfellow,* vol. 4, 92, 102, 106. For additional mention of the illustrations, see *The Crayon* (January 1859), 27–28; and S. Longfellow, *Life of Longfellow,* vol. 2, 327.

33. See H. W. Longfellow, *The Courtship of Miles Standish,* illus. John Gilbert (1859; reprint, London, 1865) and *Illustrations of Longfellow's Courtship of Miles Standish by John W. Ehninger* (New York, 1859). See L. W. Longfellow to J. W. Ehninger, November 27, 1858, *Letters of Longfellow,* vol. 4, 103–104.

34. A reviewer for *The Crayon* commented that Ehninger's "delineations" were "very happy." "New Publications," *Crayon* (January 1859):27–28.

35. For the most thorough examination of Longfellow's life, see S. Longfellow, *Life of Longfellow.* Also see Cecil Williams, *Henry Wadsworth Longfellow* (New York, 1964), and Edward Wagenknecht, *Henry Wadsworth Longfellow: His Poetry and Prose* (New York, 1986).

36. See Thomas Wortham, "Bryant and the Fireside Poets," in Emory Elliott, ed., *Columbia Literary History of the United States* (New York, 1988), 282; and Brooks, *The Flowering of New England,* 508–512.

37. Robert A. Ferguson deals with this issue in "Longfellow's Political Fears: Civic Authority and the Role of the Artist in *Hiawatha* and *Miles Standish,*" *American Literature* 50 (March, 1978):187–215. Also see Seelye, *Memory's Nation,* 378–384ff.

38. See "Poems on Slavery," in *The Poetical Works of Henry Wadsworth Longfellow,* ed. Samuel Longfellow (1886; reprint, New York, 1966), 83–97; and Thomas Wenworth Higginson, *Henry Wadsworth Longfellow* (Boston and New York, 1902), 163–211. For Longfellow's frequent expressions of distaste for Southern slavery, see H. W. Longfellow to J. G. Whittier, September 6, 1844, *Letters of Longfellow,* vol. 3, 44; H. W. Longfellow to Arthur Mills, June 12, 1850, H. W. Longfellow to Robert James Mackintosh, May 4, 1857, and H. W. Longfellow to Charles Sumner, March 13, 1854, *Letters of Longfellow,* vol. 3, 260, 425, and vol. 4, 30.

39. "It is the greatest voice, on the greatest subject, that has been uttered since we became a nation," Longfellow exclaimed after reading the speech that provoked the attack. "No matter for insults,—we feel them with you; no matter for wounds,—we also bleed in them! You have torn the mask off the faces of traitors; and at last the spirit of the North is aroused." H. W. Longfellow to Charles Sumner, May 28, 1856, February 24, 1858, May 11, 1858, *Letters of Longfellow,* vol. 3, 540; vol. 4, 65 and 77.

40. S. Longfellow, *Life of Longfellow,* vol. 2, 361; also see vol. 2, 294, 357–358, and Ferguson, "Longfellow's Political Fears, 187–215.

41. For several years, he had been struggling with the idea of writing what he called "a Puritan pastoral." At first he tried to make it into a play called "A New England Tragedy" but he soon abandoned that idea in favor of a long poem originally titled "Priscilla." "My poem is in hexameters," he wrote in his diary on December 3, 1857, "an idyl of the Old Colony times. What it will turn out I do not know; but it gives me pleasure to write it; and that I count for something." S. Longfellow, *Life of Longfellow*, vol. 2, 311, 275–276, 285, 289, 294, 310; H. W. Longfellow to Charles Deane, May 18, 1858, *Letters of Longfellow*, vol. 4, 79; Williams, *Longfellow*, 88–89, 164–168; and Wagenknecht, *Longfellow: Poetry and Prose*, 104–113.

42. "The Heroine's name is Priscilla," he told Sumner, "and so you have the chief characters and the chief incident before you, taking it for granted that you remember the anecdote." H. W. Longfellow to C. Sumner, June 3, 1858, and July 10, 1858, *Letters of Longfellow*, vol. 4, 82, 87. For earlier recountings of this tale, see Seba Smith, "Gleanings from Early New-England History," *SLM* 6 (January 1840):46–47; and "Poem," *Old Colony Messenger*, December 30, 1854.

43. Page numbers refer to Henry Wadsworth Longfellow, *Courtship of Miles Standish* (Indianapolis, 1903).

44. The author, who signed his article with the initials "S.L.C." was possibly the South Carolinian, St. Leger Carter. See S.L.C., "Miles Standish," *SLM* 28 (February 1859):118–122. For hints on identification of the author, see David K. Jackson, *The Contributors and Contributions to* The Southern Literary Messenger, *1834–1864* (Charlottesville, Va., 1936), 168.

45. Although the state had experienced an economic slump a few decades earlier, it was slowly recovering, and the region south of Jamestown was undergoing a renaissance of sorts. Not only had the port of Norfolk developed into a shipbuilding and exporting center but many of the old tobacco plantations were diversifying their crops to meet a changing market. See Martha W. McCartney, *James City County: Keystone of the Commonwealth* (James City County, Va., 1997), 279–285; and Clement Eaton, *The Growth of Southern Civilization, 1790–1860* (New York, 1961), 177–185.

46. *Richmond Enquirer*, May 19, 1857; and *Richmond Daily Dispatch*, May 19, 1857. Also see George Benjamin West, *When the Yankees Came: Civil War and Reconstruction on the Virginia Peninsula*, ed. Parke Rouse Jr. (Richmond, 1977), 19–20.

47. See *Celebration of the Two-Hundred and Fiftieth Anniversary of the English Settlement at Jamestown, May 13, 1857* (Washington, D.C., 1857), 2.

48. Ibid., 3–4, 15, 21; and "Celebration at Jamestown," *SLM* 24 (June 1857):435–436, 449.

49. *Celebration of the Anniversary*, 21–27.

50. Ibid., 29–30.

51. Ibid., 30.

52. Edward Everett, "The Birthday of Washington," in Edward Everett, *Orations and Speeches on Various Occasions* (Boston, 1859), vol. 3, 63–64.

53. For information on the campaign to save Mount Vernon, see Thomas Nelson Page, *Mount Vernon and Its Preservation* (New York, 1932); Elswyth Thane, *Mount Ver-*

non Is Ours: The Story of Its Preservation (New York, 1966); George W. Forgie, *Patricide in the House Divided: A Psychological Interpretation of Lincoln and His Age* (New York, 1979), 168–173, 183–191; William A. Bryan, "George Washington: Symbolic Guardian of the Republic, 1850–1861," *William and Mary Quarterly* 7 (January 1950):53–63; and Ruth E. Finley, *The Lady of Godey's: Sarah Josepha Hale* (Philadelphia and London, 1931), 184–189.

54. "Editor's Table," *SLM* 23 (May 1859):397.

55. *First Celebration by the Old Dominion Society of the Settlement at Jamestown, on the 13th of May, 1607* (New York, 1860), 24–25, 70, 77–78, 83.

56. Ibid., 89–91.

Chapter 10

1. Before he became an ardent abolitionist, Brown left a long legacy of erratic behavior, including several ill-fated commercial ventures in Ohio and Pennsylvania that plunged his large family into insurmountable debt. Contributing to his financial woes was the conviction that he was leading a divinely inspired mission to end slavery. For interpretations of the John Brown raid and its consequences, see Paul Finkelman, ed., *His Soul Goes Marching On: Responses to John Brown and the Harpers Ferry Raid* (Charlottesville, Va., 1995); Stephen B. Oates, *To Purge This Land with Blood: A Biography of John Brown* (Amherst, Mass., 1970 and 1984); and David M. Potter, *The Impending Crisis, 1848–1861*, completed and edited by Don E. Fehrenbacher (New York, 1976), 356–384.

2. Franklin B. Sanborn, *The Life and Letters of John Brown, Liberator of Kansas, and Martyr of Virginia* (Boston, 1891), 626–627.

3. For information on the Secret Six, see Edward J. Renehan Jr., *The Secret Six: The True Tale of the Men Who Conspired with John Brown* (New York, 1995); Jeffrey Rossbach, *Ambivalent Conspirators: John Brown, the Secret Six, and a Theory of Slave Violence* (Philadelphia, 1982); and Otto Scott, *The Secret Six: John Brown and the Abolitionist Movement* (Murphy, Calif., 1979). For a thorough discussion of Brown's connections with Massachusetts, see John Seelye's *Memory's Nation: The Place of Plymouth Rock* (Chapel Hill, N.C., 1998), 330–360ff.

4. Quoted in Renehan, *Secret Six*, 120; for other quotations, see 113 and 118.

5. "Old Browns Farewell to the Plymouth Rocks, Bunker Hill Monuments, Charter Oaks, and Uncle Thoms Cabbins," in *A John Brown Reader*, ed. Louis Ruchames (London and New York, 1959), 106.

6. In one instance, Brown killed a man in Missouri and then escorted eleven of his slaves to Canada. When in early 1858 he told Frederick Douglass of his planned incursion into Virginia, the distinguished former slave advised him that such a move would be suicidal.

7. See Craig M. Simpson, *A Good Southerner: The Life of Henry A. Wise of Virginia* (Chapel Hill, N.C., 1985), 210–218.

8. Panic, in fact, gripped the "Secret Six" after documents confiscated from Brown's possessions revealed their names. Fearing possible arrest, Sanborn, Howe, and Stearns fled to Canada; their New York colleague, Gerrit Smith, suffered a mental collapse and ended up in an insane asylum.

9. Quoted in Wendy Hamand Venet, "'Cry Aloud and Spare Not' Northern Antislavery Women and John Brown's Raid," in Finkelman, *His Soul,* 106.

10. See Simpson, *Good Southerner,* 203; and Robert E. McGlone, "John Brown, Henry Wise, and the Politics of Insanity," in Finkelman, *His Soul,* 213–252.

11. *Correspondence Between Lydia Maria Child and Gov. Wise and Mrs. Mason of Virginia* (Boston, 1860), 3–6. Also see Carolyn L. Karcher, *The First Woman in the Republic: A Cultural Biography of Lydia Maria Child* (Durham, N.C., 1994), 416–427; Jean Fagan Yellin, *Women and Sisters: The Antislavery Feminists in American Culture* (New Haven and London, 1989), 62–64; and Simpson, *Good Southerner,* 224.

12. *Correspondence Between Child and Wise,* 14–15.

13. Ibid., 16–19.

14. John Brown to Rev. Luther Humphrey, November 19, 1859, *John Brown Reader,* 139–140.

15. Ralph Waldo Emerson's speech in Tremont Temple, in James Redpath, ed., *Echoes of Harper's Ferry* (1860; reprint, New York, 1969), 67–71.

16. "Lecture by Henry D. Thoreau," in Redpath, *Echoes,* 19–20.

17. Victor Hugo to *London News,* December 2, 1859, in Redpath, *Echoes,* 268. At a meeting in Philadelphia on the day of the execution, abolitionist Theodore Tilton thanked God because "John Brown was a Puritan—the sixth in descent from the band of Pilgrims who stepped on Plymouth Rock." See "Speech of Theodore Tilton," in Redpath, *Echoes,* 274.

18. Quoted in Renehan, *Secret Six,* 294.

19. In a tribute to Brown, Whittier wrote:

> *So vainly shall Virginia set*
> *Her battle in array;*
> *In vain her trampling squadrons knead*
> *The winter snow with clay.*
> *She may strike the pouncing eagle,*
> *But she dare not harm the dove;*
> *And every gate she bars to Hate*
> *Shall open wide to Love! (*John Brown Reader, *296)*

20. "Wendell Phillips on the Puritan Principle," in Redpath, *Echoes,* 111–112, 117. Phillips also delivered a eulogy at Brown's burial on December 8 in North Elba, New York, which contained these lines: "Virginia stands at the bar of the civilized world on trial. . . . Round her victim crowd the apostles and martyrs, all the brave, high souls . . . Virginia is weak, because each man's heart said amen to John Brown.

His words,–they are stronger even than his rifles. These crushed a state. Those have changed the thoughts of millions, and will yet crush slavery." See Wendell Phillips, "Burial of John Brown," *John Brown Reader*, 282.

21. Redpath, *Echoes*, 115.

22. Stephen H. Taft, *A Discourse on the Character and Death of John Brown, Delivered in Martinsburgh, N.Y. Dec. 12 1859* (Des Moines, 1872), 15.

23. See William R. Taylor, *Cavalier and Yankee: The Old South and American National Character* (1957; reprint, Cambridge, Mass, 1979); and Jan C. Dawson, "The Puritan and the Cavalier: The South's Perception of Contrasting Traditions," *Journal of Southern History* 44 (November 1978):597–614.

24. "The New England Character," *SLM* 3 (June 1837):413.

25. William Adams, *An Address Delivered Before the New England Society in the City of New York, December 22, 1852* (New York, 1853), 6. Charles Upham also made a reference to the Civil War in his 1846 speech by declaring that the Puritan revolution erected "monuments" of "wisdom, heroism, and greatness. Those monuments are the Commonwealth of England, with the civil wars that led to it, and the Colonization of New England, terminating in the establishment of the Republic of the United States of America." Charles Upham, *An Oration Delivered Before the New England Society of New York, December 22, 1846* (New York, 1847), 15.

26. George Bancroft, *History of the United States from the Discovery of the American Continent* (1834; reprint, Boston, 1848), vol. 1, 414, 431–432. For Bancroft's political views and analysis of his historical writing, see Fred Sompkin, *Unquiet Eagle: Memory and Desire in the Idea of American Freedom, 1815–1860* (Ithaca, 1967), 175–206; Bert James Lowenberg, *American History in American Thought: Christopher Columbus to Henry Adams* (New York, 1972), 139–157; and Richard C. Vitzhum, *The American Compromise: Theme and Method in the Histories of Bancroft, Parkman, and Adams* (Norman, Okla., 1974), 12–76.

27. Henry Howe, *Historical Collections of Virginia* (Charleston, S.C., 1847), 131–132.

28. Bancroft, *History,* vol. 1, 206–207, 222–227.

29. Spencer Wallace Cone, "The Old Dominion," *SLM* 7 (July 1841):451.

30. Grenville Mellen, "Ode," in Russell, *Guide to Plymouth,* appendix, 59–60.

31. See Jan C. Dawson, "The Puritan and the Cavalier: The South's Perception of Contrasting Traditions," *Journal of Southern History* 44 (November 1978):601–609; Fred Hobson, "The Savage South: An Inquiry into the Origins, Endurance, and Presumed Demise of an Image," *Virginia Quarterly Review* 61 (Summer 1985):382–386; and Peter Gomes, "Pilgrims and Puritans: 'Heroes' and 'Villains' in the Creation of the American Past," *Proceedings of the Massachusetts Historical Society* 95 (1983):1–16.

32. James P. Holcombe, *The Election of a Black Republican President: An Overt Act of Aggression on the Right of Property in Slaves* (Richmond, 1860), 5, 10, 12, 14–15.

33. "Northern Mind and Character," *SLM* 31 (November 1860):345, 349.

34. John Esten Cooke, "A Dream of the Cavaliers," *Harper's New Monthly Magazine* 22 (January 1861):252–254, partially printed in Robert S. Tilton, *Pocahontas: The Evolution of an American Narrative* (Cambridge, Eng., and New York, 1994), 166–168.

35. Joseph Brenan, "A Ballad for the Young South," *SLM* 32 (February 1861):100–103.

36. "The Puritan and the Cavalier; or, The Elements of American Colonial Society," *De Bow's Review* 6 (September 1861):207–252.

37. "Then and Now in the Old Dominion," *Atlantic Monthly* 9 (April 1862):493–502.

38. Ibid., 500.

39. Nathaniel Hawthorne, "Chiefly About War-Matters by a Peaceable Man," *Atlantic Monthly* 10 (July 1862):50.

40. David Riggs, *Embattled Shrine: Jamestown in the Civil War* (Shippensburg, Pa., 1997), 10–36, 115–117; and Paul H. Silverstone, *Warships of the Civil War Navies* (Annapolis, Md., 1989), 24, 89, 47–48.

41. In June 1861, a battle at Big (or Great) Bethel, midway between Yorktown and Hampton, took the lives of twenty-five men from Massachusetts; thirty more were wounded or missing. A war correspondent for Plymouth's *Old Colony Memorial* reported: "The battle has begun, that is soon to decide the great contest of Freedom, the protection of the Constitution, the power of Law and Order over anarchy and rebellion, and the great principle of Democracy and its power for self-government." *Old Colony Memorial,* April 27, May 4, May 18, May 25, and June 22, 1861. Also see "A Richmond Lady" [Sallie B. Putnam], *Richmond During the War: Four Years of Personal Observation* (New York and London, 1867), 49–56, and William H. Osborne, *The History of the Twenty-Ninth Regiment of Massachusetts Volunteer Infantry, in the Late War of the Rebellion* (Boston, 1877), 37–40, 56–72; James I. Robertson Jr., *Civil War Virginia: Battleground for a Nation* (Charlottesville, Va., and London, 1991), 30; and Martha W. McCartney, *James City County: Keystone of the Commonwealth* (James City County, Va., 1997), 302–304.

42. The Standish Guards remained in Plymouth, armed and ready to fight if called, although most never returned to combat. By 1862, the Union army had been consolidated into a viable fighting force, and the Plymouth units remaining in the vicinity of Fort Monroe joined the Twenty-ninth Massachusetts Regiment, which continued to guard the mouth of the James River. *Old Colony Memorial,* July 27, 1861, and August 30, 1862.

43. Virginia experienced the longest period of occupation of all the Confederate states. See Riggs, *Embattled Shrine,* 44–45; and Stephen V. Ash, "White Virginians Under Federal Occupation, 1861–1865," *Virginia Magazine of History and Biography* 98 (April 1990):169–192.

44. Ultimately, however, the Southern navy was forced to scrap its iron monster and surrender the mouth of the James River to Union forces, after which the North controlled access to Richmond until the end of the war with a blockade that crippled Confederate president Jefferson Davis and his staff. Robertson, *Civil War Virginia,* 42–45; and Riggs, *Embattled Shrine,* 63–64.

45. Riggs, *Embattled Shrine,* 66–81; and Howard M. Hensal, *The Anatomy of Failure: The Case of Major General George B. McClellan and the Peninsular Campaign* (Montgomery, Ala., 1985).

46. Riggs, *Embattled Shrine*, 76–77, 82–84.

47. George B. McClellan, *McClellan's Own Story: The War for the Union, the Soldiers Who Fought It, the Civilians Who Directed It, and His Relations to It and to Them* (New York, 1887), 468.

48. For details on the Virginia peninsula during the war, see ibid., 37–106; McCartney, *James City County*, 312–322; and George Benjamin West, *When the Yankees Came: Civil War and Reconstruction on the Virginia Peninsula*, ed. Parke Rouse Jr. (Richmond, 1977).

49. J. H. Martin, *Smith and Pocahontas: A Poem* (Richmond, Va., 1862), 94–95. The author added a footnote to indicate this portion of the poem had been written following the battle of Bethel.

50. W.S.B., "Pocahontas; or, The Lady Rebecca," *SLM* 34 (November and December 1862):643–647.

51. See Tilton, *Pocahontas*, 172. There were warships bearing the names "Pocahontas" or "Powhatan" in both the North and the South. See ibid., 145–149, 170; and "Pocahontas and Sectionalism," available: *Crossroads,* Online, March 3, 1997.

52. With Jamestown and Plymouth characterized as historically fated foes, it is interesting to note that on June 4, 1864, the steam-tug USS *Mayflower* pulled up to the Jamestown dock to warn that Confederate snipers were attacking ships downriver. See Riggs, *Embattled Shrine*, 95; Silverstone, *Warships*, 112.

53. For details on the fall of Richmond, see A. A. and Mary Hoehling, *The Day Richmond Died* (Lanham, Md., 1981), 77–239; and Putnam, *Richmond*, 362–371.

54. Riggs, *Embattled Shrine*, 102, 105–106.

Chapter 11

1. Henry Adams to John Gorham Palfrey, October 23, 1861, and February 12, 1862, *The Letters of Henry Adams*, ed. J. C. Levenson et al. (Cambridge, Mass., and London, 1982), vol. 1, 258–259, 279–281.

2. Henry Adams to John Gorham Palfrey, March 27, 1863; May 4, 1866; July 5, 1866; July 13, 1866; and August 23, 1866; and Henry Adams to Charles Eliot Norton, August 24, 1866, *Letters of Adams*, vol. 1, 340, 506–511.

3. For Adams's opinion of Virginians, see Henry Adams, *The Education of Henry Adams* (1918; reprint, New York, 1931), 57–58.

4. Henry Adams to John Gorham Palfrey, March 20, 1862, *Letters of Adams*, vol. 1, 287–288. Also see Henry Adams to John Gorham Palfrey, February 12, 1862, *Letters of Adams*, vol. 1, 280; and Tilton, *Pocahontas*, 173–174.

5. Henry Adams to Charles Deane, November 30, 1866, *Letters of Adams*, vol. 1, 514.

6. Adams, *Education of Adams*, 222. The article received immediate notice; see Henry Adams to Charles Francis Adams Jr., February 23, 1867, *Letters of Adams*, vol. 1, 520–521.

7. Henry Adams, "Captain John Smith," *North American Review* 104 (January 1867):10–13.

8. Ibid., 14–30.

9. *Dictionary of American Biography*, under "Edward Duffield Neill."

10. Edward D. Neill, *Virginia Vetusta, During the Reign of James the First: Containing Letters and Documents Never Before Printed* (Albany, N.Y., 1885), 140–143.

11. See William Wirt Henry, "The Rescue of Captain John Smith by Pocahontas," *Potters American Monthly* 4–5 (1875):523–528; 591–592, and "The Settlement of Jamestown," *Proceedings of the Virginia Historical Society* (Richmond, 1882), 10–82.

12. Henry, "Settlement of Jamestown," 10.

13. Ibid., 16–58.

14. Ibid., 63.

15. See Laura Polanyi Striker and Bradford Smith, "The Rehabilitation of Captain John Smith," *Journal of Southern History* 28 (November 1962):474–481.

16. John Esten Cooke, *My Lady Pokahontas: A True Relation of Virginia. Writ by Anas Todkill, Puritan and Pilgrim* (1885; reprint, Boston, 1907), 1.

17. Quotations are from ibid., 20, 36–44, 53, 107.

18. *The Proceedings at the Celebration by the Pilgrim Society at Plymouth, December 21, 1870 of the Two Hundred Fiftieth Anniversary of the Landing of the Pilgrims* (Cambridge, Mass., 1871), 24–25, 60–61, 96, and 106.

19. Ibid., 123 and 131.

20. William Lloyd Garrison to the Pilgrim Society, December 19, 1870, Pilgrim Society, Plymouth.

21. *Proceedings at Plymouth*, 129.

22. For recent surveys of the colonial revival, see Karal Ann Marling, *George Washington Slept Here: Colonial Revivals and American Culture* (Cambridge, Mass., 1988), and Michael Kammen, *Mystic Chords of Memory: The Transformation of Tradition in American Culture* (New York, 1991).

23. The victors had been especially careful to preach conciliation. In his Forefathers' Day address of 1870, for example, Winthrop paid homage to Jamestown (the "elder sister" of Plymouth) and allowed that the Virginia Colony did have the first republican assembly a year before the Pilgrims landed. *Proceedings at Plymouth*, 83–84.

24. For example, Gustave Courbet had a very similar procession in *Burial at Ornans* of 1849.

25. For the reception of Boughton's painting, see Marling, *George Washington Slept Here*, 58–60.

26. When Nehlig translated this vertical composition into a horizontal lithograph, printed in sepia tones, he increased the number of figures and expanded the drama. The youthful Powhatan of the painting has become a ferocious warrior in full headdress lunging toward his intended victim, who now lies prone, his head dangling off of a rocky podium. The lithograph was issued by F. Tuchfarber and Co. of Cincinnati.

27. *Victor Nehlig's Great Historical Painting, Pocahontas, Reproduced on Stone by the Artist Himself* (Cincinnati, 1874), 5.

28. *New York Herald,* November 9, 1871, reprinted in *Nehlig's Great Historical Painting,* 8.

29. Mark Twain [Samuel Clemens], *Plymouth Rock and the Pilgrims and Other Salutary Platform Opinions,* ed. Charles Neider (New York and London, 1984), 94–98.

30. See, for example, Tryon Edwards, "Pilgrims and Puritans," *Scribner's Monthly* 12 (June 1876):212–219.

Chapter 12

1. See James F. O'Gorman, *Accomplished in All Departments of Art: Hammatt Billings of Boston, 1818–1874* (Amherst, Mass., 1998).

2. See James F. O'Gorman, "The Colossus of Plymouth, Hammatt Billings's National Monument to the Forefathers," *Journal of the Society of Architectural Historians* 54 (September 1995):282–283, 296–297.

3. Rose T. Briggs, *Plymouth Rock: History and Significance* (Plymouth, Mass., 1968), 16–18; George F. Willison, *Saints and Strangers* (New York, 1945), 424–425; and Robert D. Arner, "Plymouth Rock Revisited: The Landing of the Pilgrim Fathers," *Journal of American Culture* 6 (Winter 1983):25–35.

4. In fact, long before the monument was completed, it was already a familiar sight for New Englanders, who viewed it as an illustration designed to raise money for the monument. A drawing of it ran next to a picture taken from Bartlett's *Pilgrim Fathers* and a reproduction of Weir's *Embarkation of the Pilgrims.* See *The Illustrated Pilgrim Memorial* (Boston, 1863); and O'Gorman, "Colossus," 282–286.

5. "Monument to the Pilgrims," reprinted in the *Wide-Awake Gift: A Know-Nothing Token for 1855* (New York, 1855), 159.

6. See O'Gorman, "Colossus," 286–291.

7. The final cost of the monument was $150,000. "National Monument to the Forefathers," pamphlet, Pilgrim Society (Plymouth, Mass., n.d.); *Old Colony Memorial,* August 3, 1889; Peter J. Gomes, ed., *The Pilgrim Society, 1820–1970: An Informal Commemorative Essay* (Plymouth, Mass., 1971), 14–18; and John Seelye, *Memory's Nation: The Place of Plymouth Rock* (Chapel Hill, N.C.), 528–529, 542–545ff.

8. For a thorough study of the iconography, see O'Gorman, "Colossus," 291–296.

9. See Maurice Agulhon, *Marianne into Battle: Republican Imagery and Symbolism in France, 1789–1880* (London and New York, 1981), and Jean-Claude Lamberti, "Laboulaye and the Common Law of Free Peoples," *Liberty: The French-American Statue in Art and History* (New York, 1986), 20–25.

10. Briggs, *Plymouth Rock,* 18; Mrs. Joseph Rucker Lamar, *A History of the National Society of the Colonial Dames of America from 1891 to 1933* (Atlanta, 1934), 134–137; and Leland M. Roth, *The Architecture of McKim, Mead, and White, 1870–1920: A Building List* (New York, 1978), 122.

11. Lamar, *Colonial Dames*, 139–142.

12. Quoted in Michael Kammen, *Mystic Chords of Memory: The Transformation of Tradition in American Culture* (New York, 1991), 385.

13. In 1835, David Bullock purchased the Ambler property along with the adjoining estate of Samuel Travis, which gave him control of Jamestown Island. Four years later, Bullock sold Jamestown, which passed through several hands before ending up in the possession of William Allen, whose inheritance allowed him to extend his domain from Grove Creek to Sandy Bay. See Martha W. McCartney, *James City County: Keystone of the Commonwealth* (James City County, Va., 1997), 279–285; and Ivor Noël Hume, *The Virginia Adventure: Roanoke to James Towne, an Archeological and Historical Odyssey* (New York, 1994), 395–403.

14. In 1902, when 500 New York socialites requested permission to hold "a luncheon on the spot where Pocahontas was married to John Rolfe," APVA members debated the issue at great length before finally allowing the New Yorkers to hold their party on Virginia's "sacred" grounds. James M. Lindgren, *Preserving the Old Dominion: Historic Preservation and Virginia Traditionalism* (Charlottesville, Va., 1993), 109, 94.

15. The crumbling church tower was not the only remnant of the old Jamestown Church, for local engineers Samuel H. Yonge and W. G. Stannard had recently discovered a submerged cobblestone floor. Exact dating of those sunken underpinnings was open to question. Some believed it supported the third Jamestown Church constructed by Samuel Argall in 1617; others thought it belonged to a sanctuary built in 1647. Correspondence between Samuel Yonge and Edith Y. Wendall, Special Collections, Alderman Library, University of Virginia, Charlottesville. Also see Hume, *Virginia Adventure*, 424–431.

16. Lindgren, *Preserving the Old Dominion*, 127–129; and Lamar, *Colonial Dames*, 116–123.

17. Lamar, *Colonial Dames,* 119; and Lindgren, *Preserving the Old Dominion*, 125–126.

18. Mrs. Frank Anthony Walke, "Pocahontas and Her Descendants," *Jamestown Bulletin* (July 1905):5, and (September 1905):3; Mrs. Thomas P. Bagby, "Memorial to Pocahontas," *Jamestown Bulletin* (April 1906):7; *Pocahontas Memorial Association* (Washington, D.C., 1907), 3; and *New York Times,* February 27, 1916.

19. *New York Herald-Tribune*, December 15, 1915. Partridge was especially attuned to the wishes of his patrons, as he, too, came from a prominent colonial family. However, his antecedents had landed at Plymouth, not Jamestown, a reality the association apparently chose to overlook. By 1906, when commissioned to create the Pocahontas statue, the sculptor was commuting between his studios in New York and Milton, Massachusetts, with intermittent jaunts to London and Paris. For information on Partridge, see Robert Burns Wilson, "William Ordway Partridge," *International Studio* 31 (May 1907):lxv–lxxix; and Marjorie Pingel Balge, "William Ordway Partridge (1861–1930): American Art Critic and Sculptor," Ph.D. diss., University of Delaware, 1982.

20. William O. Partridge to Cuyler Reynolds, June 5, 1911, Albert Duveen Collection, Archives of American Art, Smithsonian Institution, Washington, D.C.; and *New York Times*, October 10, 1915.

21. See Lindgren, *Preserving the Old Dominion*, 131–132.

22. An example of earlier stereotypical sculpture is Joseph Mozier's *Pocahontas* (1854). Chrysler Museum, Norfolk, Va., and Museum of Fine Arts, Boston.

23. Pocahontas Club of Claremore, Oklahoma, *As I Recollect, 1899–1949* (Claremore, Okla., 1949), preface.

24. Maude Ward DuPriest et al., *Cherokee Recollections: The Story of the Indian Woman's Pocahontas Club and Its Members in the Cherokee Nation and Oklahoma Beginning in 1899* (Stillwater, Okla., 1976).

25. Frederick W. Bittinger, *The Story of the Pilgrim Tercentenary Celebration at Plymouth in the Year 1921* (Plymouth, Mass., 1921), 36–37; Rose T. Briggs, ed., *Picture Guide to Historic Plymouth* (Plymouth, Mass., 1963), 14.

26. At the bicentenary, Virginians had voiced their wishes for "an obelisk of granite, one hundred feet high." See *Report of the Proceedings of the Late Jubilee at Jamestown in Commemoration of the 13th May, the Second Centesimal Anniversary of the Settlement of Virginia* (Petersburg, 1807), 42.

27. *New York Times*, April 27, 1907.

28. Ibid.; *Outlook* 86 (May 4, 1907):13–15; *Harper's Weekly* 51 (May 4, 1907):634; (May 11, 1907):681–682, 694; and *Youth's Companion*, 81 (May 23, 1907):cover and 243.

29. Failure of the Richmond gentry to direct tercentennial events not only weakened the financial base of the project but fostered a prolonged period of intramural quarreling. Two years before the projected opening, the Jamestown Exposition faced potential economic disaster. The sponsoring committee appealed to Congress, which reluctantly agreed to appropriate $1,575,000. By accepting that largesse, the Virginia businessmen became pawns of Washington and had to shift the emphasis from local commerce to federal industrial and military might. See Robert T. Taylor, "The Jamestown Tercentennial Exposition of 1907," *Virginia Magazine of History and Biography* 65 (April 1957):169–180.

30. The Negro Building, designed by the black architect W. Sidney Pitman and built by African-American contractors, caused a flurry of indignation in Virginia. The state legislature threatened to boycott the Hampton Roads exposition if a Negro Building stood on the grounds. Nevertheless, it opened as scheduled, and August 3 was set aside as "Negro Day." See Tom Costa et al., *An Illustrated History of the Jamestown Exhibition* (Hampton Roads, Va., n.d.), 13; Plummer F. Jones, "The Jamestown Tercentenary Exposition," *American Monthly Review of Reviews* 35 (March 1907):122–127, 305–318; Taylor, "Jamestown Tercentennial Exposition," 182–196; *Official Guide to the Jamestown Tercentennial Exposition* (Norfolk, 1907); *The Official Blue Book of the Jamestown Ter-Centennial Exposition* (Norfolk, 1909).

31. Taylor, "Jamestown Tercentennial Exposition," 203–206.

32. See Costa, *Jamestown Exhibition*, 16–41.

33. Advertisement in *Jamestown Magazine* (June 1906); Jones, "Jamestown Tercentenary Exposition," 122–127, 305–318; *Official Guide*, and *Official Blue Book*.

34. Taylor, "Jamestown Tercentennial," 205–207; *New York Times*, April 26, 1907; and Lindgren, *Preserving the Old Dominion*, 124–125.

35. Among the artists were Howard Chandler Christy, N. C. Wyeth, Jennie Brownscombe, and Norman Rockwell; the movie is Thomas A. Edison, *Landing of the Pilgrims*, 1915.

36. The planning committee, in fact, scrapped nascent schemes for an international fair along the Boston waterfront in favor of making the celebration into a dignified historical remembrance. *Report of the Pilgrim Tercentenary Commission, January 3, 1917* (Boston, 1917), 13–20.

37. Kammen, *Mystic Chords*, 384.

38. "Observing the Pilgrim Anniversary," *American Monthly Review of Reviews* 62 (September 1920):301; and "Old Plymouth Celebrates the Pilgrim Tercentenary," *Outlook* 126 (September 15, 1920):88–89.

39. On April 15, the National Society of Mayflower Descendants gathered at Plymouth's Old Colony Theater to celebrate the "Return of the Mayflower." See Bittinger, *Story of the Pilgrim Tercentenary*, 29–34; and Karal Ann Marling, *George Washington Slept Here: Colonial Revivals and American Culture* (Cambridge, Mass., 1988), 235.

40. Bittinger, *Pilgrim Tercentenary*, 43–68; Marling, *George Washington*, 301, 324–336; and "Old Plymouth Celebrates the Pilgrim Tercentenary," *Outlook* 126 (September 15, 1920):88–89.

41. Bittinger, *Pilgrim Tercentenary*, 43–68.

42. Hermann Hagedorn, "The Pageant at Plymouth," *Outlook* 128 (August 31, 1921):697–699. Also see Stephen Eddy Snow, *Performing the Pilgrims: A Study of Ethnohistorical Role-Playing at Plimoth Plantation* (Jackson, Miss., 1993), 17–20.

43. But there were always skeptics. Ludwig Lewisohn complained in the *Nation* that "despite the marvelous lighting, despite the misleading analogies of the Greek and medieval theaters, the pageant was . . . lost somewhere between earth and sky." He did concede, however, that the symbolism of the event turned out to be "notably beautiful, vivid and impressive." Lewis Lewisohn, "The Plymouth Pageant," *Nation* 113 (August 24, 1921):210–211.

44. See Bittinger, *Pilgrim Tercentenary*, 75–81; and Marling, *George Washington*, 324–336.

Selected Bibliography

Primary Sources

Adams, Henry. *The Education of Henry Adams*. 1918. Reprint, New York: Modern Library, 1931.

Aderman, Ralph M., ed. *The Letters of James Kirke Paulding*. Madison: University of Wisconsin Press, 1962.

Anbinder, Tyler. *Nativism and Slavery. The Northern Know-Nothings and the Politics of the 1850s*. New York and Oxford: Oxford University Press, 1992.

Anonymous. *The Female American; or, The Adventures of Unca Eliza Winkfield Compiled by Herself.* 1767. Reprint, New York and London: Garland Publishing Co., 1974.

Bancroft, George. *History of the United States, from the Discovery of the American Continent*. 14th ed. Vol. 1. Boston: Charles C. Little and James Brown, 1848.

Barbour, Philip, ed. *The Complete Works of Captain John Smith*. Chapel Hill: University of North Carolina Press, 1986.

Bartlett, William H. *The Pilgrim Fathers; or, The Founders of New England in the Reign of James the First.* London: Arthur Hall, Virtue and Co., 1853.

Beecher, Lyman. *Plea for the West*. Cincinnati: Truman and Smith, 1835.

Beverley, Robert. *The History and Present State of Virginia*. Edited by Louis B. Wright. Chapel Hill: University of North Carolina Press, 1947.

Billings, Warren M., ed. *The Old Dominion in the Seventeenth Century: A Documentary History of Virginia, 1606–1689*. Williamsburg, Va., and Chapel Hill, Va.: Institute of Early American History and Culture and University of North Carolina Press, 1975.

Bradford, William. *History of Plymouth Plantation*. 2 vols. Boston: Massachusetts Historical Society and Houghton Mifflin Co., 1912.

The Bradford Manuscript: Account of the Part Taken by the American Antiquarian Society in the Return of the Bradford Manuscript to America. Worcester, Mass.: American Antiquarian Society, 1898.

Bremer, Fredrika. *America of the Fifties: Letters of Fredrika Bremer*. Edited by Adolph B. Benson. New York: American-Scandinavian Foundation, 1924.

Brougham, John. *Po-ca-hon-tas, or The Gentle Savage.* New York, 1856.

Brown, Samuel Gilman, ed. *The Works of Rufus Choate, with a Memoir of His Life.* Boston: Little, Brown and Co., 1862.

Burk, John Daly. *History of Virginia from its First Settlement to the Present Day.* 4 vols. Petersburg, Va.: Dickson and Pescud, 1804–1816.

Byrd, William. *Histories of the Dividing Line Betwixt Virginia and North Carolina.* Introduction and notes by William K. Boyd and Percy G. Adams. New York: Dover Publications, 1967.

Campbell, Charles. *History of the Colony and Ancient Dominion of Virginia.* Philadelphia: J. B. Lippincott and Co., 1860.

Cappon, Lester J., ed. *The Adams-Jefferson Letters: The Complete Correspondence Between Thomas Jefferson and Abigail and John Adams.* Chapel Hill: University of North Carolina Press, 1959.

Catalogue of Valuable Oil Paintings, Studies, and Sketches, by John G. Chapman, Artist... New York: n.p., 1848.

Celebration of the Two-Hundred and Fiftieth Anniversary of the English Settlement at Jamestown, May 13, 1857. Washington, D.C.: n.p., 1857.

Chastellux, Marquis de. *Travels in North America in the Years 1780–81–82.* 1787. English edition. Reprint, New York: New York Times and Arno Press, 1968.

Cooke, John Esten. *My Lady Pokahontas: A True Relation of Virginia: Writ by Anas Todkill, Puritan and Pilgrim.* 1885. Reprint, Boston: Houghton, Mifflin and Co., 1907.

Cummings, Thomas S. *Historic Annals of the National Academy of Design.* 1865. Reprint, New York: Kennedy Galleries, 1969.

Davis, John. *Captain Smith and Princess Pocahontas.* Philadelphia: T. C. Plowman, 1805.

_____. *The First Settlers of Virginia.* 2d ed. New York: I Riley and Co., 1806.

_____. *Travels of Four Years and a Half in the United States of America During 1798, 1799, 1800, 1801, and 1802.* 1803. Reprint, New York: Henry Holt, 1909.

Drimmer, Frederick, ed., *Captured by the Indians: 15 Firsthand Accounts, 1750–1870.* New York: Dover Publications, 1961.

Dunlap, William. *Diary of William Dunlap.* 3 vols. New York: New York Historical Society, 1931.

_____. *History of the Rise and Progress of the Arts of Design in the United States.* 3 vols. 1834. Reprint, New York: Dover Publications, 1969.

Everett, Edward. *Orations and Speeches on ... Various Occasions.* 3 vols. Boston: Little, Brown and Co., 1850–1859.

French, Benjamin Brown. *Witness to the Young Republic, A Yankee's Journal, 1828–1870.* Edited by Donald B. Cole and John J. McDonough. Hanover and London: University of New England Press, 1989.

Foote, William Henry. *Sketches of Virginia, Historical and Biographical.* First series. 1850. Reprint, Richmond, Va.: John Knox Press, 1966.

Hemans, Felicia. *The Breaking Waves Dashed High (The Pilgrim Fathers).* Illustrated by Miss L. B. Humphrey. Boston: Lee and Shepard, 1880.

Holcombe, James P. *The Election of a Black Republican President: An Overt Act of Aggression on the Right of Property in Slaves.* Richmond, Va.: Charles H. Wynne, 1860.

Howe, Henry. *Historical Collections of Virginia . . .* Charleston, S.C.: W. R. Babcock, 1847.

Hillen, Andrew, ed. *The Letters of Henry Wadsworth Longfellow.* 6 vols. Cambridge: Belknap Press of Harvard University Press, 1967–1982.

The Illustrated Pilgrim Memorial. Boston: Office of the National Monument to the Forefathers, 1860–1878.

Jefferson, Thomas. *Notes on the State of Virginia.* Chapel Hill: University of North Carolina Press, 1982.

Judd, Sylvester. *Margaret: A Tale of the Real and the Ideal, Blight and Bloom; Including Sketches of a Place Not Before Described, Called Mons Christi.* 2 vols. Boston: Phillips, Sampson and Co., 1851.

Kennedy, John P. *Memoirs of the Life of William Wirt.* 2 vols. 1850. Reprint, Buffalo, N.Y.: W. S. Hein, 1973.

Levenson, J. C., et al., eds. *The Letters of Henry Adams.* Cambridge and London: Belknap Press of Harvard University Press, 1982–1988.

Morse, Jedidiah, and Elijah Parish. *Compendious History of New England.* Charlestown, Mass.: Samuel Etheridge, 1804.

Morse, Samuel F. B. *Foreign Conspiracy Against the Liberties of the United States.* 1835. Reprint, New York: Arno Press, 1977.

Motley, John Lothrop. *Representative Selections, with Introduction, Bibliography, and Notes.* Edited by Chester Penn Higby. New York: American Book Co., 1939.

Neill, Edward D. *Virginia Vetusta, During the Reign of James the First: Containing Letters and Documents Never Before Printed.* Albany, N.Y.: Joel Munsell's Sons, 1885.

Owen, Robert Dale. *Pocahontas: A Historical Drama in Five Acts.* New York: G. Dearborn, 1837.

Palfrey, John Gorham. *History of New England.* 5 vols. Boston: Little, Brown and Co., 1858–1889.

Palmer, Beverly Wilson, ed. *The Selected Letters of Charles Sumner.* 2 vols. Boston: Northeastern University Press, 1990.

Pearson, Emily Clemens. *Cousin Franck's Household, or Scenes in the Old Dominion.* Boston: Upham, Ford and Olmsted, 1853.

_____. *Prince Paul: The Freedman Soldier.* Boston: Massachusetts Sabbath School Society, 1867.

Proceedings at the Celebration by the Pilgrim Society at Plymouth, December 21, 1870 of the Two Hundred Fiftieth Anniversary of the Landing of the Pilgrims. Cambridge, Mass.: Press of John Wilson and Son, 1871.

Ramsey, David. *History of the United States.* Philadelphia: n.p., 1816.

Redpath, James, ed. *Echoes of Harper's Ferry, 1860.* New York: Arno Press, 1969.

A Richmond Lady [Sallie B. Putnam]. *Richmond During the War: Four Years of Personal Observation.* New York: G. W. Carleton and Co.; and London: S. Low, Son and Co., 1867.

Robbins, Eliza. *Tales from American History* . . . New York: W. Burgess, 1829.

Ruchames, Louis, ed. *A John Brown Reader: The Story of John Brown in His Own Words in the Words of Those Who Knew Him and in the Poetry and Prose of the Literary Heritage.* London and New York: Abelard-Schuman, 1959.

Russell, William S. *Guide to Plymouth and Recollections of the Pilgrims.* Boston: G. Coolidge, 1846.

Sanborn, Franklin B. *The Life and Letters of John Brown, Liberator of Kansas, and Martyr of Virginia.* Boston: Roberts Brothers, 1891.

Sigourney, Lydia H. *Pocahontas and Other Poems.* London: R. Tyas, 1841.

_____. *Traits of the Aborigines of America.* Cambridge, Mass.: University Press, 1822.

Simms, William Gilmore. *The Book of My Lady, a Melange by a Bachelor Knight.* Boston: Allen and Ticknor, 1833.

Smith, Seba. *John Smith's Letters with "Picters" to Match.* New York: Samuel Coleman, 1839.

_____. *Powhatan: A Metrical Romance in Seven Cantos.* New York: Harper and Brothers, 1841.

Stirling, James. *Letters from the Slave States.* London: John W. Parker and Son, 1857.

Stith, William. *History of the First Discovery.* 1747. Spartanberg, S.C.: Reprint Co., 1965.

Stowe, Harriet Beecher. *Oldtown Folks.* Edited by Henry May. Cambridge: Belknap/Harvard University Press, 1966.

Strachey, William. *For the Colony in Virginia* . . . Edited by David H. Flaherty. 1610–1611. Reprint, Charlottesville: University Press of Virginia, 1969.

_____. *The History of Travell into Virginia Britania.* Edited by Louis B. Wright and Virginia Freund. London: Hakluyt Society, 1612.

Thacher, James. *History of the Town of Plymouth, from Its First Settlement in 1620 to the Year 1832.* Boston: Marsh Capen and Lyon, 1832.

Thackeray, William Makepeace. *The Virginians, a Tale of the Last Century.* 2 vols. London: Bradbury and Evans, 1858–1859; and New York: Macmillan and Co., 1911.

Tocqueville, Alexis de. *Democracy in America.* Edited by J. P. Mayer, translated by George Lawrence. Garden City, N.Y.: Doubleday and Co., 1969.

Tuckerman, Henry. *Book of the Artists.* 1867. Reprint, New York: James F. Karr, 1966.

The Virginia Journals of Benjamin Henry Latrobe, 1795–1798. Edited by Edward C. Carter II. 2 vols. New Haven: Yale University Press, 1977.

Waldron, William Watson. *Pocahontas, Princess of Virginia and Other Poems.* New York: Dean and Trevett, 1841.

West, George Benjamin. *When the Yankees Came: Civil War and Reconstruction on the Virginia Peninsula.* Edited by Parke Rouse Jr. Richmond, Va.: Dietz Press, 1977.

Whittier, John Greenleaf. *Anti-Slavery Poems: Songs of Labor and Reform.* 1888. Reprint, New York: Arno Press, 1969.

_____. *Legends of New England.* 1831. Gainesville, Fla.: Scholar's Facsimiles and Reprints, 1965.

Winthrop, Robert C., Jr. *A Memoir of Robert C. Winthrop.* Boston: Little, Brown and Co., 1897.

Wright, Nathalia, ed. *The Correspondence of Washington Allston.* Lexington: University Press of Kentucky, 1993.

The Writings and Speeches of Daniel Webster. Boston: Little, Brown and Co., 1903.

Young, Alexander. *Chronicles of the Pilgrim Fathers of the Colony of Plymouth, 1602–1625.* Boston: Charles C. Little and James Brown, 1841.

Secondary Sources

Anderson, Virginia Dejohn. *New England's Generation: The Great Migration and the Formation of Society and Culture in the Seventeenth Century.* Cambridge and New York: Cambridge University Press, 1991.

Anderson, William L. *Cherokee Removal: Before and After.* Athens: University of Georgia Press, 1991.

Ayers, William, ed. *Picturing History: American Painting 1770–1930.* New York: Rizzoli, 1993.

Baer, Helene G. *The Heart Is Like Heaven: The Life of Lydia Maria Child.* Philadelphia: University of Pennsylvania Press, 1964.

Baines, Dudley. *Emigration from Europe 1815–1930.* London: Macmillan Education, 1991.

Baltzell, E. Digby. *Puritan Boston and Quaker Philadelphia: Two Protestant Ethics and the Spirit of Class Authority and Leadership.* New York: Free Press, 1979.

Banner, James M., Jr. *To the Hartford Convention: The Federalists and the Origins of Party Politics in Massachusetts, 1789–1815.* New York: Knopf, 1970.

Barbour, Philip L. *Pocahontas and Her World.* Boston: Houghton Mifflin, 1970.

———. *The Three Worlds of Captain John Smith.* Boston: Houghton Mifflin Co., 1964.

Barnett, Louise K. *The Ignoble Savage, American Literary Racism, 1790–1890.* Westport, Conn.: Greenwood Press, 1975.

Barnhill, Georgia Brady, ed. *Prints of New England.* Worcester: American Antiquarian Society, 1991.

Bercovitch, Sacvan. *The American Jeremiad.* Madison: University of Wisconsin Press, 1978.

———. *The Puritan Origins of the American Self.* New York: Yale University Press, 1975.

Berkhofer, Robert F., Jr. *The White Man's Indian: Images of the American Indian from Columbus to the Present.* New York: Knopf, 1978.

Billington, Ray Allen. *The Protestant Crusade, 1800–1860: A Study of the Origins of American Nativism.* New York: Macmillan Co., 1938.

Bird, S. Elizabeth, ed. *Dressing in Feathers: The Construction of the Indian in American Popular Culture.* Boulder: Westview Press, 1996.

Breen, T. H. *Puritans and Adventurers: Change and Persistence in Early America*. New York and Oxford: Oxford University Press, 1980.

_____. *Tobacco Culture: The Mentality of the Great Tidewater Planters on the Eve of Revolution*. Princeton: Princeton University Press, 1985.

_____, ed. *Shaping Southern Society: The Colonial Experience*. New York: Oxford University Press, 1976.

Bridenbaugh, Carl. *Jamestown, 1544–1699*. New York and Oxford: Oxford University Press, 1980.

Briggs, Rose T. *Plymouth Rock, History, and Significance*. Plymouth: Pilgrim Society, 1968.

Brown, Richard D. *Massachusetts: A Bicentennial History*. New York: W. W. Norton, 1978.

Buell, Lawrence. *New England Literary Culture: From Revolution Through Renaissance*. Cambridge, London, and New York: Cambridge University Press, 1986.

Burns, Sara. *Pastoral Invention: Rural Life in Nineteenth-Century American Art and Culture*. Philadelphia: Temple University Press, 1989.

Callow, James T. *Kindred Spirits: Knickerbocker Writers and American Artists, 1807–1855*. Chapel Hill: University of North Carolina Press, 1967.

Campbell, William P. *John Gadsby Chapman*. Washington, D.C.: National Gallery of Art, 1962.

Canup, John. *Out of the Wilderness: The Emergence of an American Identity in Colonial New England*. Middletown, Conn.: Wesleyan University Press, 1990.

Carpenter, Delores Bird. *Early Encounters—Native Americans and Europeans in New England: From the Papers of W. Sears Nickerson*. East Lansing: Michigan State University Press, 1994.

Chamberlain, Georgia S. *John Gadsby Chapman, 1808–1889*. N.p.: Privately printed, 1963.

Coleman, Cynthia Tucker. *Virginia Silhouettes: Contemporary Letters Concerning Negro Slavery in the State of Virginia*. Richmond: Dietz Printing Co., 1934.

Cope, Robert S. *Carry Me Back: Slavery and Servitude in Seventeenth-Century Virginia*. Pikeville, Ky.: Pikeville College Press, 1973.

Craven, Wayne. *Colonial American Portraiture: The Economic, Religious, Social, Cultural, Philosophical, Scientific, and Aesthetic Foundations*. Cambridge: Cambridge University Press, 1986.

Craven, Wesley Frank. *The Legend of the Founding Fathers*. New York: New York University Press, 1956.

_____. *White, Red, and Black: The Seventeenth-Century Virginian*. Charlottesville: University Press of Virginia, 1971.

Dalzell, Robert F., Jr. *Enterprising Elite: The Boston Associates and the World They Made*. Cambridge: Harvard University Press, 1987.

Dameron, J. Lasley, and James W. Mathews. *No Fairer Land: Studies in Southern Literature Before 1900*. Troy, N.Y.: Whitson Publishing Co., 1986.

Davis, Richard Beale. *Intellectual Life in the Colonial South, 1585–1763.* 3 vols. Knoxville: University of Tennessee Press, 1978.

———. *Literature and Society in Early Virginia, 1608–1840.* Baton Rouge: Louisiana State University Press, 1973.

Dedmond, Francis B. *Sylvester Judd.* Boston: Twayne Publishers, 1980.

Delbanco, Andrew. *The Puritan Ordeal.* Cambridge, Mass., and London: Harvard University Press, 1989.

Demos, John. *A Little Commonwealth, Family Life in Plymouth Colony.* London, Oxford, and New York: Oxford University Press, 1970.

Douglas, Ann. *The Feminization of American Culture.* New York: Knopf, 1977.

Duberman, Martin, ed. *The Antislavery Vanguard: New Essays on the Abolitionists.* Princeton: Princeton University Press, 1965.

Dufour, Charles L. *The Mexican War: A Compact History, 1846–1848.* New York: Hawthorne Books, 1968.

The Dusseldorf Academy and the Americas. Atlanta: High Museum of Art, 1972.

Ehle, John. *Trail of Tears: The Rise and Fall of the Cherokee Nation.* New York: Anchor Books/Doubleday, 1988.

Elkins, Stanley, and Eric McKitrick. *The Age of Federalism: The Early American Republic, 1788–1800.* New York and Oxford: Oxford University Press, 1993.

Elliott, Emory. *Revolutionary Writers, Literature, and Authority in the New Republic, 1725–1810.* New York and Oxford: Oxford University Press, 1982.

Elson, Ruth Miller. *Guardians of Tradition: American Schoolbooks of the Nineteenth Century.* Lincoln: University of Nebraska Press, 1964.

Faust, Drew Gilpin. *Creation of Confederate Nationalism.* Baton Rouge: Louisiana State University Press, 1988.

Fehrenbacher, Don E. *The South and Three Sectional Crises.* Baton Rouge: Lousiana State University Press, 1980.

Finley, Ruth E. *The Lady of Godey's: Sarah Josepha Hale.* Philadelphia and London: J. B. Lippincott, 1931.

Fischer, David Hackett. *Albion's Seed: Four British Folkways in America.* New York and Oxford: Oxford University Press, 1989.

———. *The Revolution of American Conservatism: The Federalist Party in the Era of Jeffersonian Democracy.* New York: Harper and Row, 1965.

Fishwick, Marshall W. *The Virginia Tradition.* Washington, D.C.: Public Affairs Press, 1956.

Fitzpatrick, David. *Irish Emigration, 1801–1921.* Dublin: Economic and Social History Society of Ireland, 1985.

Forgie, George W. *Patricide in the House Divided: A Psychological Interpretation of Lincoln and His Age.* New York: W. W. Norton, 1979.

Formisano, Ronald P., and Constance K. Burns, eds. *Boston, 1700–1980: The Evolution of Urban Politics.* Westport, Conn.: Greenwood Press, 1980.

Foster, Stephen. *The Long Argument: English Puritanism and the Shaping of New England Culture, 1570–1700.* Williamsburg, Va., and Chapel Hill: Institute of Early American History and Culture and University of North Carolina Press, 1991.

Franklin, Wayne. *Discoverers, Explorers, Settlers: The Diligent Writers of Early America.* Chicago: University of Chicago Press, 1979.

Fraser, James W. *Pedagogue for God's Kingdom: Lyman Beecher and the Second Great Awakening.* Boston: University Presses of America, 1985.

Free, William J. *The Columbian Magazine and American Literary Nationalism.* The Hague: Mouton and Co., 1968.

Freehling, Alison Goodyear. *Drift Toward Dissolution: The Virginia Slavery Debate of 1831–1832.* Baton Rouge: Louisiana State University Press, 1982.

Freehling, William W. *The Road to Disunion.* Vol. 1, *Secessionists at Bay, 1776–1854.* New York and Oxford: Oxford University Press, 1990.

Friedman, Lawrence J. *Gregarious Saints: Self and Community in American Abolitionism, 1830–1870.* Cambridge, London, and New York: Cambridge University Press, 1982.

––––––. *Inventors of the Promised Land.* New York: Knopf, 1975.

Fryd, Vivien Green. *Art and Empire: Art, the Politics of Ethnicity in the United States Capitol, 1815–1860.* New Haven: Yale University Press, 1992.

Geller, L. D., ed. *They Knew They Were Pilgrims: Essays in Plymouth History.* New York: Poseidon Books, 1971.

Gertds, William H., and Mark Thistlethwaite. *Grand Illusions: History Painting in America.* Fort Worth, Tex.: Amon Carter Museum, 1988.

Gleach, Frederic W. *Powhatan's World and Colonial Virginia: A Conflict of Cultures.* Lincoln, Nebr., and London: University of Nebraska Press, 1997.

Goodwin, John A. *The Puritan Conspiracy Against the Pilgrim Fathers and the Congregational Church, 1624.* Boston: Cuddles, Upham and Co., 1883.

Greene, Jack P. *Interpreting Early America: Historiographical Essays.* Charlottesville and London: University Press of Virginia, 1996.

Groseclose, Barbara S. *Emanuel Leutze, 1816–1868: Freedom Is the Only King.* Washington, D.C.: Smithsonian Institution Press, 1975.

Haight, Gordon S. *Mrs. Sigourney: The Sweet Singer of Hartford.* New Haven: Yale University Press, 1930.

Hall, Virginius C. *Portraits in the Collection of the Virginia Historical Society.* Richmond: Virginia Historical Society, 1981.

Hamilton, Holman. *Prologue to Conflict: The Crisis and Compromise of 1850.* Lexington: University of Kentucky Press, 1964.

Handlin, Lillian. *George Bancroft: The Intellectual as Democrat.* New York: Harper and Row, 1984.

Handlin, Oscar. *Boston's Immigrants, 1790–1880: A Study in Acculturation.* Rev. ed. Cambridge: Belknap/Harvard University Press, 1991.

Hatch, Nathan O. *The Democratization of American Christianity.* New Haven: Yale University Press, 1989.

_____. *The Sacred Cause of Liberty: Republican Thought and the Millennium in Revolutionary New England.* New Haven and London: Yale University Press, 1977.

Hathaway, Richard D. *Sylvester Judd's New England.* University Park and London: Pennsylvania State University Press, 1981.

Hazelton, George C., Jr. *The National Capitol: Its Architecture Art and History.* New York: J. Little and Co., 1897.

Hobsbawm, Eric, and Terence Ranger, eds. *The Invention of Tradition.* Cambridge and New York: Cambridge University Press, 1983.

Honour, Hugh. *The European Vision of America.* Cleveland: Cleveland Museum, 1975.

Horn, James. *Adapting to a New World: English Society in the Seventeenth-Century Chesapeake.* Williamsburg, Va., and Chapel Hill: Institute of Early American History and Culture and University of North Carolina Press, 1994.

Howe, Daniel Walker. *The Political Culture of the American Whigs.* Chicago: University of Chicago Press, 1979.

Howorth, Lisa, ed. *The South: A Treasury of Art and Literature.* Oxford, Miss.: Center for Southern Culture/Macmillan, 1993.

Hulton, Paul. *America, 1585: The Complete Drawings of John White.* Chapel Hill: University of North Carolina Press, 1984.

Hume, Ivor Noël. *The Virginia Adventure, Roanoke to James Towne: An Archeological and Historical Odyssey.* New York: Knopf, 1994.

Isaac, Rhys. *The Transformation of Virginia, 1740–1790.* Williamsburg, Va., and Chapel Hill: Institute of Early American History and Culture and University of North Carolina Press, 1982.

Jackson, David K. *Poe and the* Southern Literary Messenger. New York: Haskell House, 1970.

Johannsen, Robert W. *To the Halls of Montezumas: The Mexican War in the American Imagination.* New York and Oxford: Oxford University Press, 1985.

Johns, Elizabeth. *Genre Painting in the Antebellum United States.* New Haven: Yale University Press, 1991.

Jordan, Winthrop D. *White over Black: American Attitudes Toward the Negro, 1550–1812.* New York: W. W. Norton, 1968.

Kammen, Michael. *In the Past Lane: Historical Perspectives on American Culture.* New York and Oxford: Oxford University Press, 1997.

_____. *Mystic Chords of Memory: The Transformation of Tradition in American Culture.* New York: Knopf, 1991.

_____. *People of Paradox: An Inquiry Concerning the Origins of American Civilization.* New York: Knopf, 1972.

_____. *A Season of Youth: The American Revolution and the Historical Imagination.* New York: Oxford University Press, 1978.

Karcher, Carolyn L. *The First Woman in the Republic: A Cultural Biography of Lydia Maria Child.* Durham and London: Duke University Press, 1994.

Kennedy, Roger G. *Architecture, Men, Women, and Money in America, 1600–1860.* New York: Random House, 1985.

Kerber, Linda K. *Federalists in Dissent: Imagery and Ideology in Jeffersonian America.* Ithaca: Cornell University Press, 1970.

King, H. Roger. *Cape Cod and Plymouth Colony in the Seventeenth Century.* Latham, Md.: University Press of America, 1994.

The Kirby Collection of Historical Paintings, Lafayette College, Easton, Pennsylvania. Easton, Pa.: Lafayette College, 1963.

Kraus, Michael. *The Writing of American History.* Norman: University of Oklahoma, 1953.

Lamar, Mrs. Joseph Rucker. *A History of the National Society of the Colonial Dames of America from 1891 to 1933.* Atlanta: Walter W. Brown Publishing Co., 1934.

Langdon, George D., Jr. *Pilgrim Colony: A History of New Plymouth, 1620–1691.* New Haven: Yale University Press, 1966.

Leary, Lewis. *John Greenleaf Whittier.* New York: Twayne Publishers, 1961.

Lemay, J. A. Leo. *The American Dream of Captain John Smith.* Charlottesville: University Press of Virginia, 1991.

———. *Did Pocahontas Save Captain John Smith?* Athens: University of Georgia Press, 1992.

———, ed. *Essays in Early Virginia Literature Honoring Richard Beale Davis.* New York: Burt Franklin and Co., 1977.

Leonard, Ira M., and Robert D. Parmet. *American Nativism, 1830–1860.* New York: Van Nostrand Reinhold Co., 1971.

Lepore, Jill. *The Name of War: King Philip's War and the Origins of American Identity.* New York: Knopf, 1998.

Levin, David. *History as Romantic Art: Bancroft, Prescott, Motley, and Parkman.* New York: Harcourt, Brace and World, 1959.

Lewis, R. W. B. *The American Adam: Innocence, Tragedy, and Tradition in the Nineteenth Century.* Chicago: University of Chicago Press, 1955.

Lindgren, James M. *Preserving Historic New England: Preservation, Progressivism, and the Remaking of Memory.* New York and Oxford: Oxford University Press, 1995.

———. *Preserving the Old Dominion: Historic Preservation and Virginia Traditionalism.* Charlottesville: University Press of Virginia, 1993.

Loewenberg, Bert James. *American History in American Thought: Christopher Columbus to Henry Adams.* New York: Simon and Schuster, 1972.

Mabee, Carleton. *The American Leonardo: A Life of Samuel F. B. Morse.* New York: Knopf, 1943.

Mails, Thomas E. *The Cherokee People: The Story of the Cherokees from Earliest Origins to Contemporary Times.* Tulsa, Okla.: Council Oak Books, 1992.

Marling, Karal Ann. *George Washington Slept Here: Colonial Revivals and American Culture.* Cambridge: Harvard University Press, 1988.

Marzio, Peter C. *The Democratic Art: Pictures for a Nineteenth-Century America: Chromolithography, 1840–1900.* Boston: D. R. Godine, 1979; and Fort Worth: Amon Carter Museum of Western Art, 1979.

Matthiessen, F. O. *American Renaissance: Art and Expression in the Age of Emerson and Whitman.* Oxford, London, and New York: Oxford University Press, 1941.

McCardell, John. *The Idea of a Southern Nation: Southern Nationalists and Southern Nationalism, 1830–1860.* New York and London: W. W. Norton and Co., 1979.

McCartney, Martha W. *James City County: Keystone of the Commonwealth.* James City County, Va.: Donning Co., 1997.

McGlinchee, Claire. *James Russell Lowell.* New York: Twayne Publishers, 1967.

McLoughlin, William G. *Cherokee Renascence in the New Republic.* Princeton: Princeton University Press, 1986.

Meinig, D. W. *The Shaping of America: A Geographical Perspective on Five Hundred Years of History.* Vol. 1, *Atlantic America, 1492–1800.* New Haven: Yale University Press, 1986.

Meyer, Jacob C. *Church and State in Massachusetts, from 1740 to 1833.* Cleveland: Western Reserve University Press, 1930.

Miller, Angela. *Empire of the Eye: Landscape Representation and American Cultural Politics, 1825–1875.* Ithaca: Cornell University Press, 1993.

Miller, David C., ed. *American Iconology: New Approaches to Nineteenth-Century Art and Literature.* New Haven: Yale University Press, 1993.

Miller, Lillian B. *Patrons and Patriotism: The Encouragement of the Fine Arts in the United States, 1790–1860.* Chicago: University of Chicago Press, 1966.

Miller, Perry. *Errand into the Wilderness.* Cambridge: Harvard University Press, 1956.

Minor, Benjamin Blake. *The Southern Literary Messenger, 1834–1864.* New York: Neale Publishing Co., 1905.

Morgan, Edmund S. *American Slavery, American Freedom: The Ordeal of Colonial Virginia.* New York and London: W. W. Norton and Co., 1975.

Moss, Michael, ed. *Robert W. Weir of West Point: Illustrator, Teacher, and Poet.* West Point, N.Y.: U.S. Military Academy, 1976.

Mossiker, Frances. *Pocahontas: The Life and the Legend.* New York: Knopf, 1976.

Mulkern, John R. *The Know-Nothing Party in Massachusetts: The Rise and Fall of a People's Movement.* Boston: Northeastern University Press, 1990.

Nissenbaum, Stephen. *The Battle for Christmas: A Cultural History of America's Most Cherished Holiday.* New York: Vintage Books, 1996.

Norton, Anne. *Alternative Americas: A Reading of Antebellum Political Culture.* Chicago: University of Chicago Press, 1986.

O'Connell, Shaun. *Imagining Boston: A Literary Landscape.* Boston: Beacon Press, 1990.

O'Connor, Thomas H. *The Boston Irish: A Political History.* Boston: Northeastern University Press, 1995.

O'Gorman, James F. *Accomplished in All Departments of Art: Hammatt Billings of Boston, 1818–1874.* Amherst: University of Massachusetts Press, 1998.

Okker, Patricia. *Our Sister Editors: Sarah J. Hale and the Tradition of Nineteenth-Century American Women Editors.* Athens: University of Georgia Press, 1995.

Osterweis, Rollin G., *Romanticism and Nationalism in the Old South.* New Haven: Yale University Press, 1949.

Pennington, Estill Curtis. *Look Away: Reality and Sentiment in Southern Art.* Atlanta: Peachtree Publishers, 1989.

———. *A Southern Collection.* Augusta, Ga.: Morris Museum, 1992.

Perry, Lewis. *Boats Against the Current: American Culture Between Revolution and Modernity, 1820–1860.* New York and Oxford: Oxford University Press, 1993.

Pessen, Edward. *Jacksonian America, Society, Personality, and Politics.* Rev. ed. Urbana and Chicago: University of Illinois Press, 1985.

Peterson, Merrill D. *Adams and Jefferson: A Revolutionary Dialogue.* Oxford and New York: Oxford University Press, 1976.

Poesch, Jessie. *The Art of the Old South: Painting, Sculpture, Architecture, and the Products of Craftsmen, 1560–1860.* New York: Knopf, 1983.

Potter, David M. *The Impending Crisis, 1848–1861.* Completed and edited by Don E. Fehrenbacher. New York: Harper and Row, 1976.

Priestley, J. B. *Victoria's Heyday.* New York: Harper and Row, 1972.

Quinn, Arthur. *A New World: An Epic of Colonial America from the Founding of Jamestown to the Fall of Quebec.* Boston: Faber and Faber, 1994.

Quinn, Arthur H. *A History of the American Drama from the Beginning to the Civil War.* New York: F. S. Crofts and Co., 1943.

Rasmussen, William S., and Robert S. Tilton. *Pocahontas: Her Life and Legend.* Richmond, Va.: Virginia Historical Society, 1994.

Remini, Robert V. *Daniel Webster: The Man and His Time.* New York: W. W. Norton, 1997.

Renehan, Edward J., Jr. *The Secret Six: The True Tale of the Men Who Conspired with John Brown.* New York: Crown Publishers, 1995.

Reynolds, David S. *Beneath the American Renaissance: The Subversive Imagination in the Age of Emerson and Melville.* Cambridge, Mass., and London: Harvard University Press, 1988.

Rickels, Milton, and Patricia Rickels. *Seba Smith.* Boston: Twayne Publishers, 1977.

Riggs, David. *Embattled Shrine: Jamestown in the Civil War.* Shippensburg, Pa.: White Mane Publishing Co., 1997.

Robert Weir: Artist and Teacher of West Point. West Point, N.Y.: U.S. Military Academy, 1967.

Robertson, Wyndham. *Pocahontas, Alias Matoaka, and Her Descendants.* 1887. Reprint, Baltimore: Genealogical Publishing Co., 1968.

Robertson, James I., Jr. *Civil War Virginia: Battleground for a Nation.* Charlottesville and London: University Press of Virginia, 1991.

Rogers, Sherbrooke. *Sarah Josepha Hale: A New England Pioneer, 1788-1879.* Grantham, N.H.: Thompson and Rutter, 1985.

Rountree, Helen C. *The Powhatan Indians of Virginia: Their Traditional Culture.* Norman and London: University of Oklahoma Press, 1989.

Ross, Alexander M. *William Henry Bartlett: Artist, Author, and Traveller.* Toronto: University of Toronto Press, 1973.

Satz, Ronald N. *American Policy in the Jacksonian Era.* Lincoln: University of Nebraska Press, 1975.

Scott, Otto. *The Secret Six: John Brown and the Abolitionist Movement.* Murphy, Cal.: Uncommon Books, 1979.

Seelye, John. *Memory's Nation: The Place of Plymouth Rock.* Chapel Hill: University of North Carolina Press, 1998.

Segal, Charles M., and David C. Stinebeck. *Puritans, Indians, and Manifest Destiny.* New York: G. P. Putnam's Sons, 1977.

Sewell, Richard H. *A House Divided: Sectionalism and Civil War, 1848-1865.* Baltimore and London: Johns Hopkins University Press, 1988.

Shackelford, George Green. *George Wythe Randolph and the Confederate Elite.* Athens and London: University of Georgia Press, 1988.

Shade, William G. *Democratizing the Old Dominion: Virginia and the Second Party System, 1824-1861.* Charlottesville and London: University Press of Virginia, 1996.

Simmons, William S. *Spirit of the New England Tribes: Indian History and Folklore, 1620-1984.* Hanover, N.H., and London: University Press of New England, 1986.

Simpson, Craig M. *A Good Southerner: The Life of Henry A. Wise of Virginia.* Chapel Hill and London: University of North Carolina Press, 1985.

Simpson, Lewis P. *Mind and the American Civil War: A Meditation on Lost Causes.* Baton Rouge: Louisiana State University Press, 1989.

Sisco, Louis Dow. *Political Nativism in New York State.* New York: Columbia University Press, 1901.

Slotkin, Richard. *Regeneration Through Violence: The Mythology of the American Frontier, 1600-1860.* Middletown, Conn.: Wesleyan University Press, 1973.

Smith, Bradford. *Bradford of Plymouth.* Philadelphia and New York: J. B. Lippincott, 1951.

Snay, Mitchell. *Gospel of Disunion: Religion and Separatism in the Antebellum South.* Cambridge and New York: Cambridge University Press, 1993.

Snow, Stephen Eddy. *Performing the Pilgrims: A Study of Ethnohistorical Role-Playing at Plimoth Plantation.* Jackson: University Press of Mississippi, 1993.

Snyder, Stephen H. *Lyman Beecher and His Children: The Transformation of a Religious Tradition.* Brooklyn, N.Y.: Carlson Publishing, 1991.

Staiti, Paul J. *Samuel F. B. Morse.* New York and Cambridge: Cambridge University Press, 1989.

Sundquist, Asebrit. *Pocahontas and Co.: The Fictional American Indian Woman in Nineteenth-Century Literature. A Study of Method.* Oslo: Solum Forlag, and Atlantic and Highlands, N.J.: Humanities Press International, 1987.

Swan, Mabel Munson. *The Anthenaeum Gallery, 1827–1873: The Boston Athenaeum as an Early Patron of Art.* Boston: Boston Athenaeum, 1940.

Taylor, William R. *Cavalier and Yankee: The Old South and American National Character.* 1957. Reprint, Cambridge: Harvard University Press, 1979.

Thane, Elswyth. *Mount Vernon Is Ours: The Story of Its Preservation.* New York: Duell, Sloan and Pearce, 1966.

Thomas, Emory M. *The Confederate Nation, 1861–1865.* New York and Cambridge: Harper and Row, 1970.

Thistlethwaite, Mark. *Painting in the Grand Manner: The Art of Peter Frederick Rothermel, 1812–1895.* Chadds Ford, Pa.: Brandywine River Museum, 1995.

Tilton, Robert S. *Pocahontas: The Evolution of an American Narrative.* Cambridge and New York: Cambridge University Press, 1994.

Truettner, William H., ed. *The West as America: Reinterpreting Images of the Frontier.* Washington, D.C.: Smithsonian Institution Press, 1991.

Tucker, Beverley D. *Nathaniel Beverley Tucker, Prophet of the Confederacy, 1784–1851.* Tokyo: Nan'un-Do, 1979.

Tucker, Louis Leonard. *Clio's Consort: Jeremy Belknap and the Founding of the Massachusetts Historical Society.* Boston: Massachusetts Historical Society, 1990.

Tyack, David B. *George Ticknor and the Boston Brahmins.* Cambridge: Harvard University Press, 1967.

Van Tassel, David. *Recording America's Past: An Interpretation of the Development of Historical Studies in America, 1607–1884.* Chicago: University of Chicago Press, 1960.

Vitzhum, Richard C. *The American Compromise: Theme and Method in the Histories of Bancroft, Parkman, and Adams.* Norman: University of Oklahoma Press, 1974.

Warren, Robert Penn. *John Greenleaf Whittier's Poetry: An Appraisal and a Selection.* Minneapolis: University of Minnesota Press, 1971.

Watts, Steven. *The Republic Reborn: War and the Making of Liberal America, 1790–1820.* Baltimore and London: Johns Hopkins University Press, 1987.

Wehle, Harry B. *Samuel F. B. Morse, American Painter.* New York: Metropolitan Museum of Art, 1932.

Weir, Irene. *Robert W. Weir, Artist.* New York: Field-Doubleday, 1947.

Welter, Rush. *The Mind of America, 1820–1860.* New York and London: Columbia University Press, 1975.

Wiebe, Robert W. *The Opening of American Society from the Adoption of the Constitution to the Eve of Disunion.* New York: Knopf, 1984.

Williams, Cecil B. *Henry Wadsworth Longfellow.* New York: Twayne Publishers, 1964.

Willison, George F. *Saints and Strangers.* New York: Reynal and Hitchcock, 1945.

Winter, William. *Life, Stories, and Poems of John Brougham.* Boston: James R. Osgood and Co., 1881.

Wood, Betty. *The Origins of American Slavery: Freedom and Bondage in the English Colonies.* New York: Hill and Wang, 1997.

Wright, Conrad Edick, ed. *Massachusetts and the New Nation.* Boston: Massachusetts Historical Society, 1992.

Wyman, Mary Alice. *Two American Pioneers: Seba Smith and Elizabeth Oakes Smith.* New York: Columbia University Press, 1972.

Yellin, Jean Fagan. *Women and Sisters: The Antislavery Feminists in American Culture.* New Haven and London: Yale University Press, 1989.

Index

Abbott, Jacob, 145
Abolitionists. *See under* Slavery
Adams, Charles Francis, 245
Adams, Henry, 245–247
Adams, John, 76, 89
Adams, John Quincy, 105–106, 159, 310(n85), 319(n11)
Adams, William (Reverend), 179, 229
"Adams and Liberty" (Paine), 94
Alcott, Bronson, 227
Alden, John, 77, 211, 212, 330(n62)
Algonquian tribes, 18, 62
Alien and Sedition Laws, 89
Allen, William, 214, 237, 344(n13)
Allston, Washington, 106, 321(n35)
Allyn, John, 88
Ambler, Richard, 47
American and Foreign Christian Union (Whittemore), 157
American Anti-Slavery Society, 226
American Colonization Society, 200
American Geography (Morse), 90
American Party, 155–157. *See also* Know-Nothing movement
American Scenery, 187
American Universal Geography (Morse), 90
Ames, Joseph Alexander, 207
Ancestors, xv, 8, 12, 145, 149, 191, 258, 271, 288(n29)
aboard the *Mayflower*, 13, 87, 88, 201, 221, 237, 272–273
remains of, 272–273

worship of, 14, 131, 172, 278
See also Forefathers' Day; Pocahontas, descendants of
Anglican Church, 39, 88, 182, 229, 320(n28)
Anne (Queen of England), 17
Antebellum period, xv, xvii, xviii, 5, 39, 40, 42, 43, 62, 69, 82, 230
Appleton, Fanny, 210
Appleton, William, 328(n44)
Appomattox, Virginia, 242
APVA. *See* Association for the Preservation of Virginia Antiquities
Argall, Samuel, 17
Aristocracy, 12, 20
Arminians, 87, 89
Art, xix, 5. *See also* Engravings; Paintings; Subscription prints
Association for the Preservation of Virginia Antiquities (APVA), 266–268, 269, 270, 273, 344(n14)
Atlantic Monthly, 202, 236–237
Austin, Samuel, 89
Autocrat of the Breakfast Table (Holmes), 202

Bacon, Nathaniel, 23
Bacon's Rebellion, 23
Bagby, Mrs. Thomas, 268
Baker, George Pierce, 277
Bancroft, George, xvi, 75, 106–107, 160, 176, 229–230, 247

Banishments, 27, 28

Baptism of Pocahontas (Chapman), 35, 36(fig. 3.1), 37, 114, 115(fig.), 120–126, 123(figs.), 151, 170, 315(n35)

Baptists, 34, 152

Barbour, Philip L., 16

Barker, James Nelson, 58–60, 62, 174, 299(nn 21, 22)

Barnes, Charlotte, 134–136, 137, 174

Barnes, Mary, 134

Barney, Edward E., 267, 280

Bartholdi, Frederic-Auguste, 263, 264

Bartlett, William H., 6–7, 187–188, 188(fig.), 189(fig. 8.8), 329(nn 55, 57, 59)

Bay Staters, xviii, 13. *See also* Massachusetts

Beaumont, Henry, 47

Beaux Arts style, 263–264

Beecher, Henry Ward, 144

Beecher, Lyman, 143–145, 153, 162, 304(n29)

Berkeley, Bishop George, 76

Berkeley, Sir William, 23

Bevan, William (Reverend), 185

Beverley, Robert, 64, 65, 69, 169, 298(n11)

Billings, Hammatt, 261–264, 262–263(figs.), 272

Billings, Joseph, 263

Bill of Rights, 8, 89

Birmingham, England, 185

Blacks, 66. *See also* Racial issues; Slavery

Blagden, George, 205

Bogart, W. S., 241

Bolling, Blair, 43–44

Bolling, John, xiii, 287(n26)

Bolling, Linneaus, 68–69

Bolling, Mrs. Robert, Jr., 56, 65

Bolling, Robert, 12, 286(n26)

Bolling, Thomas, 301(n44)

Bolling, William, 68, 69, 120–121, 301(n47)

Boston, Massachusetts, 89–90, 93–94, 96–97, 98, 101, 103, 140, 143, 150, 155, 195, 207, 221, 223, 305(n31)

Boston Clique, 196, 332(n8)

Church of the Disciples in, 153

Church of the Holy Cross in, 144

Boston Chronicle, 97

Boughton, George Henry, 253, 254(fig. 11.1), 255, 256(fig. 11.3)

Bouldin, James, 311(n1)

Brackett, Joseph Warren, 101

Bradford, William, 4, 23–28, 97, 277, 286(n14), 308(n64)

memoir of, 23–24, 76, 77, 158, 187

Bray, John, 58

Breen, T. H., 295(n66)

Brenan, Joseph, 234–235

Brewster, William, 4, 25, 160, 194, 198, 277, 308(n64)

Brooks, Charles (Reverend), 74

Brooks, Preston, 195

Brougham, John, 173–176, 326(nn 26, 28)

Brown, Hugh Stowell (Reverend), 185

Brown, John, 221–228, 337(nn 1, 6), 338(nn 8, 17, 19)

Brown, Peter, 221, 226

Brown, S. E., 85(fig. 5.7)

Browne, Robert, 24

Brownists, 24–25, 31

Brueckner, Henry, 170–171, 325(n19), 326(n23)

Bryant, William Cullen, 42–43, 45, 106, 148, 265, 321(n36)

Buchanan, James, 211, 212

Bulfinch, Charles, 144

Bulfinch, S. G., 151–152

Bullock, David, 344(n13)

Burk, John Daly, 67

Butler, Benjamin F., 238

California, 155, 324(n2)

California Society of Pilgrims, 154

Calvinism, 25, 87, 88, 91, 103, 143, 179, 222, 223, 304(n29)

Camelot, 199, 213

Campbell, Charles, 15, 168, 169, 171
Capellano, Antonio, 40, 41(fig. 3.5), 62
Capitalism, 129, 130
Capitol Rotunda, 35, 40, 114, 139, 151
Captain John Smith (Van de Passe), 52,
 53(fig.)
Captain Smith and Princess Pocahontas
 (Davis), 57, 60
Captain Smith Rescued by Pocahontas
 (Sinclair), 61(fig. 4.6)
Captain Smith Rescued by Pocahontas
 (Warren), 63(fig. 4.7)
Carmienecke, H, 83(fig. 5.6)
Cartouches, 78
Carver, John, 4, 277, 308(n64)
Catholics, 33, 37, 97, 151, 162, 182,
 261–262
  anti-Catholicism, 140, 141, 143, 144,
   145, 153, 155–157, 320(nn 18, 28)
Catlin, George, 64
Causici, Enrico, 40, 41(figs. 3.6, 37)
Cavaliers, 3, 22, 102, 171, 191, 224,
 233–234, 235, 274. *See also under*
 Puritans
Chamberlain, Georgia, 315(n41)
Channing, William Ellery, 75
Chapman, John Gadsby, 35, 36(fig. 3.1),
 37, 39, 114–126, 115(fig.),
 117–118(figs.), 151, 170, 313(nn 17,
 19, 22), 314(nn 26, 27, 30), 315(nn
 34, 35), 316(n43)
Chappel, Alonzo, 60, 61(fig. 4.5)
Charleston, South Carolina, 13
Charles II (English king), 230
Chastellux, Marquis de, 56, 65
Cherokee nation v. Georgia, 110
Cherokees, 110, 111, 271, 311(n3)
Chickasaws, 311(n3)
Child, Lydia Maria, 224–226
Children, 29
Chilton, Mary, 77, 330(n62)
China, 154–155
Chivalry, 4
Choate, Rufus, 151, 159
Choctaws, 111, 311(n3)
Christmas, 9, 10, 286(n15)

Christy, Chandler, 256(fig. 11.4)
Civil War, xvii, 11, 232, 239–242,
 286(n15), 340(nn 42, 43, 44)
  Battle at Big (or great) Bethel,
   340(n41)
Clarke, G.N.G., 77–78
Clarke, James F., 153
Classicism, 264, 265
Clay, Henry, 310(n85)
Clifford, John, 46
Clothing, 31, 37, 39, 40, 60, 62, 64, 69,
 79, 82, 84, 86, 91, 102, 116, 120,
 149, 188, 191, 207, 255, 322(n41),
 329(n59), 330(n60)
Cocke, William Archer, 235–236
Cole, Thomas, 321(n40)
Coleman, Cynthia Tucker, 269
Coles Hill burial ground, 272–273
Colonial Dames. *See* National Society of
 Colonial Dames
Colonialism, 129
Colonial Revival, 252–253, 279
Columbian Magazine, 56
Compendious History of New England
 (Morse and Parish), 90–91, 92
Compromise, 310(n82)
  Compromise of 1850, 193, 324(n2)
  See also Missouri Compromise
Cone, Spencer Wallace, 230–231
Conflict of Daniel Boone and the Indians
 (Causici), 40, 41(fig. 3.7)
Congregational Church, xix, 5, 24, 29,
 30, 87, 88, 89, 97, 143, 152, 178,
 185
Congress, 111, 165, 276, 324(n2). *See also*
 Capitol Rotunda; House of
 Representatives
Connecticut, 29
Conquistadors, 37
Constitution, 4, 43, 159, 160, 161, 194,
 232
"Conversation with Miles Standish"
 (Lowell), 203–205
Conversions, 20, 32, 65, 134. *See also*
 Pocahontas, conversion/baptism of
Cooke, John Esten, 233–234, 249–250

Cooke, Maria Heath, 315(n39)

Cooper, James Fenimore, 114

Cope, Charles, 185–187, 186(fig.), 329(nn 51, 52)

Copley, John Singleton, 309(n67)

Corbould, Edward-Henry, 62, 63(fig. 4.8), 64, 119, 300(n29)

Corné, Michele Felice, 80, 81(figs.), 82, 86, 99, 304(n21)

Coronation of Powhatan (Chapman), 116, 117(fig. 6.2)

Cotton, 185

"Council, The" (Ehninger), 208(fig. 9.2)

Courtship of Miles Standish (Longfellow), 207, 210–213, 336(nn 41, 42)

Cousin Franck's Household (Pearson), 205–207, 334(n29)

"Cradle of the New World" (Paulding), 120

Crafts, William, 320(n18)

Cranch, Richard, 76

Crawford, William, 310(n85)

Creeks, 111, 311(n3)

Critic, 150

Cromwell, Oliver, 102, 222, 226–227, 229, 230, 235

Croswell, Andrew (Reverend), 307(n58)

Croswell, Joseph, 96–98, 307(n58)

Currier, Nathaniel, 40, 84, 86(fig.)

Custis, George Washington Parke, 109–112, 113, 115, 126, 129, 134, 174, 215, 311(nn 1, 2)

Custis-Lee Mansion, 109

Daily National Intelligencer, 122, 315(n35)

Dale, R. W., 185

Dale, Sir Thomas, 20, 291(n24), 325(n19)

Darley, Felix O. C., 207

Daughters of the American Revolution, 273

Davis, Charles C., 238

Davis, John, 56–58

Davis, Judge John, 76, 92

Deane, Charles, 23, 172, 245, 246, 247

Death of Pocahontas (Stearns), 136

Deaths, 19, 340(n41)

De Bow's Review, 235

DeKay, James, 321(n36)

Democracy in America (de Tocqueville), 166–167

Democratic Party, 144

Departure of the Pilgrim Fathers (Lucy), 183(fig.), 183–184, 185

Departure of the Pilgrim Fathers from Delft Haven (Cope), 185–187, 186(fig.)

De Soto Discovering the Mississippi (Powell), 37, 38(fig. 3.4)

de Tocqueville, Alexis, 166–167

Dinner Party, The (Sargent), 101

Discourse of Virginia, A (Wingfield), 172, 245, 246

Discovery, 19

Diseases, 19, 26

Disney Studios, 51, 71, 279

District of Columbia, 324(n2)

Doña Marina, 166

Douglas, Stephen, 232

Douglass, Frederick, 337(n6)

Dow, Lorenzo, 89

"Dream of the Cavaliers, A" (Cooke), 233–234

Dunlap, William, 101, 102

Dying Hercules (S. Morse), 306(n44)

Edison, Thomas, 276

Education, 264. *See also* Public education

Edward Winslow, 100(fig.), 309(n66), 330(n59)

Ehninger, John Whetten, 207, 208 (figs.)

Elders, 29, 30

Elections, 141, 156, 232, 269, 310(n85). *See also* Voting

Eliade, Mircea, xiv–xv

Embarkation of the Pilgrims (Weir), 35, 36(fig. 3.2), 37, 39, 122, 139, 146–152, 147(fig.), 183–184, 329(nn 51, 52)

Emerson, Ralph Waldo, 193, 222, 226, 227

Endecott, John, 27

English Civil War, 229–230, 328(n45), 339(n25)

English Puritans Escaping to America (Leutze), 181(fig.), 181–182, 327(n41), 328(nn 43, 44)

Engravings, 51–54, 60–64, 77, 78, 79, 83, 85, 170–171, 181, 184, 184(fig.), 186(fig.), 188(fig.)

Erikson, Paul D., 310(n83)

"Errand in the Wilderness" (Miller), 29

Evangelicals, 87, 88, 182

Everett, Edward, 46, 105, 218, 252, 302(n2)

Faunce, Thomas, 285(n7)

Faust, Drew Gilpin, 4

Federalist Party, 89–90, 98, 102, 106, 144, 305(nn 31, 33), 309(n74)

Federal Orrery, 94

Female American, The, 298(n12)

Feminists, 302(n5)

Fendall, Philip R., 215

Fillmore, Millard, 193

Finney, Charles Grandison, 89

First Landing of the Pilgrims (Lucy), 184(fig.)

First Plymouth Church, 87–88, 103

First Sabbath of the Pilgrims, The (Matteson), 161–162, 323(n72)

First Settlers of Virginia, The (Davis), 57–58

Firth, Raymond, 8

Firth, William, 330(n60)

Food supply, 19, 20, 55

Foote, William Henry, 15

Forefathers' Day, 9, 11, 42, 74, 76, 77, 78, 79, 80, 89, 93, 95, 96, 98, 105, 106, 146, 153, 179, 194, 197, 198, 203, 205, 219, 258, 276, 286(n16), 301(n31), 308(n65), 342(n23)

Forefathers (Pilgrim) Monument, 262–264, 263(fig.), 343(nn 4, 7)

Foreign policy, 105

"Forest Maiden" (Simms), 128–129

Forest Princess, The, or Two Centuries Ago (Barnes), 134–136, 137

Forrest, Edwin, 113

Fort Monroe, 238

Fort Pocahontas, 237–238

Fort Powhatan, 238

Fort Sumter, 235

Fouke, C. C., 228

Free Kansas Movement, 222

Free-Soil Party, 195

French, Benjamin, 315(n35)

French trading posts, 26

Frost, Robert, 277–278

Frothingham, Nathaniel, 168

Fugitive Slave Law, 193, 194, 331(n2)

Gadsby, John, 114

Gallatin, Albert, 97

Galt, Edith Bolling, 269

Gardner, Henry J., 156

Garrison, William Lloyd, 165, 196, 222, 251, 332(n8)

Geer, Seth, 319(n10)

Gender, 127, 128

Generall Historie of Virginia, New England, and the Summer Isles (J. Smith), xvi, 16–17, 24, 51, 52, 53, 54, 55, 56, 60, 69, 116, 119, 120, 246, 247, 298(n12), 315(n40)

General Society of Mayflower Descendants, 272

Georgia, 110

Germany, 182, 328(n43)

"Germ of the Republic" (Morse), 142, 160, 321(n36)

Gevelot, Nicholas, 40, 41(fig. 3.8)

Gift books, 156, 207

Gilbert, John, 207, 209(figs.)

Gilmer, George, 110

Godey's Lady's Book, 11, 218

Godspeed, 19

Gold, 110

Gomes, Peter, 288(n29)

Good Times in the New World (Chapman), 116, 118(fig. 6.5), 119–120

Grant, U.S., 242

Great Awakening, 87, 89, 307(n58)

Great Migration, 29

Greenough, Horatio, 114, 322(n40)
Grigsby, Hugh, 301(nn 44, 46)
Guy Fawkes Day, 144

Hale, Sarah Josepha, 11, 218
Hall, James, 69, 86
Hall, Robert B. (Reverend), 194–195
Hamilton, Alexander, 101
Hamor, Ralph, 291(n24)
Hampton Roads. *See under* Virginia
Harding, Warren G., 278–279
Harding, Willard M. (Reverend), 263
Harpers Ferry, Virginia, 221, 222, 223,
    224, 228
Harper's New Monthly Magazine, 233
Hartford Convention, 102
Harvard College, 33, 91
Harvest Home celebration, 287(n17)
Hawthorne, Nathaniel, 179, 202, 237,
    334(n24)
Hedonism, 27
Hemans, Felicia, 73–75, 302(nn 2, 5, 6,
    7)
Hening, Elizabeth, 44
Henry, William Wirt, 248–249
Higginson, Thomas Wentworth, 222
Hill, Samuel, 78–79, 79(fig.), 99,
    308(n65)
Historians, xvi, 15, 29–30, 64, 71, 170,
    229–230, 245–249, 279, 288(n29),
    289(n12), 293(n39)
Historical Collections of Virginia (Howe),
    170
*Historical, Poetical and Pictorial American
    Scenes,* 84, 85(fig. 5.8)
*History and Antiquities of New England,
    New York, and New Jersey,* 82, 84
History and Present State of Virginia
    (Beverley), 69
History of New England (Palfrey), 172, 245
*History of the Colony and Ancient Dominion
    of Virginia,* 171
*History of the Indian Tribes of North
    America* (McKenney and Hall), 69
*History of the Protestant Episcopal Church
    in America* (Wilberforce), 23

History of the United States (Bancroft),
    106–107, 160, 229
History of the United States (Spencer), 60
Hobsbawm, Eric, 4
Hohenstein, Anton, 172, 173(fig.)
Holcombe, James P., 232
Holland, 3, 25, 32, 148, 276, 293(n39)
Holmes, Abiel, 88–89, 106
Holmes, Oliver Wendell, 13, 88, 197,
    198
Hope, James Barron, 216
Hopkins, Mark, 205
House of Representatives, 35, 105, 140,
    141, 147, 156, 310(n85)
Howard, Oliver Otis, 251
Howe, Henry, 170, 230
Howe, Julia Ward, 222, 338(n8)
Howe, Samuel Gridley, 222
Hughes, John, 157
Hugo, Victor, 227
Hunter, Joseph (Reverend), 329(n57)
Hutchinson, Thomas, 23

Immigrants, 108, 153, 157, 162, 178, 191.
    See also Irish immigrants
Imports, 20
Indentured labor, 22
Independence Day, 238
Independent Chronicle, 305(n33)
Indian Princess, The, or La Belle Sauvage
    (Barker), 58–60, 62, 174
Indian Removal Act, 108
Indians. *See* Native Americans
Inman, Henry, 37, 141, 319(n11)
Intermarriage, 65, 110. *See also*
    Miscegenation; Racial issues
Invitation to Forefathers' Day Dinner (Hill),
    78–79, 79(fig.), 86, 308(n65)
Ireland, 230
Irish immigrants, 140–141, 144–145,
    146, 152, 155

"Jack Downing" columns, 130, 131
Jackson, Andrew, 87, 110, 112, 129, 130,
    132, 230, 310(n85)
Jackson, Thomas J. (Stonewall), 242

Jacob, Henry, 184

James I (English king), 116, 158, 159, 277

James River, 21, 47, 214, 238, 340(nn 42, 44)

Jamestown colony, xiii, xiv, 3, 4, 15–18, 289(n7)
    Church tower, 7–8, 9(fig.), 47, 215, 267
    compared with Plymouth/ Massachusetts Bay colonies, 30–34, 42, 43, 47–48
    demise of, 23, 34
    founding of, xv, 268
    House of Burgesses, 21, 22, 34
    seven-man council for, 18–19
    and slavery. *See* Slavery, and Jamestown colony
    See also Jamestown, Virginia; Pocahontas; Smith, John; Virginia

Jamestown Committee, 214, 288(n31)

Jamestown Memorial Church, 267–268, 268(fig.), 271, 273, 344(n15)

Jamestown Society, 215

Jamestown, Virginia, 237–238, 239, 242, 267
    excavations at, 279, 280(fig.)
    James Fort, 281(fig. 12.8)
    Jamestown Jubilee (1857), 214, 215, 216, 217
    pilgrimages to, 4, 11–12, 214
    purchase of, 267, 280, 344(n13)
    tercentenary celebration at, 268, 269, 273
    U.S. government obelisk at, 273–274, 274(fig.)
    See also Jamestown colony

Jefferson, Thomas, 89–90, 98, 102, 309(n73)

"Jefferson and Liberty" (Paine), 94

Jefferys, Thomas, 77, 78(fig.), 84, 99

Jobs, 155

John Smith's Letters with 'Picters' to Match (S. Smith), 131

Jones, Catesby, 237

Judd, Sylvester, 10, 179–180, 327(nn 38, 39)

Kansas, 197, 198, 221

Kansas-Nebraska Act of 1854, 197

Kemble, William, 121

Kendall, James, 88

King Philip's War, 30, 113

Knickerbocker, 151

Know-Nothing movement, 143, 155–157, 162

"Lady Rebecca" (Van de Passe), 51–53, 52(fig. 4.1), 64, 121, 126, 247, 297(n1), 300(n38)

Landing of Christopher Columbus (Vanderlyn), 37, 38(fig. 3.3), 77, 151

"Landing of the Fathers, The" (Hemans), 73–74, 75

Landing of the Fathers (Sargent), 98–100, 99(fig.), 101–103, 103–104, 106, 107(fig.), 149, 308(nn 63, 64), 311(nn 87, 88)

Landing of the Forefathers (S. Morse), 91, 92(fig.), 139

Landing of the Pilgrim Fathers (Brown), 85(fig. 5.7)

Landing of the Pilgrim Fathers (Lucy), 183, 328(n46)

Landing of the Pilgrims (Causici), 40, 41(fig. 3.6)

Landing of the Pilgrims (Corné), 80, 81(figs.), 82, 86

Landing of the Pilgrims at Plymouth (Carmienecke), 83(fig. 5.6)

Landing of the Pilgrims at Plymouth (Currier), 84, 86(fig.)

Landing of the Pilgrims at Plymouth (Ormsby), 83(fig. 5.5)

Landing of the Pilgrims at Plymouth Rock (Rothermel), 188, 189(fig. 8.9), 190, 330(n63)

Lane Theological Seminary, 153, 201

Law(s), 26, 29, 160, 193, 196, 236, 264, 269
    and literacy among slaves, 200

Lawrence, Abbott, 184

Lawrence, Amos, 222

Lee, Robert E., 223, 240, 242
Lefebre de Cheverus, Jean, 144
Leonard, Nathaniel (Reverend), 88
Leopold Association, 140
Letters of the British Spy (Wirt), 65, 110
Leutze, Emanuel, 181(fig.), 181–182,
    191, 327(n41), 328(nn 43, 44)
Lewisohn, Ludwig, 346(n43)
Leyden Street (Bartlett), 188(fig.)
Liberator, The, 332(n8)
Liberia, 200
Life of George Washington (Paulding), 115
Lincoln, Abraham, 11, 211, 232, 233,
    242, 251
Literature, xx, 5, 42–45, 56–60, 67,
    73–74, 94, 120, 125–129, 130–133,
    176–178, 179–180, 201–207,
    210–213, 230–232, 233–235,
    240–241, 249–250, 276, 277–278
    romantic, 182
    See also Songs; Theatre
Liverpool, England, 185
Lodge, Henry Cabot, 276
London Morning Advertiser, 186
London News, 227
Longfellow, Henry Wadsworth, 201,
    207, 210–213, 286(n15), 335(n39),
    336(nn 41, 42)
Lord, Arthur, 265
Lossing, Benson J., 170–171, 325(n19)
Lowell, James Russell, 202, 203–205,
    212
Lucy, 183–184, 183–184(figs.), 185,
    328(n46)
Lutherans, 34
Lyford, John, 27, 97, 277, 295(n56)
Lyman, Joseph, 89

McClellan, George B., 239
McCulloch v. Maryland, 104, 312(n5)
McGowan, Shirley Custalow, 71
McKenney, Thomas, 69
McKim, Mead, and White (architectural
    firm), 265, 266(fig.), 272
McKim, Randolph Harrison, 7
McNerhany, F., 217

McRae, John, 171(fig.)
Madison, James, 102
Magnalia (Mather), 148, 321(n39)
Magruder, John B., 239
Mann, Horace, 193
Map of Virginia (Vaughan), 53, 54(fig.)
Margaret (Judd), 179–180, 327(n39)
Marriage of Pocahontas, The (Brueckner),
    170–171, 171(fig.), 325(n19),
    326(n23)
Marriage of Pocahontas, The (J. Rolfe),
    325(n17)
Martin, J. H., 240–241, 326(n22)
Mason, Margaretta, 225, 226
Masonic order, 91
Massachusetts, 40, 98, 108, 165, 202,
    217, 230, 232, 252, 253, 331(n2).
    See also Boston, Massachusetts;
    Massachusetts Bay Colony; New
    England; Plymouth colony;
    Virginia, cooperation with
    Massachusetts
Massachusetts Bay Colony, 4, 13,
    28–30, 178, 229. *See also*
    Jamestown colony, compared with
    Plymouth/Massachusetts Bay
    colonies
Massachusetts Historical Society,
    308(n65)
Massasoit, 26
Mather, Cotton, 148, 321(n39)
Matteson, Tompkins H., 160–162,
    161(fig.), 323(nn 71, 72)
Mayflower, 24, 25–26, 39, 196, 286(n14)
    celebration of landing, 9–10, 45, 103,
    106, 219, 287(n23). *See also*
    Forefathers' Day
    Mayflower compact, 4, 26, 139–162,
    194, 276
    replica of, 276
    See also under Ancestors
*Mayflower, The; or, Sketches of Scenes and
    Characters, Among the Descendants of
    the Pilgrims* (Stowe), 202
Mayflower Society, xiii
Mellen, Grenville, 231–232

Melville, Herman, 202, 334(n24)
Memorial (Mount), 321(n39)
Merry Mount settlement, 27–28
Messenger, 234
Metamora; or, the Last of the Wampanoags (Stone), 113, 326(n26)
Methodists, 34, 152
Mexico, 136, 324(nn 2, 4)
  Mexican War, 165, 204, 240
Miller, Perry, 29, 294(n55)
Miscegenation, 66, 206. *See also* Intermarriage; Racial issues
Missionaries, 152, 155, 157, 178
Missouri Compromise, 104, 197
Monitor and *Merrimac,* 239, 340(n44)
Monroe Doctrine, 105
Monrovia, 200
Monuments/memorials, 261–271, 273–274, 282, 343(nn 4, 7)
Morse, Jedidiah, 89, 90–91, 139, 140, 143, 305(nn 34, 36, 37), 306(n39)
Morse, Samuel Finley Breese, 91–93, 114, 139–143, 147, 148–149, 160, 162, 306(nn 41, 44), 318(n3), 319(n11), 322(n43)
Morton, Nathaniel, 293(n39)
Morton, Thomas, 27–28
Mount Vernon Ladies Association, 218
Mourt's Relation, 159
Mullen, Priscilla, 211, 256(fig. 11.4)
My Lady Pocahontas (Cooke), 249–250

Nantequas, 59, 124, 315(nn 40, 41)
National Academy of Design, 140, 147, 322(n43)
National Park Service, 280
National Society of Colonial Dames, 265, 267, 268, 273
National Society of Mayflower Descendants, 346(n39)
Native Americans, 14
  attitudes toward, 32, 44, 59, 71, 86–87, 113, 120, 127, 128, 257, 270
  and English settlers, 4, 10, 19, 26, 32, 40
  Indian question, 110, 112, 124, 174

raids by, 16, 20, 21, 30, 32, 62, 119
relocation of, 110, 111, 126, 129. *See also* Trail of Tears
in the South, 311(n3)
vanishing Indian, 113, 119, 131, 132, 135–136
women, 55, 57, 62, 128
See also Conversions; *individual groups*
Nativists, 155, 319(n10)
Nehlig, Victor, 253, 254(fig. 11.2), 255, 257, 342(n26)
Neill, Edward Duffield, 247–248, 249
Netherlands. *See* Holland
New England, xviii, 29, 154, 156, 159, 162, 191, 220, 230, 279, 300(n30)
  map of 1774, 77, 78(fig.), 99
  vs. Southern interests, 105
  See also Massachusetts; *under* Virginia
New England Emigrant Aid Company, 197
New England Historical Society, 211
New England Societies, 13–14, 219, 258, 271
New English Canaan, 28
New Harmony, Indiana, 129
New Mexico, 324(n2)
Newport, Christopher, 116, 132
New World Planted, A; or, The Adventures of the Forefathers of New England Who Landed in Plymouth, December, 1620 (Croswell), 96–98
New York (city), 13, 176, 263
New York Mirror, 39, 126, 142–143
New York Nativist Party, 141
New York Observer, 140
New York Tribune, 226
Norfolk Naval Station, 275
North American Review, 145, 246, 327(n36)
Norton, Andrews, 75
Norton, Charles Eliot, 246

"Ode" (Paine), 95–96
Ohio, 153
Oklahoma, 111, 126, 271. *See also* Trail of Tears

Old Colony Club, 13, 77, 95, 296(n10)
Old Colony Messenger, 156
Old Colony Memorial, 10, 101, 102, 153, 155, 340(n41)
Old Dominion, xviii, 3, 165, 166, 230. *See also* Virginia
Old Dominion Society, 219, 220, 288(n31)
Oldham, John, 27, 97, 277, 295(n56), 308(n60)
Old Jamestown, 275
Oldtown Folks (H. Stowe), 334(n23)
Oliver, Peter, 179, 327(n36)
Olmsted, Frederick Law, 167–168
Opachisco, 124, 315(nn 40, 41)
Opechancanough, 21, 62, 124, 132, 291(n27), 315(nn 40, 41)
Origin myths, xiv–xv, xix, 35, 40, 45, 86, 221
   of Massachusetts, 5–7, 42, 76, 143, 162, 165, 178, 180, 187, 191, 253
   and popular culture, 258
   restructuring, 4, 39, 282
   and slavery, 201
   of Virginia, 7–8, 15, 22, 44, 47, 60, 71, 122, 127, 129, 133, 137, 165, 166, 172, 174, 176, 199, 205, 206, 207, 228, 236, 238, 253, 271, 273
Ormsby, Waterman L., 83(fig. 5.5)
Our Country (gift book), 156
Owen, Robert, 129
Owen, Robert Dale, 127, 129–130, 174, 316(n54), 317(nn 56, 60)

Page, Thomas Nelson, 268
Paine, Robert Treat, Jr., 93–96, 307(nn 49, 55)
Paine, Robert Treat, Sr., 93, 94, 96, 307(n54)
Paine, Thomas, 93, 307(n48)
Paintings, 35–42, 68–71, 91–93, 98–103, 114–126, 136, 141, 142, 160–162, 172, 180–191, 207–209, 253–257, 276, 277, 313(n22)
Palfrey, John Gorham, 172, 245, 246
Palladium, 101

Parish, Elijah, 91
Parker, Theodore, 200, 222
Parkman, Francis, xvi
Parris, Alexander, 45, 106, 296(n12)
Parsons, Theophilus, 94
Partridge, William Ordway, 269–271, 270(fig.), 344(n19)
Patriarchs, xv, 103
Patriotism, 5, 7, 58, 112, 122, 169, 218, 252, 276, 330(n63)
Paulding, James Kirke, 115, 120, 314(n28)
Pearson, Emily Clemens, 205–207, 334(n29)
Penn's Treaty with the Indians (West), 316(n43)
Pennsylvania, 40
Percy, George, 19, 289(n7)
Periodicals, xix
Peyton, William M., 219
Philadelphia Academy of Fine Arts, 329(n52)
Phillips, Wendell, 197–198, 217, 222, 227–228, 337(n20)
Pickett, James Chamberlayne, 166
Pierce, Jane, 248
Pilgrimages. *See under* Jamestown, Virginia
Pilgrim Costumes (Bartlett), 189(fig. 8.8)
Pilgrim Fathers, The (Bartlett), 187–188, 329(n55), 330(n59)
Pilgrim Hall, 45, 46(fig.), 105, 106, 262, 296(n12)
Pilgrims, xvi, xvii, 3–4, 146, 148, 167, 200, 257–258, 332(n11)
   and abolitionists, 194, 196, 197
   Mark Twain on, 258
   mission of, 29, 45, 74, 75, 76, 91, 102, 103, 104, 105, 140, 152, 153, 251, 294(n55)
   and nature, 190
   as primary founders, 250–251, 264, 276, 279
   vs. Puritans, 88, 89, 178, 180, 187, 252, 288(n29)
   and Union victory, 251–252

use of term, xvii–xviii, 5, 178, 222,
    252
See also Mayflower; Puritans
"Pilgrims" (Sigourney), 154
Pilgrim's Daughter, The (Firth),
    330(n60)
Pilgrims Going to Church (Boughton),
    253, 254(fig. 11.1), 255
Pilgrim Society, 45, 47, 95, 106, 261,
    263, 265, 296(nn 10, 12)
Pilgrim Spirit, The (Baker), 277–279
Pitman, W. Sidney, 345(n30)
Planter class, 22. *See also* Tobacco
Playwriting. *See* Theater
Plea for the West (Beecher), 153
Plymouth colony, xiii–xiv, 23–28, 167,
    193–194
    annexation to Massachusetts Bay
        colony, 30, 34
    compared with Massachusetts Bay
        colony, 30, 178, 180, 294(n55)
    as holy territory, 6, 96
    Plymouth rock, 4, 6–7, 8, 8(fig.), 40,
        45–47, 73, 75, 77, 87, 96, 156, 195,
        261–262, 262(fig.), 265, 266(fig.),
        272, 277, 285(n7)
    See also Jamestown colony, compared
        with Plymouth/Massachusetts Bay
        colonies; *Mayflower*, Pilgrims
Plymouth, England, 276
Plymouth, Massachusetts, 261–265, 280
    Plimoth Plantation Street, 281(fig.
        12.9)
    Plymouth tercentenary at, 276–279
Plymouth Rock, 150
Pocahontas, 3, 165, 201, 228, 258, 279
    brother of, 59. *See also* Nantequas
    characterized, xv, xvi, 8, 13, 15, 16,
        44, 51–71, 58, 60, 64, 66–67,
        111–112, 122, 127, 131, 135, 166,
        169, 241, 247, 249, 250
    conversion/baptism of, 17, 20, 36(fig.
        3.1), 37, 44, 53, 111–112, 115(fig.),
        120–126, 134, 170, 215, 325(n19)
    death of, 21, 136, 248, 250

descendants of, xiii, 3, 12, 43, 56,
    64–68, 112, 125, 135, 137, 169–171,
    205, 214, 248, 269, 271, 301(n44)
Indian name of (Matoaka), 16, 53
and John Smith, 16–17, 17–18, 41(fig.
    3.5), 52(fig. 4.2), 56, 57, 61(figs.),
    63(figs.), 119, 170, 171, 175, 236,
    240, 250, 257. *See also* Smith, John,
    rescue of
marriage of, 20, 53, 66, 112, 120, 124,
    135, 170–172, 172–173, 215, 236,
    248, 249, 325(n19), 344(n14). *See
    also* Rolfe, John
portraits of, 68–71, 70(figs.), 297(n1),
    301(nn 44, 46). *See also* "Lady
    Rebecca"
rescue of English settlement by, 119,
    124
visit to England, 17, 18, 20–21, 51, 55,
    56, 64, 68, 120, 247
Pocahontas (animated film), 51, 71
Pocahontas (Partridge), 269–271, 270(fig.)
"Pocahontas" (Sigourney), 133–134
Pocahontas (R. Sully), 70(figs. 4.11, 4.12),
    71
Pocahontas (T. Sully), 70(fig. 4.10)
Pocahontas: A Historical Drama (Owen),
    129–130
Pocahontas, A Legend (M. Webster),
    125–126, 170
Pocahontas Association, 269, 270
"Pocahontas: A Subject for the
    Historical Painter" (Simms), 60,
    124–125
Pocahontas Club, 271–272
Po-ca-hon-tas, or The Gentle Savage
    (Brougham), 173–176
Pocahontas, or The Settlers of Virginia
    (Custis), 109, 111–112, 113, 126,
    129, 134, 215, 311(n1)
*Pocahontas Saving the Life of Captain John
    Smith* (Chapman), 116, 118(fig.
    6.4), 119, 125
*Pocahontas Saving the Life of Capt. John
    Smith* (Chappel), 61(fig. 4.5)

Pocahontas Saving the Life of John Smith
(Nehlig), 253, 254(fig. 11.2), 255,
257
Poe, Edgar Allan, 134
Poems on Slavery (Longfellow), 210
Polk, James, 165
Porter, Charles, 178–179
Pory, John, 31
Potawatomi Massacre, 221
Powell, William H., 37, 38(fig. 3.4)
Powhatan, 3, 18, 19, 40, 53, 55, 112, 116,
128, 130–133, 135, 175, 315(n40),
342(n26)
coronation of, 116, 117(fig. 6.2), 119,
132
death of, 21
descendants of, 269
Powhatan: A Metric Romance (S. Smith),
130–133
Powhatan Guards, 241
Powhatans, 19, 32, 64, 66, 120
Prentiss, Charles, 94, 307(n55)
Presbyterians, 34
*Preservation of Captain Smith by
Pocahontas* (Capellano), 40, 41(fig.
3.5), 62
Preston, William C., 148
Prince, Thomas (Reverend), 23
Priscilla and John Alden (Boughton),
256(fig. 11.3)
"Priscilla and John Alden" (Ehninger),
208(fig. 9.1)
"Priscilla at the Wheel" (Gilbert),
209(fig. 9.3)
Priscilla Mullen and John Alden (Christy),
257(fig. 11.4)
*Proceedings of the English Colonie in
Virginia* (J. Smith), 16
Protestants, 37, 39, 75, 87, 100, 113, 140,
143, 144, 152, 153, 154, 157, 162,
182, 267, 320(n18)
Provincetown, Massachusetts, 25
Public education, 29, 33, 89, 104, 157
"Puritan and the Cavalier, The; or, The
Elements of American Colonial
Society" (Cocke), 235

Puritan Commonwealth, The (Oliver), 179,
327(n36)
Puritans, xvii–xviii, 9, 13, 24–25, 29, 33,
91, 93, 97, 144, 146, 178–180, 191,
222, 226, 230, 235, 274, 277,
286(n15), 338(n17)
vs. Cavaliers, 227, 228, 229, 232,
236, 238
and Separatists, 187. *See also*
Separatists
See also Pilgrims, vs. Puritans

Quakers, 33, 191, 202, 203, 258

Racial issues, 64–68, 146, 172, 197, 201,
241, 248, 269. *See also* Slavery
Randolph, Edmund, 66–67, 68
Randolph, Ryland, 301(n44)
Randolph, Thomas Jefferson, 199
Rappahannock tribe, 269
Ratcliffe, John, 130
Recollections of Mexico (Thompson),
166
Reforms, 108, 130, 182, 201, 202. *See
also* Religion, reformers of
Reincarnation, 14
Religion, 7, 8, 24, 29, 32, 42, 74, 87–90,
104, 107, 122, 124, 126, 145, 149,
154, 161, 264
ideal, 180
reformers of, 87, 88–89, 162
religious diversity, 33–34
religious freedom, 3, 75, 150–151,
157, 180, 187. 197, 219, 251, 252,
258, 332(n11)
secular religion, 14
See also Anglican Church; Catholics;
Congregational Church;
Conversions; Pocahontas,
conversion/baptism of; Protestants
Republican Party, 89, 97, 156
"Rescue of John Smith" (Vaughan) 51,
53
"Return of the Pilgrims" (Frost),
277–278
Rhode Island, 29, 230

Richmond, Virginia, 43, 237, 241, 242, 267, 275

Richmond Daily Dispatch, 215

Rites/rituals, 4–5, 8, 11, 12, 14

Roanoke Island, 19

Robbins, Chandler, 5, 88

Robbins, Eliza, 148

Robertson, Wyndham, 171

Robinson, John, 25, 68, 183, 184, 277

Robinson, Mary Jane, 317(n60)

Rogers, Will, 271

Rolfe, Jane, 12, 287(n26)

Rolfe, John, xiii, 3, 12, 17, 20, 39, 43, 53, 57, 59, 66, 111, 112, 120, 124, 130

    marriage to Jane Pierce, 248

    See also Pocahontas, marriage of

Roosevelt, Franklin, 11

Roosevelt, Theodore, 274–275

Rothermel, Peter Frederick, 188, 189(fig. 8.9), 190, 191, 330(n63)

Roundheads, 102, 229, 232

Sabine, James, 145

Salvation, 39

Samoset, 26, 99, 293(n44), 308(n64)

Sanborn, Franklin, 222, 227, 338(n8)

Sargent, Henry, 98–103, 149, 190, 191, 308(nn 63, 64), 309(nn 69, 70), 311(nn 87, 88), 321(n35)

"Savage Magnanimity" (Hening), 44

Schneider, Peter, 71

Schwartz, Barry, 286(n13)

Scotland, 230

Scott, Winfield, 111, 165, 240

Secession, 161, 190, 194, 211, 233, 234, 235, 309(n74)

Secret Six, 222, 224, 228, 338(n8)

Secularization, 14, 91

Self-governance, 21, 29, 216, 277

Seminoles, 111

Sensuality, 56, 57, 58, 64, 119

Separatists, 24, 97, 158, 159, 180, 187, 264, 295(n56), 323(n64)

Seward, William, 197, 332(n11)

Sex, 57, 144. *See also* Sensuality

Shepard, Hayward, 223

Signing of the Mayflower Compact (Matteson), 160–162, 161(fig.), 323(n71)

Sigourney, Lydia Huntley, 133–134, 154

Sill, Joseph, 330(n63)

Simms, William Gilmore, 60, 124–125, 128–129, 316(n53)

Sinclair, Thomas, 61(fig. 4.6)

Sketches of Virginia (Foote), 15

Slavery, xviii, xix, 4, 34, 90, 104, 110, 137, 152, 165, 172, 173, 176, 180, 182, 190, 193, 198, 216, 219, 221, 232, 233, 239, 324(n2), 331(n2), 332(n14), 333(nn 16, 17, 19)

    abolitionists, 185, 191, 194, 195–196, 197, 199, 201–207, 210, 221–228, 251, 316(n54), 332(n8)

    and Jamestown colony, 166, 167–168, 205–207, 237

    numbers of slaves, 22

    and Virginia, 199–201. *See also* Slavery, and Jamestown colony

SLM. *See Southern Literary Messenger*

Smith, Elizabeth, 131, 317(n66)

Smith, Gerrit, 222, 337(n8)

Smith, John, xvi, 3, 26, 40, 59

    and Andrew Jackson, 130, 132

    and Brownists, 31

    description of, 290(n16)

    publications of, 16, 169, 172. *See also Generall Historie of Virginia, New England, and the Summer Isles; True Relation*

    reputation/character of, 15, 18, 67

    rescue of, 3, 17, 18, 40, 51, 53, 54–55, 60–64, 65, 66, 84, 111, 112, 116, 126–127, 132, 134, 172, 217, 228, 246–247, 255, 276, 289(n12), 300(n29). *See also individual paintings*

    See also Pocahontas, and John Smith

Smith Rescued by Pocahontas (Corbould), 63(fig. 4.8), 119

Smith, Seba, 127, 130–133, 317(n66)

Songs, 93, 94–96

South (geographical area), 105, 161, 166, 190, 200, 233, 311(n3), 332(n14), 333(n19). *See also* Civil War; Secession; Slavery; South Carolina; Virginia
South America, 105
South Carolina, 195, 211, 233
Southern Literary Messenger (SLM), 15, 43, 127, 131, 133, 168–169, 200, 213, 229, 230, 232, 241, 324(n9), 333(n19)
Southwark (London suburb), 184
Spain/Spaniards, 37, 248
Sparks, Jared, xvi
Speedwell, 25, 149, 183
Spencer, J. A., 60
Sprague, Pelig, 146
Squanto, 26, 293(n44)
Standish Guards, 238, 340(n42)
Standish, Miles, 4, 25, 28, 203–205, 207, 210–213, 308(n64)
Standish, Rose, 330(n62)
Stannard, W. G., 344(n15)
Starvation, 19, 20
Stati, Paul, 91
Statue of Liberty, 263, 264
Stearns, George L., 222, 337(n8)
Stearns, Junius Brutus, 136
Stickney, J. Henry, 262
Stirling, James, 331(n4)
Stith, William, 64, 169, 298(n11)
St. Luke's Church (Isle of Wight County, Virginia), 267
Stone, John Augustus, 113
Stowe, Calvin, 201
Stowe, Catharine and Henry, 201
Stowe, Harriet Beecher, 144, 176, 201–202, 334(n23)
Strachey, William, 247, 249, 289(n7)
Strobia, John Henry, 47
Stuart, J.E.B. (Jeb), 223
Subscription prints, 40–41, 82–87
Sullivan, William, 205, 320(n28)
Sully, Robert Mathew, 68, 69, 70(figs. 4.11, 4.12), 71

Sully, Thomas, 68, 69, 70(fig. 4.10), 301(nn 46, 47)
Summers, George W., 219
Sumner, Charles, 46, 165, 180, 193, 195–196, 210, 212, 335(n39)
Supreme Court, 104, 110
Susan Constant, 19

Taft, Stephen H., 228
Taxes, 26, 89, 230
Tea Party, The (Sargent), 101
Telegraphy, 139, 142
Terminology, xvii–xviii, 178, 222
Texas, 165
Thacher, James, 286(n16)
Thackeray, William Makepeace, 173, 176–178, 326(n32)
Thanksgiving, 10–11, 218, 251, 276, 277, 287(n18)
Theater, 58–60, 67, 75, 93, 96–98, 109, 110–113, 129, 134–136, 173–176, 215
Third Plymouth Church, 88
Thompson, John, 326(n32), 332(n14)
Thompson, Waddy, 165–166, 324(n4)
Thompson, Will, 223, 228
Thoreau, Henry David, 202, 222, 226, 227, 334(n24)
Ticknor and Fields (publisher), 207
Tilton, Robert, 241
Tilton, Theodore, 338(n17)
Tobacco, 20, 21, 22, 34, 66, 167, 291(n25), 314(n29)
Todkil, Anas, 149–150
Tourism, 261, 280
Trade, 34, 230, 309(n73)
  trading posts, 26
Trail of Tears, 111, 119, 124, 126, 127
Traits of the Aborigines of America (Sigourney), 134
Transcript, 150
Travels in North America in the Years 1780–81–82 (Chastellux), 56
Travels of Four Years and a Half in the United States of America (J. Davis), 56–57, 67

Treaties, 26
True Relation (J. Smith), 16, 169, 172, 245, 246
Trumbull, John, 35, 114, 295(n1), 313(n19), 315(n34)
Trustees of Dartmouth College v. Woodward, 104
Truth, 74
Tucker, Nathaniel Beverley, 199
Tucker, St. George, 90, 199, 305(n36), 333(n16)
Tuckerman, Henry, 302(n6)
Turkey Island portrait, 68, 69, 70(fig. 4.9), 301(nn 44, 46)
Turner, Nat, 199, 200
Twain, Mark, 258
Tyler, John, 200, 215–216, 238, 266, 305(n36)
Tyler, Lyon G., 266

Uncle Tom's Cabin (Stowe), 176, 201, 202
Unitarians, 88, 89, 144, 152, 178, 179, 306(nn 38, 39), 327(n38)
Universal suffrage, 104
Upham, Charles, 339(n25)
U.S. Centennial Exposition of 1876, 252–253
USS *Mayflower,* 341(n52)
Utah, 324(n2)

Vail, Alfred, 139
Van Buren, Martin, 141
Van de Passe, Simon, 51–53, 52(fig. 4.1), 64, 121, 126, 247, 297(n1), 300(n38)
Vanderlyn, John, 37, 38(fig. 3.3), 77, 141, 151
Vaughan, Robert, 51, 52(fig. 4.2), 53, 54(fig.), 60
Verplanck, Gulian, 148, 321(nn 35, 36)
Vespers of Palermo, The (Hemans), 75
Virginia, 40, 90, 98, 216, 266–271, 336(n45), 340(n43)
  cooperation with Massachusetts, 217–220

Hampton Roads. *See* Virginia, Tercentenary Exposition in
House of Delegates, 199, 200, 333(n17)
Isle of Wight County, 267
vs. New England, 98, 102, 120, 134, 137, 149, 165, 167–168, 172, 173, 191, 201, 213, 215, 226, 228, 234, 235–236, 279
and slavery, 199–201
Tercentenary Exposition in, 273, 274–275, 279, 345(nn 29, 30)
world's fair in. *See* Virginia, Tercentenary Exposition in
See also Jamestown colony; Jamestown, Virginia; Old Dominion
Virginia Colonization Society, 200
Virginia Company, 16, 18, 19, 20, 21, 25, 56, 130, 158, 159, 298(n12)
Virginia Dynasty, 102, 149
Virginians, The (Thackeray), 177–178
Voting, 28, 144, 269. *See also* Elections

Waddington, John, 184, 186–187
Walcot, Charles, 174
Waldron, William, 127
Wampanoags, 10, 26, 32
Ware, Henry, 91
Warning of Pocahontas, The (Chapman), 116, 117(fig. 6.3), 119
War of 1812, 102
Warren, A. C., 63(fig. 4.7)
Warren, Russell, 296(n12)
Washington, George, 109, 217–218, 287(n18)
Washington Crossing the Delaware (Leutze), 181, 327(n41)
Webster, Daniel, 103–105, 145, 154–155, 159, 193–194, 205, 310(n83), 331(n2)
Webster, Mary, 125–126, 170
Wedding of Pocahontas (Hohenstein), 172, 173(fig.)
Wedding Procession, The (Gilbert), 209 (fig. 9.4)

Weir, John Ferguson and Julian Alden, 147

Weir, Robert Walter, 35, 36(fig. 3.2), 37, 39, 122, 139, 141, 146–152, 147(fig.), 162, 183–184, 191, 320(n32), 321(nn 35, 39, 40), 322(nn 41, 43)

Wesley, John, 87

West (geographical area), 40, 43, 113, 136, 143, 152, 153, 154, 155, 165

West, Benjamin, 100, 306(n44), 316(n43)

Wheelwright, Edward M., 267

Whelpley, P. M., 145

Whig, 199

Whig Party, 144, 155, 159

Whitaker, Alexander (Reverend), 122

White, John, 53, 62

White, Peregrine, 149

Whitefield, George, 87

White superiority, 197

Whittemore, T. (Reverend), 156–157

Whittier, John Greenleaf, 202–203, 337(n19)

Wide Awake Gift, The (gift book), 156

Wilberforce, Samuel, 23

William and Mary College, 11, 33, 214, 266

William Penn's Treaty with the Indians (Gevelot), 40, 41(fig. 3.8)

Williamsburg, Virginia, 11, 23, 34, 239

Wilmot, David, 324(n2)

Wilson, Edith Bolling, 12, 269

Wilson, Henry, 156

Wilson, James, 159

Wilson, Woodrow, 12

Wingfield, Edward Maria, 19, 172, 245, 246, 249, 298(n12)

Winslow, Edward, 100(fig.), 308(n64), 309(n66), 330(n59)

Winthrop, John, 5–6, 28, 146

Winthrop, Robert, 5–6, 146, 251, 314(n29), 342(n23)

Wirt, William, 65–66, 110, 312(n5)

Wise, Henry Alexander, 114, 215, 216–217, 223–225, 239

Women, 111, 112, 126–127, 129, 130, 131, 133, 137, 174, 176, 191, 202, 264, 267, 270, 291(n23), 302(n5), 314(n29), 317(nn 60, 66), 325(n19), 333(n16). *See also under* Native Americans

Worcester, Samuel W. (Reverend), 153

Worcester v. Georgia, 110–111

World War I, 275

Wortham, Thomas, 210

Wright, Frances, 129, 317(n60)

Yonge, Samuel H., 344(n15)

Young, Philip, 290(n12)

Zolla, Elemire, 289(n12)